About the Author

For the past twenty-five years CHARLES MACDONALD has occupied top executive positions in major corporations. He was a member of the world headquarters staff of ITT Corporation in New York under Harold Geneen's inspired (and inspiring) management. He was Director of Business Planning for ITT's North American Area, and Chairman of the ITT Economic Advisory Council for this area.

He was vice president of planning and marketing for Western Union during its conversion from an old-line telegraph company into a modern electronic telecommunications organization, employing communications satellites and high-speed computer switching devices. While there, he had total profit responsibility for Western Union's operations in the seven Northeastern states—a job heavily oriented to sales and customer service. During this period he had the opportunity to refine and validate in an actual operating situation the principles of self-appraisal by checklist, which are the basis of this manual.

In addition, he has held a number of industrial engineering, marketing, and sales management positions in small business firms. For several years he owned and managed his own advertising agency specializing in industrial accounts. Currently he heads a management consulting firm serving industrial clients in the Northeast.

Charles Macdonald is the author of *MBO Can Work! How to Manage by Contract* (McGraw-Hill, New York, 1981), and has also written several articles for technical management publications.

The author presently resides at Barnegat Bay in New Jersey.

i

THE MARKETING AUDIT WORKBOOK

CHARLES R. MACDONALD

Institute for Business Planning
A Prentice-Hall Company
Englewood Cliffs, N.J. 07632

Library of Congress Cataloging in Publication Data

Macdonald, Charles R.
 The Marketing Audit Workbook (formerly published as
 24 Ways to Greater Business Productivity)

 1. Marketing management—Handbooks, manuals, etc.
2. Advertising management—Handbooks, manuals, etc.
3. Sales management—Handbooks, manuals, etc.   4. Customer
service—Handbooks, manuals, etc.   I. Title.
II. Title: Twenty-four ways to greater business productivity.
HF5415.13.M25   658.8   81-7096

AACR2

ISBN 0-87624-364-2

This publication is designed to provide accurate and authoritative information in regard to the subject matter covered. It is sold with the understanding that the publisher is not engaged in rendering legal, accounting, or other professional service. If legal advice or other expert assistance is required, the services of a competent professional person should be sought.

 —From a Declaration of Principles jointly adopted by a Committee of the American Bar Association and a Committee of Publishers and Associations

Printed in the United States of America

10 9 8 7 6 5 4 3

How This Manual
Can Help You

This marketing and sales self-audit manual is for the professional marketeur who is earnestly seeking ways to improve the firm's total marketing performance and productivity. It is also useful to managers of such marketing functions as market research, distribution, field sales, or customer service, who want to improve their individual performance—and thereby enhance their value to the organization.

The manual contains detailed checklists and guiding instructions to use in making "productivity audits" of your marketing organization and operations. It covers the full range of marketing and sales activities, from "Organizing for Market Leadership" to "Post-Sale Customer Service." Along the way, the manual provides for auditing such vital activities as new-product and new-market planning and development, market research and analysis, advertising and sales promotion, sales management, product distribution, customer communications, and others—a total of two dozen functions in all.

Several of these functions will not be found on the conventional marketing organization chart. Some of them require the coordinated efforts of two or more managers, and some may be part-time activities of managers who have other responsibilities. Nevertheless, each one is important to your firm's marketing success—and a company that neglects them may quickly find itself outmaneuvered by its competitors.

A SELF-AUDIT SELF-SCORING MANUAL

The manual is structured in a way that permits the manager responsible for each of the functions to do a "self-audit" of the function and to score and rate the results. If desired, all the audits can be conducted by you, as the top-level manager of the marketing function. The *self-audit*, however, has been found to be far and away more productive, not only because it is less taxing on you, but because your individual managers learn more about their own jobs through the self-audits. They also tend to become more personally committed to the resulting improvement goals when they themselves do the auditing and rating of their own functions.

It must be emphasized that the manual is not intended to tell you how to do your job. The manual presumes that you and your subordinates are mature, competent, and experienced marketing professionals who "know your trade." If you are typical of most marketing people, however, you are subject to enormous pressures from every side to get things done. Where you probably need help is in deciding which things to do first, which to do later, and which should not be done at all. So the checklists and the accompanying analysis and recommendations simply help you set priorities—they are guides to *doing the right something*, rather than *doing something right*.

NOT A THEORY BUT A PRACTICAL MANAGEMENT TOOL THAT WORKS

The systematic and honest self-appraisal of all marketing activities, together with the application of the principles and management practices recommended in this manual, can improve a company's marketing performance significantly. The results can quickly find their way to the firm's bottom line. It has worked for others:

- *Case History 1*: A west coast manufacturer of measuring and control instruments increased net income by more than 80 percent by pruning its product line of over 500 slow-moving types and sizes that were consuming salesperson's time and selling expenses.

- *Case History 2*: A producer of metal stampings increased its volume of business by over 100 percent—and its profit by an even higher percentage—just by doing a superior job of sales analysis and then concentrating selling efforts on the best existing customers. Previously its sales efforts were being wasted on attempts to move into distant markets in the mistaken belief that its present markets were saturated.

- *Case History 3*: An ailing communications products sales and service organization reversed a downward trend in sales and profit by instituting a first-class sales training and sales incentive program where both had been lacking before.

- *Case History 4*: A well-known technology company, selling to industrial markets, recently discovered that the day is past when a company could make a product in the lab and then say, "Now how are we going to sell it?" The firm recently applied systematic marketing research and planning to a new product—including, to them, a revolutionary step of *asking customers what they needed*. Even before the technical people went to work in the lab, the firm's advertising agency was involved, helping to design the product. In the first six months following introduction of the new product, the company's dealers sold over $2 million of it. The old traditional methods of industrial selling, the firm's marketing director estimates, would have produced sales of about $300 thousand.

Other examples are given throughout the manual. There is no intention to claim that the manual approach can salvage a dying business or one whose top management is incompetent. The self-audit can't save a business whose product quality is bad, or one that is in the wrong markets. It may be too late to save a couple of auto manufacturers who failed to heed the signal sent out by the Arabs back in 1973 that the age of the over-powered and overweight vehicle was over. And probably nothing will help the firm whose chief executive doesn't believe in market research, who sets corporate goals and strategies without consulting the marketing manager, who considers sales training a waste of money, or who cuts the new-product development budget in order to make a better bottom line.

But for management that is sincerely seeking ways to improve productivity throughout the organization, this manual can help to make the enterprise more effective where it really counts—in the marketplace.

A MARKETING CONSULTANT AT YOUR FINGERTIPS

Today competent marketing consultants command fees of several hundred dollars to one thousand a day—and generally they earn their cost many times over in savings or in increased sales and profit.

This manual is not intended to replace or to do away with marketing consultants, of course. What it *can* do is to help you identify and define marketing problems while they are in their early developing stages—when the cost of resolving them is low. The manual is also intended to help you spot opportunities while they, too, are in their formative stage—so they can be exploited before the competition gets there. Thus you can often avoid the need to hire an expensive consultant later on to come in and resolve the problem or to combat entrenched competition.

THE CHECKLIST SELF-AUDIT IS EASY TO DO

The checklists are designed to make your self-audit easy. An hour or so each day spent reviewing your particular operation should enable you to complete your self-audit within a few days. (It is desirable to do so away from the distractions of your daily workplace, if possible.)

The checklists are designed to guide you through the appraisal of your function in the most productive way. They provide you with a comprehensive list of points to consider, covering all aspects of functional management—from the delegation of authority to the availability of re-sources. Each point on the checklists is stated in the form of a positive statement that expresses an "ideal" condition you should strive for. For example, one point under Advertising reads, "Specific goals for advertising and sales promotion are included in the marketing plan." Obviously, when goals are "specific," people are more likely to know what is expected from them; when these goals are expressed *in writing* and contained in an important marketing document, they are more likely to be taken seriously. (As you know, most advertising failures result from the lack of clear objectives, not from the lack of effort or sincerity on the part of your advertising people.)

If you honestly believe this statement is generally true of your advertising function, simply put a checkmark in the "yes" column. If you feel that the statement is not really true—that your marketing plan does not include specific goals for advertising—check the "no" column. If you consider the statement to be partially true—that the marketing plan contains some goals but they are not really specific—or if you feel it is true only in some cases, check the "S/P" (sometimes or partially) column.

The next two pages give detailed instructions and an example of *how to use the checklists, how to evaluate your answers*, and *how to rate and score your responses*.

Each checklist is followed by a brief interpretation of WHAT THE RATING SIGNIFIES, as well as suggestions as to WHAT TO DO NOW.

HOW TO USE THE CHECKLISTS

For each of the statements in the Checklist, compare the condition of your function to the "ideal" as described in the statement. Then:

1. If you consider the statement to be *generally true* of your function, check the YES column.

2. If you consider the statement to be *untrue* of your function, check the NO column.

3. If you consider the statement to be *less than true* (but not totally untrue) of your function, check the SOMETIMES OR PARTIAL column.

4. If the statement does not apply to your particular situation, write "Not Applicable" across the response spaces (or simply draw a line through them).

5. If you lack the data for a definite response, write in "Not Answerable" or "Don't Know."

HOW TO EVALUATE YOUR RESPONSES

When you have completed the checklist, glance over your responses, keeping these points in mind:

1. A negative answer is always unfavorable because it indicates a problem within the function: the greater the number of NOs, the more serious the situation.

2. A positive response is always a good indication. But too many YES answers could indicate that your review is not objective enough.

3. Too many SOMETIMES OR PARTIALLY answers can point to internal weaknesses or to a lack of firm direction.

4. A lot of "Not Applicable" answers could indicate that you are avoiding the issue.

5. A large number of "Not Answerable" or "Don't Know" answers could be symptomatic of inadequate records or data bases.

HOW TO RATE AND SCORE YOUR RESPONSES

When you are satisfied with your responses in general, you are ready to score the Checklist. For your convenience, a self-explanatory Scoring and Rating Block follows each Checklist. This block not only tells you whether the condition of your function is satisfactory, but it also gives you a measure of its effectiveness.

Here's how to total up the points for inclusion in the Scoring and Rating Block:

1. Total up the number of points you scored:
   a. For each YES, give yourself one point.
   b. For each NO, give yourself zero.
   c. For each SOMETIMES OR PARTIALLY, give yourself a half-point.
   d. For each "Not Applicable" answer, give yourself zero and deduct one from the number of items on the Checklist.
   e. For each "Not Answerable" or "Don't Know" answer, give yourself zero.

2. Next divide the total number of points you score by the total number of items (statements) on the Checklist (less items marked "Not Applicable"). You'll get a 1.0 for a perfect score and a fraction for anything less.

3. Multiply the result of step 2 by 100 to arrive at the percentage for your score.

What is a satisfactory rating? A rating of less than 65 percent is unacceptable and calls for an improvement program: Obviously, the lower the rating, the more drastic the action required.

A brief "how-to" example of this Scoring and Rating system follows . . .

EXAMPLE

	YES (1)	NO (0)	S/P* (½)

1. Field sale reports designed to provide information on sales progress contain data on the following topics:

   a. sales calls and sales presentations made by salespersons and sales agents,   ✓

   b. bids, quotations, and proposals made,   ✓

   c. new orders booked,   ✓

   d. lost business, and reasons for the loss,   ✓ (NO)

   e. accomplishments toward future orders,   ✓ (S/P)

   f. performance in filling orders, handling complaints, and otherwise servicing individual customers,   ✓

   g. action taken in response to customer requests, such as sending samples, spec sheets, etc.,   ✓

   h. accomplishments of significance and value to other members of the sales force.   ✓ (S/P)

*SOMETIMES OR PARTIALLY

TOTAL POINTS $\boxed{5}$ + 0 + $\boxed{1}$

= $\boxed{6}$

RATING

$$\frac{\text{Enter number of points scored} \quad \boxed{6}}{\text{Enter number of items on checklist} \quad \boxed{8}} = .75 \times 100 = \boxed{75}\ \%$$

Introduction

MARKET LEADERSHIP AND MARKETING POWER

The principal purpose of this manual is to help you move your company into a position of leadership and power in its chosen markets—and keep it there despite the agressive efforts of competition to dislodge it.

Market leadership and marketing power are achieved only by firms in which the marketing function and its managers have enough influence and "clout" within the organization that there is a strong marketing orientation throughout the company. *This manual is intended to help you move your marketing function into a position of internal power—and keep it there despite the well-intentioned efforts of your colleagues to make their functions dominant instead.*

Market leadership means that your company has the capability to influence, or even to control, the decisions and actions of the other market factors. Marketing power means that your firm is a major factor to be reckoned with by any competitor who seeks to expand its position in your markets. Leadership and power signify that your competitors must consider your potential response whenever they make an important strategic decision or tactical move that affects your markets. And they must also respond to your competitive moves—or risk the loss of market standing.

This kind of potency and prestige is gained not simply through bigger ad budgets and a larger sales force, but by creative thinking and innovative action—by brains, not brawn. The large companies may have more bucks, but they have no corner on intelligence. Accordingly, it is possible for a small firm to become a significant power even in a market populated by giant companies.

SMALL COMPANIES CAN BE GIANT KILLERS

Business history is filled with cases wherein newcomers took on large established corporations in the markets they dominated—and beat them at their own game. Here are a few examples:

- Previously unknown firms with the unlikely names of "Apple" and "Wang" have recently become market leaders in small computers and word processors.

- A relatively small company called Savin has taken on giant Xerox Corporation to become a market power in copiers.

- Federal Express took on the entire airline industry, as well as the established parcel delivery companies—not to mention the U.S. Postal Service—to become the market leader in priority package delivery.

- A man named Freddie Laker defied the all-powerful International Air Travel Association to become a major factor in the trans-Atlantic travel market (at the same time bringing down the cost of air travel to the point where more people can afford it).

WHAT IS THEIR COMMON DENOMINATOR?

The large established companies may have more money, better facilities, and superior technical capabilities—but all their resources couldn't stop these energetic, enterprising young organizations from capturing substantial shares of the markets they once dominated. What gave these "upstart" companies their competitive edge was *marketing—strong, agressive, and innovative marketing.*

THE VIEW FROM THE TOP

As manager of marketing (whatever your title and rank), you quite naturally consider yourself and your marketing organization to be innovative, energetic, forceful, and progressive. You also believe, I'm sure, that you and your group are perceived by others in the same well-deserved terms of approbation.

It may come as a shock, however, to learn that not all of your colleagues and superiors share your positive opinion of the marketing function and of marketing people. Here is another less approving view:

> Marketing people are afraid to take a chance. They don't have enough new ideas. Marketers too often look for the quick sales results instead of satisfying longer-range objectives. What is more, they don't understand the financial consequences of their actions.

So say the top executives of some thirty of America's largest and most successful corporations, according to a survey by a professor of marketing at Dartmouth. The survey goes on to say that some CEOs perceive their marketing managers as myopic, unimaginative, and lacking in foresight. Others say their marketers are deficient in innovative and entrepreneurial thinking, the very qualities one would expect most in a marketing person. One chief accused his marketers, especially those with MBAs, of over-caution, saying, "They won't stick their necks out . . . they play it safe."

A major concern expressed by these top executives is the failure of marketing people to keep their productivity in step with the rising costs of advertising, market development, and sales promotion. Another is their "fixation" on sales volume rather than on profitability and long-term growth.

WHETHER THEY'RE RIGHT OR WRONG, YOU HAVE A PROBLEM

Of course you don't agree with these negative views of marketing and marketing people. Not every chief executive feels this way, either. But whether they're right or wrong is not the issue—the very fact that a lot of high executives do perceive marketers in a less-than-positive manner is evidence that you have a very serious "image" problem to overcome. It is clear that you must restore lost confidence and credibility before you can exercise the kind of influence and internal "clout" you need. You have to demonstrate that you are capable of leading the company in the right direction—into the right markets with the right products—before you can expect that your marketing objectives and strategies will be endorsed by your superiors, accepted by your associates in other functions, and followed by other members of the organization.

How do you accomplish this turnabout? How do you regain marketing's waning prestige and reassert marketing's diminished authority and power to lead the organization? How, in short, do you "clean up your act" as the firm's manager of marketing?

THE KEY IS PRODUCTIVITY

It starts with recognition that the productivity of a business begins in the marketplace, not on the production line, the shop floor, or in the engineering lab. The technical people—bless their hearts—can invent the most ingenious, efficient, and advanced product known to man. The production department can turn out the product at a fantastic rate. But if the output of all this engineering brain-power and production know-how doesn't fill a user or consumer need, then the engineers and manufacturing people are not really productive—and neither is the company.

For it is only by fulfilling the needs and wants of customers that a business is truly productive. In this regard, the productivity of a business is really *competitiveness*. Filling needs is the only real purpose and "reason for being" of the enterprise, and marketing is the cutting edge of the organization in this effort.

THE CHALLENGE TO MARKETING

The decade of the 1980's is shaping up to be the most challenging and demanding period in history for marketing managers. It is a time of unprecedented change in every aspect of business operation and management. For one, the energy "crisis" is altering the economics of energy production and consumption in ways that are impacting our lifestyles and our future security.

The new energy economics make obsolete every machine, every vehicle, every structure, and every device that uses or produces power, light, heat, or motion. American industry today is a "vehicle built to operate on $3 a barrel oil—puffing along with an inefficient engine, with the body leaking vast amounts of energy," according to two highly regarded energy authorities at Harvard University. As a consequence, during the next ten years or so, virtually every product we own and every process we use must be redesigned or rebuilt to make it energy-efficient and energy-productive.

In effect, the entire U.S. industrial economy must be overhauled within the decade.

This "reindustrialization" task is a staggering one. The situation is so critical it has been described as a matter of national survival. To accomplish the task is a grave challenge to American management. A particularly heavy burden of responsibility for the turnaround falls on professional marketing managers and on the marketing function—as the pace-setting arm of the business organization.

THE NEW "MARKETEUR"

What is needed is a resurgence of entrepreneurial spirit throughout our business institutions. In the forefront of the effort must be the professional marketing managers who "make it all happen" by seeking out the new needs and wants of consumers in an energy-conscious economy, and then making sure that producers respond with products and services that meet these needs.

I have coined a term to describe the marketing professional who will rise to this challenge. It is *marketeur*. A marketeur is a unique blend of marketer and entrepreneur. He (or she) is a seeker after new market opportunities, a rare combination of specialist and innovator, and a producer of creative approaches to marketing problems.

If you are one of this new breed of marketeur—if the thought of facing up to the challenge of the 1980's turns you on—then this "self-audit and self-scoring manual" is offered with the intention and the hope that it will help you to manage your marketing function better and more productively in the months and years ahead.

Contents

7   Planning and Developing Markets

Section III   Managing Marketing Intelligence

8   How to Research and Analyze Market Demand

9   Evaluating Competitor Strengths and Weaknesses

Section **V**   Managing
Product Distribution 243

14   Keeping Distribution Attuned
to the Changing Marketplace 245

15   Selling Through Resellers—
Indirect Distribution 265

Section **VI**   Managing the
Selling Effort 287

16   How to Train the Sales Force 291

17   How to Improve Productivity of the
Individual Salesperson 309

Section ■

How to Manage
Total Marketing

There is almost universal acceptance that marketing should be the prime mover of the business enterprise. Peter Drucker states it plainly, "There is only one valid definition of business purpose: to create a customer . . . and the business enterprise has only two basic functions—marketing and innovation."[1]

MARKETING STARTS AT THE TOP

Accepting this assertion as true, responsibility for marketing starts with the company's chief executive officer and, through delegation of authority, becomes a prime responsibility of every manager. In this sense, marketing management is the direction and control of all activities having as their purpose the satisfaction of customer needs, activities not only within the marketing organization but in every function of the business.

Unfortunately, definitions as global and noble as this tend to generate "motherhood" statements, and platitudes about objective-setting, market leadership, and employee motivation. It is unfair to this vital business function to take this easy approach, instead of getting down the hard-rock of identifying tasks, responsibilities, and accountabilities of marketing managers. Accordingly, this section of the Marketing and Sales Manual takes a more focused and more pragmatic view of marketing management. For purposes of this appraisal it is defined as:

The direct planning, organization, direction, and control of people and activities within the marketing organization, and the "indirect management" of people in the other functions through persuasion,

[1]Drucker, Peter F., Management "New York: Harper & Row, 1973."

1

influence, and motivation, *to the end that all company resources are used in the most productive way to make and keep the firm competitive in the marketplace.*

The overriding purpose of the appraisal is to ensure that the marketing function takes the lead in developing objectives, strategies, and plans; promotes a market-orientation for all company personnel and activities; and organizes for maximum marketing effectiveness. Above all, it is to ensure that the marketing resources and strengths of the company are equal to or better than those of the strongest competitor because this is where the dollar payoff is.

NEED FOR MARKETING INNOVATION

In his stimulating book, *The Profitable Product*, Walter Talley makes a strong case for marketing innovation, saying that it can contribute as much to business success as product or technological innovation. Even more, he states, innovation in marketing is a quicker route to higher profitability, as utilization of assets is increased and ROI is improved through creative new sales of present products produced by facilities already in place.[2]

Examples of creative marketing are changes in product distribution to make locations and hours of service and sale more convenient to customers; the shift to self-service even for such products as gasoline; and the strong trend to marketing computers and word processors through retail outlets. Many of these innovations require little or no new investment in facilities and equipment; many in fact, reduce costs of distribution and sales.

THE FOUR MAIN FUNCTIONS OF TOTAL MARKETING

For appraisal purposes, we are grouping the principal marketing management activities, tasks, and responsibilities under four broad but nonetheless specific topics:

1. organizing for market leadership,
2. developing marketing objectives and strategies,
3. coordinating and controlling marketing activities, and
4. developing marketing personnel.

[2]Englewood Cliffs, N.J.: Prentice Hall Inc., 1965.

Chapter 1

Organizing for Market Leadership

Organizing the firm to achieve leadership in the markets in which the company participates is a very definite and specific activity, although it is not always viewed as such. It involves more than simply filling the boxes on the marketing department's organization chart: It comprehends every function of the business, and it involves every forward plan and virtually every major company decision. One of the most important aspects of this activity is the development of a "market-orientation" throughout the entire organization: that is, a sensitivity and awareness of the customer by every employee in every transaction.

MARKET LEADERSHIP PAYS OFF

The rewards of market leadership are high, and those firms that enjoy market leadership are extraordinarily profitable. It is not necessarily a function of size. A firm may be recognized as a market leader even though it has only a nominal share of the markets it participates in, while another much larger company in terms of assets and total sales may not be. The difference is more a matter of momentum. Whatever its size, the market leader can be recognized by these signs:

1. high return on investment,
2. faster-than-average growth rate,
3. high level of customer service, and
4. reputation for new-product and marketing innovation.

TWO EXAMPLES OF OUTSTANDING MARKET LEADERS AND HOW THEY DID IT

A prime example of a large and well-established company that is a true market leader is Procter & Gamble in household products. Although it is far beyond the age when many firms become senile, at 143 years it is growing faster than ever. In the past 10 years, its earnings have tripled. The current fiscal years shows sales growth of 16 percent, to over $8 billion, and net income increase of over 13 percent. Why has the company never lost touch with its customers despite its massive size? Constant consumer research and highly organized handling of user information keeps the firm up on the ever-changing tastes of the consuming public. Products carry a toll-free telephone number so customers can call in immediately any comments or complaints. P&G will contact, by phone or in person, about a million and a half people this year, in order to obtain first-hand opinions about the company and its products. Complaints, often considered a nuisance by many firms, are treated as a valuable marketing asset.

Procter & Gamble became a market leader by *organizing* for leadership—by listening to its customers and heeding what they say in an organized fashion. There is nothing happenstance about its market leadership: It is designed into the entire organization.

At the other end of the size and age spectrum is a market leader of quite a different sort. Federal Express was established only seven years ago, but now operates one of the largest fleets of aircraft in the world, delivering priority packages overnight to more than 218,000 customers throughout the country. In this brief span of time, the company has grown to over $250 million in annual revenues, and $21 million in net income. In the first six months of fiscal 1980, revenues are up by a phenomenal 71 percent. Federal Express has carved out this position of market leadership by providing a service that the passenger airlines were overlooking, even though they had the facilities to fill the need. Its reward is a 30 percent share of the market for high-priority small package freight.

Clearly, both of these firms understand and practice true *marketing*, and do not confuse it with sales. Levitt has defined *marketing* as "a total integrated effort to discover, create, arouse, and satisfy unfilled customer needs." When the entire organization is dedicated to this principle, market leadership follows.

THE OTHER SIDE OF THE COIN: BUSINESS FAILURES

Business history is filled with stories about companies that failed to follow these principles; firms with reputations for their technological and production capabilities, but who lacked the ability to sense the pulse of the consumer. They went "down the tube" because they failed to produce the products that the marketplace wanted. Few people, for instance, contend that Chrysler does not produce good products—cars that are as well engineered and well built as those of Ford, GM, or most imports. Chrysler's problem—and to a great extent that of the whole U.S. auto industry—is that the domestic auto manufacturers continued to turn out oversize and overweight vehicles long after the consumer had signaled a preference for small, light, fuel-efficient cars. The industry is paying the price that business must pay when it ignores the customer.

KEY OBJECTIVE OF THE SELF-AUDIT

The principal purpose of this section of the self-audit, *Organizing for Market Leadership*, is to ensure that the marketing organization has sufficient influence and power with top management and other functions of the business that every company decision is made and every company resource is employed to further the market leadership of the firm.

4

HOW TO USE THE CHECKLISTS

For each of the statements in the Checklist, compare the condition of your function to the "ideal" as described in the statement. Then:

1. If you consider the statement to be *generally true* of your function, check the YES column.

2. If you consider the statement to be *untrue* of your function, check the NO column.

3. If you consider the statement to be *less than true* (but not totally untrue) of your function, check the SOMETIMES OR PARTIAL column.

4. If the statement does not apply to your particular situation, write "Not Applicable" across the response spaces (or simply draw a line through them).

5. If you lack the data for a definite response, write in "Not Answerable" or "Don't Know."

HOW TO EVALUATE YOUR RESPONSES

When you have completed the checklist, glance over your responses, keeping these points in mind:

1. A negative answer is always unfavorable because it indicates a problem within the function: the greater the number of NOs, the more serious the situation.

2. A positive response is always a good indication. But too many YES answers could indicate that your review is not objective enough.

3. Too many SOMETIMES OR PARTIALLY answers can point to internal weaknesses or to a lack of firm direction.

4. A lot of "Not Applicable" answers could indicate that you are avoiding the issue.

5. A large number of "Not Answerable" or "Don't Know" answers could be symptomatic of inadequate records or data bases.

HOW TO RATE AND SCORE YOUR RESPONSES

When you are satisfied with your responses in general, you are ready to score the Checklist. For your convenience, a self-explanatory Scoring and Rating Block follows each Checklist. This block not only tells you whether the condition of your function is satisfactory, but it also gives you a measure of its effectiveness.

Here's how to total up the points for inclusion in the Scoring and Rating Block:

1. Total up the number of points you scored:
   a. For each YES, give yourself one point.
   b. For each NO, give yourself zero.
   c. For each SOMETIMES OR PARTIALLY, give yourself a half-point.
   d. For each "Not Applicable" answer, give yourself zero and deduct one from the number of items on the Checklist.
   e. For each "Not Answerable" or "Don't Know" answer, give yourself zero.

2. Next divide the total number of points you score by the total number of items (statements) on the Checklist (less items marked "Not Applicable"). You'll get a 1.0 for a perfect score and a fraction for anything less.

3. Multiply the result of step 2 by 100 to arrive at the percentage for your score.

What is a satisfactory rating? A rating of less than 65 percent is unacceptable and calls for an improvement program: Obviously, the lower the rating, the more drastic the action required.

A brief "how-to" example of this Scoring and Rating system follows . . .

EXAMPLE

	YES (1)	NO (0)	S/P* (½)

1. Field sale reports designed to provide information on sales progress contain data on the following topics:

   a. sales calls and sales presentations made by salespersons and sales agents,   ✓

   b. bids, quotations, and proposals made,   ✓

   c. new orders booked,   ✓

   d. lost business, and reasons for the loss,   ✓ (NO)

   e. accomplishments toward future orders,   ✓ (S/P)

   f. performance in filling orders, handling complaints, and otherwise servicing individual customers,   ✓

   g. action taken in response to customer requests, such as sending samples, spec sheets, etc.,   ✓

   h. accomplishments of significance and value to other members of the sales force.   ✓ (S/P)

*SOMETIMES OR PARTIALLY

TOTAL POINTS   5   + 0 +   1

$$= 6$$

RATING

$$\frac{\text{Enter number of points scored} \quad \boxed{6}}{\text{Enter number of items on checklist} \quad \boxed{8}} = .75 \times 100 = \boxed{75 \%}$$

1-A
ORGANIZATION, ADMINISTRATION, AND OPERATION

	YES (1)	NO (0)	S/P* (½)

1. The process of organizing marketing activities is considered to be a vital company activity and an important function of marketing. _____ _____ _____

2. The organization is reviewed at least once a year, and changes are made to improve marketing effectiveness. _____ _____ _____

3. As part of the review, the business mission, or charter, of the marketing department is reviewed and up-dated. _____ _____ _____

4. The marketing function is sufficiently high in the company organizational structure so as to have proper power and influence with peer functions and with the executive office. _____ _____ _____

5. The manager of marketing (whatever the title) reports to the top executive of the company. _____ _____ _____

6. The marketing budget includes an allocation for all expenses of this activity. _____ _____ _____

7. Organization charts showing the reporting relationships of marketing and other functions are up-to-date and reflect the actual situation. _____ _____ _____

8. The organization chart of the marketing function itself is complete, up-to-date, and reflects the real situation. _____ _____ _____

9. The function is staffed by marketing professionals well-informed about the company's products, markets, and competitors. _____ _____ _____

10. Marketing management is represented in all top executive committees and in all top level conferences. _____ _____ _____

11. The organization is designed to encourage marketing creativity and innovation by individuals. _____ _____ _____

12. The organization makes maximum use of product management, multi-functional task groups, and matrix-type organizations to assure that all points of view are considered in marketing decisions. _____ _____ _____

13. The manager of marketing heads up or chairs a formal cross-functional group composed of high level representatives of engineering, production, financial control, distribution, and other key business functions. _____ _____ _____

14. This group meets on a fixed schedule, works to an agenda, and issues action assignments. _____ _____ _____

15. This group was established for the purpose of asserting marketing leadership in matters involving:

   a. new products, _____ _____ _____

   b. product pricing, _____ _____ _____

   c. product modifications, _____ _____ _____

   d. product pruning, _____ _____ _____

   e. entry into new market areas, _____ _____ _____

   f. customer service, and _____ _____ _____

   g. diversification actions. _____ _____ _____

*SOMETIMES OR PARTIALLY

	YES (1)	NO (0)	S/P* (½)

16. The marketing manager devotes at least 10 percent of his time to organizational matters. _____ _____ _____

17. The marketing manager actively promotes a market-orientation throughout the entire organization, through constant contact (30-40 percent of the time) with other functions. _____ _____ _____

18. The development of interfunctional organizations, such as task groups and committees, is considered part of the task of organizing marketing. _____ _____ _____

19. Organizing for marketing leadership and marketing control of new product developments is also part of the task. _____ _____ _____

20. Marketing management follows good principles of organization:

   a. keep it simple, keep it "lean and clean," _____ _____ _____

   b. organize along lines of responsibility and accountability, _____ _____ _____

   c. organize for action, and _____ _____ _____

   d. keep it flexible. _____ _____ _____

*SOMETIMES OR PARTIALLY

TOTAL POINTS [ ] + 0 + [ ]

= [ ]

RATING

Enter number of points scored [ ]
———————————————————————— = × 100 = [ ] %
Enter number of items on checklist [ ]

WHAT THE RATINGS SIGNIFY

A less-than-acceptable rating in this section indicates that the marketing function may lack the "clout" needed to influence and persuade other functions and top management to follow its recommendations. As a consequence, decisions may be made on matters affecting product designs, pricing, advertising programs, sales incentive programs, customer relations, acquisitions, and diversifications, and future market direction without proper consideration of market conditions, marketing objectives and strategies, and actual customer attitudes and perceptions of the company.

Lacking strong direction from marketing, the sales force could be generating high dollar volume by selling the low-margin, easy-to-sell products, instead of the newer, higher margin items that increase company profit. The engineering people may be pushing the new products invented in the lab simply because they are intrigued by the technological challenge they represent—with the danger that the market may reject them. The advertising department may be creating dramatic (and expensive) sales promotion campaigns for products that marketing has found are no longer in demand.

In the absence of good marketing guidance, top executive decisions may be made to acquire companies with product lines that don't fit the firm's marketing capabilities and strengths. Market research may be conducted in the executive conference room, where it tends to confirm that the products the company presently sells are what the customers want—or worse, that the idea for a new product that the chairman of the board thought up at the breakfast table is a sure winner!

WHAT TO DO NOW   The marketing organization must set objectives and priorities to build or restore its power base within the organization. The following actions are essential:

1. *Analyze the results* of the self-audit to determine which factors are most critical to the effectiveness of marketing.

2. *Concentrate on two or three critical factors.* Set goals for these few important factors and others will follow.

3. *Build support* for your objectives with the managers of the other functions by keeping them informed. Persuade them that they will benefit from a strong marketing organization.

4. *Get your boss on your side.* Make a "partner" for yourself by convincing him or her that a strong and influential marketing organization can help achieve his or her objectives.

5. *Create an information power base. Information* is the new source of power in the business organization. Become the information center, the organizer and dispenser of reliable, up-to-date information—the kind that others need to get their jobs done. Make sure that marketing is always identified as the source of the information. Share it freely with other managers, but insist on a *quid pro quo*—an equal sharing in return of credible information that marketing needs, such as:

   - status of new project developments from engineering,
   - customer attitudes and preferences, from sales and customer service,
   - progress on new production facilities and expansions,
   - proposed organization changes,
   - status of important government legislation, and
   - the forward plans of other functions, so their impact on marketing can be assessed.

6. *Campaign for an adequate share of company resources.* Let your boss know what is needed—realistically—to meet the objectives you have set, in the form of funding, capital investment, personnel, outside services, and support from the other service functions like data processing, communications, etc. Don't agree to achieve important objectives without firm assurance that the resources it takes will be available.

7. *Staff your marketing organization with professionals.* Build respect for the function by assuring that every task is done in a professional manner, and that all contacts with others reflect this professionalism.

1-B
AUTHORITY, RESPONSIBILITY, AND ACCOUNTABILITY

	YES (1)	NO (0)	S/P* (½)
1. The manager of marketing has written formal delegated authority to commit company funds and assign tasks for reports and studies he considers necessary for making product and market decisions, such as:			
a. new-product testing,	———	———	———

*SOMETIMES OR PARTIALLY

   b. customer surveys,

   c. market studies,

   d. comparative product evaluations, and

   e. business environment (economic) reports.

2. Through a position description or a policy statement, the manager of marketing is held responsible:

   a. to staff and manage an organization whose purpose is to identify, penetrate, and maintain a strong position in selected markets, and

   b. to create a "market-orientation" for the unit as a whole, and to assure that all major decisions have had adequate marketing input.

3. By means of a company policy statement or other formal document, responsibility for product-line profitability and ROI is assigned to the manager of marketing. This does not relieve the line manager of the responsibility.

4. The marketing manager is held accountable for:

   a. serious loss of market share by existing products,

   b. failure of new-product introductions,

   c. loss or marginal products in the line resulting from ineffective marketing organization.

*SOMETIMES OR PARTIALLY

TOTAL POINTS   ☐ + 0 + ☐

= ☐

RATING

Enter number of points scored ☐

Enter number of items on checklist ☐

= ☐ × 100 = ☐ %

WHAT THE RATINGS SIGNIFY

An unsatisfactory rating on the first point indicates that the manager of marketing (whatever the title) lacks the authority to spend the money that marketing needs to collect, analyze, and disseminate the vital information needed to support its recommendations to management. It is possible that a recommendation that lacks a base of factual support could be approved on faith—more often, however, it is rejected and the manager tends to lose some credibility with each rejection.

A low rating on the next point can mean that others in the organization may not be aware of the extent of the manager's responsibility to build and maintain a strong marketing organization. What is worse, others may not know that his or her charter includes the responsibility to make sure that the information that marketing provides to others is used productively. How can other managers be forced to use the information? They cannot, of course. But the manager of marketing can assure that the information is valid, accurate, timely, and complete—and so useful that others would be foolish not to use it.

A less-than-acceptable rating on the third and fourth points may indicate that the authority apparently granted to the manager may not be real, and that his or her responsibility could be less firm than it appears to be. Unless marketing managers are held accountable for profitability of the product line, along with line managers, they can walk away from problems caused by their decisions. Unless they are held accountable for serious mistakes and failures, their authority and responsibility are really meaningless, because they can "get off the hook" by blaming circumstances, bad luck, or subordinates. Only when managers have to live with the consequences of every decision is their authority genuine and their responsibility firm.

WHAT TO DO NOW

1. *Exert pressure directly on the boss,* and indirectly on others, to get formal, written delegation of authority to expend company funds, enter into contracts in the name of the company, and utilize company assets—up to clearly specified limits—without the need for specific approval on each occasion.

2. *Draft a position description* or policy statement defining responsibilities and work through established channels to get it approved.

3. *Spell out the accountability of each person* so there is less chance for misunderstanding and blame-shifting. Realistically, no manager will demand to be held accountable for mistakes and failures—on the other hand, it must be made clear that a manager who dodges responsibility and repeatedly tries to shift the blame to others will not be considered seriously when a position of higher responsibility opens up.

1-C
MEASUREMENTS, CONTROL REPORTS AND PERFORMANCE RECORDS

	YES (1)	NO (0)	S/P* (½)
1. The effectiveness of the marketing organization is measured and evaluated regularly and continuously.	___	___	___
2. This effectiveness is measured by comparing actual performance and results to certain benchmarks or standards, such as:			
a. product-line profit margins,	___	___	___
b. penetration of new markets,	___	___	___
c. new-product content of sales, and	___	___	___
d. new-product success ratio.	___	___	___
3. Internal records and reports are prepared and maintained on a routine basis for the purpose of:			

*SOMETIMES OR PARTIALLY

	YES (1)	NO (0)	S/P* (½)

a. keeping the marketing organization staffed with competent people ___ ___ ___

b. assuring that all marketing personnel know and understand their roles and responsibilities, ___ ___ ___

c. keeping tasks and assignments on cost and time schedules, ___ ___ ___

d. keeping departmental expenditures within budget, ___ ___ ___

e. directing and controlling outside purchased services, ___ ___ ___

f. assuring that all meetings have a productive purpose and result including agenda and action assignments, ___ ___ ___

g. assuring that good market information is made available for top-level meetings. ___ ___ ___

4. Control reports give "early warning" to marketing management about organizational problems and deficiencies that could adversely affect product-line profitability or ROI. ___ ___ ___

5. A predetermined set of corrective actions for problem situations takes place automatically, without the active intervention of the marketing manager (such as requiring a revised "cost-to-complete" estimate when an outside contractor overruns costs-to-date by an established percentage). ___ ___ ___

*SOMETIMES OR PARTIALLY

TOTAL POINTS [ ] + 0 + [ ]

= [ ]

RATING

$$\frac{\text{Enter number of points scored} \quad [\quad]}{\text{Enter number of items on checklist} \quad [\quad]} = \quad \times 100 = \boxed{\quad} \%$$

WHAT THE RATINGS SIGNIFY

A less-than-satisfactory rating in this section of the self-audit check-list indicates that the base of information used to manage the marketing organization may be deficient. The reports and records prepared by the marketing staff may be out of date because of changes in organization and responsibilities since they were designed, or the control reports are not useful because they contain only history, not information for effective decision-making.

When the staff and the manager lack good records and reports on the progress of department projects, expenditures vs. budgets, performance vs. plans, and the status of major problems, the organization's effectiveness can be seriously impaired. And if the department's internal controls are inadequate, it can't be expected to play a leading role in the marketing direction of the entire company.

WHAT TO DO NOW

1. *Call upon the Systems and Procedures people*, or the MIS specialists in the organization, to help define the information needs of the marketing

group and set up the procedures to capture the data. This does not necessarily mean that a computerized information system is needed—often a simple manual system will do the job.

2. *Assign responsibility* to an individual to get the records and reporting system up to standard.

3. *Get rid of* all reports and records that do not help to improve the marketing function's effectiveness—that is, that do not cause someone to take productive action.

1-D
OPERATING PERFORMANCE HISTORY

	YES (1)	NO (0)	S/P* (½)
1. Based on a review of control reports and records for the past year, the marketing organization has proved to be effective, as evidenced by:			
a. success in meeting marketing objectives,	———	———	———
b. completion of all major projects on time and within budgeted costs,	———	———	———
c. improved market shares for major products,	———	———	———
d. improved product-line return on sales and ROI,	———	———	———
e. improved ratio of marketing expense to sales,	———	———	———
f. improved marketing reputation of the company as measured by consumer surveys,	———	———	———
g. successful introduction of at least one major new product (and no failures),	———	———	———
h. successful development of at least one new market for existing products, and	———	———	———
i. reduction in number of loss and marginal products.	———	———	———

*SOMETIMES OR PARTIALLY

TOTAL POINTS ☐ + 0 + ☐

= ☐

RATING

Enter number of points scored ☐
———————————————————————— = ☐ × 100 = ☐ %
Enter number of items on checklist ☐

WHAT THE RATINGS SIGNIFY   A low rating here is evidence that the marketing organization has a poor "track record" in meeting its past commitments and living up to its obligations to the company. As a result, the department will tend to have a low level of credibility with top management and other functional managers in making commitments for the future.

1. There is only one way for marketing to regain its lost credibility. That is the hard way—by meeting every deadline and completing every project on time and within cost budgets. Only good performance will restore a reputation tarnished by failures and unsatisfactory results. In the meantime, it is good policy to avoid further over-commitment; to build a record of success by setting modest goals and meeting them.

2. *Advertise your successes* with your boss and with others. One of the best ways to do this is to issue a weekly "Progress Report" covering all the activities of the marketing function. Distribute the report to other functional managers so they can know what is being accomplished.

3. *Rebuild the confidence of the staff.* A record of repeated failures can tear down the morale of people to the point where they are often afraid to take on assignments. A record of success, on the other hand, can lead to more and greater success.

1-E
TOP-LEVEL SUPPORT AND GUIDANCE

	YES (1)	NO (0)	S/P* (½)

1. The executive office demonstrates active support for marketing as an organized function, and for efforts to promote a strong market-orientation throughout the total organization. Support, guidance, and recognition are evidenced by:

    a. budget approval,

    b. published policy statements,

    c. endorsement of interfunctional team projects and programs,

    d. appointment of marketing manager to top-level committees,

    e. participation in marketing plan reviews, and

    f. recognition and reward for outstanding accomplishment.

*SOMETIMES OR PARTIALLY

TOTAL POINTS ☐ + 0 + ☐

= ☐

RATING

Enter number of points scored ☐
——————————————————————— = × 100 = ☐ %
Enter number of items on checklist ☐

A low rating on this point signifies that the marketing function either has low visibility or low believability with the executive office. In either case, the organization is in trouble, because without backing and recognition by the front office, marketing can hardly expect to get the other functions of the business to support its programs and policies.

WHAT TO DO NOW   If marketing's problem is low visibility because the current corporate emphasis is on technology, or financial control, or growth through acquisition, there is no easy solution or quick fix. What is required is a long-range program to persuade top management that an unbalanced approach to corporate development is dangerous and that over-emphasis on any one function to the exclusion of others often leads to serious difficulty in the future.

If, on the other hand, the marketing organization is held in low esteem because of poor performance, then the task is to rebuild top management's confidence in the function by taking the remedial actions discussed under the previous point, Operating Performance History.

1-F
INNOVATION IN METHODS AND TECHNIQUES

	YES (1)	NO (0)	S/P* (½)
1. Marketing management evaluates and utilizes up-to-date organizational techniques to organize and adapt activities to meet customer needs. Management actively keeps up-to-date through:			
a. seminars, conferences and workshops,	———	———	———
b. professional associations,	———	———	———
c. review of current literature,	———	———	———
d. industry contacts,	———	———	———
e. outside specialists,	———	———	———
f. solicitation of new ideas from personnel at all levels, and	———	———	———
g. budgets provide funds for such activities.	———	———	———
2. The computer is used to store, process and display market data, sales data, and project status.	———	———	———

*SOMETIMES OR PARTIALLY

TOTAL POINTS   [ ] + 0 + [ ]

= [ ]

RATING

Enter number of points scored [ ]
———————————————————————— = × 100 = [ ] %
Enter number of items on checklist [ ]

WHAT THE RATINGS SIGNIFY

An unsatisfactory rating in "Innovation" indicates that marketing management is not keeping up with the state-of-the-art in modern organizational management. Failure to keep up with changing times can lead to isolation: The marketing organization can become ingrown and complacent, believing that the way it operates is the only way and the best way. While this is going on, the more progressive and outward-looking firms are becoming the market leaders.

WHAT TO DO NOW

1. *Get to know* what the most progressive companies are doing, by attending seminars and workships such as those run by various associations.

2. *Keep in constant contact* with other marketing professionals by joining the professional societies and attending meetings. (This can also help should you want to change jobs someday.)

3. *Make your staff members responsible* to review the current professional publications, keep notes on any good ideas they find, and present these as recommendations at staff meetings. This is excellent training in addition to being useful.

4. If the computer is not being used, *get to know the information systems and computer operations people.* They're in business to help you, and they're usually willing and able to improve your information handling at little cost.

5. *Make sure* that the next annual operating budget includes an allocation for the costs of these activities, by justifying the expense with results. Out-of-town seminars are often regarded by management with suspicion—make sure that every one attended leads to specific improvement action that benefits the company.

1-G
INTERFUNCTIONAL COMMUNICATIONS AND COORDINATION

	YES (1)	NO (0)	S/P* (½)
1. Marketing managers are encouraged to participate in activities involving other functions.	___	___	___
2. Managers of other functions are encouraged to take part in marketing activities, as members of cross-functional task groups led by marketing.	___	___	___
3. Close working relations are maintained at several organizational levels with other functions, especially field sales, to resolve day-to-day problems.	___	___	___
4. Marketing personnel accompany field sales representatives on sales calls at least once a month.	___	___	___

*SOMETIMES OR PARTIALLY

TOTAL POINTS   ☐ + 0 + ☐

= ☐

RATING

Enter number of points scored ☐

Enter number of items on checklist ☐

= × 100 = ☐ %

16

This is a two-way street. You and your marketing people should be actively involved in non-marketing activities, especially engineering and development, quality assurance, even financial control—in order to bring to marketing tasks a broader view of the business. Conversely, managers from other functions should be invited to participate in marketing planning and other marketing activities in order that they will add a marketing outlook to the work they do.

A low rating indicates that this two-way exchange of viewpoints is not taking place. As a consequence, marketing and non-marketing people may be functioning in isolation from each other, or even worse, they may be working at cross-purposes.

WHAT TO DO NOW

1. *Set up a program* of active contact and communication with sales, production, quality control, customer service, engineering, and other company functions.
2. *Contacts must be encouraged* at every organizational level, not just at the department head level, in order to break down the walls between functions.
3. *Invite people from other functions* to attend marketing meetings—you may be surprised at some of the good ideas they'll contribute when encouraged to participate.
4. Most importantly, *make sure that marketing people get out of the office* and accompany sales people on customer calls. There is no better way for your staff members to learn what customers actually think about the company and its products.

1-H
FUNCTIONAL IMPROVEMENT PROGRAM

	YES (1)	NO (0)	S/P* (½)
1. There is an active, on-going interfunctional team effort to improve organizational effectiveness, with major efforts directed toward:			
a. improved market-orientation and customer-responsiveness throughout the entire organization, and	———	———	———
b. new organizational forms designed to encourage innovation and creativity in marketing.	———	———	———
2. The following functions are represented on the team, depending on the task:			
a. product management,	———	———	———
b. field sales,	———	———	———
c. personnel and organizational development, and	———	———	———
d. information systems.	———	———	———

*SOMETIMES OR PARTIALLY

TOTAL POINTS

$$\boxed{} + 0 + \boxed{}$$
$$= \boxed{}$$

RATING

Enter number of points scored $\boxed{}$
——————————————————————— $=$ $\boxed{} \times 100 = \boxed{} \%$
Enter number of items on checklist $\boxed{}$

WHAT THE RATING SIGNIFIES

In order to organize the enterprise and to achieve market leadership, it is necessary to look at new, more adaptable form of organization—not just for the marketing department but for the company as a whole. Most business organizations, according to John Gardner, are designed to solve problems that no longer exist.

This does not mean that the conventional hierarchy—the classic pyramid—should be discarded in favor of a new "matrix organization." The matrix is popular at the moment, but it is not always appropriate: It can often cause more problems than it solves. What is needed is a less rigid, more flexible form of organization—one that can change easily as circumstances require—while still offering people the organizational stability and security they need.

One such mechanism is the team or task group that crosses functional lines. It is important that this group be assigned to solve a specific problem or spearhead a single improvement program, and then "self-destruct" when the project is completed. In the case of marketing, the task group is an excellent personnel development medium, as well as a helpful way to make the company more marketing conscious.

WHAT TO DO NOW

1. Try the team approach on a limited-scope project on an informal basis at first. When results justify, the process can be formalized.

2. Select a couple of functions that are most likely to cooperate, and choose an improvement project with a low controversy level to insure success.

3. Give public credit for the ideas that others contribute. It costs nothing and builds real cooperation.

1-1
RESOURCES

	YES (1)	NO (0)	S/P* (½)
1. Marketing management is kept informed about the company's objectives, policies, plans, and programs, through key meetings and access to appropriate business plans, capital budgets, and business development plans.			

*SOMETIMES OR PARTIALLY

	YES (1)	NO (0)	S/P* (½)

2. Based on this knowledge, marketing resources are judged to be adequate to meet the organizational needs of the department and the company during the next three, six, and twelve months, in terms of:

   a. budget funding, _____ _____ _____

   b. management time, _____ _____ _____

   c. staff assistance, _____ _____ _____

   d. support from personnel, _____ _____ _____

   e. computer time and capacity, and _____ _____ _____

   f. support from other functions. _____ _____ _____

*SOMETIMES OR PARTIALLY

TOTAL POINTS   [ ] + 0 + [ ]

= [ ]

RATING

Enter number of points scored [ ]
———————————————————————————— = × 100 = [ ] %
Enter number of items on checklist [ ]

WHAT THE RATINGS SIGNIFY

If the answer to point 1 is "no," then it is not possible to respond to point 2 with any confidence. Perhaps more than any other function of the business, marketing management must be informed about company goals, overall growth strategies, and forward plans. Knowledge and information are marketing's stock in trade.

Lacking the vital information it needs, marketing management cannot state with assurance that its resources are adequate to meet the needs of the company in the period ahead; when this is the case, the chances of getting additional resources are not good.

WHAT TO DO NOW

1. First, if lack of information is the problem, it may be because marketing management has failed to tell others what kind of information it needs. The first task is to identify exactly the kind and amount of information needed.

2. Second, a case has to be made *why* the information is needed, in terms of how it will be used to strengthen the firm's market activity.

3. Third, an active effort must be made to go after and get the needed information, on the basis that the department is entitled to it. In some cases, it must be demanded. In few cases will it come without effort on the part of marketing people.

4. If the problem is not lack of information but lack of physical and human resources—money, facilities, people, support from other functions, etc.—then marketing management has to perform the task of planning. This involves several specific steps:

19

a. Identify what resources are short of needs, and

b. determine the cost of the needed resources, for example, one market research assistant at $15,000/year.

c. Justify the cost with specific benefits. For example, "undertake two critical market studies needed to position the company in the $12 billion home energy conservation market in 198-."

d. Sell the boss on the plan. Without his support, the program to get the needed resources has little chance of success.

e. Enlist the support of other functional managers—sales, engineering, production, information systems, etc. They will then know what you expect from them during the coming months and what they can expect from you in return.

Chapter **2**

How to Develop Marketing Objectives And Strategies

The process of developing challenging marketing objectives and innovative marketing strategies is at the heart of marketing leadership.

THE FOUR MAIN STEPS IN THE PROCESS

1. Identifying the forces in the environment that affect profitability,
2. relating these to specific company strengths,
3. setting specific and demanding objectives, and
4. developing innovative marketing strategies to exploit opportunities and build on company strengths.

These activities add up to a marketing planning process that is complex and demanding. Process is the key word—it is not a one-shot effort, it is an on-going, year-round, continuous program. The process takes time and concentrated effort. It also requires standardized procedures, schedules, and a budget allocation.

Above all, marketing innovation has to be actively and aggressively sought after; it doesn't just happen because the marketing department holds a brain-storming session now and then, or a suggestion box was nailed to the office wall. Marketing innovation, like technical innovation, has to be organized and managed.

GROWTH THROUGH INNOVATION

A small business can be just as innovative as a large corporation—frequently more so. A small firm, in fact, *must* be innovative because it has less resources to employ when it comes to head-to-head competition with a bigger and financially stronger company. Nine times in ten, the enterprise that grows from small beginnings to become large and prosperous does so through brain-power. Sometimes, unfortunately, the kind of innovative marketing thinking and creative freedom that made the company grow is discouraged after it reaches a certain size—and then it tends to stop growing.

KEY OBJECTIVE OF THE SELF-AUDIT

The principal purpose of this section is to provide assurance that the marketing function—indeed the entire company—actively develops challenging marketing objectives and follows innovative marketing strategies; and has the mechanism to keep them in phase with changing conditions. To this end, the audit should examine with a critical eye the capability of the department to collect and use *information*—the only sound basis on which to establish these critical statements of business direction.

HOW TO USE THE CHECKLISTS

For each of the statements in the Checklist, compare the condition of your function to the "ideal" as described in the statement. Then:

1. If you consider the statement to be *generally true* of your function, check the YES column.

2. If you consider the statement to be *untrue* of your function, check the NO column.

3. If you consider the statement to be *less than true* (but not totally untrue) of your function, check the SOMETIMES OR PARTIAL column.

4. If the statement does not apply to your particular situation, write "Not Applicable" across the response spaces (or simply draw a line through them).

5. If you lack the data for a definite response, write in "Not Answerable" or "Don't Know."

HOW TO EVALUATE YOUR RESPONSES

When you have completed the checklist, glance over your responses, keeping these points in mind:

1. A negative answer is always unfavorable because it indicates a problem within the function: the greater the number of NOs, the more serious the situation.

2. A positive response is always a good indication. But too many YES answers could indicate that your review is not objective enough.

3. Too many SOMETIMES OR PARTIALLY answers can point to internal weaknesses or to a lack of firm direction.

4. A lot of "Not Applicable" answers could indicate that you are avoiding the issue.

5. A large number of "Not Answerable" or "Don't Know" answers could be symptomatic of inadequate records or data bases.

HOW TO RATE AND SCORE YOUR RESPONSES

When you are satisfied with your responses in general, you are ready to score the Checklist. For your convenience, a self-explanatory Scoring and Rating Block follows each Checklist. This block not only tells you whether the condition of your function is satisfactory, but it also gives you a measure of its effectiveness.

Here's how to total up the points for inclusion in the Scoring and Rating Block:

1. Total up the number of points you scored:
   a. For each YES, give yourself one point.
   b. For each NO, give yourself zero.
   c. For each SOMETIMES OR PARTIALLY, give yourself a half-point.
   d. For each "Not Applicable" answer, give yourself zero and deduct one from the number of items on the Checklist.
   e. For each "Not Answerable" or "Don't Know" answer, give yourself zero.

2. Next divide the total number of points you score by the total number of items (statements) on the Checklist (less items marked "Not Applicable"). You'll get a 1.0 for a perfect score and a fraction for anything less.

3. Multiply the result of step 2 by 100 to arrive at the percentage for your score.

What is a satisfactory rating? A rating of less than 65 percent is unacceptable and calls for an improvement program: Obviously, the lower the rating, the more drastic the action required.

A brief "how-to" example of this Scoring and Rating system follows . . .

EXAMPLE

	YES (1)	NO (0)	S/P* (½)

1. Field sale reports designed to provide information on sales progress contain data on the following topics:

   a. sales calls and sales presentations made by salespersons and sales agents, ✓ YES

   b. bids, quotations, and proposals made, ✓ YES

   c. new orders booked, ✓ YES

   d. lost business, and reasons for the loss, ✓ NO

   e. accomplishments toward future orders, ✓ S/P

   f. performance in filling orders, handling complaints, and otherwise servicing individual customers, ✓ YES

   g. action taken in response to customer requests, such as sending samples, spec sheets, etc., ✓ YES

   h. accomplishments of significance and value to other members of the sales force. ✓ S/P

*SOMETIMES OR PARTIALLY

TOTAL POINTS

$$\boxed{5} + 0 + \boxed{1}$$

$$= \boxed{6}$$

RATING

$$\frac{\text{Enter number of points scored} \quad \boxed{6}}{\text{Enter number of items on checklist} \quad \boxed{8}} = .75 \times 100 = \boxed{75}\ \%$$

24

	YES (1)	NO (0)	S/P* (½)
1. The development of marketing objectives and strategies is recognized as a high-priority company activity that has top management endorsement and support.	_____	_____	_____
2. The activity is recognized on the organization charts and in managers' position descriptions as an important function of marketing or product management.	_____	_____	_____
3. The work is done under the personal direction of the marketing manager, or product manager.	_____	_____	_____
4. The marketing budget includes an allocation for this activity, covering internal expenses and outside intelligence services if required.	_____	_____	_____
5. The budget is based on a critical review and evaluation of all tasks involved.	_____	_____	_____
6. Managers involved are trained in the principles of objective-setting and strategy-development, and are well informed about the company's products and markets.	_____	_____	_____
7. The establishment of marketing objectives and strategies is accomplished through a systematic, formal process guided by a written procedure.	_____	_____	_____
8. Every level of marketing management is involved at some point in the process.	_____	_____	_____
9. One or more managers are freed from other tasks and dedicated to this effort for an extended period of time.	_____	_____	_____
10. A definite schedule is established for the task, in terms of duration and completion date.	_____	_____	_____
11. Marketing objectives and strategies are based on sound knowledge and up-to-date information—not on intuition, guesswork, and speculation.	_____	_____	_____
12. Marketing objectives:			
a. Marketing objectives are reviewed and revised annually, as part of marketing planning.	_____	_____	_____
b. Marketing objectives have been established by product line for:			
1. share of available market,	_____	_____	_____
2. sales and revenue growth,	_____	_____	_____
3. margin in dollars and percent of sales,	_____	_____	_____
4. new product contribution, and	_____	_____	_____
5. product phase-out.	_____	_____	_____
c. Quantitative marketing objectives are established in a sequence such as this:			
1. first, based on market potential assuming no constraints,	_____	_____	_____
2. second, revised downward to reflect known limitations on resources available, and	_____	_____	_____
3. third, revised upward to provide a "stretch" factor.	_____	_____	_____

*SOMETIMES OR PARTIALLY

	YES (1)	NO (0)	S/P* (½)

d. Objectives are clearly stated in writing, and have an explicit time factor.

e. The sum of all product line objectives exceeds the company total objective by a factor for contingencies.

f. Marketing objectives are in harmony with overall company objectives, strategies, policies, and long-range plans.

g. Marketing objectives have been modified in some respects by the subsequent process of developing marketing strategies.

13. Marketing strategies:

a. Marketing strategies are innovative in nature, couched in action terms, and oriented to growth and improved profitability.

b. Strategies are developed only after a critical assessment of marketing strengths and weaknesses relative to competition.

c. Strategies are designed to build on current strengths, not merely to correct weaknesses.

d. Strategies are developed through a process of discussion, debate, and consideration of all alternatives.

e. Each key marketing strategy is accompanied by a "fall back" strategy for contingency use.

f. The Unit is prepared to abandon a strategy that appears headed for failure or is too expensive, and adopt a new approach.

g. Strategies are defined in writing and "tested" for comprehension, logic, feasibility of execution, and probability of success.

h. Marketing strategies selected are communicated to managers of all other functions to utilize in developing action plans, schedules, and cost projections.

14. Marketing objectives and strategies are treated as "company confidential" information of the highest order.

*SOMETIMES OR PARTIALLY

TOTAL POINTS   [ ] + 0 + [ ]

= [ ]

RATING

Enter number of points scored   [ ]

────────────────────────────────

Enter number of items on checklist   [ ]

= [ ] × 100 = [ ] %

WHAT THE RATING SIGNIFIES   A less-than-satisfactory rating for this section is an indication that management might be selling this important activity short—by failing to treat the development of marketing objectives and strategies as a *separate, discrete, on-going, business function* that must be organized, funded, and managed. As a result, the objectives and strategies the company is following may not be realistic.

If they're not realistic, the chances are small that they will be realized—or if they are realized, they could lead you to a wrong result. Objectives and strategies are achievable and realistic only when they are (1) based on adequate and up-to-date information about the company's markets, customers, and competitors, (2) they are developed on an organized, methodical, and thoughtful manner, with input from other business functions (and not on a hit-or-miss, last minute basis to meet a deadline for the annual business plan).

If neither of these two conditions apply, then it follows that marketing objectives and strategies *cannot be innovative.* Innovation means "new and different;" if you don't have accurate up-to-date information about what your competition is doing, you can't know if what you're planning to do is really different. What is more, if you don't have enough time to analyze the information you get, you're taking a chance that the strategies you adopt may work in your competitor's favor instead of yours.

A low rating may also indicate that your objectives and strategies may be unrealistic because they are out of joint with present company strengths and available resources. This is dangerous. Objectives that are clearly beyond the capabilities of people to achieve are counter-productive, because people may quit trying. Strategies dependent on resources that are unavailable can lead you down blind alleys from which there is no way out.

WHAT TO DO NOW

1. If the problem is that management doesn't look on this activity as an important separate function, the task ahead is an educational one. In this situation, you should build a case for the company's *need* for marketing objectives that are realistic and achievable, and for more innovative marketing strategies. To support your case, it's very possible that you can find evidence of *past failures to meet objectives* and a history of *strategies that went wrong.*

2. If the problem is lack of good, current marketing information on which to base marketing objectives and strategies, you should set as one of your major objectives the creation of a good data bank during the next six to twelve months. This is not a job you can do overnight.

   In addition to information on markets, industries, and competitors, you need an up-to-date "inventory" of your company's strengths and capabilities. Next you need a method for gathering data on current trends and developments in your industry and your markets, and organizing the data into useful information.

   The computer can't do this for you, but it is an indispensible means to store the information, manipulate it many ways quickly, and recall it whenever you need it.

3. If the problem is lack of a system for handling information, you may have to call on the company's information systems specialists for help. If your budget can stand it, a good analyst can earn his or her salary many times over by ensuring that the data you get is converted into useful information.

4. Whatever the problem, marketing innovation requires a constant, free-flowing stream of ideas from every member of the organization. The marketing department does not have a corner on new ideas—other functions should be actively encouraged to contribute their best thinking. Every idea, no matter how bizarre it may seem at first, should be

considered. The best of them should be tested in the market place on a controlled experiment basis—then modified by experience before putting them into effect.

5. *Caution*: Don't let yourself become so infatuated with one approach that you neglect other possibilities. Have backup strategies ready to call up when it appears that your way is blocked.

2-B
AUTHORITY, RESPONSIBILITY AND ACCOUNTABILITY

	YES (1)	NO (0)	S/P* (½)
1. Authority has been delegated to the manager of marketing to expend company funds and assign tasks necessary to develop and publish marketing objectives and strategies.	___	___	___
2. Delegation of authority is made firm and binding through:			
a. budget allocation,	___	___	___
b. job title, and	___	___	___
c. position description.	___	___	___
3. Responsibility is firmly assigned to the manager of marketing to:			
a. staff and manage an organization capable of developing forceful and innovative marketing objectives and strategies,	___	___	___
b. develop and administer sound procedures and controls to guide and govern the function,	___	___	___
c. publish approved objectives and strategies prior to the start of the operating year, as part of the marketing plan.	___	___	___
4. The manager is held accountable for:			
a. failure to provide proper guidance to marketing and sales personnel for their annual planning and operations,	___	___	___
b. failure to provide marketing leadership to other functions, in the form of challenging marketing objectives and strategies,	___	___	___
c. and in the final analysis for failure to increase penetration of markets of major importance to the company.	___	___	___

*SOMETIMES OR PARTIALLY

TOTAL POINTS [ ] + 0 + [ ]

= [ ]

RATING

Enter number of points scored [ ] = × 100 = [ ] %

Enter number of items on checklist [ ]

WHAT THE RATING SIGNIFIES

Negative answers to points 1 and 2 can indicate that the manager of marketing may not have real authority to spend company funds for this activity, even though he may think he has. As a consequence, he or she may be accused of spending money unwisely, or even foolishly, when conducting a three-day "strategy" meeting at a remote conference center, or subscribing to a costly outside market intelligence service.

The manager could be in big trouble if, after answering "no" to these points, he answers "yes" to points 3 and 4. There is nothing more dangerous for a manager than to be responsible and accountable for results of an activity for which he lacks authority.

WHAT TO DO NOW

1. Insist on clear and explicit delegation of authority and position descriptions that spell out exactly what your spending limits are for all important aspects of your function. The more specific these are, the more positive and decisive you can be in getting your job done. You should approach this as your right—a necessary condition to getting your job done.

2. Have these validated and supported by a specific line item in your operating budget for the task of developing marketing objectives and strategies.

3. If you are the manager of marketing in fact, but your title doesn't make that clear to others, you should take steps to get a position title that does.

2-C
MEASUREMENTS, CONTROL REPORTS AND PERFORMANCE RECORDS

	YES (1)	NO (0)	S/P* (½)
1. The effectiveness of the company's marketing objectives and strategies is measured and compared to specific benchmarks of performance and results, regularly and continuously.	___	___	___
2. The following benchmarks are used regularly to measure and evaluate the effectiveness of marketing objectives and strategies:			
a. improvement in market shares of the company's products,	___	___	___
b. trend in return on investment,	___	___	___
c. positioning of new products and development of new markets—actual performance vs. forecasts, and	___	___	___
d. progress toward identified future markets of interest is known.	___	___	___
3. The size and potential of all major markets of interest is known.	___	___	___
4. Market surveys and studies of all major company markets are made or up-dated at least every 2 years.	___	___	___
5. Surveys are routinely analyzed for evidence of changes in user needs and preferences that could affect strategies.	___	___	___

*SOMETIMES OR PARTIALLY

	YES (1)	NO (0)	S/P* (½)

6. Competitive and industry intelligence is actively gathered and routinely analyzed for evidence of new product and market activities by competitors.

7. Field sales reports are analyzed for trends and relationships.

8. Reports and surveys showing significant changes in markets or competitive developments alert management automatically to the need for re-appraisal of objectives and strategies.

*SOMETIMES OR PARTIALLY

TOTAL POINTS ☐ + 0 + ☐

= ☐

RATING

Enter number of points scored ☐

Enter number of items on checklist ☐

= × 100 = ☐ %

WHAT THE RATING SIGNIFIES

Negative answers to the first two points indicates that the effectiveness of your objectives and strategies is not being evaluated methodically. If this is so, then you cannot know with any certainty whether they are working or not. If you're not sure whether they're working, the chances are high that you will keep on following them long after they have been outdated by external events. A couple of American auto makers insisted that what the public wanted was large size and high power, and followed that market strategy almost to insolvency, even while the evidence against it was piling up in their dealers' lots and showrooms in the form of unsold cars.

A low rating in the rest of this section usually confirms that *information* is not being effectively used as a basis for keeping your objectives and strategies up to date—either it is lacking or it is not being analyzed properly.

WHAT TO DO NOW

1. According to Peter Drucker control is really measurement; so if you want to control an activity, you must measure it. This means that you must set up measurement criteria—benchmarks, milestones, etc.—and compare performance to them regularly. In principle, the more often you measure performance, the better it is—in this case, by measuring them frequently, your objectives and strategies become more easily and quickly adapted to changing conditions. Unless you take a regular "physical examination" of your function, you might have to conduct a "*post mortem*" to determine the cause of its demise!

2. In order to keep your objectives and strategies "in tune" with changing circumstances, you need a *systematic process* for collecting and analyzing information about what is happening, both within the organization and outside it. This requires assigning a responsible person, or persons,

to the task (not necessarily full time, of course) of ensuring that your information is accurate, timely and meaningful.

2-D
OPERATING PERFORMANCE HISTORY

	YES (1)	NO (0)	S/P* (½)

1. During the past several years there has been an improving trend in:

    a. penetration of major markets, as measured by market shares,

    b. overall ROI,

    c. number of new products successfully introduced,

    d. new-product sales volume (products less than 3 years old), and

    e. sales volume in new markets in which the company did not participate 3 years ago.

2. Major objectives established in the past have essentially been met, according to a review of the records for the past year.

3. The principal strategies chosen to achieve last year's objectives have:

    a. been followed in their essential elements, and

    b. have proved to be effective.

4. Most recent marketing objectives and strategies were approved by top management essentially on schedule.

5. There have been no important moves by competitors during the past year that were not anticipated and considered in formulating objectives and strategies.

6. No company strategy was disclosed to competition either inadvertently or through information "leaks" within the company. (Answer yes if true.)

*SOMETIMES OR PARTIALLY

TOTAL POINTS   ☐ + 0 + ☐

= ☐

RATING

Enter number of points scored   ☐

————————————————   =   × 100 = ☐ %

Enter number of items on checklist   ☐

WHAT THE RATING SIGNIFIES   If you have a problem answering these points, it may be because your measurements and control reports are deficient (see previous section).

A low score in this section normally means that the objectives and strategies you set in the past were either out of phase with your market and competitive environments, or they were beyond your functional resources and capabilities to achieve them. In other words, your objectives and strategies were at fault, not your performance.

WHAT TO DO NOW

1. The only sure cure for past failure is to isolate and correct the basic problem. Treating symptoms, or solving the wrong problem, can consume your energies and get you nowhere.

2. Make a thorough, honest, and painstaking review and analysis of your past functional performance in relation to your past objectives and strategies. Chances are you'll find out that poor performance was a result of inadequate or out-of-date information; and objectives and strategies that were based on intuition, conjecture, biased opinion which is often wrong, and guesswork instead of hard facts.

2-E
TOP-LEVEL SUPPORT AND GUIDANCE

	YES (1)	NO (0)	S/P* (½)
1. The executive office provides active support, guidance, and recognition to the process of developing marketing objectives and strategies, through:			
a. budget approval,	_____	_____	_____
b. executive review and approval of objectives and strategies,	_____	_____	_____
c. personal guidance to marketing and product management during the process,	_____	_____	_____
d. participation in progress review meetings during implementation,	_____	_____	_____
e. recognition and reward for outstanding accomplishment, and	_____	_____	_____
f. published policy statements.	_____	_____	_____

*SOMETIMES OR PARTIALLY

TOTAL POINTS [   ] + 0 + [   ]

= [   ]

RATING

Enter number of points scored [   ]

───────────────────────────────── = × 100 = [   ] %

Enter number of items on checklist [   ]

WHAT THE RATING SIGNIFIES

Support from the front office is essential to successful development and achievement of marketing objectives and strategies because these statements support and reinforce the goals and strategies of the entire organization. If the top executive does not play an active and visible role in this activity, by approving the proposed goals and strategies and by periodically reviewing progress toward them, then managers of other functions may not take them seriously—and marketing may fail.

WHAT TO DO NOW

1. This kind of support comes only if your chief executive is convinced that you have the capability to set challenging objectives and develop innovative strategies that put the company out front in the competitive race—*out front where the profits are greater.*

2. This is a sort of Catch-22 situation: You need top level support to be successful—but you must be successful to get the support. However, you do have control if you have the authority and the resources. The resource you need most of all is creative people. With a staff (however small) of intelligent, energetic, and innovative people, you can't miss—without it, you're "dead in the water!"

2-F
INNOVATION IN METHODS AND TECHNIQUES

	YES (1)	NO (0)	S/P* (½)

1. Marketing management actively keeps informed about new techniques for developing marketing objectives and strategies, through:

   a. seminars, workshops, and conferences,

   b. professional associations,

   c. outside specialists,

   d. industry contacts,

   e. review of current literature, and

   f. budgets include funds for such activities.

2. Competent outside specialists are utilized to keep marketing people informed about markets and competition.

3. Latest OR techniques of modeling, statistical analysis, probability theory, and gaming are employed *when appropriate to the problem.*

4. The computer is utilized to store, process, and display information needed in formulating objectives and strategy.

*SOMETIMES OR PARTIALLY

TOTAL POINTS ☐ + 0 + ☐

= ☐

RATING

Enter number of points scored ☐

Enter number of items on checklist ☐

= × 100 = ☐ %

WHAT THE RATING SIGNIFIES   A less-than-acceptable score here indicates that marketing management may be running the risk of becoming isolated from the mainstream—by failing to look outside the company for new tools, techniques, and

33

management methods to improve operations. The world is changing rapidly, and the manager who doesn't keep up with what is happening outside his company is going to be left behind the parade. This is especially true of marketing managers. It may take three or four hours a week—or even more—of a manager's time to keep up with the literature alone. In addition, he should set aside perhaps 5 to 10 percent of his time to attend marketing seminars and workshops and update his professional skills through education. Functional budgets should provide for these activities, or else they won't be done—*and the company will be the loser* for it. The most innovative firms recognize this. International Harvester, for example, *pays its managers a bonus* for joining professional societies.

(*Note*: It is important from a personal standpoint to keep up your industry contacts—for the day when you might find your career path blocked in your present firm—and a move to another company is indicated.)

WHAT TO DO NOW

1. If your budget doesn't cover the expenses of outside seminars, consulting fees, etc., start now to build a case for getting them in next year's budget. Meanwhile, take advantage of all free and low-cost outside sources of information. There are many, including the cheapest source of all—the public library. Collect the annual reports of your competitors and prospects, and analyze them carefully—they are often a gold mine of information.

2. Before you employ a consultant, check him out carefully, and define his task in very specific terms. Above all, base his or her fee on *specific and verifiable results*, not on the amount of time spent on your premises.

3. If you use a data processing service company, make sure they're qualified to do the analysis and programming job you need. And demand *full* service, not simply computer time. The business is highly competitive—shop and bargain for the best terms. If your own firm has an internal computer operation, it might pay you to get an outside quotation on your job to keep them "honest."

4. This is "what *not* to do" advice; *do not use* highly technical methods of "scientific management" except on very large and complex problems where the cost is justified.

2-G
INTERFUNCTIONAL COMMUNICATIONS AND COORDINATION

	YES (1)	NO (0)	S/P* (½)
1. Cross-functional teams, task forces, or review committees are employed to bring other viewpoints into the process of developing marketing objectives and strategies.	____	____	____
2. Teams meet on a fixed schedule, work to an agenda, and issue action assignments.	____	____	____
3. Draft objectives and strategies are reviewed with management of other company functions so that plans can be "harmonized" among marketing, manufacturing, engineering, and others.	____	____	____

*SOMETIMES OR PARTIALLY

TOTAL POINTS

□ + 0 + □

= □

RATING

Enter number of points scored □

———————————————————— = × 100 = □ %

Enter number of items on checklist □

WHAT THE RATING SIGNIFIES   A low rating on this section indicates that the firm's marketing objectives and strategies may be out of joint with the other key functions of the business—engineering, sales or production. If so, there is no way they will ever be realized. Or if they are, they may be achieved at a high cost to the company in the form of contention and damaging competitiveness between functions, and loss of cooperation during implementation.

WHAT TO DO NOW   Make absolutely sure that the other functions participate in the development of these critical company statements of future intent. It's your initiative to do so, and your responsibility. It's also to your advantage—not only will the goals be better, but the other functional managers are more likely to provide the cooperation needed to make them successful (and far less likely to criticize if things should go wrong!)

2-H
FUNCTIONAL IMPROVEMENT PROGRAM

	YES (1)	NO (0)	S/P* (½)
1. There is an active, organized, on-going interfunctional team effort to improve the quality of marketing objectives and strategies and the process of developing them. Major efforts on a task basis are directed toward:			
a. more active involvement in the process by other functional managers,	———	———	———
b. improved relevance of objectives and strategies to the realities of the marketplace,	———	———	———
c. more emphasis on return on investment,	———	———	———
d. more innovative marketing strategies, and	———	———	———
e. an organized "marketing R&D" effort.	———	———	———
2. The following functions are represented on the team, as required by the particular task:	———	———	———
a. field sales,	———	———	———

*SOMETIMES OR PARTIALLY

	YES (1)	NO (0)	S/P* (½)
b. research, development, and engineering,	___	___	___
c. production,	___	___	___
d. information systems, and	___	___	___
e. all marketing functions, especially product management.	___	___	___

*SOMETIMES OR PARTIALLY

TOTAL POINTS [ ] + 0 + [ ]

= [ ]

RATING

Enter number of points scored   [ ]
———————————————————————————— = × 100 = [   ] %
Enter number of items on checklist   [ ]

WHAT THE RATING SIGNIFIES

Very few firms have this kind of organized approach to functional improvement. A low rating, therefore, should be viewed as a signal that your function could benefit from more involvement and input from the other functions, not as a critical deficiency.

WHAT TO DO NOW

It's not easy to get other functional managers involved with your activities. You'll have to demonstrate to them that they will gain from their expenditure of time, so a little preparation is in order.

1. Define the benefits that each of them will get from better marketing objectives and more innovative strategies. (If you can't do this, don't go any further.)
2. Then actively sell them the benefits—you may be pleasantly surprised at the cooperation you will get.

2-I
RESOURCES

	YES (1)	NO (0)	S/P* (½)
1. Marketing management is routinely kept informed about company objectives, policies, plans, and programs through:			
a. participation in meetings,	___	___	___
b. access to business development plans,	___	___	___
c. access to capital budgets, and	___	___	___
d. operating reports.	___	___	___

*SOMETIMES OR PARTIALLY

	YES (1)	NO (0)	S/P* (½)

2. Based on this knowledge and the foregoing appraisal, marketing resources are judged to be adequate to meet the company needs for effective marketing objectives and strategies during the next three, six, and twelve months, in terms of:

a. manpower,

b. capabilities,

c. budget funding,

d. outside services,

e. computer time and capacity, if applicable, and

f. other functional support.

*SOMETIMES OR PARTIALLY

TOTAL POINTS ☐ + 0 + ☐

= ☐

RATING

Enter number of points scored ☐

Enter number of items on checklist ☐

= × 100 = ☐ %

WHAT THE RATING SIGNIFIES

Negative answers to point 1 are evidence of a serious problem. There's no way in the world you can set meaningful marketing objectives and develop innovative marketing strategies unless you keep well-informed about the current overall goals and programs of the company.

Without this top-level guiding input, your functional output cannot be good, and your function can't be productive. Not only that, but you cannot even know whether your resources are adequate to meet the needs of the company in the period ahead.

WHAT TO DO NOW

1. If you lack access to the top-level information you need, you must *demand it*. Don't take it for granted that someone higher will decide what you need to know. If you have the responsibility, you have the right to the resources—including information—it takes to carry it out.

2. If you lack the other resources—such as funding, manpower, support—you need an action plan to get them. What is needed is the kind of plan that commits you to accomplish specific goals by a specified time. Only then can you make a pitch to get the resources it takes to carry out the plan. Having a plan doesn't guarantee success—but *not* having a plan is an almost certain guarantee of failure!

Chapter **3**

How to Coordinate
And Control
Marketing Activities

In the most progressive and successful firms, marketing is the leading edge of the organization. Marketing has the dominant role in the shaping of over-all goals and business strategy, and has a strong voice in all major decisions involving the allocation of company resources.

THE KEY FACTORS: COMMUNICATION AND SELF-CONTROL

This is a heavy responsibility. It requires that marketing activities be well coordinated with all the other functions of the organization, in addition to being well controlled and coordinated internally. Communication is a key element. To ensure this vital coordination and control, the manager of marketing should regard it as a separate function within the marketing department—one that must be organized, staffed, and funded. It takes time and effort, and costs money to produce control reports, hold coordination meetings, measure performance, distribute information, and prepare and control schedules.

There is another type of control needed, as well. If marketing is to be really productive, a large measure of *self-control* is needed by its people. Otherwise, marketing management has to spend so much time on internal control that coordination with others is neglected. So all marketing people should be encouraged to control their activities to the maximum.

KEY AIM OF THE SELF-AUDIT

The main purpose of the self-audit is to ensure that marketing activities are coordinated with all other business functions in a way that ensures a strong market-orientation throughout the whole organization, and a leading role for marketing in all company decisions that affect its future.

The secondary objective of the appraisal is to provide assurance that the marketing function is under good control. It should not be a restrictive type of control that stifles initiative and self-development, but a kind of self-control that encourages initiative and innovation by all personnel.

HOW TO USE THE CHECKLISTS

For each of the statements in the Checklist, compare the condition of your function to the "ideal" as described in the statement. Then:

1. If you consider the statement to be *generally true* of your function, check the YES column.
2. If you consider the statement to be *untrue* of your function, check the NO column.
3. If you consider the statement to be *less than true* (but not totally untrue) of your function, check the SOMETIMES OR PARTIAL column.
4. If the statement does not apply to your particular situation, write "Not Applicable" across the response spaces (or simply draw a line through them).
5. If you lack the data for a definite response, write in "Not Answerable" or "Don't Know."

HOW TO EVALUATE YOUR RESPONSES

When you have completed the checklist, glance over your responses, keeping these points in mind:

1. A negative answer is always unfavorable because it indicates a problem within the function: the greater the number of NOs, the more serious the situation.
2. A positive response is always a good indication. But too many YES answers could indicate that your review is not objective enough.
3. Too many SOMETIMES OR PARTIALLY answers can point to internal weaknesses or to a lack of firm direction.
4. A lot of "Not Applicable" answers could indicate that you are avoiding the issue.
5. A large number of "Not Answerable" or "Don't Know" answers could be symptomatic of inadequate records or data bases.

HOW TO RATE AND SCORE YOUR RESPONSES

When you are satisfied with your responses in general, you are ready to score the Checklist. For your convenience, a self-explanatory Scoring and Rating Block follows each Checklist. This block not only tells you whether the condition of your function is satisfactory, but it also gives you a measure of its effectiveness.

Here's how to total up the points for inclusion in the Scoring and Rating Block:

1. Total up the number of points you scored:
   a. For each YES, give yourself one point.
   b. For each NO, give yourself zero.
   c. For each SOMETIMES OR PARTIALLY, give yourself a half-point.
   d. For each "Not Applicable" answer, give yourself zero and deduct one from the number of items on the Checklist.
   e. For each "Not Answerable" or "Don't Know" answer, give yourself zero.
2. Next divide the total number of points you score by the total number of items (statements) on the Checklist (less items marked "Not Applicable"). You'll get a 1.0 for a perfect score and a fraction for anything less.
3. Multiply the result of step 2 by 100 to arrive at the percentage for your score.

What is a satisfactory rating? A rating of less than 65 percent is unacceptable and calls for an improvement program: Obviously, the lower the rating, the more drastic the action required.

A brief "how-to" example of this Scoring and Rating system follows . . .

EXAMPLE

	YES (1)	NO (0)	S/P* (½)

1. Field sale reports designed to provide information on sales progress contain data on the following topics:

   a. sales calls and sales presentations made by salespersons and sales agents, ✓

   b. bids, quotations, and proposals made, ✓

   c. new orders booked, ✓

   d. lost business, and reasons for the loss, ✓ (NO)

   e. accomplishments toward future orders, ✓ (S/P)

   f. performance in filling orders, handling complaints, and otherwise servicing individual customers, ✓

   g. action taken in response to customer requests, such as sending samples, spec sheets, etc., ✓

   h. accomplishments of significance and value to other members of the sales force. ✓ (S/P)

*SOMETIMES OR PARTIALLY

TOTAL POINTS $\boxed{5}$ + 0 + $\boxed{1}$

= $\boxed{6}$

RATING

$$\frac{\text{Enter number of points scored} \quad \boxed{6}}{\text{Enter number of items on checklist} \quad \boxed{8}} = .75 \times 100 = \boxed{75}\%$$

40

3-A
ORGANIZATION, ADMINISTRATION, AND OPERATION

	YES (1)	NO (0)	S/P* (½)
1. Coordination of marketing activities with other functions of the business is recognized as an important company activity that has top management endorsement and support.	———	———	———
2. The manager of marketing spends a substantial portion, about 20 percent, of his time on this activity.	———	———	———
3. Marketing management follows an organized approach and systematic, written operating procedures to assure internal control and coordination with other functions.	———	———	———
4. Coordination and control of marketing activities is considered important enough to be organized as a separate function within marketing (not necessarily full-time).	———	———	———
5. Coordination and control are achieved by means of:			
a. marketing plans,	———	———	———
b. written procedures,	———	———	———
c. weekly staff meetings,	———	———	———
d. interdepartmental meetings,	———	———	———
e. exchange of activity reports,	———	———	———
f. operating committee meetings,	———	———	———
g. meeting minutes and action assignments,	———	———	———
h. weekly and monthly progress reports,	———	———	———
i. budget controls on spending,	———	———	———
j. project control reports,	———	———	———
k. performance reports,	———	———	———
l. position descriptions,	———	———	———
m. productivity standards, and	———	———	———
n. project specifications and schedules.	———	———	———
6. The marketing budget includes an allocation for this activity, covering internal expenses and outside services, if required.	———	———	———
7. Managers are encouraged and expected to:			
a. set their own objectives, consistent with company goals,	———	———	———
b. help to establish standards for their operations,	———	———	———
c. correct deviations from standard, and	———	———	———
d. report only those deviations that are beyond their own control range to upper management.	———	———	———

*SOMETIMES OR PARTIALLY

TOTAL POINTS □ + 0 + □

}

= □

RATING

Enter number of points scored □

——————————————————————————— = □ × 100 = □ %

Enter number of items on checklist □

WHAT THE RATING SIGNIFIES

A less-than-acceptable rating indicates that the marketing function may not be assertive enough in playing its role as the leading edge of the organization. Coordination is used here in an active, not a passive sense; that is, marketing should take the initiative to ensure that the other functions of the business follow marketing's lead.

This means that product engineering should be working on the new product that marketing management has recommended, based on good market surveys. It means that product distribution and the sales force should be stocking and selling the brands that marketing has determined are the most in demand—and consequently tend to have the highest profit margins. This determination should be based on up-to-date market demand analyses, analysis of current sales, and the latest margin analysis made by the controller's department.

It also means that production should be producing these same products, and not simply turning out goods because they have idle facilities.

WHAT TO DO NOW

Coordination and control require *communication*.

1. First, your marketing plans should get the widest circulation consistent with company security, because they are the key medium for asserting marketing's leadership.

2. Open up your marketing meetings to the other functions. Make sure that they are productive meetings and that you are in control of the agenda!

3. Make yourself available and helpful to the other functions. Make sure that the other members of the marketing staff have good day-to-day contact with other functional people on their level.

4. Finally, preface every market survey with a firm recommendation for action by other functions. Unless you do, chances are either that nothing will be done, or that someone will act on his own interpretation of the data, which might be 100 percent wrong.

3-B
AUTHORITY, RESPONSIBILITY, AND ACCOUNTABILITY

	YES (1)	NO (0)	S/P* (½)
1. Authority has been delegated in writing to the marketing manager to expend company funds and assign tasks necessary to assure a high degree of coordination and control of marketing activities, internally and with other company functions.			

*SOMETIMES OR PARTIALLY

	YES (1)	NO (0)	S/P* (½)

2. Through policy statement or position description, responsibility is assigned to the marketing manager to staff and manage an organization to control and coordinate marketing activities throughout the company.

3. Responsibility is firmly assigned to the marketing manager for establishing control procedures and standard practices and enforcing them.

4. Responsibility is assigned to an individual to administer the procedures and standard practices, to record meeting proceedings, and to maintain control reports and records.

5. Responsibility for individual performance and results is vested in each individual (self-control).

6. Self-control requires each person to accept accountability for meeting personal goals, and for operating within predetermined standards of performance and expense budgets.

7. The marketing manager is held accountable for serious failure to meet departmental goals, or to accomplish projects and programs on time. This includes projects led by marketing that involve other departments, which result from inadequate coordination and control.

*SOMETIMES OR PARTIALLY

TOTAL POINTS   ☐ + 0 + ☐

= ☐

RATING

Enter number of points scored ☐
——————————————————— = × 100 = ☐ %
Enter number of items on checklist ☐

WHAT THE RATING SIGNIFIES

A low rating in this section is a "red flag" warning of trouble ahead. Unless you have firm and explicit authority to spend the funds required to set up and operate the controls and produce the reports needed—and unless people know exactly what their responsibilities are in this important function—the work won't be done and coordination and control will suffer.

WHAT DO TO NOW

If you feel that you lack sufficient authority or resources:

1. Make sure that your own house is in order. Test your subordinate's knowledge of their responsibilities and their understanding of what they are accountable for.

2. Insist that they have full and speedy "feedback" on their own performance, so they don't have to wait for you to tell them how they're doing.

3. When you're satisfied that your operation is efficient and productive, you can go after the authority you lack—with confidence. Sell your own boss first; if he can't give it to you, get him to carry your message higher.

3-C
MEASUREMENTS, CONTROL REPORTS AND PERFORMANCE RECORDS

	YES (1)	NO (0)	S/P* (½)

1. The effectiveness of marketing coordination and control is measured and evaluated regularly and continuously.

2. The following criteria of performance and results are used to measure effectiveness:

   a. acceptance by others of marketing's recommendations,

   b. success in meeting marketing plan objectives,

   c. accomplishment of marketing projects on time and within budget,

   d. meeting department goals and budgets, and

   e. achievement of individual staff members' goals.

3. Project controls are maintained showing actual performance against plan, and expenditures vs. budget.

4. Control reports show current status of major programs, actual performance toward marketing objectives and strategies, and status of new product developments.

5. Major deviations from plans and standards are flagged automatically for management attention.

6. Reports on sales, gross margins, new orders, selling expenses, order backlogs, cancellations, and lost business are routinely received and analyzed for significance to marketing activities.

7. Reports, market surveys, and special studies on products and markets, are abstracted, cross-indexed, and filed for quick and frequent reference.

8. Expenses of the activity are routinely compared with budget, and major variances analyzed for corrective action.

*SOMETIMES OR PARTIALLY

TOTAL POINTS ☐ + 0 + ☐ = ☐

RATING

Enter number of points scored ☐ / Enter number of items on checklist ☐ = ☐ × 100 = ☐ %

WHAT THE RATING SIGNIFIES

This is a function that is not generally measured because it is not considered to be a separate function. The fact is, marketing coordination and control is one of the most critical activities of the business, especially in the highly competitive world of the eighties.

Negative answers to points 1 and 2 indicates that this may be the case. If so, the company runs the risk of falling behind in the competitive race through lack of marketing coordination

A low rating on the rest of this section is an indication that control is lax because controls are missing.

WHAT TO DO NOW

1. Good control depends on information. Lack of control may come from one of two failings—lack of information, or failure to use the information that is available. Either way, you need a person to manage information, that is, someone who has the ability to collect, organize, analyze, and interpret data.

2. The computer can help, but it takes a human to do the necessary thinking. If you can get the work done by calling on the information systems department, you might save money, but it may be better to have someone right in your own department.

3-D
OPERATING PERFORMANCE HISTORY

	YES (1)	NO (0)	S/P* (½)
1. A review and analysis of control reports and records has been made for at least one year past.	___	___	___
2. During the past year, marketing has met or exceeded overall departmental objectives.	___	___	___
3. Total expenses have been on budget, plus or minus an acceptable margin.	___	___	___
4. Individual projects (market surveys, etc.) have been completed essentially within original cost and time schedule.	___	___	___
5. Individual managers have essentially met their personal goals, with few cases of intervention by the marketing manager.	___	___	___
6. Major company-wide programs that are led by marketing, such as new business ventures, have essentially met target goals.	___	___	___

*SOMETIMES OR PARTIALLY

TOTAL POINTS [ ] + 0 + [ ]

= [ ]

RATING

Enter number of points scored [ ]

Enter number of items on checklist [ ]

= × 100 = [ ] %

WHAT THE RATING SIGNIFIES

A less-than-acceptable rating indicates that past performance was unsatisfactory relative to goals and standards. This does not necessarily prove that performance was poor—it is possible that the previous objectives were set so high that they were unattainable. It is also possible that the function lacked the resources needed to attain the goals and meet the budgets.

1. Before any other action is taken, detailed analysis should be made of past performance vs. budgets and goals, to identify the real cause of unsatisfactory performance. Unless the underlying problem is isolated, you may be treating surface symptoms only, while the basic problem remains to fester.

2. In the meantime, you should be cautious about making new commitments, or setting new objectives. Time enough for that after you have done your analysis. Then make sure that your functional objectives are realistic and can be achieved. Success in reaching these will build your people's confidence—and enthusiasm—to tackle more challenging goals.

3-E
TOP-LEVEL SUPPORT AND GUIDANCE

	YES (1)	NO (0)	S/P* (½)
1. The executive office demonstrates active interest in marketing coordination and control through:			
a. executive statements in published policy and in management meetings that recognize marketing as the "leading edge" of the organization,	___	___	___
b. participation in key marketing conferences,	___	___	___
c. budget approval for this activity,	___	___	___
d. informed comments on departmental progress reports,	___	___	___
e. appointment of marketing managers to head up cross-functional project teams, and	___	___	___
f. recognition and reward for outstanding effort and accomplishment.	___	___	___

*SOMETIMES OR PARTIALLY

TOTAL POINTS   ☐ + 0 + ☐

= ☐

RATING

Enter number of points scored ☐
───────────────────────────── =   × 100 = ☐ %
Enter number of items on checklist ☐

Negative answers to these points is evidence that marketing is lower on the organizational totem pole than some other function. As a consequence, you may find that the technical people, or sales, or manufacturing, are leading the company into product lines that suit the engineering talents on hand, or the production facilities available, or the particular desires of the sales force in the field—*instead of what customers really want.*

It is not unusual for this to occur—it happens every day. And if it continues long enough, it can get the firm into big trouble. Statistics show that thousands of companies fail every year—and many, if not most, of these go down the tube because of failure to produce and sell what the market really wants and needs—failure to listen to what customers and prospects are saying about the company and its products.

Business history is filled with stories of companies that produced marvels of technology—and went bankrupt. The General Dynamics Series 880 and 990 jetliners of the 1950's were very advanced airplanes technically, but they cost the company $500 million in losses and also put the company out of the commercial airliner business, probably forever, because they were out of phase with the airline market at that time.

WHAT TO DO NOW

1. Mount a determined campaign to increase marketing's visibility to the executive office.

2. Make sure the boss reads every horror story about companies that failed because they neglected the marketplace. Make sure, as well, that he sees every success story of companies that put marketing and the customers' needs on the top of the list—companies like Procter & Gamble, 3M, Texas Instruments, and International Harvester.

3. Build a selling story to "sell" your own top management as thoroughly as you would for your best customer.

3-F
INNOVATION IN METHODS AND TECHNIQUES

	YES (1)	NO (0)	S/P* (½)
1. Management actively seeks better ways to control and coordinate marketing activities, through:			
a. seminars, workshops, conferences,	___	___	___
b. professional associations,	___	___	___
c. review of current literature,	___	___	___
and budgets provide funds for such activities.	___	___	___
2. The computer is used for control whenever it is determined to be cost-effective.	___	___	___
3. Latest operations research (OR) techniques are investigated for application, and used where appropriate (only on large complex problems where their high cost can be justified.)	___	___	___

*SOMETIMES OR PARTIALLY

TOTAL POINTS [ ] + 0 + [ ]

= [ ]

RATING

Enter number of points scored [ ]

Enter number of items on checklist [ ]

= × 100 = [ ] %

The most innovative companies are not often the most successful. This applies not only to their creative marketing methods, but also to the innovative ways in which they control their marketing activities. As markets become more diverse and fractionated, and distribution becomes complex (and more costly), older methods are no longer adequate to the task of coordinating marketing activities and controlling the marketing plan. New methods for collecting, organizing, and communicating information are needed.

The computer alone can't control people's activities, but it can store, process, and display the information you need for control, and it can speed up important feedback on marketing performance so you can make quicker control decisions. If you're not presently taking advantage of these computer capabilities, you may not be in full control of the situation.

Operations research techniques are appropriate in situations with many, many variables, and large numbers of transactions—problems that are not all that uncommon today in firms with extensive product lines and international distribution.

WHAT TO DO NOW

1. Managers in successful firms like to talk about their successful techniques. Watch for seminars conducted by them, articles written by them, and adapt their methods whenever they're appropriate to your situation.

2. Make a professional analysis of your information needs, using either the services of your Information Systems people or an outside information specialist. Do not give your problem to a computer technician until then. If you do, you might end up with a computer program that does a very efficient job of processing garbage.

3. If you have large, complex problems, consider using the proven O.R. techniques that are available. But don't give the job to an amateur.

3-G
INTERFUNCTIONAL COMMUNICATIONS AND COORDINATION

	YES (1)	NO (0)	S/P* (½)
1. Inasmuch as the function being evaluated is directly concerned with interdepartmental coordination, close and active communication and personal contact is maintained at several organizational levels with other functions of the business.	___	___	___
2. A minimum of 20 percent of the department manager's time is spent on coordination with other functions.	___	___	___
3. The marketing manager actively promotes coordination and cooperation through attitudes of mutual trust and good faith.	___	___	___

*SOMETIMES OR PARTIALLY

TOTAL POINTS ☐ + 0 + ☐

{ = ☐

RATING

Enter number of points scored ☐

Enter number of items on checklist ☐

= × 100 = ☐ %

WHAT THE RATING SIGNIFIES A low rating in this section negates a high rating in every other. It could mean that you haven't been entirely honest with yourself up to this point.

WHAT TO DO NOW
1. Review your answers to the other sections of the self-appraisal. Then set up an action program to improve your communications at every level of the organization. Maybe you should be spending even more than 20 percent of your time on this activity.
2. Think carefully about point 3—unless you and every member of your staff are sincere and honest with others, you can't expect them to trust and cooperate with you.

3-H
FUNCTIONAL IMPROVEMENT PROGRAM

	YES (1)	NO (0)	S/P* (½)

1. There is an active, on-going interfunctional effort to improve marketing coordination and control. Principal efforts are directed toward:

   a. a sincere marketing orientation throughout the organization, ___ ___ ___

   b. participation by all levels of management, ___ ___ ___

   c. a higher degree of employee "self-control," ___ ___ ___

   d. more involvement in planning and objective-setting, and ___ ___ ___

   e. improved automatic controls. ___ ___ ___

2. The program involves every other business function. ___ ___ ___

*SOMETIMES OR PARTIALLY

TOTAL POINTS ☐ + 0 + ☐

{ = ☐

RATING

Enter number of points scored ☐

Enter number of items on checklist ☐

= × 100 = ☐ %

49

This is really the essence of marketing coordination and control—an active and continuous program to get all functions working toward the same purpose, the productive fulfillment of customer needs. *When this is done, profit follows as surely as night follows day.*

WHAT DO TO NOW

If you have made an honest appraisal at this point, and have set up improvement plans to strengthen your coordination and control, then you are on your way to productive results.

3-1
RESOURCES

	YES (1)	NO (0)	S/P* (½)
1. Marketing management is fully and currently informed about the company's objectives, strategies, policies, and plans through:			
a. access to appropriate strategic and business development plans,	___	___	___
b. participation in key management meetings,	___	___	___
c. direct access to top executives, and	___	___	___
d. access to current management control reports.	___	___	___
2. The marketing department has adequate staff and sufficient budget support to assure that marketing activities are properly controlled and coordinated with others, based on the foregoing information about the company's objectives and plans for the next three, six, and twelve months. Other resources are considered to be adequate including:	___	___	___
a. management time,	___	___	___
b. capabilities,	___	___	___
c. control systems,	___	___	___
d. computer time and capacity, and	___	___	___
e. other functional support.	___	___	___

*SOMETIMES OR PARTIALLY

TOTAL POINTS [ ] + 0 + [ ]

= [ ]

RATING

Enter number of points scored   [ ]
_____   =   × 100 = [ ] %
Enter number of items on checklist [ ]

WHAT THE RATING SIGNIFIES

1. If the marketing staff lacks this kind of information, it is cut off from the life blood of the organization, and will not function for very long. If you're not getting it, it may be that others don't know you need it.

2. If some of these resources are not available, you run the risk of failure to achieve the kind of marketing coordination and control the company needs to survive in a highly competitive world.

WHAT TO DO NOW

1. You must have access to this vital information because, without it, your function may be impotent. First prove that you're entitled to it—establish your need in terms of getting the job done. Get your direct boss to support your case, because such backing is essential.

2. Resources normally flow to the person who promises to use them most productively. Build a case—set objectives and develop a plan—for getting the resources you need. Then make good on your promises.

51

Chapter **4**

Developing
Marketing Personnel

A marketing organization can have every quality required for success, except one; and because it lacks that single quality, it will eventually fail. The department may have a very efficient organization, a highly experienced staff, and an ample operating budget, and yet may fail to accomplish its long-range objectives—*if it neglects to develop its people.*

Japanese management recognized this early. Employees of major Japanese companies are provided with far-reaching education and training programs throughout their careers, plus periodic job rotation to broaden their outlooks. The high productivity and marketing competitiveness of Japanese auto, steel, and electronics manufacturers can be attributed to this development activity.

Failure to develop people can have a serious effect on any organization over a prolonged period of time. The effect is particularly harmful to a marketing organization because marketing people are out on the cutting edge of the organization where the pressures and stresses are high and constant—unrelenting change is the norm. That is why "Developing Marketing Personnel" is included in this manual as a separate section.

Human resource development is a relatively recent phenomenon. It is only in the past generation or so that the corporation recognized that it had both the need and the obligation to contribute to the personal and professional development of its people. Earlier, this was considered to be the sole responsibility of the person himself. Today, it is a shared responsibility.

PERSONNEL DEVELOPMENT MUST BE MANAGED

As with any other important activity within the contemporary organization, the development of people must be a structured and managed process. Objectives must be set and a plan followed. Provision must be made for the costs and expenses required, authority must be delegated, responsibilities firmly assigned, accountability made clear, and standardized procedures must be documented. What is more, the performance of people must be measured and controlled.

This may read like a prescription for a rigid and authoritarian approach to personnel development. To the contrary, it is a recommendation for a structured and disciplined approach that provides a firm foundation for flexibility and adaptability in its application.

It must be recognized, however, that all personnel development is "self-development." All the organization can do is to provide the resources and the environment—the rest is up to the individual.

The most productive and rewarding type of personnel development may be when a person is placed in a situation that stretches his or her capabilities to the fullest. When an individual is given a task that is somewhat beyond his or her current capabilities—an assignment that person is considered not quite ready for—the individual, his superior, and the enterprise all benefit. The person gains through the discovery of internal resources he may not have been aware of, the individual's boss gains a more competent and mature subordinate, and the company gains a *manager.*

To give such an assignment is an act of trust and faith. There is risk involved, to be sure—the risk of failure. This risk is minimized when the person's superior provides the kind of support, guidance, and encouragement that all add up to "leadership."

KEY OBJECTIVE OF THE SELF-AUDIT

The principal purpose of this section is to ensure that all marketing people are encouraged and given the opportunity to develop their professional and personal capabilities through education and training, participation in higher management level activities, and exposure to broadening influences through rotation and cross-functional task group assignments.

HOW TO USE THE CHECKLISTS

For each of the statements in the Checklist, compare the condition of your function to the "ideal" as described in the statement. Then:

1. If you consider the statement to be *generally true* of your function, check the YES column.

2. If you consider the statement to be *untrue* of your function, check the NO column.

3. If you consider the statement to be *less than true* (but not totally untrue) of your function, check the SOMETIMES OR PARTIAL column.

4. If the statement does not apply to your particular situation, write "Not Applicable" across the response spaces (or simply draw a line through them).

5. If you lack the data for a definite response, write in "Not Answerable" or "Don't Know."

HOW TO EVALUATE YOUR RESPONSES

When you have completed the checklist, glance over your responses, keeping these points in mind:

1. A negative answer is always unfavorable because it indicates a problem within the function: the greater the number of NOs, the more serious the situation.

2. A positive response is always a good indication. But too many YES answers could indicate that your review is not objective enough.

3. Too many SOMETIMES OR PARTIALLY answers can point to internal weaknesses or to a lack of firm direction.

4. A lot of "Not Applicable" answers could indicate that you are avoiding the issue.

5. A large number of "Not Answerable" or "Don't Know" answers could be symptomatic of inadequate records or data bases.

HOW TO RATE AND SCORE YOUR RESPONSES

When you are satisfied with your responses in general, you are ready to score the Checklist. For your convenience, a self-explanatory Scoring and Rating Block follows each Checklist. This block not only tells you whether the condition of your function is satisfactory, but it also gives you a measure of its effectiveness.

Here's how to total up the points for inclusion in the Scoring and Rating Block:

1. Total up the number of points you scored:
   a. For each YES, give yourself one point.
   b. For each NO, give yourself zero.
   c. For each SOMETIMES OR PARTIALLY, give yourself a half-point.
   d. For each "Not Applicable" answer, give yourself zero and deduct one from the number of items on the Checklist.
   e. For each "Not Answerable" or "Don't Know" answer, give yourself zero.

2. Next divide the total number of points you score by the total number of items (statements) on the Checklist (less items marked "Not Applicable"). You'll get a 1.0 for a perfect score and a fraction for anything less.

3. Multiply the result of step 2 by 100 to arrive at the percentage for your score.

What is a satisfactory rating? A rating of less than 65 percent is unacceptable and calls for an improvement program: Obviously, the lower the rating, the more drastic the action required.

A brief "how-to" example of this Scoring and Rating system follows . . .

EXAMPLE

	YES (1)	NO (0)	S/P* (½)

1. Field sale reports designed to provide information on sales progress contain data on the following topics:

   a. sales calls and sales presentations made by salespersons and sales agents,   ✓

   b. bids, quotations, and proposals made,   ✓

   c. new orders booked,   ✓

   d. lost business, and reasons for the loss,   ✓ (NO)

   e. accomplishments toward future orders,   ✓ (S/P)

   f. performance in filling orders, handling complaints, and otherwise servicing individual customers,   ✓

   g. action taken in response to customer requests, such as sending samples, spec sheets, etc.,   ✓

   h. accomplishments of significance and value to other members of the sales force.   ✓ (S/P)

*SOMETIMES OR PARTIALLY

TOTAL POINTS $\boxed{5}$ + 0 + $\boxed{1}$

= $\boxed{6}$

RATING

$$\frac{\text{Enter number of points scored} \quad \boxed{6}}{\text{Enter number of items on checklist} \quad \boxed{8}} = .75 \times 100 = \boxed{75}\ \%$$

4-A
ORGANIZATION, ADMINISTRATION, AND OPERATION

	YES (1)	NO (0)	S/P* (½)

1. The personal and professional development of marketing people (as well as those in other functions) is recognized in published policy statements as a vital company activity. ___ ___ ___

2. Personnel development is recognized in managers' position descriptions as an important function of marketing. ___ ___ ___

3. The marketing budget includes an allocation for this activity, covering internal activities and fees for outside services, if required. ___ ___ ___

4. The budget was based on a critical review and analysis of department resources and needs. ___ ___ ___

5. Marketing managers at all levels actively work at personnel development. ___ ___ ___

6. The department has a formalized program of personnel development, guided by written procedures. ___ ___ ___

7. Activities covered by the program include:

   a. education and training, ___ ___ ___

   b. financial support (tuition refunds), ___ ___ ___

   c. attendance at seminars, conferences, workshops, ___ ___ ___

   d. organizational development (OD), ___ ___ ___

   e. MBO programs, ___ ___ ___

   f. performance reviews and potential appraisals, ___ ___ ___

   g. staff meeting attendance, ___ ___ ___

   h. exposure at management meetings, ___ ___ ___

   i. opportunities to make high level presentations, ___ ___ ___

   j. participation in task groups, ___ ___ ___

   k. participation in business planning, ___ ___ ___

   l. participation in market surveys, ___ ___ ___

   m. rotation through the organization, ___ ___ ___

   n. transfers between field and staff, ___ ___ ___

   o. opportunities to assume more responsibility, and ___ ___ ___

   p. delegating to subordinates during absence at conferences, travel, vacations. ___ ___ ___

8. Meetings of all marketing function people are held at least quarterly for the purpose of exchanging views. ___ ___ ___

9. All managers are expected to take an active part in meetings, including making presentations on their activities. ___ ___ ___

10. Marketing managers participate in an incentive compensation plan based, in part, on performance in developing personnel. ___ ___ ___

*SOMETIMES OR PARTIALLY

	YES (1)	NO (0)	S/P* (½)
11. A mix of promotion from within and outside recruiting is used to fill marketing slots.	___	___	___
12. Women and minority employees are given equal advancement opportunity.	___	___	___
13. Representation of these two groups in management has increased during the past year.	___	___	___
14. Performance reviews are held with each member of the department, at least once a year.	___	___	___
15. Marketing management utilizes up-to-date MBO principles throughout the organization.	___	___	___
16. Participation in business planning is required by several levels of marketing management, including attendance at plan review meetings to the extent possible.	___	___	___
17. Marketing management actively encourages participation in worthwhile seminars, conferences, workshops, distributor forums, and dealer symposiums.	___	___	___
18. Staff meetings are held weekly.	___	___	___
19. Managers are required to submit weekly and monthly progress reports.	___	___	___
20. Marketing people are expected to participate in joint sales calls on customers and prospects with field sales representatives.	___	___	___
21. Internal training and re-training sessions are held on a regular basis.	___	___	___
22. Marketing people are expected to attend sales training sessions at least once a year.	___	___	___
23. Marketing works within guidelines and policies issued by the personnel department.	___	___	___

*SOMETIMES OR PARTIALLY

TOTAL POINTS ☐ + 0 + ☐

= ☐

RATING

Enter number of points scored ☐

Enter number of items on checklist ☐

= ☐ × 100 = ☐ %

WHAT THE RATING SIGNIFIES

A less-than-satisfactory rating indicates that personnel development may not be considered to be an important function within the marketing organization. If this conclusion is true, then not only is the long-term viability of the organization threatened, but the department's present productivity is probably lower than it should be.

Many, if not most, of the activities designed to develop the personal and professional capabilities of people tend to improve their performance in the near-term. An example of this is *Management by Objectives*. MBO can develop people's future capabilities and potential in a major way—it also improves their current performance by focusing their efforts on measurable, high-quality output—on *results*, not just on activity.

WHAT TO DO NOW

1. A deficiency in this function is generally a long-term problem—it didn't happen overnight, and it can't be cured quickly. If your operating budget doesn't include an allocation of funds for personnel development, plan to get one into next year's expense budget.

2. Meanwhile, make sure that people are doing all the things to develop their capabilities and potential that don't cost much money. There are many of these, both inside the company and outside. The American Management Association (AMA) has published a sixty-page catalog of development goals,* many of which cost little to implement.

3. Most importantly, encourage your people to develop *themselves*, through outside courses of study and reading. Insist that everyone participate actively in meetings, by making brief presentations on their progress—and not just passively attend them.

4. It is also important for marketing people to accompany sales representatives or service reps on customer calls every once in a while. Nothing broadens the outlook like a little exposure to the "real world" of customers and prospects.

4-B
AUTHORITY, RESPONSIBILITY, AND ACCOUNTABILITY

	YES (1)	NO (0)	S/P* (½)
1. Authority has been delegated to the manager of marketing to expend company funds and assign tasks necessary to assure the fullest possible personal and professional development of all people within marketing.	___	___	___
2. Responsibility is firmly assigned in writing to the marketing manager for implementation of enlightened personnel policies within marketing.	___	___	___
3. Responsibilities are clearly assigned to individual managers to develop personnel reporting directly to them.	___	___	___
4. The marketing manager is held accountable for failure of the marketing function to meet its departmental objectives, or to meet its obligations to other company functions, because of sub-standard performance by individuals or groups within the department.	___	___	___
5. The manager is also held accountable for failure to meet the department's Affirmative Action Plan objectives.			

*SOMETIMES OR PARTIALLY

TOTAL POINTS ☐ + 0 + ☐

= ☐

RATING

Enter number of points scored ☐

Enter number of items on checklist ☐

= × 100 = ☐ %

* The Manager's Guide to Developing Subordinate Managers, an AMA Management Briefing, (AMACOM, a division of American Management Associations, New York, 1980.)

WHAT THE RATING SIGNIFIES

A less-than-satisfactory rating is evidence that the organization is not sincere about human resources development. Unless authority is clearly delegated to the manager to spend money—and the delegation is backed up by a line item in the expense budget—it will not be done, despite all the pious statements by the executive office. And unless responsibility is clearly assigned to subordinate managers to develop their people, they will work on more pressing tasks. Finally, unless the department head is held accountable for failure to meet objectives caused by sub-standard performance of people, he can blame other people instead of his own failure to develop them fully.

WHAT TO DO NOW

1. Assuming that the company as a whole follows modern and enlightened policies of human resources management, you should ensure that these are known and understood by everyone in your group. If it does not, then your company is in serious trouble!

2. Make sure that every manager reporting to you knows that he or she is responsible for carrying them out, under pain of penalty for failure.

3. Be sure to *reward* managers who do a superior job of developing their subordinates, by public recognition, or increased responsibility, or incentive compensation. There is no finer motivation than genuine approval and sincere praise.

4-C
MEASUREMENTS, CONTROL REPORTS AND PERFORMANCE RECORDS

	YES (1)	NO (0)	S/P* (½)
1. The effectiveness of marketing's personnel development is measured and evaluated regularly and continuously.	___	___	___
2. The effectiveness is measured by comparing it with several benchmarks of performance and results such as the department's performance in:	___	___	___
a. attracting, retaining, and promoting superior people,	___	___	___
b. motivating employees to self-development, and	___	___	___
c. accomplishing challenging objectives.	___	___	___
3. The performance and the potential of each employee are reviewed at least once a year, in a one-on-one "counseling" session with his or her superior.	___	___	___
4. The developmental needs of each are identified by the superior, and recommendations are made to the employee for action.	___	___	___
5. Records are routinely kept of employees progress, accomplishments, and participation in self-developmental activities.	___	___	___
6. Organization charts, position descriptions, and manning tables are kept current.	___	___	___

*SOMETIMES OR PARTIALLY

TOTAL POINTS ☐ + 0 + ☐

}

= ☐

RATING

Enter number of points scored ☐

————————————————— = ☐ × 100 = ☐ %

Enter number of items on checklist ☐

**WHAT THE RATING
SIGNIFIES**

If the function is not measured regularly, it can't be effective. What is worse, you won't even know that it's not effective. And if the benchmarks used to measure it are not purposeful, goals-oriented performance criteria, then the measurements are not useful for improving productivity.

If the answers to points 3 and 4 are negative, then your people may not know what is expected of them in the way of self-development. Almost everyone needs some form of coaching. They may also feel that the company has no real interest in their personal development, despite all other indications that it does.

WHAT TO DO NOW

1. If the responses to points 3 and 4 were negative, or if the performance reviews that are made are perfunctory, one of the most important actions to take is to institute an intensive program of employee performance review and potential appraisal throughout your department. Nothing else will pay such high dividends in productivity.

2. Even worse than no program is one in which supervisors with poor interpersonal skills and little sensitivity use the performance review meeting to criticize their subordinates' performance and find fault with their attitudes and behavior. You may not even know that this is being done—until demoralized people quit or ask for transfers.

3. Managers need training for this—take advantage of the many courses available at low cost through colleges, associations, and training organizations.

4-D
OPERATING PERFORMANCE HISTORY

	YES (1)	NO (0)	S/P* (½)
1. An analysis has been made of control reports and records for the past year or so, to determine how effective marketing has been in developing its personnel.	——	——	——
2. This analysis shows that during the past year:			
a. at least one management position was filled by promotion from within,	——	——	——
b. at least one position was filled from field sales,	——	——	——
c. at least one position was filled from outside.	——	——	——

*SOMETIMES OR PARTIALLY

	YES (1)	NO (0)	S/P* (½)

3. During the past year there have been:

    a. no losses of exceptional people, except through promotion, and   _____   _____   _____

    b. no major positions left unfilled for longer than three months.   _____   _____   _____

    (Answer "yes" if these are true.)

4. During the past year, more than one management position was filled by a woman or a minority person.   _____   _____   _____

5. Every employee was reviewed by his or her boss at least once, and recommendations accepted for self-development activities.   _____   _____   _____

6. At least 25 percent of department personnel are actively pursuing educational advancement.   _____   _____   _____

*SOMETIMES OR PARTIALLY

TOTAL POINTS   [ ] + 0 + [ ]

= [ ]

RATING

$$\frac{\text{Enter number of points scored} \quad [\ ]}{\text{Enter number of items on checklist} \quad [\ ]} = \quad \times\ 100 = \boxed{\quad \%}$$

WHAT THE RATING SIGNIFIES

A less-than-acceptable rating here indicates that the department is not actively and aggressively pursuing human resources development. It may indicate, as well, that there is little movement of people in and out of the department, and within the group. A dynamic and vital marketing function is constantly feeding marketing-oriented people into other functions. It is one of the important training grounds for developing top executives.

A marketing group of any size should also be a conduit to bring people into the company from other companies and other industries, in order to prevent insularity and to gain the benefit of other viewpoints.

WHAT TO DO NOW

If the past is to serve as a useful guide to the future, you should use this analysis of past experience to set up a program of personnel development that is both effective and affordable. You need professional guidance on this, either from your own personnel section or from a competent outside specialist.

4-E
TOP-LEVEL SUPPORT AND GUIDANCE

	YES (1)	NO (0)	S/P* (½)

1. The executive office demonstrates active support, guidance, and recognition of marketing personnel development (as part of overall company personnel development) by providing:

*SOMETIMES OR PARTIALLY

	YES (1)	NO (0)	S/P* (½)
a. budget approval of funds for education, training, organizational development,	___	___	___
b. support of MBO programs,	___	___	___
c. guidance through participation in training and O.D. sessions,	___	___	___
d. recognition and reward for outstanding effort and accomplishment, and	___	___	___
e. published policy statements endorsing personnel development.	___	___	___

*SOMETIMES OR PARTIALLY

TOTAL POINTS [ ] + 0 + [ ]

= [ ]

RATING

Enter number of points scored [ ]
_____ = × 100 = [ ] %
Enter number of items on checklist [ ]

WHAT THE RATING SIGNIFIES

A less-than-satisfactory rating here usually confirms earlier low ratings by signifying that the company as a whole does not actively endorse personnel development. If the executive office does not demonstrate support by *participating actively and visibly* in personnel development, then the chairman's usual statements in the annual report to the effect that "our loyal and dedicated employees are our most important resource" is just a meaningless stereotype—annual report platitudes.

WHAT TO DO NOW

This is a tough one. If the front office doesn't really believe in human resources development, there is not much you can do as an individual to change its attitude. If you sincerely believe that it is important, you can do some things without top-side support. It's possible, on the other hand, that you'll be so frustrated that your best bet might be to find a more progressive environment for your talents.

4-F
INNOVATION IN METHODS AND TECHNIQUES

	YES (1)	NO (0)	S/P* (½)
1. Marketing management actively seeks new and better techniques to stimulate departmental personnel to improve skills and knowledge.	___	___	___
2. Management uses many sources for ideas to improve the department's personnel development, among them:			
a. seminars on human resources development,	___	___	___
b. survey of current literature,	___	___	___

*SOMETIMES OR PARTIALLY

	YES (1)	NO (0)	S/P* (½)
c. outside specialists,	___	___	___
d. solicitation of suggestions from personnel at all levels,	___	___	___
e. contacts in other firms and other industries, and	___	___	___
f. budgets include funds for such activities.	___	___	___
3. The computer is used to record, store, and display information on employee skills, education, and qualifications, for use in filling open positions and promotion.	___	___	___

*SOMETIMES OR PARTIALLY

TOTAL POINTS   [ ] + 0 + [ ]

= [ ]

RATING

Enter number of points scored [ ]
─────────────────────────────── = × 100 = [ ] %
Enter number of items on checklist [ ]

WHAT THE RATING SIGNIFIES   Human resources development is the most vital and fastest growing aspect of business management. It takes time and effort to keep up with developments in the field. If you are not putting any effort into this, but are simply waiting for direction from your personnel function, then you are imposing limits *on your own* development as a manager. If, on the other hand, you can manage and develop people well, you probably can handle much higher responsibility.

WHAT TO DO NOW   Take every opportunity to hone your skills in managing people. Every college and university offers courses; so do a variety of management organizations. Insist that your subordinate managers do the same. Your "return on investment" of time can be very high.

4-G
INTERFUNCTIONAL COMMUNICATIONS AND COORDINATION

	YES (1)	NO (0)	S/P* (½)
1. In the process of developing marketing personnel, the manager of marketing and key department people maintain a close day-to-day working relationship with people in other functions, including:			
a. field sales,	___	___	___
b. personnel,	___	___	___
c. sales training,	___	___	___
d. organization development, and	___	___	___
e. information systems.	___	___	___

*SOMETIMES OR PARTIALLY

	YES (1)	NO (0)	S/P* (½)

2. Additionally, the department maintains active communications with other functions of the business in order to assure a reservoir of new marketing talent, as well as to broaden the business knowledge of marketing people.

3. Progress in developing people is reported in the department's regular Progress Reports, which are distributed to the managers of other key functions.

*SOMETIMES OR PARTIALLY

TOTAL POINTS [ ] + 0 + [ ]

= [ ]

RATING

Enter number of points scored [ ] = × 100 = [ ] %

Enter number of items on checklist [ ]

WHAT THE RATING SIGNIFIES

A close working relationship and a free flow of communication among functions is an important aspect of human resources development. It provides the exposure to other functional operations so necessary to effective marketing coordination. It also can broaden the outlook of people and give them a better perspective on the business as a whole. A low rating here can mean that your people may become narrow functional specialists with a limited view of the importance of marketing in the total picture.

WHAT TO DO NOW

1. Assign each of your subordinates the responsibility to set up and maintain regular contact with a key person in each of the other functions.

2. Bring your subordinates together regularly to exchange information, and to keep you informed about what's going on at lower levels of the organization. Unquestionably, your people will benefit—and you may end up the best informed manager in the whole company.

4-H
FUNCTIONAL IMPROVEMENT PROGRAM

	YES (1)	NO (0)	S/P* (½)

1. There is an active, on-going interfunctional team effort to improve personnel development in marketing (as part of the overall company effort). Major efforts are directed toward:

a. more "self-control" by all personnel,

b. improved management by objectives (MBO),

c. more meaningful performance review and appraisal,

d. broader and more active participation in planning and decision making,

*SOMETIMES OR PARTIALLY

64

e. more participation in cross-functional team activities, and

f. more exposure of personnel to top management and vice versa.

*SOMETIMES OR PARTIALLY

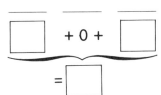

TOTAL POINTS ☐ + 0 + ☐

= ☐

RATING

Enter number of points scored ☐

―――――――――――――――――――――

Enter number of items on checklist ☐

= × 100 = ☐ %

WHAT THE RATING SIGNIFIES

Most management authorities agree that "self-control" is the most effective kind of control. It's not for everyone, to be sure, but for those people in your organization who are self-confident, mature, and competent the opportunity to control their own activities is the best kind of management and personal development. This type of person hopefully forms the majority.

Making decisions is a necessary part of a person's development; so is making mistakes. But the great benefits gained both to the company and the individual far outweigh the cost of mistakes. Of course, if mistakes happen often, or become serious, then a review of that person's self-control is in order.

Participation in long-range planning is also a superb development mechanism. The most productive managers are those who can look ahead, anticipate events, and prepare for them. Allowing your subordinates to take part in planning is good training for this.

A less-than satisfactory rating indicates that marketing people could gain from participation in activities that cross functional lines.

WHAT TO DO NOW

1. You should be working constantly with your personnel people on this, as the knowledgeable professionals in management development.

2. Without a formal team effort, you should try to get your people assigned to task groups set up to improve other functional activities, such as product quality control or the like. The knowledge and insight they will gain will help both them and the department.

4-1
RESOURCES

	YES (1)	NO (0)	S/P* (½)

1. Marketing resources, including budget funding, are adequate to permit expenditure of management time and funds required to develop marketing personnel.

2. The department's workload is known for the next three, six, and twelve months—

*SOMETIMES OR PARTIALLY

based on budgets, marketing plans, and business plans—and other resources are known to be adequate including:

a. computer support,

b. other functional support,

c. training support, and

d. support from the personnel department.

TOTAL POINTS [ ] + 0 + [ ]

= [ ]

RATING

Enter number of points scored [ ]

————————————————————————— = × 100 = [%   ]

Enter number of items on checklist [ ]

WHAT THE RATING SIGNIFIES

A low rating here indicates that you lack a basic level of resources needed to develop your subordinates. As a consequence, your best people may become frustrated and move on to other departments or other companies where they feel they will have more opportunity to grow, professionally and personally.

WHAT TO DO NOW

1. In the face of these limitations, you've got to call upon people's ingenuity—on which there is no limit. There are many everyday activities that develop personal and professional capabilities, provided they are conducted with such a purpose in mind. Staff meetings, for example, are an excellent means for informing department personnel about broad company issues and programs—and in the process, developing their outlook. It costs nothing to invite lower-level people into these meetings every once in a while on a rotating basis.

2. Meanwhile, conduct a campaign to get more resources for next year, especially a budget allocation for training and education.

3. If your company has a tuition refund program, encourage your people to take full advantage of it. Both they and the company will benefit.

THE BOTTOM LINE: TOTAL MARKETING

Market leadership brings tremendous rewards to the company and to the managers who help to create it. It also has a price. Part of the price is the expense of organizing, staffing, and operating a marketing function of professionals who know the company, its customers, competitors, and products. Part of the price, too, is the cost of listening to the customer.

Another part of the price for market leadership is the need to periodically review and evaluate the marketing organization; to analyze its strengths and weaknesses candidly and objectively; and to set up improvement programs designed to make it more productive. Organization alone is not enough, of course. Market leadership requires a process as well—a process for developing marketing objectives that challenge and energize the entire company and for establishing competitive strategies that are both innovative and workable. The process must also provide for coordinating and controlling all marketing activities throughout the organization so that marketing considerations are guiding and for developing the capabilities of all individuals involved so that they contribute their full intelligence and maximum energies to the overall goals of the enterprise.

That is the purpose of the self-audit. Conducted once a year, it helps marketing management to move the firm into a position of market leadership and keep it there.

SUMMARY OF SELF-AUDIT RATINGS
AND FUNCTIONAL IMPROVEMENT GOALS

If you wish, you may summarize the ratings for each function at the end of each section, on this "Summary Rating" form. (A "function" is the equivalent of a chapter.) The rating is simply an arithmetic average of the ratings on Checklists A through I—that is, the total divided by 9. This form also provides space for listing the Improvement Goals for each function.

Under each function, enter the rating percentage for each Checklist section, A through I. "Function Number 1," for example, is the first (1st) chapter in the section, regardless of its number in the book—5, 11, or so on. The Summary Rating is the total of each column divided by 9, to give you an average rating for the total function. The lower portion of the form can be used to list your improvement goals for each function.

	FUNCTION NUMBER					
CHECKLIST	**1** %	**2** %	**3** %	**4** %	**5** %	**6** %
A	_____	_____	_____	_____	_____	_____
B	_____	_____	_____	_____	_____	_____
C	_____	_____	_____	_____	_____	_____
D	_____	_____	_____	_____	_____	_____
E	_____	_____	_____	_____	_____	_____
F	_____	_____	_____	_____	_____	_____
G	_____	_____	_____	_____	_____	_____
H	_____	_____	_____	_____	_____	_____
I	_____	_____	_____	_____	_____	_____
SUMMARY RATING (%)	_____	_____	_____	_____	_____	_____

IMPROVEMENT GOALS

_____

_____

_____

_____

_____

_____

_____

_____

(Use separate sheet as required)

Section **II**

Managing
Marketing Innovation

This section of the Marketing and Sales Audit is concerned with the successful commercial exploitation of new product and new market opportunities for the company. Its principal concern is with the marketing aspects of new-product planning and development.

HOW A NEW PRODUCT "IDEA" IS CONVERTED INTO PROFITABLE SALES

1. identification of a market need,
2. development of a "concept" to fill the need,
3. precise expression of this concept in words and symbols,
4. rigorous testing of the concept to determine its acceptability to the market,
5. evaluation of the concept in terms of value to the company, and "fit" with business mission, objectives, and capabilities,
6. modification or rejection of the concept when test and evaluation results dictate,
7. further development of the concept into a commercial specification for a product, and
8. development of a product and marketing plan.

(Note: The technical invention, creative engineering development, and innovative design of the product to meet the commercial specifications are covered under R.D.&E., and are not the direct concern of this section.)

69

NEED FOR MARKETING FOCUS

Control by marketing throughout the entire planning and development process is essential to avoid the all-too-common preoccupation with engineering and hardware to the exclusion of the market—the product-focus that in Peter Drucker's words, "produces miracles of technology but disappointing market rewards." The planning and development of new products and new markets are among the most important tasks and responsibilities of business management. With regard to the company's future growth and profitability, these activities are far and away the most critical. It is not putting it too strongly to say that they are essential to the very survival of the enterprise.

Peter Drucker states the case for new product innovation in these strong words, "an established company which, in an age demanding innovation, is not capable of innovation is doomed to decline and extinction."

Appraisal of these activities, then, must be made in this context. Accordingly, the appraisal can only be made by the top executive of the unit, assisted by his top operating managers of marketing, R&D, financial control, and operations. Before proceeding with the review of new-product and new-market developments, it is well to restate and review some fundamentals. These are expressed in terms of resources an organization must have *today*, and tasks management must undertake *today*, in order to "insure its future" in a highly competitive world.

NINE CRITICAL FACTORS FOR SUCCESS IN NEW-PRODUCT AND NEW-MARKET DEVELOPMENT:

The following "Critical Factors for Success" in new product and market innovation have been developed from the experience of companies noted for new-product planning and development.

It also draws upon the author's experience in marketing management with several progressive business firms, as well as the ideas of well-regarded business educators and consultants.

It is important to note here that the term "innovation" is used in its broad marketing, economic and social sense, not solely in terms of new technology.

1. MANAGEMENT COMMITMENT. A strong, active, and highly visible commitment by the executive office to the principle that product innovation is a top-priority activity throughout the company. This commitment should be evidenced by:
   a. published policy statements,
   b. financial support in operating, R.&D., and capital budgets,
   c. active participation in new-product progress review meetings, and
   d. recognition and reward for outstanding innovation.

2. AN ORGANIZATION DESIGNED FOR INNOVATION. A "market-focused" organization that is responsive to customer needs, not organized simply to make and sell today's products.

   In this connection, a classic study of new-product development by Booz, Allen identifies the major cause of new-product failure as the business organization that is structured along rigid functional lines, with little or no communication between marketing and engineering, and between engineering and production.

   Many of these failures occurred in companies with reputations for their sales capabilities. Unfortunately, they confused sales with marketing and failed to look beyond today's products (which sales people generally feel most comfortable with).

3. "... AND MARKETING SHALL LEAD THEM." Strong leadership by marketing of new-product and new-market innovation is essential. Basic to successful new-product management is acceptance by all managers that the company is in business to produce what the market wants, not to sell whatever it finds easiest and most interesting to make. This is an old bromide, but failure to observe it is one of the prime causes of new-product failure.

Unfortunately, product innovation is inherently a self-centered activity. It is easy, almost natural, to look *inward*—what do *we* need? Success demands a look outward to the marketplace; a willingness to listen to the consumer. This is marketing's responsibility; but it also requires a market-orientation on the part of all business functions in the organization.

Marketing leadership requires considerably more than a statement by the executive office that the marketing department will be involved in all new-product decisions. It requires firm delegation of authority to commit company funds for innovation, to override the inherent desire of R.D.&E. people to push development of products that appeal to them technically, and sometimes to demand that a new product be scrapped after a lot of money has been spent on it because market conditions no longer justify its development.

4. KNOW THE ODDS. Most new products fail. The odds against a new-product idea becoming a commercial success are about 100 to 1, according to professional studies. In certain industries the odds are higher—chemical products are about 500 to 1. In pharmaceutical products the odds may run as high as 6,000 to 1.

The implications of these statistics is not to avoid risk by sticking with today's products, but rather to establish a planning and development process that encourages the taking of risk while at the same time assures that the risk is calculated at various stages.

In short, organizing for success means recognizing that the price is many failures. The point is to recognize them early, when the cost of write-off is tolerable.

5. BUILD ON STRENGTHS. Risk in new-product and new-market innovation increases in relation to the degree that the new product departs from company know-how and experience in engineering, manufacturing, marketing, and distribution. The more a product differs from those the company now makes and sells, the higher the risk that it will not contribute to profit.

This is not an argument to avoid all risk. Nor is it intended to say that one should not innovate new products but should only make minor changes in existing products. It is rather a reason to know one's own strengths and to build on them.

If a company's greatest strength is in distribution, then new products that fit well into that distribution chain stand the greatest chance of success. A new product that requires a totally new kind of sales outlet would very likely be a high risk. A company with years of experience and know-how in selling to OEMs would be ill advised to introduce new products that must be sold directly to the consumer.

For a company with limited technical capability to take on development of a new product requiring new technology is to ask for serious trouble, by diverting management attention to problems that it may not be equipped to deal with.

This advice may sound simplistic, even absurd, but the fact is companies constantly fail to stick to what they do best—and sometimes as a consequence, they fail to survive. Corporate fall-out is increasing, and many firms go down the tube simply because they fail to know and build on their own strengths.

6. COURAGE AND CONVICTION. Most new-product ideas at their inception are fragile things and must be handled carefully. They often sound trivial at first—and so are easy targets for the sharpshooters in the organization. Courage and conviction are needed in order to support and encourage these new ideas until they either become viable product concepts, or until they fail the "screen test" of market potential.

On the other hand, a decision to *terminate* a product development when evidence shows that it will lead to a dead-end requires an even higher kind of management courage. Once a development is under way it has a tendency to take on a life of its own, and often develops a momentum that makes it ride over evidence that market conditions have changed.

Unfortunately, market research does not come with a lifetime guarantee. Early assumptions become obsolete; early findings are invalidated by later evidence. Moreover, conditions can change remarkably during the months or years of new-product planning and development. More than money is involved. People's judgment, pride, and jobs are tied up with a development.

Expenditures made previously do not constitute by themselves a valid reason for proceeding further. These are "sunk costs" that should not be factored into a comparative economic evaluation of new-product opportunities vs. products in development.

7. INNOVATE WITH A PURPOSE. The decision to innovate new products and markets is not up to the company to make. It has been made by events. Customer needs, competition, and technology are all changing so rapidly that it has no choice whether or not to innovate. It's important, however, that it be done with a defined purpose and known objectives.

First purpose is survival of the enterprise. Survival of a business requires that the enterprise generate a certain minimum profit. The minimum amount of profit required by a business can be determined through analysis, but that is the concern of other sections of the guide. What is essential to our present purpose is to realize that there are constant, unrelenting pressures and forces on every business enterprise that tend to put it out of business. As consumer needs, perceptions and social norms change the market operates to cause many older, more mature products and markets to decline in profitability, even though sales volume may remain the same.

The healthy enterprise must constantly replenish and renew itself with a flow of new products and markets in order to maintain the minimum profit needed for survival.

Associated with this is the need to make the hard decisions to abandon older products that have become a drag on profitability. All too often, we tend to do this only as a last resort, after trying everything to save a marginal product. Perhaps the question—"why not eliminate the product from the line?" should be asked first, instead of last. Perhaps signals from the marketplace are not being heeded—the decline in profitability may be proclaiming that external factors have eliminated or reduced the *need* for the product.

If this is the case—and only by listening to the customer can it be known—then the felony may be compounded by trying to doctor up the product or to hypo the market. Tinkering with a product that should be abandoned is like seeking a solution without knowing what the problem is.

8. AVOID GLOBAL SOLUTIONS AND TECHNOLOGICAL "BREAKTHROUGHS." Most new-product innovation does not require revolutionary technology. The vast majority of successful new products, even those in high technology companies, require only creative exploitation of available technology.

Too often, managers of research and development become victims of their desire to impress the world by pushing the state-of-the-art so far and so fast that they end up in a kind of technological quicksand that devours dollars and absorbs the energies of competent people.

Market research people often have a tendency to come up with global problems that, if taken seriously, would require a revolution of technology to solve. The way to avoid this is to demand that marketing so define the market need and so limit the problem for the technical people that they can address their creative talents to solvable problems, and not to finding a way to "solve the German U-boat problem by setting the ocean on fire."

9. AVOID "CONFERENCE ROOM" MARKET RESEARCH. Some of the most notorious new-product "bombs" originate in the wide-ranging minds of top executives as they sit around the conference table on the fourteenth floor of headquarters, remote from the real marketplace. Marketing professionals enjoy telling the classic story about the company that launched a new dog food with massive advertising and sales promotion. When it failed to sell, the chief exec asked the marketing manager why. "It seems," he replied, "that the dogs won't eat it."

Unfortunately, there is considerable truth behind this old joke. The New York Times recently reported that Max Factor, a prestigious cosmetics company, introduced a new perfume named "Just Call Me Maxi" with considerable fanfare and a ten million dollars advertising program. The report goes on to say, ". . . suddenly, in the weeks before Christmas, sales dropped off drastically and stores returned seven million dollars worth of the fragrance, reporting that "customers did not like the scent." No joke to Max Factor; the episode cost the company five million dollars, according to informed sources.

KEY AIM OF THE SELF-AUDIT

The principal objectives of the appraisal are to assure:

1. that the company has an organized function aggressively, systematically, and continuously working to weed out of the product line those products with unsatisfactory profit margins and little promise for the future, and to replace them with new products that will make a higher profit contribution to the company,

2. that the search for new products is directed and led by marketing, not by technical or manufacturing considerations,

3. that there is an active search for new markets for existing products, and ways to exploit them through innovative market development, and

4. that there are strong and independent controls on the product/market planning and development cycle; that events and changes in markets, competition, and other external factors are closely monitored; that internal progress is regularly reviewed; and that necessary management decisions are made at "go/no go" points in the cycle.

COVERAGE OF THE SELF-AUDIT

The following sections cover the three basic elements of the Product/ Market Development function:

a. Evaluating and Pruning the Product Line.
b. Planning and Controlling New Product Development.
c. Planning and Developing Markets.

Each section contains detailed checklists for making a self-appraisal.

Chapter **5**

How to Evaluate
And Prune the
Product Line

INVIGORATING THE PRODUCT LINE

The importance of keeping the company's product line fresh and vigorous has been stressed repeatedly. No other activity is so critical to the overall productivity of the firm. No other single factor contributes more to its long-term growth and profitability. This requires the systematic identification and elimination of loss and marginal products from the line, and their replacement with new, high-margin products. The process can be likened to pruning deadwood from a living plant and grafting on new growth to keep the plant vital.

HOW TO DETERMINE WHAT PRODUCTS SHOULD BE ELIMINATED.

Products to be eliminated may be the older ones past their prime and in the declining stage of their demand cycle. Typically, these products have low gross margins, low returns on investment, and little or no growth potential. Other candidates for elimination are those new-product introductions of previous years which either failed to get off the ground or, if they did take off, lacked sufficient market power to gain altitude.

In larger, multi-product line firms, a group of associated products or an entire product line may be considered for discontinuance. A line that is based on obsolete technology may require an enormous investment of engineering expenditures to catch up with the state of the art—it might be better strategy to "leap-frog" to an advanced technology, while the current line is being phased out. Pressures on prices and erosion of profit margins may be caused by excess industry capacity—if that excess is to extend far into the future, the best strategy may be to discontinue the line.

Most managers applaud a policy of adding new products to the line, but many resist to the bitter end the abandonment of current ones. Yet it is just as important to the company to weed out of the line low-margin products as it is to add new high-margin ones—and to do this, not just once in a while, but on a systematic, continuous, planned basis. This is not an

75

argument against retaining an older product in order to "milk it" for cash flow to nurture new products in their early period. The exploitation of "cash cows" is an important part of a sound growth strategy.

A product once in the line is painfully difficult to eliminate, despite evidence that it is only marginally profitable, even unprofitable—despite proof that market demand has shifted to other products. A product has a way of building a constituency within the organization over time—managers whose jobs may be affected by its discontinuance, or last-ditch defenders of the "full line" marketing concept.

SUBTRACT BEFORE YOU ADD

Failure to prune the line of these profit drains can offset much, if not all, of the benefit gained from adding new products. The loss and low-margin products continue to depress total product line profitability. Facilities, capital, and personnel are tied up with their production and sale and management time is diverted from more productive uses to deal with the problems that marginal products often cause. Even worse consequences can come from misguided attempts to revive a dying product—to restyle it, to repackage it, to stimulate sales through price-cutting or incentives, or to experiment with new advertising platforms. These efforts can devour money, manpower, and management attention, and drain the organization of its productivity.

It is unfortunate that many managers prefer to deal with these problems rather than with the larger issues of growth and development. If the efforts to save a moribund product were directed toward increasing sales of the most profitable products in the line, the return on effort expended could be very high indeed. Even if a massive effort could double sales of a marginal product from, say $500,000 to $1,000,000, it would contribute less volume to the company than a modest 10 percent increase in sales of a $10 million product—and far less profit margin.

Product-line proliferation is one of those management problems that cannot be solved but must be lived with. A complicating factor is the need for two very different kinds of product pruning decisions: First, a decision in principle to abandon a marginal product; and then a decision (or set of decisions) on how and when to phase it out. The first decision is a strategic one; the second is usually operational or tactical. It is not uncommon for the first decision to be made but not the second. In some instances, products are made and sold *years* after top management decided to drop them.

Meanwhile, new products continue to be added to the line and the catalog gets larger and larger. The process is a kind of creeping growth that may not even be noticed until a new manager comes in and discovers to his dismay that the product line contains some 2,000 sizes, shapes and styles, of which about 150 account for 85 percent of sales (and, not infrequently, over 100 percent of the line's profit).

PRODUCT PRUNING CAN BE PROFITABLE

Most progressive firms have effective new-product planning and development control systems. What is lacking in many organizations are controls on product proliferation, controls designed to encourage systematic phasing-out of products that have no future. Product pruning and new-product additions must be regarded as two aspects of the same issue, the maintenance of a healthy product line. As older, low-margin product sales decline and the products are eventually phased out, their place in the line should be taken by new products with a higher margin contribution. This process maintains and increases overall product-line profitability, and the firm's order book is kept high in profit margin content.

HOW TO USE THE CHECKLISTS

For each of the statements in the Checklist, compare the condition of your function to the "ideal" as described in the statement. Then:

1. If you consider the statement to be *generally true* of your function, check the YES column.

2. If you consider the statement to be *untrue* of your function, check the NO column.

3. If you consider the statement to be *less than true* (but not totally untrue) of your function, check the SOMETIMES OR PARTIAL column.

4. If the statement does not apply to your particular situation, write "Not Applicable" across the response spaces (or simply draw a line through them).

5. If you lack the data for a definite response, write in "Not Answerable" or "Don't Know."

HOW TO EVALUATE YOUR RESPONSES

When you have completed the checklist, glance over your responses, keeping these points in mind:

1. A negative answer is always unfavorable because it indicates a problem within the function: the greater the number of NOs, the more serious the situation.

2. A positive response is always a good indication. But too many YES answers could indicate that your review is not objective enough.

3. Too many SOMETIMES OR PARTIALLY answers can point to internal weaknesses or to a lack of firm direction.

4. A lot of "Not Applicable" answers could indicate that you are avoiding the issue.

5. A large number of "Not Answerable" or "Don't Know" answers could be symptomatic of inadequate records or data bases.

HOW TO RATE AND SCORE YOUR RESPONSES

When you are satisfied with your responses in general, you are ready to score the Checklist. For your convenience, a self-explanatory Scoring and Rating Block follows each Checklist. This block not only tells you whether the condition of your function is satisfactory, but it also gives you a measure of its effectiveness.

Here's how to total up the points for inclusion in the Scoring and Rating Block:

1. Total up the number of points you scored:
   a. For each YES, give yourself one point.
   b. For each NO, give yourself zero.
   c. For each SOMETIMES OR PARTIALLY, give yourself a half-point.
   d. For each "Not Applicable" answer, give yourself zero and deduct one from the number of items on the Checklist.
   e. For each "Not Answerable" or "Don't Know" answer, give yourself zero.

2. Next divide the total number of points you score by the total number of items (statements) on the Checklist (less items marked "Not Applicable"). You'll get a 1.0 for a perfect score and a fraction for anything less.

3. Multiply the result of step 2 by 100 to arrive at the percentage for your score.

What is a satisfactory rating? A rating of less than 65 percent is unacceptable and calls for an improvement program: Obviously, the lower the rating, the more drastic the action required.

A brief "how-to" example of this Scoring and Rating system follows . . .

EXAMPLE

	YES (1)	NO (0)	S/P* (½)

1. Field sale reports designed to provide information on sales progress contain data on the following topics:

   a. sales calls and sales presentations made by salespersons and sales agents, — ✓ (YES)

   b. bids, quotations, and proposals made, — ✓ (YES)

   c. new orders booked, — ✓ (YES)

   d. lost business, and reasons for the loss, — ✓ (NO)

   e. accomplishments toward future orders, — ✓ (S/P)

   f. performance in filling orders, handling complaints, and otherwise servicing individual customers, — ✓ (YES)

   g. action taken in response to customer requests, such as sending samples, spec sheets, etc., — ✓ (YES)

   h. accomplishments of significance and value to other members of the sales force. — ✓ (S/P)

*SOMETIMES OR PARTIALLY

TOTAL POINTS $\boxed{5}$ + 0 + $\boxed{1}$

= $\boxed{6}$

RATING

$$\frac{\text{Enter number of points scored} \quad \boxed{6}}{\text{Enter number of items on checklist} \quad \boxed{8}} = .75 \times 100 = \boxed{75}\ \%$$

5-A
ORGANIZATION, ADMINISTRATION, AND OPERATION

	YES (1)	NO (0)	S/P* (½)
1. An annual in-depth product-line evaluation is recognized as a vital company activity that has top management endorsement and support.	_____	_____	_____
2. The activity is recognized in managers' position descriptions as an important function of marketing.	_____	_____	_____
3. The marketing budget includes an allocation for internal expenses of this activity, and outside services if required.	_____	_____	_____
4. Business plans and marketing plans include product-line evaluation as key inputs.	_____	_____	_____
5. The unit has formalized procedures and follows a prescribed schedule for making annual product-line evaluations and "pruning" the line of deadwood.	_____	_____	_____
6. An in-depth evaluation of the product line has been made within the past year.	_____	_____	_____
7. Evaluation covered all products in the line.	_____	_____	_____
8. The evaluation is based in part upon up-to-date surveys conducted among users of the products, that is, the evaluation is market-oriented.	_____	_____	_____
9. Surveys were designed and conducted by professional market research people, either in-house or on a consulting basis.	_____	_____	_____
10. Surveys covered key buying factors such as:			
a. product characteristics—features and benefits,	_____	_____	_____
b. service considerations, and	_____	_____	_____
c. economic factors.	_____	_____	_____
11. Surveys rated products in terms of:			
a. ability to meet customer needs,	_____	_____	_____
b. comparison with strongest competitor, and	_____	_____	_____
c. alternatives open to customer (example: gas heater vs. electric heater).	_____	_____	_____
12. The surveys covered a sufficient size and diversity of users to give valid and representative data.	_____	_____	_____
13. Survey results were used to make recommendations to:			
a. eliminate products from the line,	_____	_____	_____
b. add features and benefits through product revision,	_____	_____	_____
c. extend line with new products, and	_____	_____	_____
d. propose new products that an associated unit might investigate for market potential.	_____	_____	_____
14. The product line evaluation is also based upon an analysis of the products from a producer viewpoint; that is, upon manufacturing, marketing, cost, and other internal considerations.	_____	_____	_____

*SOMETIMES OR PARTIALLY

	YES (1)	NO (0)	S/P* (½)

15. Evaluation covered the following factors for each product in the line:

   a. The sales trend since inception of the product has met expectations.

   b. Profit margins are known by product from the accounting records.

   c. Profit margins are satisfactory in dollars and in percent of sales.

   d. Sales have substantially met sales forecasts during past year.

   e. Forecasted growth in sales and margins is acceptable in terms of total product line objectives.

   f. The product contributes an appropriate and balanced percentage share of the total sales and profit margin of the entire line.

   g. Selling costs are in line with industry norms and with similar products.

   h. Share of the market is known.

   i. Share of the market is acceptable.

   j. Product is projected to give an acceptable share of market within the business plan period.

   k. Product fits well with other products in the line, and with the assigned business mission of the unit.

   l. The product can stand alone in the marketplace and is not too dependent on other products in the line for support.

   m. The product is free from serious safety, user liability, or environmental problems.

   n. The product has at least one unique feature or user benefit that can be exploited by the sales and advertising departments.

   o. The product is a good fit with manufacturing facilities and processes.

   p. The product has good acceptance by sales personnel, distributors, and dealers.

   q. The product is profitable for:

      a. manufacturing,

      b. salesman,

      c. distributor, and

      d. dealer.

   r. The product line in total is free from:

      a. loss leaders,

      b. too many options and choices of size, color, capacity, etc.,

      c. the "full-line" fallacy.

   s. Production and inventory costs are not excessive.

   t. An assessment has been made of the impact to the product line and the company if the product is dropped from the line.

*SOMETIMES OR PARTIALLY

	YES (1)	NO (0)	S/P* (½)

16. The individual products contributing 75–80 percent of the product-line profit margin have been identified, as well as those producing only 20–25 percent of the total profit margin.   _____   _____   _____

17. Of these, the products that show a loss or marginal profit on sales have been isolated for analysis.   _____   _____   _____

18. Within this special group, some products have been identified as "deadwood," and isolated as candidates for elimination from the product line.   _____   _____   _____

19. One or more of these products has been recommended for phase-out during the next year.   _____   _____   _____

20. Policy requires executive approval of all product discontinuances before implementation.   _____   _____   _____

*SOMETIMES OR PARTIALLY

TOTAL POINTS   ☐ + 0 + ☐

= ☐

RATING

Enter number of points scored ☐

Enter number of items on checklist ☐

=   × 100 = ☐ %

WHAT THE RATING SIGNIFIES

A less-than-acceptable rating is evidence that management does not consider it important to weed out the product "losers" from the "winners." The danger is that the product line will grow and grow to the point that it becomes unmanageable—and very expensive to maintain. High inventory costs, high selling expenses, and high production costs for short runs can eat up profits like a visiting relative.

The sales people love a full line—so they can offer the product in forty sizes, fourteen styles, and seven colors. Trouble is, the customer finds out he can design the product, so he'll ask for size number forty-one, style number fifteen, and a two-color combination—and most sales reps couldn't care less how much it costs to produce.

WHAT TO DO NOW

1. A very practical and effective way to cut the product line down to size is to put the sales force on an incentive program that pays a higher commission for selling standard sizes and styles in larger quantities, and a low commission for specials in small quantities. When their income depends on it, sales people will push the products that produce the profit margins, and the losers will weed themselves out. Of course, if it turns out that the standards don't sell, then you have a serious marketing and product design problem.

2. Be prepared to hear screams from sales, product distribution, and others when you cut products from the line. Someone's ox is gored every time the line is cut. But keep in mind that something like 80 to 85

percent of the products in the line usually account for only 15–20 percent of total profit margin. They also account for 80 percent of the costs and expenses.

3. A well-designed customer survey can often help to support your case for product phase-outs, by showing how market demand has shifted away from the products you have identified. Make sure that the survey is professionally designed, tested, and conducted, so you'll have confidence that the results are valid.

5-B
AUTHORITY, RESPONSIBILITY, AND ACCOUNTABILITY

	YES (1)	NO (0)	S/P* (½)
1. Authority has been delegated to the marketing manager, in writing, to expend company funds and assign tasks necessary to assure that the company's product line is regularly and systematically evaluated and "pruned" for the purpose of keeping it profitable.	_____	_____	_____
2. Through a policy statement or position description, responsibility is firmly assigned to the marketing manager for staffing and managing an organization to evaluate the company's product line.	_____	_____	_____
3. Responsibility is firmly assigned to the marketing manager for:			
a. an annual evaluation of the product line,	_____	_____	_____
b. firm recommendations for deletions from the line, and	_____	_____	_____
c. pressure for management decisions on these recommendations.	_____	_____	_____
4. The manager is held accountable for any serious			
a. decline in product-line profitability,	_____	_____	_____
b. increase in number of loss and marginal products,	_____	_____	_____
c. excess inventories caused by product proliferation,	_____	_____	_____
d. slow-moving product caused by dealer or distributor resistance (or sales force resistance), or	_____	_____	_____
e. decline in market shares.	_____	_____	_____

*SOMETIMES OR PARTIALLY

TOTAL POINTS [ ] + 0 + [ ]

= [ ]

RATING

Enter number of points scored [ ]
─────────────────────────────── = [ ] × 100 = [ ] %
Enter number of items on checklist [ ]

Adding products to the line is easy, compared to the task of cutting a product out of the line. It will not get done unless marketing has the power to override other functions who have a vested interest in the product. A low rating on the first three points indicates that this power may be lacking. A low score on point four indicates that the manager of marketing is not held accountable for all the adverse consequences of failure to prune the line—so there is little reason to put his or her job on the line to get it done, despite opposition.

WHAT TO DO NOW

1. It's to your advantage to have a lean and clean product line. It's easier to manage, because you can concentrate marketing time and talent on fewer items, and thus do a better job of marketing. You'll also find it easier to add new products with real promise and profit potential to the line.

2. It's also a good deal more profitable than an excessively full product line, with many, many models, styles and sizes. You will get the authority you need only by proving this to top management. Fortunately, it *can* be proved by a thorough analysis of costs and expenses, product by product. You need the cooperation of the controller for the basic analysis. Then you have to calculate and assign certain costs that the accounting system normally doesn't pick up—such as high sales costs for small special orders, high production set-up costs and scrap losses for manufacturing small lots, and high costs for maintaining product catalogs and spec sheets.

3. It's important to avoid a "crisis" approach—an arbitrary across-the-board cut of 25 percent, or 50 percent, of the low volume products from the line, without a sound financial analysis. This approach can kill off some good products that haven't been properly marketed, or some new products that haven't yet reached their potential.

5-C
MEASUREMENTS, CONTROL REPORTS AND PERFORMANCE RECORDS

	YES (1)	NO (0)	S/P* (½)
1. The effectiveness of the product-line evaluation and pruning process is measured and evaluated regularly and continuously.	——	——	——
2. This effectiveness is determined by comparing actual product performance and results to certain standards, benchmarks, or targets, such as product line:			
a. profit margins,	——	——	——
b. selling expenses,	——	——	——
c. inventory carrying costs,	——	——	——
d. distribution costs, and	——	——	——
e. production costs.	——	——	——

*SOMETIMES OR PARTIALLY

3. The effectiveness of the product-line evaluation process is also determined by its ability to keep the line free of loss and marginal products, despite opposition and resistance by people in sales, engineering, manufacturing, and distribution who may have a "vested interest" in the products. _____ _____ _____

4. Records and control reports provide product management, on a continuous basis, with information that:

   a. gives early warning of declining market demand and profitability, _____ _____ _____

   b. alerts management to the need for changes in the product line, _____ _____ _____

   c. stimulates action to meet a competitive threat, or to exploit an opportunity. _____ _____ _____

5. History and forecasts of market demand and sales prepared by market research and sales analysis are used in PL evaluation. _____ _____ _____

6. Accounting reports of product costs and profit margins are used in PL evaluation. _____ _____ _____

7. Reports are prepared showing all pertinent facts about loss and marginal products, together with recommended action, and disposition. _____ _____ _____

8. When no action is taken on recommendations within 3 months, marketing management is alerted for further action. _____ _____ _____

*SOMETIMES OR PARTIALLY

TOTAL POINTS [ ] + 0 + [ ]

= [ ]

RATING

Enter number of points scored [ ]

Enter number of items on checklist [ ]

= × 100 = [ ] %

WHAT THE RATING SIGNIFIES

A less-than acceptable rating in this section indicates that the essential information needed to make sound product abandonment decisions may not be available or up-to-date. As a consequence, a product may be cut out of the line for the wrong reasons—because the chairman of the board doesn't like the style, or the taste, or the color—rather than because it is unprofitable and has no future potential.

WHAT TO DO NOW

The recommendation to drop a product from the line is only a step in the right direction. Even when the recommendation is supported by massive evidence that the product is a loser, it takes conviction and persistence to see that the product is in fact abandoned.

1. You must keep pressure on other people to ensure that they follow through on your recommendation—even though top management has endorsed it. If you don't, you're liable to find it still in the catalog—maybe under a different name and number—two years from now.

2. Almost every product that is discontinued leaves a residue of unusable assets, like specialized production equipment—or even people who have built jobs around the product. The assets have to be disposed of at least loss—and the human resources involved have to be taken care of. It is your responsibility to ensure that this is done, as part of your product-abandonment recommendation.

5-D
OPERATING PERFORMANCE HISTORY

	YES (1)	NO (0)	S/P* (½)
1. An in-depth analysis has been made of functional control reports and records for at least one year past.	___	___	___
2. Based on the facts revealed by the analysis, the function has done a satisfactory job in the past of evaluating and pruning the product line.	___	___	___
3. In the current product line, 20 to 25 percent of products were not in the line 5 years previous.	___	___	___
4. During the past year, at least 5 percent of existing products were eliminated from the line as a result of the evaluation.	___	___	___
5. A satisfactory number of new-product developments have been initiated as a result of evaluation ("satisfactory number" should be defined).	___	___	___
6. No major product has shown a severe unanticipated drop in market share.	___	___	___
7. Product-line profit margin has shown an improving trend.	___	___	___
8. The number of loss and marginal products in the line has declined by a satisfactory percentage.	___	___	___

*SOMETIMES OR PARTIALLY

TOTAL POINTS   ☐ + 0 + ☐

= ☐

RATING

Enter number of points scored   ☐
———————————————————————   =   × 100 =   ☐ %
Enter number of items on checklist   ☐

WHAT THE RATING SIGNIFIES

Progressive and innovative companies set goals for new products, in terms of total product line content. 3M, for example, requires that 25 percent of the products in a division's product line be new, that is, they were not in the line five years earlier. Obviously, older, marginally-profitable products have to be dropped to make room for the new high-margin products. A low rating here indicates that these standards are not being met. If it continues this way, the product line can become overloaded with marginal products and competitively weak.

WHAT TO DO NOW

1. If past performance was unsatisfactory, make an analysis to pinpoint the causes. Discuss the results with your subordinates and your peers in other key functions; their insights can be helpful. With their support, set your priorities to improve performance.

2. Get your boss on your side. By building a solid base of consensus and support in advance, your program has a much greater chance of success.

5-E
TOP-LEVEL SUPPORT AND GUIDANCE

	YES (1)	NO (0)	S/P* (½)
1. The company has a published policy that older, low-margin or loss products with low potential for the future should be eliminated from the product line.	____	____	____
2. The executive office demonstrates active support, guidance, and recognition of the product line evaluation function through:			
a. budget approval for related costs and expenses,	____	____	____
b. review of recommendations for product-line changes,	____	____	____
c. expeditious decisions on recommendations to phase-out loss/marginal products,	____	____	____
d. informed comments on progress reports, and	____	____	____
e. recognition and reward for outstanding accomplishment.	____	____	____

*SOMETIMES OR PARTIALLY

TOTAL POINTS ☐ + 0 + ☐

= ☐

RATING

$$\frac{\text{Enter number of points scored} \quad \boxed{}}{\text{Enter number of items on checklist} \quad \boxed{}} = \boxed{} \times 100 = \boxed{\quad \%}$$

WHAT THE RATING SIGNIFIES

If the company has no firm policy on product discontinuance, your efforts should be directed toward getting one written and published. Without its support, you may find it impossible to get any action by other functions. If the policy exists, but is not being validated by visible support from the front office, it may be because you have failed to demand it as a condition of performance and results.

WHAT TO DO NOW

1. Write a draft policy and push it up through channels. It may be that no one topside is aware of the lack of a firm policy. Then follow through with well-considered and documented recommendations for discontinuance of outmoded products.

2. Insure your initial success by starting with products that no one will defend— never pick controversial ones with a built-in constituency at first.

3. Have a follow-up financial analysis made a year or so afterward, to document your good judgment and get credit for your accomplishment. Your only reward may be that the next one will be easier; nevertheless, it's worth the effort.

5-F
INNOVATION IN METHODS AND TECHNIQUES

	YES (1)	NO (0)	S/P* (½)
1. Marketing management actively pursues new methods, tools, and techniques to improve its evaluation of the product line, and make product pruning more effective, through:			
a. seminars and workshops,	____	____	____
b. use of outside specialists,	____	____	____
c. review of current literature,	____	____	____
d. professional societies,	____	____	____
e. solicitation of ideas from people in all functions and at all levels.	____	____	____
f. budgets include funds for such activities.	____	____	____
2. Competent outside intelligence services are employed to supplement in-house market research capabilities.	____	____	____
3. Up-to-date analytical techniques are used for making in-depth comparisons between the Unit's products and those of competitors.	____	____	____
4. The computer is used to store, process, and display information on sales, profit margins, market shares, growth rates by product line.	____	____	____
5. Operations research techniques of modeling and statistical analysis are considered for use in making P.L. evaluations.	____	____	____

*SOMETIMES OR PARTIALLY

TOTAL POINTS   ☐ + 0 + ☐

= ☐

RATING

Enter number of points scored ☐

─────────────────────────────   = ☐ × 100 = ☐ %

Enter number of items on checklist ☐

WHAT THE RATING SIGNIFIES   An effective evaluation of the product line depends on up-to-date knowledge of products, markets, and competitors. A low rating indicates that information may not be sought after and used as well as it should. If this conclusion is borne out by further investigation then the decision to drop a product may be based on conjecture rather than facts.

WHAT TO DO NOW

1. Find out what the most innovative and successful firms are doing. Fortunately, when people do a thing well they like to talk about it, in seminars, books, and articles in management journals.
2. Build a file (if one doesn't already exist) on each major product, showing the history of the product from its inception to date.
3. Chart volume, billings, and gross margin on a time-series graph as far back as records allow, and watch the trends carefully for early warning signals of decline.

5-G
INTERFUNCTIONAL COMMUNICATIONS AND COORDINATION

	YES (1)	NO (0)	S/P* (½)
1. Managers responsible for product-line evaluation:			
a. have active and direct contact with field sales personnel,	___	___	___
b. have accompanied direct sales representatives on joint sales calls,	___	___	___
c. work closely with people in sales analysis and market research,	___	___	___
d. work closely with value engineering and cost accounting,	___	___	___
e. attend top-level meetings in which loss and marginal products are reviewed and are given access to minutes of meetings on the subject.	___	___	___
2. Before making a firm recommendation to phase-out a product, marketing actively solicits the opinions of manufacturing, sales, engineering, distribution, and financial control.	___	___	___
3. Opposing views on product discontinuances are included in recommendations to the executive office.	___	___	___

*SOMETIMES OR PARTIALLY

TOTAL POINTS ☐ + 0 + ☐

= ☐

RATING

Enter number of points scored ☐
————————————————————————— = × 100 = ☐ %
Enter number of items on checklist ☐

WHAT THE RATING SIGNIFIES

The preceding section of the appraisal dealt with facts. This one is concerned with opinion. The opinions of managers in other functions are valuable input to a product abandonment decision, because they are often based on knowledge that marketing may not have access to directly, such as knowledge of new technology or a new way to reduce product costs. A low rating here indicates that these opinions may be overlooked; and an opportunity to revive the product and give it new life in the marketplace by redesign, substitution of new materials, or reduced costs may be lost.

WHAT TO DO NOW

1. The procedure for phasing out products should provide for input from all functions affected. If it doesn't you should take action to correct it.

2. Product line evaluation is a continuous process that requires a constant flow of information from many sources, both inside and outside the organization. You should, accordingly, make a special effort to maintain good, on-going communication with the other functions, especially with field sales, customer service, and accounting.

3. Small bits of data regularly dropped into your product files can add up to important information at decision time.

5-H
FUNCTIONAL IMPROVEMENT PROGRAM

	YES (1)	NO (0)	S/P* (½)
1. There is an active, on-going interfunctional team effort to improve the product-line evaluation process. Specific efforts on a task basis are directed toward:			
a. better identification of loss and marginal products as candidates for product-line "pruning,"	___	___	___
b. improved flow of information on markets and products from field sales and customer service, and	___	___	___
c. improved information on profitability by product.	___	___	___
2. Members of the team, depending on the task, include:			
a. cost accounting,	___	___	___
b. field sales,	___	___	___
c. market research, and	___	___	___
d. value engineering.	___	___	___

*SOMETIMES OR PARTIALLY

TOTAL POINTS ☐ + 0 + ☐

= ☐

RATING

Enter number of points scored ☐
——————————————————— = × 100 = ☐ %
Enter number of items on checklist ☐

WHAT THE RATING SIGNIFIES Good product-line evaluation is, perhaps more than any other activity, a team effort. Many points of view should be brought into the decision to drop or retain a product. The best way—perhaps the only way—to ensure that this is done is to formalize the process, by setting up a formal task group to meet regularly to review loss and marginal products for abandonment.

WHAT TO DO NOW

1. You need a top-side decision to set up the team, or task group, with you as its leader. This requires, first, a well-drawn recommendation, supported by facts. Second, the recommendation must be endorsed by your boss. Third, nominate a high quality group of managers from the other functions—the best you can get. (Of course, make sure in advance that they are agreeable to serve on the task force.)

2. Insure success by picking your product candidates for discontinuance carefully, as noted under point E earlier.

5-1
RESOURCES

	YES (1)	NO (0)	S/P* (½)
1. Managers responsible for evaluating and pruning the product line are kept informed about company objectives, strategies, policies, and programs, through access to:			
a. appropriate business plans,	___	___	___
b. marketing plans,	___	___	___
c. budgets,	___	___	___
d. new-product development plans, and	___	___	___
e. current operating reports.	___	___	___
2. Workload is known for the next three, six, and twelve months, based on plans and budgets; and resources are considered to be adequate to meet company needs, in terms of:			
a. manpower,	___	___	___
b. capabilities,	___	___	___
c. computer time and capacity,	___	___	___
d. budget funding, and	___	___	___
e. access to outside services.	___	___	___

*SOMETIMES OR PARTIALLY

TOTAL POINTS   ☐ + 0 + ☐

= ☐

RATING

Enter number of points scored ☐

───────────────────────────────── = ☐ × 100 = ☐ %

Enter number of items on checklist ☐

WHAT THE RATING SIGNIFIES

First, unless managers are kept informed about the direction the company is taking, and about basic marketing strategies being pursued, their recommendations for product phase-out may run counter to approved strategy.

Second, the process of evaluating the product line takes time and costs money. It is money well-spent, of course. But unless managers responsible for the process have the resources they need, they can't be held accountable for results.

WHAT TO DO NOW

1. Make sure that your product evaluation managers or task group have access to company information to the maximum extent consistent with company.

2. Insist on a *plan* for product-line evaluation and pruning. Obviously the plan can't name the specific products that will be recommended for phase-out, but it should identify the specific objective criteria that will be used to make the evaluation, and set some specific targets for product-line improvement. The plan should also include a specific schedule of review meetings, so all affected persons can plan to attend. In addition, it should be quite specific in terms of estimated dollar cost savings, increased product-line profit margins, expenses associated with the program, and resources needed.

Chapter

Planning and Controlling New-Product Development

This is the management function that serves to keep the enterprise vital and strong—and adapted to change in a rapidly changing world. It is one of the most demanding and complex of management activities. It is extremely difficult to do well, but terribly easy to do badly. When it is done badly, or not done at all, it can drag the company down. When it is done well, it can make the organization profitable beyond imagining. Also when it is done well, the rewards to owners and management can be enormous, both financially and in personal satisfaction.

SEVERAL GUIDELINES YOU SHOULD FOLLOW IN PLANNING NEW PRODUCT DEVELOPMENT

As a management process, it is many things. It is a process of great risk-taking. It is a process of looking forward from today's products and processes, identifying the supposed needs of people at some future time, and betting company resources on the choice. It is a process of looking out from the internal organization to the firm's several external environments—its markets, industries, and competitors; the business economy in which it functions, the legislative and regulatory bodies that make many of the rules it must live by; and the society it serves. Then it involves assessing the implications to the company of events and developments in these environments.

Planning and controlling new-product development is a unique combination of innovative, free-wheeling idea generation, and highly-structured procedures and controls for converting these ideas into viable products.

It requires, first of all, a free and full flow of ideas from many sources. This can only take place in a company atmosphere that encourages innovation, that is receptive and hospitable to new ideas. Next, it requires a system of incentives to stimulate creative thinking, recognition and consideration of every contribution, and reward for those ideas that result in new products.

NEED FOR A POSITIVE ATTITUDE

The process must include a method for testing new ideas while they are in conceptual form. This must be a positive phase of encouragement for the ideas, of looking for user benefits, rather than a negative one of screening out and of rejecting ideas because they initially don't measure up to a set of rigorous financial standards.

The process should take the survivors of this initial concept testing and start them through a structured and phased development process. At specific points along the way, each project should undergo an intensive review in the light of then-current information about the marketplace, the latest state of technology, and other environmental conditions. Market considerations must be the overriding factors in these reviews and a positive attitude is necessary. Funding should be associated with these phases, of course, in order to minimize the risks.

The entire process should be carried out within the framework of schedules and costs specified in a definitive new-product development plan prepared by marketing before the start of the business year. This plan cannot identify specific products, of course, but it should set firm criteria for their selection, in terms of anticipated market demand.

KEY AIM OF THE SELF-AUDIT

The main purposes of the appraisal are to ensure that (1) marketing considerations drive the new-product development process; (2) that ideas for new products are welcomed regardless of source; and (3) the process is directed and controlled from the top of the organization, because only the chief executive has the power to integrate all parts of the organization into the concerted company-wide effort that produces profitable new products.

HOW TO USE THE CHECKLISTS

For each of the statements in the Checklist, compare the condition of your function to the "ideal" as described in the statement. Then:

1. If you consider the statement to be *generally true* of your function, check the YES column.
2. If you consider the statement to be *untrue* of your function, check the NO column.
3. If you consider the statement to be *less than true* (but not totally untrue) of your function, check the SOMETIMES OR PARTIAL column.
4. If the statement does not apply to your particular situation, write "Not Applicable" across the response spaces (or simply draw a line through them).
5. If you lack the data for a definite response, write in "Not Answerable" or "Don't Know."

HOW TO EVALUATE YOUR RESPONSES

When you have completed the checklist, glance over your responses, keeping these points in mind:

1. A negative answer is always unfavorable because it indicates a problem within the function: the greater the number of NOs, the more serious the situation.
2. A positive response is always a good indication. But too many YES answers could indicate that your review is not objective enough.
3. Too many SOMETIMES OR PARTIALLY answers can point to internal weaknesses or to a lack of firm direction.
4. A lot of "Not Applicable" answers could indicate that you are avoiding the issue.
5. A large number of "Not Answerable" or "Don't Know" answers could be symptomatic of inadequate records or data bases.

HOW TO RATE AND SCORE YOUR RESPONSES

When you are satisfied with your responses in general, you are ready to score the Checklist. For your convenience, a self-explanatory Scoring and Rating Block follows each Checklist. This block not only tells you whether the condition of your function is satisfactory, but it also gives you a measure of its effectiveness.

Here's how to total up the points for inclusion in the Scoring and Rating Block:

1. Total up the number of points you scored:
    a. For each YES, give yourself one point.
    b. For each NO, give yourself zero.
    c. For each SOMETIMES OR PARTIALLY, give yourself a half-point.
    d. For each "Not Applicable" answer, give yourself zero and deduct one from the number of items on the Checklist.
    e. For each "Not Answerable" or "Don't Know" answer, give yourself zero.
2. Next divide the total number of points you score by the total number of items (statements) on the Checklist (less items marked "Not Applicable"). You'll get a 1.0 for a perfect score and a fraction for anything less.
3. Multiply the result of step 2 by 100 to arrive at the percentage for your score.

What is a satisfactory rating? A rating of less than 65 percent is unacceptable and calls for an improvement program: Obviously, the lower the rating, the more drastic the action required.

A brief "how-to" example of this Scoring and Rating system follows . . .

EXAMPLE

	YES (1)	NO (0)	S/P* (½)

1. Field sale reports designed to provide information on sales progress contain data on the following topics:

   a. sales calls and sales presentations made by salespersons and sales agents, ✓

   b. bids, quotations, and proposals made, ✓

   c. new orders booked, ✓

   d. lost business, and reasons for the loss, ✓ (NO)

   e. accomplishments toward future orders, ✓ (S/P)

   f. performance in filling orders, handling complaints, and otherwise servicing individual customers, ✓

   g. action taken in response to customer requests, such as sending samples, spec sheets, etc., ✓

   h. accomplishments of significance and value to other members of the sales force. ✓ (S/P)

*SOMETIMES OR PARTIALLY

TOTAL POINTS $\boxed{5}$ + 0 + $\boxed{1}$

= $\boxed{6}$

RATING

$$\frac{\text{Enter number of points scored} \quad \boxed{6}}{\text{Enter number of items on checklist} \quad \boxed{8}} = .75 \times 100 = \boxed{75}\%$$

6-A
ORGANIZATION, ADMINISTRATION, AND OPERATION

	YES (1)	NO (0)	S/P* (½)

1. The planning and control of new product development is recognized as one of the most vital company activities, and an important function of marketing.

2. The activity is directed and controlled by the chief executive of the company (or division), as chairman of the new product committee or board.

3. The express purpose of the committee is to promote, fund, monitor, and control the development of new products from initial concept through commercial market offering.

4. The function of new-product planning and development control is recognized on the organization charts and in managers' position descriptions as a full-time activity within the marketing department, or as a separate marketing function reporting to the chief executive.

5. If part of the marketing department, the manager of new-product planning and development control reports to the manager of marketing.

6. The manager of new-product planning and development control routinely attends top-level meetings on these matters, as well as those on facilities expansion, capital budgeting, product reliability and quality assurance, and business planning.

7. The function is managed and staffed by experienced professional marketeers who know the company's products, markets, and competition.

8. The marketing department prepares a one-year new-product development program plan, as part of the overall marketing plan.

9. The new-product development program plan is used as a guide throughout the year.

10. All new-product development projects are approved, funded, guided, and controlled by formal, up-to-date procedures and standard practices.

11. The internal organization is structured to function as the lead and liaison organization for the company throughout the planning and development process.

12. The function has a formal budget allocation covering internal expenses and outside services, if required.

13. The manager of marketing, and/or the new-product development manager, plays a key role in the activities of the new product committee, second only to the chief executive.

14. The committee has high-level representation from *all* functions of the business.

15. The group meets on a fixed schedule to review all new-product development projects from inception to completion.

16. The group works to a prepared agenda, and issues action assignments, which are followed-up until completed.

17. All new-product development projects are funded in stages.

*SOMETIMES OR PARTIALLY

	YES (1)	NO (0)	S/P* (½)

18. Funding approval for each stage is given only after committee review and approval of progress to date. ___ ___ ___

19. Funding approval for each stage is also dependent upon:

    a. continued favorable conditions in the market, ___ ___ ___

    b. a favorable economic outlook, ___ ___ ___

    c. review of the competitive, technological, and regulatory environments, and agreement that threats can be managed, and ___ ___ ___

    d. assessment of financial and other business risks. ___ ___ ___

*SOMETIMES OR PARTIALLY

TOTAL POINTS   [ ] + 0 + [ ]

= [ ]

RATING

$$\frac{\text{Enter number of points scored} \quad [\ ]}{\text{Enter number of items on checklist} \quad [\ ]} = \quad \times 100 = [\quad] \%$$

WHAT THE RATING SIGNIFIES

If new-product planning and development is not fostered, directed, and controlled at the very top level of the organization, whether company or division, then there is a very high risk that the firm will have a poor record in bringing new products to market. And if the marketing people don't have the strongest influence on the selection of new product candidates, there is an even greater risk that the failure rate in the marketplace will be high.

Furthermore, if new-products are not guided and monitored throughout their development, and funded in stages, there is a real danger that the process will get out of control.

If any or all of these "ifs" are evidenced by a low rating on this section, then it is almost certain that the firm's profitability and growth rate are declining.

WHAT TO DO NOW

As manager of marketing you have an obligation to ensure that new high-margin products with strong market demand are constantly brought on-stream, to replace older, low-margin products near the end of their product life-cycle and with small potential for the future.

1. To fulfill this obligation, you first need lots of organizational "clout," in order to get people in every other function and on every other organizational level to work together in the complex process of planning, selecting, and developing new products.

2. How do you get this power? You start by asking for it—by demanding it, if necessary, as an essential condition to getting your job done. As a first step, you should prepare a strong case for your position, drawing

on the documented experiences of business firms that have successful new product programs. You should also document some bad examples—perhaps your own company. Then you have to sell your case to a lot of other people—including your chief executive.

3. If this doesn't work, either your case is not convincing or your company top management's concern for the firm's future is not genuine—in which case, you had better seek a more promising environment for your talents.

4. You also need a sound new-product development program plan, with schedules and estimated costs. This is the primary responsibility of marketing, not engineering, because the program should be driven by market considerations. In addition, you need well-structured procedures for shepherding a number of new products through the (sometimes lengthy) process of planning and development. Again, you should heed the people who do this well—the 3Ms, the International Harvesters, the Procter & Gambles, the Texas Instruments, etc.

5. On top of this, you need a superior staff of marketers reporting to you; a high-class Engineering and Development group to carry the projects through design and development; and a financial control staff to watchdog the costs.

6. Finally, you need to encourage a flow of new-product ideas from everyone in the organization—from the CEO to the building custodian. You do this only by recognizing and rewarding people, and by proving to them that their ideas were sincerely considered.

6-B
AUTHORITY, RESPONSIBILITY, AND ACCOUNTABILITY

	YES (1)	NO (0)	S/P* (½)
1. Authority has been delegated in writing to the chief executive of the company (or division) to expend company funds, invest capital, and assign tasks necessary to assure a flow of high-margin new products into the product line.	___	___	___
2. As chairman of the new-product committee, the chief executive of the company (or division) has authority to commit company resources to further work on a project, to redirect the development effort, or to terminate a project.	___	___	___
3. The manager of marketing is responsible for staffing and managing an organization to keep the committee up-to-date on markets, competitors, and business conditions.	___	___	___
4. Other functional heads are responsible for keeping the committee informed on events, developments, and trends in their respective areas, i.e., financial, technological, regulatory, etc., that can affect new-products in planning and development.	___	___	___
5. Responsibility is firmly assigned to the manager of marketing (or the new-products manager) to coordinate and administer the directives of the chairman of the new-product committee.	___	___	___

*SOMETIMES OR PARTIALLY

	YES (1)	NO (0)	S/P* (½)

6. Responsibilities are clearly assigned to other functional heads to implement directives in their functional areas.   _____ _____ _____

7. The chief executive is held accountable for:

   a. serious failure to meet business plan objectives for new-product sales and margins,   _____ _____ _____

   b. serious delays or cost overruns on new-product development projects,   _____ _____ _____

   c. failure to terminate or redirect efforts on projects when evidence shows that the market is no longer receptive to the new product.   _____ _____ _____

8. The manager of marketing (or the new-products manager) is held accountable for serious delays, excessive costs, or non-acceptance of new product developments resulting from poor administration or coordination or from failure of marketing to provide adequate and timely information to the new-product committee.   _____ _____ _____

*SOMETIMES OR PARTIALLY

TOTAL POINTS $\boxed{}$ + 0 + $\boxed{}$

= $\boxed{}$

RATING

Enter number of points scored $\boxed{}$

Enter number of items on checklist $\boxed{}$

= × 100 = $\boxed{}$ %

WHAT THE RATING SIGNIFIES

This appraisal section assumes that the chief executive of the company (or division) is considered responsible for new-product planning and development. Only the top executive has the authority and the command of resources needed for effective results in this critical activity. This authority should not be redelegated. It also assumes that the chief executive should chair a new-product committee, or review board or task force. Whatever it is called, it is made up of the managers of all key functions.

A low rating in this section indicates that authority and responsibility are lower in the organization than is required for effective new-product planning and development, or is dispersed instead of centralized. If this is so, then there may be a lot of finger-pointing when a new product bombs in the marketplace—or the wrong head will roll for the failure.

WHAT TO DO NOW

1. As manager of marketing with responsibility to position new products in the marketplace, you could find it a bit difficult to tell your top boss, the CEO, that he or she is part of the problem. However, if the CEO doesn't take the time to oversee the new product activity properly, or if the CEO believes he or she can delegate authority for this to a subordinate—the company can suffer serious consequences. (Obviously in a large divisionalized corporation, authority can be delegated to division presidents or general managers for new products in their product lines.)

2. You could proceed by building a concensus among the top functional managers for a process that requires participation and the decision power of the top executive's office. Only when you're sure of their support should you make your pitch to the boss.

6-C
MEASUREMENTS, CONTROL REPORTS AND PERFORMANCE RECORDS

	YES (1)	NO (0)	S/P* (½)
1. The effectiveness of planning and control of new-product developments is measured and evaluated regularly and continuously.	___	___	___
2. This effectiveness is measured by comparing actual performance and results to targets, benchmarks, or standards, such as:			
a. product line profit margins,	___	___	___
b. new-product content of order input and billings ("new" is defined as less than five years old), and	___	___	___
c. meeting time and cost schedules in project plans.	___	___	___
3. The growth in sales of each new product and its profit contribution to the line are tracked separately for intense management review during the 5 years after market introduction.	___	___	___
4. External trends and events are monitored on a regular basis, and those with significance to products in development are highlighted for attention of the new-products committee. Assessment reports are made of changes in:	___	___	___
a. markets,	___	___	___
b. competition,	___	___	___
c. the economy,	___	___	___
d. demographic and social factors,	___	___	___
e. technology,	___	___	___
f. consumer preferences, and	___	___	___
g. regulation and legislation.	___	___	___
5. Records are maintained showing internal progress of each new product under development, and comparison of actual performance with budgets and schedules is made on a regular basis:	___	___	___
a. progress to date,	___	___	___
b. costs to date,	___	___	___
c. technical problems,	___	___	___
d. materials or process problems,	___	___	___
e. costs to complete,	___	___	___

*SOMETIMES OR PARTIALLY

	YES (1)	NO (0)	S/P* (½)
f. time to complete,	____	____	____
g. changes in economics of the project, and	____	____	____
h. relative worth of project vs. others, and vs. new opportunities.	____	____	____

6. The implications of changes in external factors, such as the introduction of a new product by a competitor, are assessed by the committee. Consideration is given to:

a. changing the pace of development,	____	____	____
b. changing product characteristics, and	____	____	____
c. terminating development of the product.	____	____	____

7. Excessive cost overruns, technical hang-ups, schedule delays, or changes in the relative economics of a project are also assessed by the committee, in terms of their impact on the development program.   ____ ____ ____

*SOMETIMES OR PARTIALLY

TOTAL POINTS   ☐ + 0 + ☐

= ☐

RATING

Enter number of points scored ☐
————————————————— = × 100 = ☐ %
Enter number of items on checklist ☐

WHAT THE RATING SIGNIFIES

A less-than-satisfactory rating indicates that the company is running high risk that a new product could be obsolescent before it reaches the market. In today's fast moving competitive marketplace, a new product development project can be "blind-sided" by events and developments in another company, another industry, or even another country. Unless the organization has a system for gathering information, analyzing it, and assessing its significance to projects in development, company management is like the crew of a ship or airplane navigating without instruments.

It's always an unpleasant shock to discover that a new product half-way through development has become obsolete by a change in customer needs, a technological breakthrough, a competitor getting to market first, or new government legislation or regulation. The only thing worse is not discovering it—or discovering it *after* the product reaches the general market.

WHAT TO DO NOW

1. Your information system should be designed to give you early warning of events—a kind of management DEW-line—so you can do something about it before it's too late. The earlier you terminate a dead-end development the less it costs.

2. Your project control system also should be designed to alert you when it appears that costs are going out of control, or scheduled milestones will be seriously missed, or technical problems threaten the success of the project.

6-D
OPERATING PERFORMANCE HISTORY

	YES (1)	NO (0)	S/P* (½)

1. A review and analysis have been made of control reports and records for at least one year past. ___ ___ ___

2. This review of records and reports for the past year shows that:

   a. at least one new product was introduced last year and produced sales of $1 million (annual rate at year end), ___ ___ ___

   b. a minimum of 25 percent of sales came from products not in line five years earlier, ___ ___ ___

   c. all developments under way are less than 10 percent over cost-to-complete estimates, ___ ___ ___

   d. all developments under way are less than three months behind schedule, ___ ___ ___

   e. all developments under way have been in progress less than two years, and ___ ___ ___

   f. a minimum of 25 new-product ideas were considered for development. ___ ___ ___

(The figures above may be changed to fit the size and characteristics of the company being appraised.)

*SOMETIMES OR PARTIALLY

TOTAL POINTS   [   ] + 0 + [   ]

= [   ]

RATING

Enter number of points scored [   ]
───────────────────────────────────── =   [   ] × 100 = [   ] %
Enter number of items on checklist [   ]

WHAT THE RATING SIGNIFIES   If the answer to point 1 is negative, then it is not possible to respond to point 2 with assurance. If the review has been made, and the response to point 2 is unsatisfactory, it is evidence that planning and control of new-product development projects may be inadequate.

WHAT TO DO NOW

1. A satisfactory output of new products from the engineering and development section depends, first of all, on a substantial flow of new product ideas into the development hopper. It may take from ten to one hundred ideas, or even more, to produce one viable new product. These ideas can come from any direction. Your own engineering, sales or production people are an excellent source. Your own customers can be one of the best sources—they often use your product in ways your engineers didn't think of, and this can stimulate ideas for other products.

2. Every new product development is a roll of the dice—hedge your bets by cutting off a development quickly when your information shows that it won't work, or it won't sell, or it will cost too much to be profitable—and put the money into more promising products.

6-E
TOP-LEVEL SUPPORT AND GUIDANCE

	YES (1)	NO (0)	S/P* (½)
1. The executive office demonstrates active support, guidance, and recognition of planning and control of new product development through:			
a. personal direction of the new-product development review process,	————	————	————
b. approval of capital projects for new products,	————	————	————
c. approval of expense budgets for new product development,	————	————	————
d. company policy statements endorsing the activity,	————	————	————
e. a significant investment of executive time, and	————	————	————
f. recognition and reward for outstanding accomplishment.	————	————	————

*SOMETIMES OR PARTIALLY

TOTAL POINTS   ☐ + 0 + ☐

= ☐

RATING

Enter number of points scored ☐

─────────────────────────────   = ☐ × 100 = ☐ %

Enter number of items on checklist ☐

WHAT THE RATING SIGNIFIES

When the top executive gets behind the new-product program and gives it his personal support, great things can happen. When he doesn't, a great many potentially profitable product ideas will never see the light of day, and a lot of talented people may become frustrated.

If this rating is low, then the kind of active, *visible* support the program needs is not coming from the front office.

WHAT TO DO NOW

1. This appraisal is closely related to the earlier appraisal of authority and responsibility. The action recommended there is appropriate to this section.
2. Build a concensus of agreement that top-level support is essential to new-product success—even to corporate survival—then sell it to the CEO. Failure on your part to do so is failure to meet your responsibility to the enterprise.

6-F
INNOVATION IN METHODS AND TECHNIQUES

	YES (1)	NO (0)	S/P* (½)
1. Management employs the computer to store, process, and display information needed for planning and control of new-product development.	————	————	————
2. Outside sources of information on future markets and technology are used to assess new-product opportunities.	————	————	————

3. Latest market research techniques for testing product concepts, and measuring consumer demand are utilized.

4. Management actively seeks new methods and techniques for improving the new-product success ratio, through:

    a. seminars, workshops, conferences,

    b. professional associations,

    c. industry and customer contacts,

    d. outside specialists,

    e. review of current literature, and

    f. solicitation of ideas from personnel at all levels and

    g. budgets provide funds for such activities.

*SOMETIMES OR PARTIALLY

TOTAL POINTS   ☐ + 0 + ☐

= ☐

RATING

Enter number of points scored / Enter number of items on checklist = ☐ × 100 = ☐ %

WHAT THE RATING SIGNIFIES   This section seeks to determine whether the organization is being innovative in managing innovation. A low rating indicates that it is not.

WHAT TO DO NOW

1. No other function of the business is so dependent on fresh new ideas. Open up every channel of communication with people, both inside and outside the organization.

2. Challenge all of your people to innovate—then recognize and reward them when they do.

3. Record every suggestion, no matter how offbeat—and track its progress through the steps in the process of evaluation, planning, and development.

4. Continue to bring these up for discussion at new-product meetings, because they can stimulate people to think more creatively.

6-G
INTERFUNCTIONAL COMMUNICATIONS AND COORDINATION

	YES (1)	NO (0)	S/P* (½)

1. New-product management actively maintains day-to-day close working relations at several organizational levels with:

   a. research, development, and engineering,

   b. field sales (including joint sales calls),

   c. market research,

   d. production engineering,

   e. quality assurance,

   f. financial control,

   g. legal, and

   h. customer service.

2. Formal communications with other functions is achieved through:

   a. new-product review meetings,

   b. new-product progress reports,

   c. the new-product review committee, and

   d. business planning and operating committee meetings.

*SOMETIMES OR PARTIALLY

TOTAL POINTS   ☐ + 0 + ☐

= ☐

RATING

Enter number of points scored ☐
—————————————————————— = ☐ × 100 = ☐ %
Enter number of items on checklist ☐

WHAT THE RATING SIGNIFIES   Good lines of communication between all functions is an important requisite for high productivity in any organization. It is absolutely essential for planning and controlling new-product development, because every function of the business is involved in the process. Too often, new-product development is considered the province only of the research, development and engineering function, and the other functions learn about the new product when it's ready to go into production—or even later when it is displayed at the annual trade show. If the rating is low in this section, new products may lack the valuable contribution of information, insight, and experience that other functions have to offer.

WHAT TO DO NOW   1. The earlier that people get involved with a new-product development, the more they can contribute to its successful development. The advertising function is an example. Antony Jay, in *Management and Machia-*

velli, says that management should get the advertising people involved at the beginning, so that "the desirable and appetizing qualities they specialize in applying could be built into the product instead of into the commercial."

2. It's important, of course, that all people participate in a positive and constructive manner. You have to set the example—and you must come down hard on people who contribute nothing but criticism and disapproval of the products and the process.

6-H
FUNCTIONAL IMPROVEMENT PROGRAM

	YES (1)	NO (0)	S/P* (½)
1. There is an active, on-going interfunctional team effort to improve the new product planning and development process, principally in the form of a high-level new-product committee or board of review composed of representatives of other business functions. Specific efforts are directed toward:			
a. more relevant and timely input from the marketplace,	___	___	___
b. better assessment of its implications to the company,	___	___	___
c. more effective control of project costs and schedules, and	___	___	___
d. earlier market testing and refinement of new-product concepts.	___	___	___
2. All major functions are represented on the team.	___	___	___

*SOMETIMES OR PARTIALLY

TOTAL POINTS   [ ] + 0 + [ ]

= [ ]

RATING

Enter number of points scored [ ]
————————————————————— = [ ] × 100 = [ ] %
Enter number of items on checklist [ ]

WHAT THE RATING SIGNIFIES   It was noted earlier in these comments that a cross-functional new-product review board or team is essential to effective new-product planning and development. It is not stating the case too strongly to say that without it the function will fail—and eventually, so will the company.

WHAT TO DO NOW   1. In addition to its primary task of shepherding new products through development, the team should constantly be looking for new methods, tools, control systems, and organizational structures that will make the new-product development process more effective and productive.

	YES (1)	NO (0)	S/P* (½)

1. New-product management is kept informed about company objectives, policies, plans, and programs through access to appropriate business plans, budgets, and executive directives.

2. Based on these and other inputs, resources for planning and control of new-product development are considered to be adequate to meet the needs of the business over the next three, six, and twelve months, in terms of:

   a. manpower,

   b. capabilities,

   c. budget support,

   d. engineering and development resources,

   e. access to outside resources,

   f. computer time and capacity, and

   g. support from other company functions.

*SOMETIMES OR PARTIALLY

TOTAL POINTS [ ] + 0 + [ ] = [ ]

RATING

Enter number of points scored [ ] / Enter number of items on checklist [ ] = [ ] × 100 = [ ] %

WHAT THE RATING SIGNIFIES

Obviously, new-product management cannot function without up-to-date information about the company's goals, business development strategies, and policies. Lacking such knowledge, the group might do a superb job of developing the wrong products!

Although this is an appraisal of marketing capabilities, and does not cover the actual engineering design and development of new products—that is covered in under RD&E—*it is marketing's responsibility to know* whether or not the engineering and development resources of the company are adequate to carry out the new-product development program marketing has designed to make the company a leader in the marketplace.

WHAT TO DO NOW

1. Your annual new-product development program plan should be the basis for evaluating resources. The plan will undoubtedly reflect some give-and-take and trade-offs between desires and reality.

2. It is normal for plans to change as the program progresses—just make sure that the changes are recorded and their impact on costs and schedules is controlled.

Chapter 7

Planning and
Developing Markets

This appraisal covers three phases of market development. One, developing present markets—that is, achieving greater market penetration by current products; two, developing new markets for existing products; and three, developing markets for a new product. Each requires a somewhat different approach, within an overall framework of structured market planning.

A THREE-PHASE PROCESS

The first phase is simply achieving greater penetration of existing markets and present customer accounts through innovative marketing strategies and tactics.

The second phase is a move into a new market by products currently in the product line. This involves an organized search for potential new outlets, and follow-on actions to stimulate demand for the product. The nature of these actions will vary, of course, with the particular characteristics of the new market. If the company has had no previous experience with the new market, however, there is a risk that these actions may not be the correct ones. For this reason, it is important to study the new market intensively, and identify the "critical factors for success" possessed by the most successful firms in the particular market. There are usually not more than two or three of these critical factors. If you have them, the lack of some other things seem not to matter; if you don't have them, it doesn't matter what other great things you have, you can't succeed in the market.

For example, if you're moving a brand into supermarkets from specialty stores, you'd better have the capability for wide distribution and stocking, and the attractive packaging that gets good shelf positioning because the package is now the sales clerk. This is true, as well, if you're moving to direct consumer selling from OEM sales. If you don't have these capabilities, it doesn't matter how good your product tastes, or looks, or works, how efficiently you produce it, or how good your advertising is—because your prospects won't be able to find your product when they want to buy it.

The third phase—developing markets for a new product—is an even more exacting task. The search for new markets should start even before the new product goes into development, when it is just a concept. If markets cannot be found at this point, or if market research fails to show sufficient market potential for sales volume and profitability, then the product idea should go no further. Assuming that promising markets exist, then the process of market development should begin the moment that the new product goes into design—and should continue until the developed product is in production. Actually, in fact, it should never stop, but should continue until the product reaches the end of its life cycle and is quietly laid to rest.

INFORMATION IS THE KEY

Planning and developing markets is an intellectual activity that functions on information. Good market research is the key and this is covered in the next section of the manual. A market is never created out of nothing—markets are developed only by learning what real needs are "out there," and then providing the products and services that meet these needs better than anyone else.

KEY AIM OF THE APPRAISAL

The principal objective of the appraisal is to ensure that the company follows a systematic and organized process of (1) searching out potential new markets, (2) analyzing these markets to determine what factors are critical to success, and (3) matching company strengths to these market requirements on a realistic basis.

HOW TO USE THE CHECKLISTS

For each of the statements in the Checklist, compare the condition of your function to the "ideal" as described in the statement. Then:

1. If you consider the statement to be *generally true* of your function, check the YES column.

2. If you consider the statement to be *untrue* of your function, check the NO column.

3. If you consider the statement to be *less than true* (but not totally untrue) of your function, check the SOMETIMES OR PARTIAL column.

4. If the statement does not apply to your particular situation, write "Not Applicable" across the response spaces (or simply draw a line through them).

5. If you lack the data for a definite response, write in "Not Answerable" or "Don't Know."

HOW TO EVALUATE YOUR RESPONSES

When you have completed the checklist, glance over your responses, keeping these points in mind:

1. A negative answer is always unfavorable because it indicates a problem within the function: the greater the number of NOs, the more serious the situation.

2. A positive response is always a good indication. But too many YES answers could indicate that your review is not objective enough.

3. Too many SOMETIMES OR PARTIALLY answers can point to internal weaknesses or to a lack of firm direction.

4. A lot of "Not Applicable" answers could indicate that you are avoiding the issue.

5. A large number of "Not Answerable" or "Don't Know" answers could be symptomatic of inadequate records or data bases.

HOW TO RATE AND SCORE YOUR RESPONSES

When you are satisfied with your responses in general, you are ready to score the Checklist. For your convenience, a self-explanatory Scoring and Rating Block follows each Checklist. This block not only tells you whether the condition of your function is satisfactory, but it also gives you a measure of its effectiveness.

Here's how to total up the points for inclusion in the Scoring and Rating Block:

1. Total up the number of points you scored:
   a. For each YES, give yourself one point.
   b. For each NO, give yourself zero.
   c. For each SOMETIMES OR PARTIALLY, give yourself a half-point.
   d. For each "Not Applicable" answer, give yourself zero and deduct one from the number of items on the Checklist.
   e. For each "Not Answerable" or "Don't Know" answer, give yourself zero.

2. Next divide the total number of points you score by the total number of items (statements) on the Checklist (less items marked "Not Applicable"). You'll get a 1.0 for a perfect score and a fraction for anything less.

3. Multiply the result of step 2 by 100 to arrive at the percentage for your score.

What is a satisfactory rating? A rating of less than 65 percent is unacceptable and calls for an improvement program: Obviously, the lower the rating, the more drastic the action required.

A brief "how-to" example of this Scoring and Rating system follows . . .

EXAMPLE

	YES (1)	NO (0)	S/P* (½)

1. Field sale reports designed to provide information on sales progress contain data on the following topics:

   a. sales calls and sales presentations made by salespersons and sales agents, ✓

   b. bids, quotations, and proposals made, ✓

   c. new orders booked, ✓

   d. lost business, and reasons for the loss, (NO) ✓

   e. accomplishments toward future orders, (S/P) ✓

   f. performance in filling orders, handling complaints, and otherwise servicing individual customers, ✓

   g. action taken in response to customer requests, such as sending samples, spec sheets, etc., ✓

   h. accomplishments of significance and value to other members of the sales force. (S/P) ✓

*SOMETIMES OR PARTIALLY

TOTAL POINTS 5 + 0 + 1

$= 6$

RATING

$$\frac{\text{Enter number of points scored} \quad \boxed{6}}{\text{Enter number of items on checklist} \quad \boxed{8}} = .75 \times 100 = \boxed{75}\%$$

111

7-A
ORGANIZATION, ADMINISTRATION AND OPERATION

	YES (1)	NO (0)	S/P* (½)

1. Planning and development of markets for the company's present products and planned new products are endorsed and supported by top management as vital company activities.

2. These activities are recognized on the organization charts and in managers' position descriptions as important functions of marketing and/or product management.

3. The activities are managed and staffed by experienced professionals trained in market planning and development and informed about the company's products, markets, and competition.

4. The marketing budget has an allocation to cover expenses of these functions, including outside services if required.

5. Planning and development of markets are conducted as an integrated and organized process, guided and governed by written procedures and schedules.

Market Planning

6. Market planning is conducted as an annual activity. The product of the planning is the annual marketing plan.

7. Market planning involves all functions within marketing, and draws on other functions of the business for information and analysis.

8. Key information sources for market planning include:

   a. customers,

   b. market studies and surveys,

   c. government statistics,

   d. industry publications,

   e. competitors' annual reports,

   f. distributors and dealers,

   g. field sales people,

   h. sales analysis, and

   i. service personnel.

9. The marketing plan is structured to show separately plans to develop:

   a. markets for planned new products, and

   b. new markets for existing products.

10. The marketing plan is distributed to other functions prior to the start of business planning, and serves as a key input to the planning of engineering, production, sales, and other business functions.

Market Development

11. Market development is conducted on a year-round basis, guided and governed by the annual marketing plan, procedures, and standard practices.

	YES (1)	NO (0)	S/P* (½)

12. Market development, or implementation of the marketing plan, is a function of marketing and/or product management. ___ ___ ___

13. Developing new markets for existing products, and developing markets for new products, involves other functions of the business, including (depending on the type of product):

   a. advertising and sales promotion, ___ ___ ___

   b. product publicity, ___ ___ ___

   c. field sales, ___ ___ ___

   d. application engineering, ___ ___ ___

   e. product distribution, and ___ ___ ___

   f. packaging. ___ ___ ___

14. Market development for a new product begins early, when the proposed new product is in the idea stage. ___ ___ ___

15. New-product market development continues throughout the product design and engineering development process. ___ ___ ___

16. To develop markets, marketing employs all accepted techniques to stimulate initial and on-going demand for the product, including as appropriate:

   a. advertising, ___ ___ ___

   b. sales promotion, ___ ___ ___

   c. sampling, ___ ___ ___

   d. sales calls, ___ ___ ___

   e. "Phone Power," ___ ___ ___

   f. field sales, ___ ___ ___

   g. price reductions or rebates, ___ ___ ___

   h. engineering or application assistance, ___ ___ ___

   i. dealer promotions, and ___ ___ ___

   j. private branding. ___ ___ ___

17. Information gained from these efforts is fed back for analysis and use in preparing follow-on merchandising programs. ___ ___ ___

*SOMETIMES OR PARTIALLY

TOTAL POINTS   [ ] + 0 + [ ]

= [ ]

RATING

Enter number of points scored [ ] = × 100 = [ ] %

Enter number of items on checklist [ ]

113

WHAT THE RATING SIGNIFIES

A less-than-acceptable rating is evidence of a lack of structure and organization of the market planning and development activity. If this is so, then it follows almost certainly that the company is not fully exploiting the markets available to it. Furthermore, the most profitable markets may be overlooked or undeveloped. What is worse, management may *not even know* that its declining volume and profit is the result of failure to develop markets adequately. What can follow is a severe cost-cutting program that can further weaken the firm's ability to find and develop markets—and a vicious circle of declining marketing productivity is set in motion.

WHAT TO DO NOW

1. Assuming that you have good products, all that good planning and development of markets needs is good people and a good process.

    Both of these, in turn, depend on a constant flow of good information. If you lack any *one* of these three essentials, you should set a near-term objective to put it in place.

2. If you lack *two* of these essentials you're in serious trouble, and it's going to take an expensive remedial program to correct your problem. If you lack all three, forget it—your situation is hopeless.

3. All of these essentials cost money and if your budget doesn't cover them, you'd better start now to get an allocation in next year's budget.

4. One of the worst things you can do—short of calling in consultants when you don't know your problem—is to try to revive a dying market by price cutting, product redesign, more advertising, or sales incentive programs. Better to put the money into finding and developing a new market.

7-B
AUTHORITY, RESPONSIBILITY AND ACCOUNTABILITY

	YES (1)	NO (0)	S/P* (½)
1. Authority has been delegated in writing to the marketing manager to expend company funds and assign tasks necessary to ensure that the company's business is conducted on the basis of:			
a. a sound and aggressive annual marketing plan, and	___	___	___
b. aggressive implementation of the plan in developing markets for existing products, and positioning new products for maximum growth and profitability.	___	___	___
2. Responsibility has been firmly assigned to the marketing manager for staffing and managing an organization to prepare an annual marketing plan for the unit.	___	___	___
3. Responsibility has been firmly assigned to product or market managers for development of marketing plans for their product lines or markets.	___	___	___
4. Responsibilities are clearly assigned to the same individuals for implementation of the marketing plan.	___	___	___

*SOMETIMES OR PARTIALLY

5. Authority has been delegated to product managers (or market managers) to expend company funds and to coordinate other functions' activities, as necessary to develop their respective markets. _____ _____ _____

6. Responsibilities are clearly assigned to managers of advertising and sales promotion, field sales, sales administration, and distribution, for effective development of markets for existing products, and profitable positioning of new products. _____ _____ _____

7. The marketing manager is held accountable for serious loss of sales volume, profit margins, and market shares, resulting from failure to develop effective marketing plans, or from failure to develop the company's markets properly. _____ _____ _____

8. The marketing manager is also held accountable for failure of new products to achieve planned goals for sales, profit margin, and market share, resulting from inadequate planning or market development. _____ _____ _____

9. Product managers (or market managers) share in the accountability for their respective market areas. _____ _____ _____

*SOMETIMES OR PARTIALLY

TOTAL POINTS [ ] + 0 + [ ]

= [ ]

RATING

Enter number of points scored [ ]

Enter number of items on checklist [ ]

= × 100 = [ ] %

WHAT THE RATING SIGNIFIES

A good job of planning and developing markets can't be done "on the cheap." But, as they say about good advertising, it doesn't cost—it pays. It starts with clear-cut authority to spend the funds necessary to collect, organize, and analyze information about potential markets; to prepare an effective marketing plan; and to maintain a staff of professional marketing people.

Responsibility has to be clearly assigned to individuals for developing new markets, or they will tend to cling to the same old markets because they're used to them. And accountability should be identified, so people will know clearly that reward for accomplishment will be accompanied by penalty for failure.

WHAT TO DO NOW

1. The managers who prepare marketing plans should have the responsibility to carry them out; to accomplish their objectives, to meet their schedule dates, and to live with their cost estimates. There are a couple of dangers in this. One is that an eager manager may over-promise, with the consequent risk of failing to meet unrealistic goals and schedules. The other is that a manager may play it cute by setting low objectives and easy targets to assure his own success, but which do little for the company.

2. Because the marketing plan is so important as a baseline for developing new markets, you must avoid these two traps by questioning every

input to these plans for validity and soundness. Make sure that assumptions are clearly defined, so that managers can't slip off the hook by claiming that circumstances have changed since they wrote the plan.

3. Then if a manager repeatedly fails to meet agreed-upon goals, and products continue to lose market share, you'll know what changes to make.

7-C
MEASUREMENTS, CONTROL REPORTS AND PERFORMANCE RECORDS

	YES (1)	NO (0)	S/P* (½)
1. The effectiveness of the market planning and development process is measured and evaluated regularly and continuously.	___	___	___
2. This effectiveness is measured by comparing actual performance and results with benchmarks, targets, or standards, such as:			
a. product-line profit margins,	___	___	___
b. market shares,	___	___	___
c. new-product content of order input and billings ("new" is defined as less than five years old), and	___	___	___
d. meeting objectives and target dates in marketing plans.	___	___	___
3. Sales reports and accounting records are routinely received and analyzed for significance to market development activities.	___	___	___
4. Reports are designed to give "early warning" of market developments and trends that affect the unit's existing products, and to stimulate management action to:			
a. exploit new-market opportunities, and	___	___	___
b. combat competitive threats to market position.	___	___	___
5. Feedback from initial market development is used to modify new products if necessary to meet the requirements of the markets.	___	___	___
6. New-product control reports give information on trends, changes, and market developments that can impact the development of markets for new products. Reports are designed to:			
a. alert management to the need for changes in the timing or direction of the new-market development, and	___	___	___
b. trigger action to modify the program.	___	___	___
7. Expenses of the market planning and development activity are routinely recorded and compared with budget.	___	___	___

*SOMETIMES OR PARTIALLY

TOTAL POINTS   [   ] + 0 + [   ]

= [   ]

RATING

Enter number of points scored [   ]
—————————————————————— = × 100 = [   ] %
Enter number of items on checklist [   ]

The real measure of effectiveness for this function is improvement in product-line profit margins. This is what market-planning and development is all about. The reason for developing new markets for existing products, and for developing markets for new products is to capitalize on higher demand that brings higher gross margins. It's not simply to increase volume—higher volume can sometimes cause more problems than it is worth. An example is a situation where a manufacturer expands capacity to meet higher volume only to find that the additional fixed costs and increased need for working capital offset the benefits of increased output.

The purpose of all measurements and controls, therefore, is to ensure that product-line profit margins are improved as a result of the market planning and development process.

WHAT TO DO NOW

1. Make it clear to all managers involved in planning and developing markets that the primary objective of their activities is to improve *overall product-line gross profit margins*. This helps to focus their activities on markets that are more promising from a profitability viewpoint—and helps to prevent the unproductive kind of activities aimed at "increasing our share of market" that all-too-frequently are achieved at a high cost.

2. Set up all measurements and controls to reinforce this objective—and eliminate everyone that doesn't.

7-D
OPERATING PERFORMANCE HISTORY

	YES (1)	NO (0)	S/P* (½)
1. An analysis has been made of control reports and records for at least one year past.	___	___	___
2. This review shows that there has been a satisfactory improvement in overall product-line profit margins.	___	___	___
3. During the past year, at least _____ significant new markets for existing products were identified and explored.	___	___	___
4. At least _____ of these markets were developed in a significant way.	___	___	___
5. At least _____ new markets were penetrated to a significant extent with "first purchases" by one or more major users.	___	___	___
6. There has been no serious loss of sales of a major product because of failure to detect changes in the market. (Answer "Yes" if true.)	___	___	___
7. Records show at least one significant market entry of a new product (minimum sales of $_____ million annual rate at year end).	___	___	___
8. There were no cases where a new product reached the final stages of development, and then failed to achieve targeted sales volume. (Answer "Yes" if true.)	___	___	___
9. The expense budget has essentially been met for the past year. (The figures above should be adapted to the size and characteristics of the company being reviewed.)	___	___	___

TOTAL POINTS   □ + 0 + □

☐ ‗‗‗‗‗‗ { = □

RATING

Enter number of points scored   □
‗‗‗‗‗‗‗‗‗‗‗‗‗‗‗‗‗‗‗‗‗‗‗‗‗ = ☐ × 100 = ☐ %
Enter number of items on checklist   □

WHAT THE RATING SIGNIFIES

An unsatisfactory rating is a signal that corrective action is needed to improve the market planning and development process. The past is not always an infallible guide to the future, of course, but poor performance in the recent past can't simply be brushed off with the attitude that "we'll do better in the future."

WHAT TO DO NOW

1. The *reasons* for past failures should be analyzed, and a corrective action program set up.

2. Look especially at *trends* in product profit margins. If they're flat or steadily declining, a deeper analysis should be made. If your accounting system is able to track profit margins by market segments, you should sort out the most promising market areas for further development.

3. Don't try to bolster the sagging markets unless you have a very compelling reason—it could cost you dearly by diverting your resources away from the really promising markets.

7-E
TOP-LEVEL SUPPORT AND GUIDANCE

	YES (1)	NO (0)	S/P* (½)
1. The executive office demonstrates active support, guidance, and recognition of the market planning and development activity, by means of:			
a. budget approval,	‗‗‗	‗‗‗	‗‗‗
b. policy statements,	‗‗‗	‗‗‗	‗‗‗
c. review and approval of marketing plans and recommendations for market development programs,	‗‗‗	‗‗‗	‗‗‗
d. participation in progress review meetings,	‗‗‗	‗‗‗	‗‗‗
e. informed comments on progress reports, and	‗‗‗	‗‗‗	‗‗‗
f. recognition and reward for outstanding accomplishment.	‗‗‗	‗‗‗	‗‗‗

*SOMETIMES OR PARTIALLY

$\boxed{} + 0 + \boxed{}$

$= \boxed{}$

RATING

Enter number of points scored $\boxed{}$ $=$ $\times\ 100 = \boxed{}$ %

Enter number of items on checklist $\boxed{}$

WHAT THE RATING SIGNIFIES

If your CEO demonstrates by his actions that he is sincerely supportive of your function, consider yourself blessed. If not—if he gives it only "lip service" and doesn't actively take part in the process—your task is to convert him into a believer.

WHAT TO DO NOW

1. Take every opportunity to "educate" the top executive and his key executives in the critical need to develop new markets. Send up every success story of companies that do a superior job of market planning and development—especially those of competitors. Send up, also, the "horror stories" of firms that fail because they neglect this—there are many of these. Don't be subtle—on every one draw a firm conclusion and make a firm recommendation for strengthening your activity.

2. Market planning and development costs money—but it's one of the best investments the boss can make in the future growth and profitability of the enterprise. Point out how it can also pay off in the short-term, by identifying where market demand is declining—so near-term sales and marketing efforts can be redirected to more profitable areas.

7-F
INNOVATION IN METHODS AND TECHNIQUES

	YES (1)	NO (0)	S/P* (½)
1. Management actively keeps informed about better ways to plan and develop markets, through:			
a. seminars, workshops, conferences,	———	———	———
b. outside specialists,	———	———	———
c. professional associations,	———	———	———
d. review of current literature,	———	———	———
e. industry contacts,	———	———	———
f. solicitation of ideas and suggestions from personnel at all levels, and	———	———	———
g. budgets provide funds for such activities.	———	———	———

*SOMETIMES OR PARTIALLY

	YES (1)	NO (0)	S/P* (½)

2. Management actively searches for and evaluates new research and survey methods to obtain market data for marketing planning.

3. Management actively searches for and utilizes new marketing techniques to stimulate market interest and demand.

4. The computer is used to store, process, and display information on markets, products, and development programs.

*SOMETIMES OR PARTIALLY

TOTAL POINTS ☐ + 0 + ☐

= ☐

RATING

Enter number of points scored ☐

Enter number of items on checklist ☐

= × 100 = ☐ %

WHAT THE RATING SIGNIFIES

Market planning and development is above all an innovative activity. It's vitally important for marketing management to stay abreast of new developments in the state-of-the-art, through regular contact with people in other companies and other industries. Trends and developments in what is called the "sociocultural" environment—that of social and cultural interaction among people—that are especially important to market planning and development. Regardless of what your company produces and sells, whether nuclear power reactors or bubble gum, your business is affected by changes in the way that people live, work, play, and communicate with each other. Marketing people, perhaps more than people of any other function, must be tuned in to these changes.

WHAT TO DO NOW

1. Make sure that all of your managers actively take part in outside activities, keep up with the professional literature, and stay up with current events.

2. See that your budget has funds for seminars, workshops, and other development activities.

3. Make sure that the most value is obtained for the money by requiring every manager to report fully to others on what he or she has gained from these activities, and how the knowledge is being put to work to improve the function.

7-G
INTERFUNCTIONAL COMMUNICATIONS AND COORDINATION

	YES (1)	NO (0)	S/P* (½)

1. During preparation of annual marketing plans, marketing personnel routinely maintain close working relations with other functions of the business, including:

   a. field sales, ——— ——— ———

   b. RD & E, ——— ——— ———

   c. advertising and sales promotion, and ——— ——— ———

   d. product distribution. ——— ——— ———

2. Marketing actively solicits help from other functions in identifying opportunities to enter new markets. ——— ——— ———

3. Market planning and development managers periodically accompany field sales people and customer service people on customer calls. ——— ——— ———

4. Close and continuous contact is maintained with other functions at several organizational levels during implementation of the marketing plan, to assure that the full resources of the company are used to develop markets. ——— ——— ———

*SOMETIMES OR PARTIALLY

TOTAL POINTS [ ] + 0 + [ ]

= [ ]

RATING

Enter number of points scored [ ]
―――――――――――――――――――――――   = [ ] × 100 = [ ] %
Enter number of items on checklist [ ]

WHAT THE RATING SIGNIFIES   A low rating in this section should alert marketing management that the market planning and development activity may be neglecting the important information and insight that other functional managers can contribute. Field sales and customer service people especially should be deeply involved in the process, because they are the eyes and ears of the company in its relations with customers.

WHAT TO DO NOW
1. It's up to you to initiate this essential coordination. The other functional managers have their own problems and concerns, and can't be expected to get involved with market planning and development unless you make it worth their while.
2. For one thing, make it a point to provide them with helpful information. Second, invite them to participate in your meetings. Third, give every suggestion from others full and serious consideration—and give public recognition to persons who contribute useful ideas.
3. Finally, take every opportunity to "pick the brains" of other functional managers through personal contact.

7-H
FUNCTIONAL IMPROVEMENT PROGRAM

	YES (1)	NO (0)	S/P* (½)

1. There is an active, on-going interfunctional team effort to improve the effectiveness of market planning and development. Principal efforts on a project basis, are directed toward:

	YES (1)	NO (0)	S/P* (½)
a. more relevant and timely input from the marketplace,	_____	_____	_____
b. better information feedback from field sales and service,	_____	_____	_____
c. more innovative approaches to market development,	_____	_____	_____
d. improved methods of testing markets for product acceptance.	_____	_____	_____

2. The team has representation from (depending on project):

	YES (1)	NO (0)	S/P* (½)
a. field sales,	_____	_____	_____
b. customer service,	_____	_____	_____
c. information systems,	_____	_____	_____
d. RD & E, and	_____	_____	_____
e. advertising and promotion.	_____	_____	_____

*SOMETIMES OR PARTIALLY

TOTAL POINTS [ ] + 0 + [ ]

= [ ]

RATING

Enter number of points scored
————————————————————— [ ] = × 100 = [ ] %
Enter number of items on checklist [ ]

WHAT THE RATING SIGNIFIES   This section is an extension of the previous one. By *formalizing* communications, assurance is provided that all points of view are built into the market planning and development process.

WHAT TO DO NOW

1. If the rating is low on the previous section, consider forming a team to conduct an on-going evaluation of the market development process. You can't lose by doing this, and you stand to gain a lot by getting the other functions involved.

2. You might do this informally at first. After you have some results to show, you can propose that the team be set up on a formal basis.

7-1
RESOURCES

	YES (1)	NO (0)	S/P* (½)
1. Marketing is kept informed about the company's objectives, policies, plans, and programs through involvement in business planning, capital budgeting, and business development.	___	___	___
2. Resources for market planning and development are considered to be adequate to meet the needs of the company over the next three, six, and twelve months, in terms of:			
a. manpower,	___	___	___
b. operating budget,	___	___	___
c. capabilities,	___	___	___
d. market research,	___	___	___
e. advertising and sales promotion,	___	___	___
f. sales support,	___	___	___
g. outside services,	___	___	___
h. computer and information systems support, and	___	___	___
i. functional support.	___	___	___

*SOMETIMES OR PARTIALLY

TOTAL POINTS   ☐ + 0 + ☐

= ☐

RATING

Enter number of points scored ☐
———————————————————————— = ☐ × 100 = ☐ %
Enter number of items on checklist ☐

WHAT THE RATING SIGNIFIES

If the answer to point 1 is negative, the function is in trouble. There is no way that marketing can do a productive job of market planning and development unless managers know the overall strategic direction of the enterprise. Without this guidance, there is a serious danger that the markets selected for development could be at cross purposes to the business strategies adopted by the executive office. Information is rapidly becoming the most important resource of business management; for market planning and development, *it is the life blood* of the function. You can have every other resource—money, manpower, and a key to the executive washroom—but unless you have factual, accurate, and comprehensive information to work with, you can't be productive.

WHAT TO DO NOW

1. In today's fast-moving marketplace, information is perishable, and has a short shelf-life. Make sure the information you get is up-to-date, and used while it is still valid.

2. One of your most important resources is *brain power*. Make sure your budget provides for salaries and incentive compensation that will attract the top talents in market planning and development.

THE BOTTOM LINE

The single product firm cannot survive for long in today's fast-changing business environment. Neither can the company that is dependent on a single market for the bulk of its business.

At the other extreme, the enterprise that attempts to "be all things to all customers," by offering the most complete range of product options, sizes, types, and applications, soon finds itself unable to compete cost-wise with competitors that serve selected segments of their markets with a moderate range of products.

What is required is balance between the risk of dependence on a single product that may become obsolete and the high operating costs associated with carrying a full line of products.

BEWARE OF THE "FULL-LINE" SYNDROME

A well-known maker of controls and measuring instruments enjoyed a reputation for offering a full line of products for the industry. The company—call it the Complete Controls Company—had continued to add new types, styles, and sizes to its catalog without ever discontinuing older products. As a consequence, they were suffering from a severe case of "product proliferation".

The symptoms were swollen inventories, high carrying costs, small orders and short production runs, and extremely high selling expenses—not to mention a very expensive product catalog. Profit margins were declining at an alarming rate.

A new general manager called for an audit of all functions involved, to be conducted by the responsible managers, using the checklist approach. Application of "Pareto's Law," otherwise known as the 80/20 rule, showed that over 85 percent of sales volume—and well over 100 percent of profit margins—were generated by less than 30 percent of the items in the product line. After further analysis identified the slow-moving and obsolete products, the catalog was reduced by over two hundred items. Certain of the sales reps were unhappy to be deprived of the capability to give their customers everything they asked for, but management was adamant about pruning the line. A revised sales compensation scheme that provided high commissions on standard items helped to restore the salesmen's morale.

The outcome was an improvement in earnings of better than eighty percent during the next twelve months. Inventories were cut by $2 million and selling expenses by over 15 percent, despite higher sales commissions to sales reps and agents. The increased income was plowed back into new products that further enhanced the company's growth and profitability.

SUMMARY OF SELF-AUDIT RATINGS
AND FUNCTIONAL IMPROVEMENT GOALS

If you wish, you may summarize the ratings for each function at the end of each section, on this "Summary Rating" form. (A "function" is the equivalent of a chapter.) The rating is simply an arithmetic average of the ratings on Checklists A through I—that is, the total divided by 9. This form also provides space for listing the Improvement Goals for each function.

Under each function, enter the rating percentage for each Checklist section, A through I. "Function Number 1," for example, is the first (1st) chapter in the section, regardless of its number in the book—5, 11, or so on. The Summary Rating is the total of each column divided by 9, to give you an average rating for the total function. The lower portion of the form can be used to list your improvement goals for each function.

	FUNCTION NUMBER					
CHECKLIST	**1** %	**2** %	**3** %	**4** %	**5** %	**6** %
A	_____	_____	_____	_____	_____	_____
B	_____	_____	_____	_____	_____	_____
C	_____	_____	_____	_____	_____	_____
D	_____	_____	_____	_____	_____	_____
E	_____	_____	_____	_____	_____	_____
F	_____	_____	_____	_____	_____	_____
G	_____	_____	_____	_____	_____	_____
H	_____	_____	_____	_____	_____	_____
I	_____	_____	_____	_____	_____	_____
SUMMARY RATING (%)	_____	_____	_____	_____	_____	_____

IMPROVEMENT GOALS

_____

_____

_____

_____

_____

_____

_____

_____

(Use separate sheet as required)

Section

Managing Marketing Intelligence

Market research is an organized and systematic effort to acquire, interpret and project information about present and prospective markets of interest to the firm, in order to decide on courses of action that will improve the company's competitive performance in those markets.

THREE KEY COMPONENTS OF MARKET RESEARCH

Market research is not a single function, but rather is made up of several separate and distinct component activities. These are:

1. *Market demand analysis* is systematic research and analysis of all factors that affect demand for the firm's present and planned offerings—and reasoned projection of these into the future. Market demand analysis goes to the question: Does the company know enough about its present and prospective customers—their needs, interests, buying habits, purchasing policies, decision-makers, and their perceptions of the company—to reach and serve them profitably?

2. *Competitor evaluation* is systematic collection and analysis of intelligence about the other sellers in the firm's market or markets. Competitor evaluation is intended to answer the question: Does the company have sufficient knowledge of its competitors' strengths and weaknesses, products, services, selling capabilities, and sales methods, to compete effectively against them?

3. *Sales Analysis* is systematic analysis of internal sales performance data, the factors that affect the company's performance, and projection of new order input and sales into the period ahead. Sales analysis is performed to answer the question: Does the company have enough information about its own selling efforts to ensure that these efforts are effective and competitive, now and in the future?

MARKET RESEARCH ACTIVITIES ARE EVERYONE'S BUSINESS

There is an unfortunate tendency to view market research in a limited sense; to think of it in terms of such routine activities as collecting market information from published sources, compiling industry and company sales statistics, or conducting occasional trade interviews. These activities are important, but do not begin to describe the full scope of what market research can and should be.

In its broadest sense, market research is *the identification of the specific courses of action that should be taken by the total enterprise, not just the marketing department, to affect customer purchasing decisions.* It is through the objective insights into market needs and competitive conditions gained through professional market research that the company is enabled to determine what products and services it should offer, at what price, and under what conditions, in order to be profitably successful in the marketplace.

Once these basic determinations are made, other critical decisions flow from them; such as what technical capabilities and facilities are required, what physical resources are needed to produce the desired output, how the organization must be structured to utilize these resources most productively, and what financial resources are required to make it all work.

Market research is inherent in every marketing activity, from planning to advertising to selling. In fact, even though they may not think of it in these terms, individual salespersons conduct "market research" in their daily work as they identify prospective customers, evaluate their needs and interests, compare competitive offerings, develop effective sales approaches, establish and maintian key account profiles, analyze why the sale was made or lost, and review their own performance for possible improvement.

NEED FOR OUTWARD ORIENTATION

An all-too-common affliction of market researchers is to be inward-directed. Rather than seeing a customer, they tend to look at a reflection of their own product-oriented biases. Rather than seeing needs, they tend to see only outlets for existing products. Levitt pointed out in his classic, "Marketing Myopia," written long before the automobile industry got into deep trouble, that "Detroit never really researched the customers' wants—they researched preferences between the kind of things they had already decided to offer . . . "

The overriding purpose of market research is to provide management with information on which to make sound marketing decisions with confidence. This includes decisions about market needs not fulfilled by existing products. Information should cover demand, present and prospective, for the company's present and planned products; competition, existing and potential, and analysis of sales performance.

Chapter **8**

How to Research
And Analyze
Market Demand

Market demand analysis *is a systematic and comprehensive inquiry into the buyer's side of a market; a deep probing into all factors that significantly affect customer demand.* In order to measure its effectiveness, market demand analysis should be evaluated as an *organized process for producing essential information about and projections of customer demand*, rather than a specific methodology for analyzing a particular market or market segment.

TO GET THE RIGHT ANSWERS YOU MUST ASK THE RIGHT QUESTIONS

Market demand analysis seeks to respond to the basic issues of business operation: What is the market for the products produced and planned by the company? How much of these products will be purchased by *all buyers* from *all sellers*? Of this aggregate, what portion is available to the firm? Of the "available market," what portion or share can be captured? In order to respond with confidence to these issues, a host of related questions must be addressed:

1. How are the markets for the company's products defined and identified? What are their major component market segments? What is the size of these markets?
2. How fast have they been growing? What is their likely future growth rate? What factors are likely to influence growth for better or worse?
3. Which classes of customers buy what, and why? What brands are preferred, and why? At what prices, and why?

4. How is the product bought—through what channels of distribution, and why?

5. How is the product used? What are its alternatives? Is demand independent or derived, that is, dependent on the sale of the customer's product?

6. What are the key buying influences affecting the sale of the product?

   a. What are the factors that influence customer purchasing decisions, and what is the relative importance of these factors?

   b. Who are the people in customers organizations who influence purchasing decisions, and what is their relative importance?

   c. What associated services are important to customers?

   d. What problems are customers experiencing that the company, through its efforts, should seek to minimize?

   e. What are the customers' principal opportunities that the company, through its efforts, should seek to maximize?

   f. To what extent are the above factors changing, and why?

KEY AIM OF THE SELF-AUDIT

The fundamental objective of the appraisal is to ensure that management is provided with pertinent and timely information about present and prospective customer demand for the company's products and services, in order to make sound marketing decisions. Without such information, there can be no logical basis for the development of marketing objectives, strategies, and marketing plans; without marketing plans, the firm lacks the essential guidance to be successful. The saying, "Know your customer," is the first rule of market demand analysis, as it is of marketing as a whole.

HOW TO USE THE CHECKLISTS

For each of the statements in the Checklist, compare the condition of your function to the "ideal" as described in the statement. Then:

1. If you consider the statement to be *generally true* of your function, check the YES column.
2. If you consider the statement to be *untrue* of your function, check the NO column.
3. If you consider the statement to be *less than true* (but not totally untrue) of your function, check the SOMETIMES OR PARTIAL column.
4. If the statement does not apply to your particular situation, write "Not Applicable" across the response spaces (or simply draw a line through them).
5. If you lack the data for a definite response, write in "Not Answerable" or "Don't Know."

HOW TO EVALUATE YOUR RESPONSES

When you have completed the checklist, glance over your responses, keeping these points in mind:

1. A negative answer is always unfavorable because it indicates a problem within the function: the greater the number of NOs, the more serious the situation.
2. A positive response is always a good indication. But too many YES answers could indicate that your review is not objective enough.
3. Too many SOMETIMES OR PARTIALLY answers can point to internal weaknesses or to a lack of firm direction.
4. A lot of "Not Applicable" answers could indicate that you are avoiding the issue.
5. A large number of "Not Answerable" or "Don't Know" answers could be symptomatic of inadequate records or data bases.

HOW TO RATE AND SCORE YOUR RESPONSES

When you are satisfied with your responses in general, you are ready to score the Checklist. For your convenience, a self-explanatory Scoring and Rating Block follows each Checklist. This block not only tells you whether the condition of your function is satisfactory, but it also gives you a measure of its effectiveness.

Here's how to total up the points for inclusion in the Scoring and Rating Block:

1. Total up the number of points you scored:
    a. For each YES, give yourself one point.
    b. For each NO, give yourself zero.
    c. For each SOMETIMES OR PARTIALLY, give yourself a half-point.
    d. For each "Not Applicable" answer, give yourself zero and deduct one from the number of items on the Checklist.
    e. For each "Not Answerable" or "Don't Know" answer, give yourself zero.
2. Next divide the total number of points you score by the total number of items (statements) on the Checklist (less items marked "Not Applicable"). You'll get a 1.0 for a perfect score and a fraction for anything less.
3. Multiply the result of step 2 by 100 to arrive at the percentage for your score.

What is a satisfactory rating? A rating of less than 65 percent is unacceptable and calls for an improvement program: Obviously, the lower the rating, the more drastic the action required.

A brief "how-to" example of this Scoring and Rating system follows . . .

EXAMPLE

	YES (1)	NO (0)	S/P* (½)

1. Field sale reports designed to provide information on sales progress contain data on the following topics:

	YES (1)	NO (0)	S/P* (½)
a. sales calls and sales presentations made by salespersons and sales agents,	✓		
b. bids, quotations, and proposals made,	✓		
c. new orders booked,	✓		
d. lost business, and reasons for the loss,		✓	
e. accomplishments toward future orders,			✓
f. performance in filling orders, handling complaints, and otherwise servicing individual customers,	✓		
g. action taken in response to customer requests, such as sending samples, spec sheets, etc.,	✓		
h. accomplishments of significance and value to other members of the sales force.			✓

*SOMETIMES OR PARTIALLY

TOTAL POINTS $\boxed{5}$ + 0 + $\boxed{1}$

$= \boxed{6}$

RATING

Enter number of points scored $\boxed{6}$

Enter number of items on checklist $\boxed{8}$ = .75 × 100 = $\boxed{75\ \%}$

8-A
ORGANIZATION, ADMINISTRATION AND OPERATION

	YES (1)	NO (0)	S/P* (½)

1. Market demand analysis is recognized on the organization charts and in managers' position descriptions as an important marketing activity, and an important function of market research. ___ ___ ___

2. The function is supervised and staffed by marketing professionals (who may have other responsibilities). They are trained in modern techniques of market demand analysis, and informed about the company's products and markets. ___ ___ ___

3. The market research budget has an allocation covering internal expenses for market demand analysis and outside market intelligence services, if required. ___ ___ ___

4. The manager of marketing research routinely participates in marketing staff meetings, marketing planning meetings, new-product and new-market project reviews, and sales meetings. ___ ___ ___

5. The collection, analysis, dissemination, and use of market demand data and forecasts are guided and governed by written procedures. ___ ___ ___

6. Market demand analyses and forecasts are treated as "company confidential" material by all personnel. ___ ___ ___

7. Consistent use is made of market demand analyses by top management in deciding whether and how to introduce new products, and to enter new markets. ___ ___ ___

8. Changes in market demand are continuously monitored throughout the new-product/new-market development process, so that changes in timing and direction can be made as needed. ___ ___ ___

9. Basic data required for determining market demand and customer buying characteristics is maintained on a current basis in market research files. ___ ___ ___

10. The following sources are regularly used in conducting market demand analyses:

    a. contacts with direct sales personnel, ___ ___ ___

    b. interviews with customers and prospects, ___ ___ ___

    c. sales agents, distributors, and dealers, ___ ___ ___

    d. government reports, ___ ___ ___

    e. trade association publications and other industry sources, ___ ___ ___

    f. business editors and writers, financial analysts, other outside professionals, and ___ ___ ___

    g. data maintained within the marketing department and other business functions. ___ ___ ___

11. Field sales reports are reviewed and analyzed on a routine basis. ___ ___ ___

12. In all major market demand analyses conducted during the past year:

    a. objectives were clearly defined, ___ ___ ___

    b. the method of analysis was spelled out in a written work plan, ___ ___ ___

    c. a time and cost estimate was prepared and actual performance was later compared with these estimates, ___ ___ ___

*SOMETIMES OR PARTIALLY

    d. questionnaires, correlations, sampling, interview guides and aids were professionally designed and used,

    e. all data collected was tested for validity and accuracy.

13. The following types of market demand analyses are conducted annually:

    a. size and growth trends of current major markets by product category and customer class,

    b. the near-term outlook for these markets,

    c. three- to five-year projections of current and prospective major markets, and

    d. evaluation of at least one major new market for management consideration.

14. All major market demand analyses completed:

    a. reflect a clear understanding of the objectives of the work,

    b. state major premises,

    c. identify sources of data,

    d. indicate the reliability of data,

    e. draw logical conclusions, and

    f. include firm recommendations for action.

15. All major market demand analyses:

    a. forecast the future nature and extent of the market, including market prices,

    b. analyze the market into significant segments,

    c. identify the buying motives of each segment,

    d. identify who makes actual buying decisions,

    e. reflect the impact of current economic factors,

    f. organize and synthesize the resulting analysis into logical conclusions, and

    g. anticipate management's information requirements about market demand.

16. Major market demand analyses identify and evaluate the importance of all factors that influence customer buying decisions, such as:

    a. product suitability to customer needs,

    b. product reliability and quality,

    c. guarantees and warranties,

    d. product information (advertising and sales promotion, product literature, customer training, technical assistance in use, etc.),

    e. terms of sale,

    f. product availability,

    g. after-sale service, and

    h. associated features (packaging, appearance, design, etc.).

*SOMETIMES OR PARTIALLY

	YES (1)	NO (0)	S/P* (½)

17. Market demand analyses clearly identify the people or positions in customer organizations that have the most influence on purchasing decisions, including the individuals responsible for:

    a. product specifications, performance requirements, inventory levels, etc.,   ——— ——— ———

    b. product acceptance, test, incoming inspection and quality control, etc.,   ——— ——— ———

    c. actual product use, such as master mechanics, maintenance foremen, or construction superintendents,   ——— ——— ———

    d. the customer's purchasing organization, and   ——— ——— ———

    e. the actual buying decision-makers.   ——— ——— ———

18. Market demand analyses identify problems customers currently have with the company's products, and specify efforts to rectify these.   ——— ——— ———

19. Market demand analyses and forecasts are utilized for planning and control purposes, such as:

    a. establishing business plan objectives and strategies,   ——— ——— ———

    b. preparing product plans,   ——— ——— ———

    c. sales planning, including allocation of sales territories,   ——— ——— ———

    d. directing and controlling field sales force activities, and   ——— ——— ———

    e. sales training.   ——— ——— ———

20. Market demand analyses are distributed to affected and authorized personnel.   ——— ——— ———

21. A majority of recommendations made were accepted and acted upon by management.   ——— ——— ———

22. All market demand analysis work performed by outside individuals (consultants, research agencies, or other firms) was based upon:

    a. a clear and agreed to written statement of objectives and purpose, and   ——— ——— ———

    b. a written proposal stating time, cost, and tasks to be done.   ——— ——— ———

23. All outside market research was monitored during its conduct by marketing personnel to assure conformance with needs.   ——— ——— ———

24. All outside market research was evaluated in writing regarding:

    a. its value relative to its cost, and   ——— ——— ———

    b. the competence of the outside service.   ——— ——— ———

*SOMETIMES OR PARTIALLY

TOTAL POINTS   ☐ + 0 + ☐

= ☐

RATING

Enter number of points scored ☐
——————————————————————   =   × 100 = ☐ %
Enter number of items on checklist ☐

A less-than-acceptable rating in this section indicates a serious lack of management knowledge of and concern about the factors that have the most significance to the growth and profitability of the firm—the nature, size, and growth rates of the markets that nourish the company. Indeed, the very survival of the enterprise depends on management's ability to search out and identify promising markets and to direct it into the most rewarding of these.

The company may have the finest technical staff and research laboratories in the industry, its production facilities may be second to none, and its sales force may be the largest and most aggressive in the field—yet, if it lacks the capability to continuously, methodically, and intelligently research and analyze the markets for its output, sooner or later it will surely fail. A business firm that lacks factual and timely knowledge of actual and potential markets can spend millions of dollars on new product research and development, and construction of automated factories, and may be only "rearranging the deck chairs on the Titanic!"

WHAT TO DO NOW

1. As manager of marketing (or manager of market research) in a situation such as this, the task ahead of you can be a difficult and lengthy one. The task goes beyond getting an executive OK to conduct market demand analysis. It is to develop a market awareness and a marketing orientation throughout the entire organization.

   It is only fair to point out that the risk of failure is high, particularly if the top levels of management are heavily biased toward the technical and engineering activities, or are purely financial types. If you succeed, however, the rewards to both you and the enterprise can be gratifying.

2. In order to get top management's attention, you might have to employ the classic "mule and two-by-four" approach. Make a projection of the company's sales and income on a basis that the markets the company is presently serving are the only markets the company will be serving in the future. If this shows a significant decline in revenues and earnings during the next five years or so—as it could under the circumstances assumed here—you just might shock management into adopting more aggressive marketing policies.

3. Build a file of company case histories: cases of business failure caused by marketing short-sightedness, and success stories of leading companies who regard marketing as the cutting edge of the entire organization. Publicize them internally at every opportunity, and cite them in every meeting.

4. Distribute copies of Levitt's famous *Harvard Business Review* article, "Marketing Myopia." This has since been widely reprinted and adopted as classic case material in many sales training courses.

8-B
AUTHORITY, RESPONSIBILITY AND ACCOUNTABILITY

	YES (1)	NO (0)	S/P* (½)
1. Authority has been delegated to the manager of market research, through allocation of budget funds and a written position description, to expend company funds for the purpose of staffing and managing an organization to perform market demand analysis.	⎯⎯	⎯⎯	⎯⎯
2. Responsibility is firmly assigned to the manager for making informed projections of future demand for the company's products.	⎯⎯	⎯⎯	⎯⎯
3. The manager is also responsible for making firm recommendations as to courses of action the company should follow to develop and exploit markets for its products.	⎯⎯	⎯⎯	⎯⎯
4. The manager is held accountable for any significant			
a. loss of market share by existing products,	⎯⎯	⎯⎯	⎯⎯
b. failures of new-product developments, and	⎯⎯	⎯⎯	⎯⎯
c. failures of new-market entries that result from lack of timely information, or invalid information about the company's markets.	⎯⎯	⎯⎯	⎯⎯
5. The manager is also held accountable for any serious cost overruns or schedule delays on market demand analysis projects.	⎯⎯	⎯⎯	⎯⎯

*SOMETIMES OR PARTIALLY

TOTAL POINTS ☐ + 0 + ☐

= ☐

RATING

$$\frac{\text{Enter number of points scored} \quad \boxed{}}{\text{Enter number of items on checklist} \quad \boxed{}} = \boxed{} \times 100 = \boxed{} \%$$

WHAT THE RATING SIGNIFIES

Failure of management to delegate adequate authority to spend money, failure to assign firm responsibility for results, or failure to specify clear accountability for the adverse consequences of non-performance are indicators that management may place a low value on market demand analysis.

Further evidence of this is failure to require managers to put their jobs on the line—to "put their money where their mouths are"—by demanding that market analysis be accompanied by firm recommendation for action. This could be the most serious failure of all, because without this demand the manager could evade real responsibility to provide marketing guidance to the company.

WHAT TO DO NOW

1. Authority follows responsibility—not the other way around. Demonstrate your responsibility by prefacing every market demand analysis with a firm, clearly expressed, unqualified, and unequivocal recom-

mendation for action. If your recommendations are sound, the authority will follow.

2. Your recommendation should be the first paragraph in your report. The market demand analysis is only supporting data for your position. To make your readers wade through twenty or thirty pages of tables, charts, and text before they discover what it is you want to do is not only unfair but irresponsible.

8-C
MEASUREMENTS, CONTROL REPORTS AND PERFORMANCE RECORDS

	YES (1)	NO (0)	S/P* (½)
1. The effectiveness of the market demand analysis function is measured frequently.	___	___	___
2. This effectiveness is measured by comparing actual performance and results to specific benchmarks, standards, or targets, such as:			
a. performance of markets selected for development,	___	___	___
b. accuracy of market forecasts, and	___	___	___
c. validity of the buying influences identified.	___	___	___
3. The effectiveness of the market demand analysis activity is further determined by its ability to:			
a. improve the planning for production and distribution of existing products,	___	___	___
b. improve the planning for expansion of facilities for existing products,	___	___	___
c. improve the planning and development of new products and markets.	___	___	___
4. Reports and records of production and sales of existing products are routinely analyzed for significance to market demand analysis.	___	___	___
5. Post-completion audits are made of expansion projects, new-product development projects, and market development projects to compare actual results with market demand forecasts used in the original proposals.	___	___	___
6. The actual costs of purchased market research are routinely compared with the estimates used for approval of the expenditure.	___	___	___
7. Cost of outside work is periodically compared with estimates of what it would cost if done internally.	___	___	___
8. Operating costs are compared with budget monthly, and major variances are analyzed for corrective action.			

*SOMETIMES OR PARTIALLY

TOTAL POINTS   ☐ + 0 + ☐

= ☐

RATING

Enter number of points scored   ☐
────────────────────────────────   = ☐ × 100 = ☐ %
Enter number of items on checklist ☐

WHAT THE RATING SIGNIFIES

Forecasting the shape and size of future market demand is a difficult and complex task, and subject to many variables. Some market researchers prefer long-range market projections to short-term forecasts in the belief that before the time arrives when the forecast's accuracy can be checked, they will be long gone from the scene. To prevent this kind of responsibility-avoidance, all market demand analyses should contain both elements, and the short-range forecasts should be checked periodically to ensure responsible forecasting.

A low rating can mean that performance is not measured regularly and systematically, or that data needed for making the measurements is not available. Either way, the company lacks a means to keep market forecasters honest and responsible.

WHAT TO DO NOW

1. Just as the first requirement for a good market demand forecast is good data, the first requirement for determining *whether the process is effective* is good information to compare results with.

   You can't wait until a project is completed to assess performance. Then it's too late to do anything about it. You need performance standards, progress milestones, and targets against which to measure current performance and current progress toward goals.

2. Generally speaking, the more frequently you measure performance the better your chances are to improve it. (This can be carried to extremes, of course, and care must be exercised against a practice of "pulling the plant up by its roots every day to see how it's growing.")

8-D
OPERATING PERFORMANCE HISTORY

	YES (1)	NO (0)	S/P* (½)
1. A review and analysis has been made of control reports and records for at least one year past for the purpose of assessing past performance.	_____	_____	_____
2. This review shows no evidence of any serious failure by the company's production and distribution system to meet customer demand caused by inadequate or invalid market demand information. (Answer "yes" if true.)	_____	_____	_____
3. This review shows no evidence of excessive unsold inventories of products caused by poor market demand information. (Answer "yes" if true.)	_____	_____	_____
4. During the past year, there have been no serious failures of new-product or market development projects resulting either from lack of timely market demand information or invalid information. (Answer "yes" if true.)	_____	_____	_____
5. Post-completion audits* of market demand projections show the information given to be substantially complete and accurate, and relevant to the company's needs.	_____	_____	_____

*SOMETIMES OR PARTIALLY

*After completion and market entry of new-product/market projects.

	YES (1)	NO (0)	S/P* (½)

6. Surveys and studies made during the past year were comprehensive and credible, and were completed essentially on time and within cost estimates. _____ _____ _____

7. The function has substantially met its operation budget for the past year. _____ _____ _____

*SOMETIMES OR PARTIALLY

TOTAL POINTS   ☐ + 0 + ☐

= ☐

RATING

Enter number of points scored ☐
─────────────────────────────────── = × 100 = ☐ %
Enter number of items on checklist ☐

WHAT THE RATING SIGNIFIES

A less-than-acceptable rating in this section may indicate the need for a redirection of functional effort from activity to results. The department may have made a great many market surveys and analyses, written volumes of reports to management, and participated in countless studies, and yet have failed completely to carry out its assigned business mission. Because the effectiveness of the market demand analysis function is determined—when the chips are down and all bets are in—by *results*; by the company's performance in satisfying customer needs without excessive inventories of goods and at a profit; positioning new products successfully, and penetrating new markets with high promise. All else is merely the means to these ends.

WHAT TO DO NOW

1. If your organization doesn't already follow "management by objectives," or some variation thereof, you should consider setting up a mini-MBO program for your functional people. First, ask each individual to review his or her own area of activity and set some improvement goals for the next three, six and twelve months.

2. Have them put four or five of these goals down on paper—the format and their writing skill doesn't count—and review them periodically as they go along.

3. At the end of six months or so, sit down with each staff member and ask him or her to review performance toward these goals. Give praise generously for improvement and progress; offer coaching where it's needed; use criticism sparingly; *never* reproach or ridicule the person for failure to perform.

4. There's a great deal more to MBO than this, but a simple program like this can help enormously to focus attention on results instead of mere activity.

8-E
TOP-LEVEL SUPPORT AND GUIDANCE

	YES (1)	NO (0)	S/P* (½)

1. The executive office demonstrates active support for the market demand analysis function, by providing:

   a. budget approval for operating expenses and outside services,

   b. guidance through participation in review meetings of production plans, sales plans, and business plans,

   c. guidance by reading and commenting on progress reports, and

   d. recognition and reward for outstanding accomplishment.

*SOMETIMES OR PARTIALLY

TOTAL POINTS ☐ + 0 + ☐

= ☐

RATING

Enter number of points scored ☐
————————————————————— = × 100 = ☐ %
Enter number of items on checklist ☐

WHAT THE RATING SIGNIFIES

The best way that the executive office can show its support (outside of delegating authority and providing budget funds for operation) is by actively participating in meetings where plans and progress are discussed.

All forward plans—whether strategic plans, new-product development plans, marketing plans, sales plans or production plans—should contain at their core market demand analyses and projections. These projections should be regularly "tested" by hard questioning from top executives, because sales forecasts on which strategies and action plans are based are derived from them. If these projections are not sound and credible, if they can't hold up under scrutiny, the sales forecasts are suspect and so are the derived strategies and plans.

When this executive "probing" is done in a non-critical, constructive manner, it can only result in better market demand analysis and forecasting. A low rating here indicates that the executive office may not be providing this essential guidance.

WHAT TO DO NOW

It is important that the persons responsible for making market demand analysis and forecasts are periodically exposed to the kind of testing discussed here. Not only does it improve the quality of the work, but it is the best kind of management development for the individual.

8-F
INNOVATION IN METHODS AND TECHNIQUES

	YES (1)	NO (0)	S/P* (½)

1. Management actively searches for better ways to collect, interpret, and forecast market data through:

   a. participation in seminars and workshops,

   b. surveys of management literature,

   c. professional association meetings,

   d. industry contacts,

   e. solicitation of ideas and suggestions from personnel at all levels, and

   f. use of outside specialists and

   g. budgets that provide for such activities.

2. The computer is used to store, process and display information on market size and growth rates, company shares of market, and market characteristics.

3. The computer is used to project (by product line) market growth and company sales growth, and to determine their correlation.

4. Management employs modern statistical decision theory and modeling techniques wherever they are appropriate to the market demand analysis task.

*SOMETIMES OR PARTIALLY

TOTAL POINTS ☐ + 0 + ☐

= ☐

RATING

Enter number of points scored ☐

Enter number of items on checklist ☐

= ☐ × 100 = ☐ %

WHAT THE RATING SIGNIFIES

Market demand analysis is a demanding intellectual activity. It is both a science and an art, and its techniques are advancing rapidly. Unless marketing management keeps up with these advances, systematically and purposefully, there is a high probability that its output will be less valid than it could be, and the marketing strategy recommendations derived from the data may be unsound.

WHAT TO DO NOW

1. All personnel involved with market demand analysis should be encouraged—should be required, in fact—to keep up with the state-of-the-art.

2. The department budget should include an adequate amount of funds for these activities. This is an *investment*, not an *expense*.

8-G
INTERFUNCTIONAL COMMUNICATIONS AND COORDINATION

	YES (1)	NO (0)	S/P* (½)

1. Personnel conducting market demand analysis maintain close working relations with other functions of the business, including:

   a. field sales, _____ _____ _____

   b. information systems, _____ _____ _____

   c. customer service, _____ _____ _____

   d. product planners, and, _____ _____ _____

   e. product distribution. _____ _____ _____

2. Market data that can be useful in day-to-day operations is distributed at once to field sales, product planning, distribution, production, quality assurance, value analysis, and cost accounting. _____ _____ _____

*SOMETIMES OR PARTIALLY

TOTAL POINTS   [ ] + 0 + [ ]

= [ ]

RATING

Enter number of points scored [ ]
———————————————————— = [ ] × 100 = [ ] %
Enter number of items on checklist [ ]

WHAT THE RATING SIGNIFIES

Market demand analysis consumes data and produces information. Good analysis requires enormous amounts of data of almost infinite variety—not just numbers—from a wide range of sources. Virtually every function of the business can contribute, particularly those in close constant contact with customers, such as, field sales, customer service and application engineering. In return, the activity produces information of great value to the ongoing workings of these and other functions.

Negative responses to these points indicates that this vital information interchange is not effective.

WHAT TO DO NOW

1. If you're not getting the input you need from other internal functions, perhaps it's because (a) they don't know you need it, (b) they don't see what's in it for them, or (c) you don't give them what they need.

2. Whatever the reason, you should (a) define exactly what data and information you need, (b) give the possessor of the data a good reason to give it to you, and (c) reciprocate by giving useful information in return.

3. Don't wait until you need information to set up a relationship with others. Establish a series of contacts at various levels by assigning your people to interface regularly with their organizational opposites in other

functions. You're certain to learn things you never would if your only contacts were with the department heads.

8-H
FUNCTIONAL IMPROVEMENT PROGRAM

	YES (1)	NO (0)	S/P* (½)
1. There is an active, ongoing interfunctional team effort to improve the quality of market demand analysis. Principal efforts on a task basis are directed toward:			
a. more accurate long- and short-range forecasting,	_____	_____	_____
b. better market segmentation, both demographic and psychographic,	_____	_____	_____
c. improved two-way communications between market research and other business functions.	_____	_____	_____
2. Functions participating are (depending on the task):			
a. field sales,	_____	_____	_____
b. customer service,	_____	_____	_____
c. information systems,	_____	_____	_____
d. product planning, and	_____	_____	_____
e. other marketing functions.	_____	_____	_____

*SOMETIMES OR PARTIALLY

TOTAL POINTS ☐ + 0 + ☐

= ☐

RATING

$$\frac{\text{Enter number of points scored} \quad \boxed{}}{\text{Enter number of items on checklist} \quad \boxed{}} = \boxed{} \times 100 = \boxed{} \%$$

WHAT THE RATING SIGNIFIES   This section is intended to assure the appraiser that several varied points of view are brought to bear on improvement tasks, on a formalized basis. When this perspective is lacking, there is a danger of biased, one-dimensional solutions that frequently contain the seeds of new problems.

WHAT TO DO NOW   1. The task objectives should be set only after group discussion to insure they will reflect all functional viewpoints and a measure of commitment by each team member. Display them on a large sheet of paper in a conspicuous place.

2. With improvement goals clearly articulated and agreed-to, the task

elements should be precisely defined and assigned *in writing*. Each member should have a copy.

3. Getting the job accomplished is now largely a matter of team leadership and self-control.

4. It is important to recognize and reward team members for their contributions, even if the reward is only a sincere "thanks and well done."

8-1
RESOURCES

	YES (1)	NO (0)	S/P* (½)
1. The manager of market research is kept informed about company objectives, plans and programs, through access to appropriate business plans, marketing plans, sales plans, new-product and market project plans, and budgets.	___	___	___
2. Based on this knowledge, resources are considered adequate to meet the company's needs for market demand analysis during the next three, six, and twelve months in terms of:			
a. manpower,	___	___	___
b. capabilities,	___	___	___
c. budget funding,	___	___	___
d. outside intelligence services,	___	___	___
e. information systems support,	___	___	___
f. computer time and capacity,	___	___	___
g. other functional support, and	___	___	___
h. communications.	___	___	___

*SOMETIMES OR PARTIALLY

TOTAL POINTS ☐ + 0 + ☐

= ☐

RATING

Enter number of points scored ☐

Enter number of items on checklist ☐

= × 100 = ☐ %

WHAT THE RATING SIGNIFIES   The most critical resource needed is a strong capability to handle information; to collect, organize, analyze, process, and display information so that it will cause managers to act in a productive way. This can only happen when the significance and importance of the information to the operation of the business are made apparent to others. The talent and intelligence to do this resides only in people, not in computers, and it is not the most common of commodities.

The other critical resource needed, therefore, is a working environment that can attract and retain top quality people. When you have these two resources, others seem to follow.

WHAT TO DO NOW

1. First, make sure that the department environment is hospitable to innovation and creativity; that it is free of overly restrictive rules, regulations, and controls.

2. Get the very best people you can. In this function, people are your assets, your primary stock in trade. Mediocrity can cost you dearly in wasted effort and poor output.

3. Set high standards. Good people want to work to high standards.

4. Operate the function on a basis of self-controls to the maximum extent.

Chapter

Evaluating Competitor Strengths And Weaknesses

Competitiveness of a business must be measured in two ways. First and foremost, competitiveness of a seller is determined by end-users and consumers, who rate prospective sellers in terms of relative abilities to satisfy their needs. Those sellers who best meet requirements are competitive; those who do not, are not. Thus, the ultimate test of competitiveness is the response of sellers to the demands of buyers, and is decided in the marketplace.

Secondly, competitiveness is determined by the ability of a business enterprise to meet buyer's demands. In every industry, there are certain *critical requirements for success* that must be met by participants in that industry if they are to survive. These requirements, which may be capital investment, technical capability, or strong distribution, differ from industry to industry. Heavy equipment manufacture is very capital-intensive, data processing requires a high-technology competence, and the cosmetics business calls for unique marketing talents. Participants with serious weaknesses in the critical requirements of their particular industry are simply not capable of being truly competitive in the long run.

While competitiveness is measured in the final analysis by response to customer demand, *ability to meet that demand*, particularly over the longer term, is determined by strength in those areas that are critical for success in the industry. Both aspects of competitiveness are covered in this appraisal.

147

KNOW THY COMPETITION —LEGALLY!

The purpose of evaluating competition is to learn as much of significance as is ethically possible about present and potential competitors in order that the company may take appropriate action to be competitive with those enterprises. Ideally, the company should know as much about its competitors as it does about itself, but achieving this ideal is not only impractical but has legal implications as well.

This analysis of the company's competitive position should be prepared at least annually. The evaluation should serve as a basic source document for sales planning, product planning, marketing planning and business planning, as well as an important reference for use by other functions.

KEY AIM OF THE APPRAISAL

The principal objective of the appraisal is to assure that management is provided with pertinent and timely information on present and potential competitors, in order to make sound marketing decisions. In order to survive and prosper in a rapidly changing market environment, the function should be as competitive as, or better than, the other participants in the marketplace.

HOW TO USE THE CHECKLISTS

For each of the statements in the Checklist, compare the condition of your function to the "ideal" as described in the statement. Then:

1. If you consider the statement to be *generally true* of your function, check the YES column.

2. If you consider the statement to be *untrue* of your function, check the NO column.

3. If you consider the statement to be *less than true* (but not totally untrue) of your function, check the SOMETIMES OR PARTIAL column.

4. If the statement does not apply to your particular situation, write "Not Applicable" across the response spaces (or simply draw a line through them).

5. If you lack the data for a definite response, write in "Not Answerable" or "Don't Know."

HOW TO EVALUATE YOUR RESPONSES

When you have completed the checklist, glance over your responses, keeping these points in mind:

1. A negative answer is always unfavorable because it indicates a problem within the function: the greater the number of NOs, the more serious the situation.

2. A positive response is always a good indication. But too many YES answers could indicate that your review is not objective enough.

3. Too many SOMETIMES OR PARTIALLY answers can point to internal weaknesses or to a lack of firm direction.

4. A lot of "Not Applicable" answers could indicate that you are avoiding the issue.

5. A large number of "Not Answerable" or "Don't Know" answers could be symptomatic of inadequate records or data bases.

HOW TO RATE AND SCORE YOUR RESPONSES

When you are satisfied with your responses in general, you are ready to score the Checklist. For your convenience, a self-explanatory Scoring and Rating Block follows each Checklist. This block not only tells you whether the condition of your function is satisfactory, but it also gives you a measure of its effectiveness.

Here's how to total up the points for inclusion in the Scoring and Rating Block:

1. Total up the number of points you scored:
    a. For each YES, give yourself one point.
    b. For each NO, give yourself zero.
    c. For each SOMETIMES OR PARTIALLY, give yourself a half-point.
    d. For each "Not Applicable" answer, give yourself zero and deduct one from the number of items on the Checklist.
    e. For each "Not Answerable" or "Don't Know" answer, give yourself zero.

2. Next divide the total number of points you score by the total number of items (statements) on the Checklist (less items marked "Not Applicable"). You'll get a 1.0 for a perfect score and a fraction for anything less.

3. Multiply the result of step 2 by 100 to arrive at the percentage for your score.

What is a satisfactory rating? A rating of less than 65 percent is unacceptable and calls for an improvement program: Obviously, the lower the rating, the more drastic the action required.

A brief "how-to" example of this Scoring and Rating system follows . . .

EXAMPLE

	YES (1)	NO (0)	S/P* (½)

1. Field sale reports designed to provide information on sales progress contain data on the following topics:

   a. sales calls and sales presentations made by salespersons and sales agents,

   b. bids, quotations, and proposals made,

   c. new orders booked,

   d. lost business, and reasons for the loss,

   e. accomplishments toward future orders,

   f. performance in filling orders, handling complaints, and otherwise servicing individual customers,

   g. action taken in response to customer requests, such as sending samples, spec sheets, etc.,

   h. accomplishments of significance and value to other members of the sales force.

*SOMETIMES OR PARTIALLY

TOTAL POINTS 5 + 0 + 1

$$= 6$$

RATING

$$\frac{\text{Enter number of points scored} \quad 6}{\text{Enter number of items on checklist} \quad 8} = .75 \times 100 = 75 \%$$

9-A
ORGANIZATION, ADMINISTRATION, AND OPERATION

	YES (1)	NO (0)	S/P* (½)

1. Competitor evaluation is recognized on the organization charts and in managers' position descriptions as a vital marketing activity, and an important function of market research. _____ _____ _____

2. The function is supervised and staffed by marketing professionals (who may have other responsibilities) trained in modern techniques of competitor evaluation and informed about the company's products, markets, and competitors. _____ _____ _____

3. The market research budget has an allocation covering internal expenses for competitor evaluation and fees for outside intelligence services, if required. _____ _____ _____

4. The collection of information about competitors and the evaluation and dissemination of this information are guided and governed by written procedures. _____ _____ _____

5. Consistent use is made of competitor analyses by top management in deciding whether, how, and when to introduce new products and enter new markets. _____ _____ _____

6. Changes in the competitive situation are continuously monitored throughout the new-product/new-market development process, so that changes in timing and direction can be made as needed. _____ _____ _____

7. The following types of basic data required for evaluating major competitors are maintained in the marketing research files on a current basis:

   a. annual and interim shareholder reports, _____ _____ _____

   b. 10K reports to the Securities and Exchange Commission, _____ _____ _____

   c. newspaper and trade publication items on competitors, _____ _____ _____

   d. competitors' advertising, new product releases, sales promotion literature, etc., and _____ _____ _____

   e. industry studies by government agencies and private organizations, such as research firms, financial analysts and professional associations. _____ _____ _____

8. Personnel conducting competitor evaluations:

   a. use customers' key buying factors as a basis for comparing the firm's product offering with competitors', and _____ _____ _____

   b. use field sales reports as a basis for keeping current on competitor activities. _____ _____ _____

9. Competitive information is routinely received from:

   a. field sales, _____ _____ _____

   b. distribution, _____ _____ _____

   c. customer service, _____ _____ _____

   d. advertising and sales promotion, _____ _____ _____

   e. technical department, _____ _____ _____

   f. quality control, and _____ _____ _____

   g. others—comptroller, industrial relations, legal, etc. _____ _____ _____

*SOMETIMES OR PARTIALLY

10. Managers of other company functions—technical, legal, manufacturing, quality control, engineering, etc.—are asked to specify the types of competitive information they need. ___ ___ ___

11. Competitive information is routinely:

    a. screened for source, reliability, redundancy, etc., ___ ___ ___

    b. related to other information for added significance, and ___ ___ ___

    c. filed properly for future reference. ___ ___ ___

12. Management is promptly advised of significant competitive developments. ___ ___ ___

13. Competitor evaluations contain written summaries of key information and projections about each major competitor, and these summaries are available to management and other functions. ___ ___ ___

14. A separate file is maintained on each major competitor. ___ ___ ___

15. For all important competing products, files contain:

    a. samples, pictures, ___ ___ ___

    b. product literature, specification sheets, selling prices, terms of sale, and ___ ___ ___

    c. product use information. ___ ___ ___

16. Product comparisons are routinely made to establish product advantages and disadvantages in:

    a. functional design, ___ ___ ___

    b. features (including customer options), ___ ___ ___

    c. appearance (including packaging, etc.), ___ ___ ___

    d. reliability and service life, and ___ ___ ___

    e. user operating costs (including depreciation, maintenance, service, parts, etc.). ___ ___ ___

17. The following types of competitor analyses are conducted regularly:

    a. total market and share by major competitor, ___ ___ ___

    b. competitive practices and competitive outlook, ___ ___ ___

    c. evaluation of the relative strengths and weaknesses of competitors, ___ ___ ___

    d. ranking of the company and major competitors in terms of specific buying factors important to customers, ___ ___ ___

    e. financial position of the company versus its principal competitors. ___ ___ ___

18. Competitor evaluations routinely and promptly detect and report to management significant competitive developments. ___ ___ ___

19. Competitor evaluations regularly assess the relative strengths and weaknesses of the company and competitors in these critical capabilities:

    a. marketing (including sales, customer service, etc.), ___ ___ ___

    b. technical or engineering, ___ ___ ___

*SOMETIMES OR PARTIALLY

c. manufacturing, and   _____   _____   _____

d. financial, installation, etc.   _____   _____   _____

20. Competitor analyses are regularly used to:

   a. develop sales plans, new-product plans, marketing plans and business plans,   _____   _____   _____

   b. validate marketing standards, such as using information on competitors' on-time delivery performance to confirm or question the company's delivery standards, and   _____   _____   _____

   c. check and improve competitiveness of other business functions, that is, to accelerate product development programs, upgrade quality requirements, change terms of credit, etc.   _____   _____   _____

21. The majority of recommendations made were accepted and acted upon by management.   _____   _____   _____

*SOMETIMES OR PARTIALLY

TOTAL POINTS   ☐ + 0 + ☐

= ☐

RATING

Enter number of points scored   ☐
—————————————————————   = ☐   × 100 = ☐ %
Enter number of items on checklist   ☐

WHAT THE RATING SIGNIFIES

A less-than-satisfactory rating in this section indicates that the process of gathering and analyzing competitive intelligence may not be as well organized and administered—hence, not as *productive*—as it should be.

Most publicly-owned corporations disclose a lot of information about themselves, both formally and informally. People love to talk about their accomplishments in articles, news releases and annual reports; and at technical and professional conferences, trade shows and seminars. A good industrial intelligence activity can learn a great deal about its competitors simply by reading and listening systematically.

The process is not unlike military espionage, where small bits of data from many, many sources are brought together and analyzed until patterns and trends emerge, and enemy activities can be determined. All this doesn't make for a very exciting spy novel, but it's by far the largest part of the espionage business.

Sales and customer service personnel are excellent sources of competitor information, provided they are trained and incentivized to look and listen purposefully, and to convey their observations back to a central point for assembly and analysis. Obviously, these observers must be given firm ground rules to follow, to avoid illegal industrial spying.

Every other business function has a contribution to make to the competitive evaluation process, as well. The role of each should be carefully defined and their activities controlled.

Information alone has little value. All the information in the world is useless unless a conclusion is drawn from it, and firm recommendations are made for action to be taken. Furthermore, it is only to the extent that these recommendations are accepted and acted upon that they have real value to the enterprise. This requires a high degree of credibility by top management in the recommendations made and the information on which they are based—in other words, a high degree of confidence in the people who manage and perform the function. A low rating may indicate that this credibility and confidence are lacking. If this is the case, the function has a serious hurdle to overcome.

WHAT TO DO NOW

1. The process of competitor evaluation should be organized, staffed, and managed as every other business function. This does not necessarily mean that it has to be a full time activity. Lacking structure, however, there's a danger that the work won't be done.

2. Competitor evaluation costs money. The department budget should include an allocation for these expenses, and it should be detailed. Expenses incurred by other functions for the work they do for you in this area ought to be reimbursed on a transfer basis, in order to ensure their willing participation.

3. Make sure that your functional output is used. To ensure this, you have to stand behind every recommendation you make. This is not always the most comfortable place to stand, to be sure, but it is essential to build credibility and confidence in your product by its users.

9-B
AUTHORITY, RESPONSIBILITY AND ACCOUNTABILITY

	YES (1)	NO (0)	S/P* (½)
1. Authority has been delegated to the manager of marketing research, through allocation of budget funds and a written position description, to expend money for the purpose of staffing and managing an organization to perform competitor evaluations.	___	___	___
2. The manager is responsible for collecting, organizing, analyzing, evaluating, and interpreting all information relevant to present and potential competition for the company's business.	___	___	___
3. The manager is also responsible for making firm recommendations as to courses of action the company should pursue to enhance its competitiveness.	___	___	___
4. The manager is held accountable for serious losses of business to competitors, resulting from lack of timely information, or from invalid information, about the company's competition.	___	___	___
5. Managers of other company functions are responsible to collect and evaluate information about major competitors as it applies to their areas of functional responsibility.	___	___	___

*SOMETIMES OR PARTIALLY

TOTAL POINTS ☐ + 0 + ☐

‎⎵

= ☐

RATING

Enter number of points scored ☐ = ☐ × 100 = ☐ %

Enter number of items on checklist ☐

WHAT THE RATING SIGNIFIES Negative answers to these appraisal points indicates that firm authority to employ the firm's resources, firm responsibility for performing tasks, and firm accountability for results may be lacking. If any or all of these conditions apply, the necessary work will not be done regardless of how well the function is staffed.

WHAT TO DO NOW

1. Make sure that your people know and understand exactly what is expected of them and what the penalty is for failure to perform.

2. Not everyone is mature enough to accept accountability. Persons who can't should not be given the responsibility. No one should be allowed to walk away from failure with impunity.

3. If you have built into your operation these two essentials, you will produce results. The third essential—delegation of authority—normally will follow because authority tends to gravitate to those who produce results.

4. *Warning*: Competitor evaluation is a sensitive function. There is sometimes a fine line between this essential business function and industrial espionage, which is unethical and illegal. Make sure that your people understand this well because if they don't, they could get you in a pile of trouble.

9-C
MEASUREMENTS, AND CONTROL REPORTS AND PERFORMANCE RECORDS

	YES (1)	NO (0)	S/P* (½)
1. The effectiveness of the competitor evaluation function is measured and evaluated regularly.	___	___	___
2. This effectiveness is measured by comparing actual performance and results to specific benchmarks, or targets, such as:			
a. actual outcome of predictions made about the behavior of competitors,	___	___	___
b. actual results of following competitive strategies recommended, and	___	___	___
c. gains in shares of market vis-a-vis principal competitors.	___	___	___

*SOMETIMES OR PARTIALLY

	YES (1)	NO (0)	S/P* (½)

3. The effectiveness of the competitor evaluation activity is also measured by:

   a. timeliness of reports,

   b. credibility of assumptions and information inputs,

   c. validity of analyses and findings,

   d. firmness of recommendations, and

   e. soundness of supporting data.

4. Comparisons are made regularly of sales by product line vs. major competitors, in terms of percentage gains over prior periods.

5. Records are kept of market shares vs. competitors by product line, when available.

6. Reports are routinely received on business lost to competitors, and analyzed for reasons and significance.

7. Expenses of the competitor evaluation activity are routinely compared with budget, and major variances are analyzed for corrective action.

*SOMETIMES OR PARTIALLY

TOTAL POINTS

☐ + 0 + ☐

= ☐

RATING

Enter number of points scored ☐
_____ = × 100 = ☐ %
Enter number of items on checklist ☐

WHAT THE RATING SIGNIFIES

The effectiveness of the competitor evaluation process cannot be measured by the number of analysts on the payroll, or the volume of the competitor information files, or even by the number of reports issued. Effectiveness means *productivity*, not simply *activity*. Productivity means results in the marketplace, nothing else. Only when the market strategies that are recommended as a direct result of superior competitive evaluation give the company a marketing advantage, can the function be considered effective.

A low rating in this section is a strong indication that activity may be given more emphasis than results.

WHAT TO DO NOW

1. Make clear to all people involved that the only measure of their effectiveness is the *validity of their recommendations for marketing action,* and that their research, analyses, and evaluations are just *support* for these.

2. Expect that mistakes will be made. No one has a crystal ball that is so clear that their predictions are infallible. Competitors are people—and people do not always behave in predictable ways.

3. Tolerate mistakes only to a point, however. Demand a high "batting average" that will result in overall marketing success for the company.

9-D
OPERATING PERFORMANCE HISTORY

	YES (1)	NO (0)	S/P* (½)
1. A review has been made of the competitor evaluation activity for the past year or longer, for the purpose of assessing its performance.	___	___	___
2. This review shows that performance has been generally effective, and that all major objectives have been met.	___	___	___
3. The review also shows no evidence of any serious defections by major customers or losses of sizeable orders to competitors, resulting from lack of timely information or invalid information on competition. (Answer "yes" if true.)	___	___	___
4. During the past year, there have been no serious failures to meet objectives of the sales plan, or failures of new-product/market development projects, as a result of basing these plans and projects upon competitive information furnished by the function. (Answer "yes" if true.)	___	___	___
5. During the past year, there have been gains in sales volume and market shares by the company's principal product lines.	___	___	___
6. The expense budget has essentially been met for the past year.	___	___	___

*SOMETIMES OR PARTIALLY

TOTAL POINTS [ ] + 0 + [ ]

= [ ]

RATING

Enter number of points scored [ ]

Enter number of items on checklist [ ]

= × 100 = [ ] %

WHAT THE RATING SIGNIFIES

This section serves as a confirming appraisal to test the validity of the previous sections.

A history of failed marketing strategies or faulty predictions about competitors' behavior in the marketplace signals the need for an immediate overhaul of the competitor evaluation process. It matters little how superior the market demand analysis may be, or how effective the selling effort—if competitor intelligence is deficient, then it won't be long before the company will be blindsided by the introduction of an exciting new product or a clever new marketing ploy by another participant in the market.

WHAT TO DO NOW

1. If an inordinate number of objectives were not met during the past year or so, consider scaling down your expectations. Failure to meet goals tends to have a demoralizing effect on people—even when it is the fault of an unrealistic objective, not their performance.

2. Do a post-mortem on major cases of lost business, to determine where the competitor evaluation process went wrong. Search for basic causes, not for scapegoats to pin the blame on.

9-E
TOP-LEVEL SUPPORT AND GUIDANCE

	YES (1)	NO (0)	S/P* (½)

The executive office demonstrates active support of the activity by providing:

a. budget approval,

b. endorsement of marketing strategy recommendations,

c. guidance through participation in marketing planning and progress review meetings,

d. guidance through informed comments on reports and studies, and

e. recognition and reward for outstanding accomplishment.

*SOMETIMES OR PARTIALLY

TOTAL POINTS   ☐ + 0 + ☐

= ☐

RATING

Enter number of points scored ☐

Enter number of items on checklist ☐

= × 100 = ☐ %

WHAT THE RATING SIGNIFIES

The most critical evidence of executive support is, of course, delegation of spending authority. The most *visible* evidence is public endorsement of the marketing strategies proposed by the competitor evaluation group. When this is lacking, the function cannot be effective.

WHAT TO DO NOW

1. Past performance, not promises of future results, is the only basis on which the CEO can reasonably be expected to accept and endorse the recommendations of the group. If the previous section had a low rating on past performance, it is going to take time and a superior performance record to restore confidence in your function.

2. Meanwhile, make doubly sure that your recommendations are realistic. Make sure, also, that their supporting documentation is factually accurate, complete, and well organized.

9-F
INNOVATION IN METHODS AND TECHNIQUES

	YES (1)	NO (0)	S/P* (½)

1. There is an active search for better ways to collect and interpret competitive data through:

   a. participation in seminars and workshops on the subject, ⎯⎯ ⎯⎯ ⎯⎯

   b. review of management literature, ⎯⎯ ⎯⎯ ⎯⎯

   c. outside specialists, ⎯⎯ ⎯⎯ ⎯⎯

   d. professional associations, ⎯⎯ ⎯⎯ ⎯⎯

   e. industry contacts, ⎯⎯ ⎯⎯ ⎯⎯

   f. solicitation of ideas and suggestions from personnel at all levels, including dealers and distributors, ⎯⎯ ⎯⎯ ⎯⎯

   g. budgets should provide funds for such activities. ⎯⎯ ⎯⎯ ⎯⎯

2. The computer is used to store, process, and display information on the size, growth rate, profitability, market shares, market coverage, location of principal facilities, and products of the company's major competitors. ⎯⎯ ⎯⎯ ⎯⎯

3. The computer is also employed to project the company's and competitors sales trends in order to determine loss or gain in market shares of major products. ⎯⎯ ⎯⎯ ⎯⎯

*SOMETIMES OR PARTIALLY

TOTAL POINTS ☐ + 0 + ☐

= ☐

RATING

Enter number of points scored ☐

Enter number of items on checklist ☐

= × 100 = ☐ %

WHAT THE RATING SIGNIFIES   No one organization has a corner on the best methods for evaluating competition. An organized search for new techniques will pay off handsomely in more useful and timely data about competitors' behavior and customers' attitudes toward them. A low rating could mean that the techniques presently being used are outdated.

WHAT TO DO NOW

1. Don't overlook the contribution that lower-level personnel can make when properly motivated and rewarded; especially field sales, engineering support, and customer service people.

2. Among the most useful knowledge about competitors is information on management and organization changes. This often signals changes in business direction and marketing strategy. Much of this is published—some directly from the competitor himself.

3. The computer is virtually indispensible as a means for storing and

159

rapidly recalling competitor data. Properly programmed, the computer can detect patterns of behavior and trends that could escape manual analysis.

9-G
INTERFUNCTIONAL COMMUNICATIONS AND COORDINATION

	YES (1)	NO (0)	S/P* (½)

1. The manager of the function maintains close and continuing contact with other functions of the business; in particular:

   a. sales, for first-hand reactions of customers to the company's products and services, first-hand reports on competitors' actions, and for information exchange, _____ _____ _____

   b. product distribution, for input from dealers and distributors of the products, _____ _____ _____

   c. technical, for testing and evaluation of competitors' products, _____ _____ _____

   d. customer service, for field reports on customers' experience with competitors' service capabilities, _____ _____ _____

   e. advertising and P.R., for evaluation of competitors' sales promotion efforts and materials, _____ _____ _____

   f. legal, for counsel on intelligence-gathering restrictions, and _____ _____ _____

   g. other marketing functions, for coordination of efforts. _____ _____ _____

2. Competitive intelligence that can be of immediate tactical value is promptly passed on to field sales, product distribution, and other functions. _____ _____ _____

*SOMETIMES OR PARTIALLY   **TOTAL POINTS**   [ ] + 0 + [ ]

= [ ]

RATING

Enter number of points scored [ ]

Enter number of items on checklist [ ]

= × 100 = [   ] %

WHAT THE RATING SIGNIFIES   No one can predict where a vital bit of information about a competitor may come from, so it is essential to have many, many points of contact. This section seeks to assure the appraiser that a good two-way flow of information exists between competitor evaluation analysts and all other functions. A low rating here indicates that important information may be "falling between the cracks."

WHAT TO DO NOW   1. Not only the manager, but all personnel involved should have assigned points of contact with other functions.

2. Bring all people together frequently for round-table discussions of competition. Insist that every attendee contribute information and opinion and those who do not should be penalized by being uninvited to the next meeting.

3. Control the agenda tightly. Record the main points discussed and make firm action assignments for follow-up of significant items.

4. Although dealers and distributors are not direct employees, they are an important source of competitor information. Use it well.

9-H
FUNCTIONAL IMPROVEMENT PROGRAM

	YES (1)	NO (0)	S/P* (½)
1. There is an active, on-going interfunctional team effort to improve the quality and value of competitive intelligence, with emphasis on:			
a. better observation and reporting by field sales, customer service, field engineering, product distribution, and others in the field,	——	——	——
b. better integration and analysis of information from various sources,	——	——	——
c. quicker tactical feedback of analyses to field people for action, and	——	——	——
d. more active participation in intelligence-gathering and analysis by other functions.	——	——	——
2. The team is composed of representatives from the following functions, depending on the particular task:			
a. sales,	——	——	——
b. technical,	——	——	——
c. product distribution,	——	——	——
d. quality assurance,	——	——	——
e. advertising and P.R.,	——	——	——
f. information systems, and	——	——	——
g. customer service.	——	——	——

*SOMETIMES OR PARTIALLY

TOTAL POINTS ☐ + 0 + ☐

= ☐

RATING

Enter number of points scored ☐

Enter number of items on checklist ☐

= × 100 = ☐ %

Good competitive intelligence has value to just about every function of the business. Consequently, each should have an incentive to join in an effort to improve the process.

A good rating on this section is a strong plus; and a low score should signal a need to get a message across to other people that they have a real stake in the process, and should contribute to it.

WHAT TO DO NOW

1. Make an effort to persuade top management that a cross-functional team effort can enhance the value of competitive intelligence.

2. Better still, select a project that has a high probability of success and do a project informally—then use the results to get executive endorsement for an organized effort.

3. Get agreement from the other functional managers that they will participate. The best way to do this is to "line up your ducks" in advance. (The worst way is to announce "The boss says you gotta help me on this . . .")

9-1
RESOURCES

	YES (1)	NO (0)	S/P* (½)
1. Market research personnel are kept informed about the company's objectives, policies, plans, and programs through access to appropriate business plans, capital budgets, new-product plans, and marketing plans.	_____	_____	_____
2. Based on this knowledge, market research resources are considered to be adequate to meet the company's needs for competitor evaluations during the next 3, 6 and 12 months in terms of:			
a. budget funding,	_____	_____	_____
b. manpower,	_____	_____	_____
c. capabilities,	_____	_____	_____
d. outside intelligence services,	_____	_____	_____
e. computer time and capacity, and	_____	_____	_____
f. other functional support.	_____	_____	_____

*SOMETIMES OR PARTIALLY

TOTAL POINTS ☐ + 0 + ☐

= ☐

RATING

Enter number of points scored ☐

───────────────────────────── = × 100 = ☐ %

Enter number of items on checklist ☐

**WHAT THE RATING
SIGNIFIES**

Good competitive evaluation is a *mining* type of operation, in which a ton of ore may be refined into an ounce of valuable product. The processing is crucial—and it takes resources. The resources in this situation are the money and brain power it takes to collect vast amounts of data, analyze it for significance, organize it into a meaningful format, draw conclusions, and make recommendations for action. Neither the money nor the intelligence alone will do the job—both are needed.

WHAT TO DO NOW

1. Use the mining analogy with your people. Point out that the "ore" is without value unless and until it is processed.

2. A critical input to the process is current information about your own company—its overall goals, its policies, and its forward plans. Lacking this, your recommendations might be at cross-purposes to the direction of the enterprise.

163

Chapter 10

How to Analyze
And Forecast Sales

Sales analysis is *a systematic process of collecting, organizing, evaluating, and interpreting actual sales data, for the purpose of projecting the firm's sales performance in the period ahead.* It is an analytical process intended to expose significant trends and relationships among the multitude of factors affecting sales effectiveness in order that sales management may take action to improve future performance.

NUMBERS AREN'T EVERYTHING

Sales analysis requires considerably more than the mere compiling of numbers. Effective sales analysis is explanatory and prescriptive as well. Sales analysis should reflect both good judgment in the selection of factors to be measured, as well as clear cause-and-effect thinking in the development and presentation of findings and conclusions. The evaluative and interpretative aspects of sales analysis, therefore, are emphasized in this appraisal, rather than the mere compilation and assembly of data. It presumes that the actual recording and accumulating of most sales data will be performed by people in other functions, such as accounting, sales management and customer service. The sales analysis function is responsible, of course, to prescribe the types of information to be recorded and the form in which it should be accumulated.

LOOKING IN-LOOKING OUT: KEY DIFFERENCES BETWEEN SALES AND MARKET DEMAND ANALYSIS

Sales analysis and market demand analysis are similar in certain respects, yet there is a fundamental difference between the two. Market demand analysis is concerned primarily with the *total market* for a product or service and is therefore largely *external* in nature, whereas sales analysis is concerned primarily with the company's own sales performance in that market and is therefore largely *internal* in nature. Each function is related to and contributes to the other, however, because while the company's sales are part of the total market, a measure of the total market's performance is needed in order to evaluate the firm's performance in that market.

The essential purpose of the sales analysis function is to furnish those who plan and direct sales activities with sound information and recommendations for action to improve sales and profit performance. Analysis of sales performance is not limited to the sales analysis function, since all personnel who are responsible, directly or indirectly, for achieving sales objectives must constantly analyze the factors affecting their own work. It is the sales analysis function, however, that concentrates in this area to permit maximum application of specialized skills and training.

KEY AIM OF THE SELF-AUDIT

The principal objective of the appraisal is to provide assurance that all information on order input and sales performance is gathered, organized, analyzed, and evaluated systematically and promptly in order to provide sales and marketing management with timely data for making decisions to improve sales and profitability in the period ahead.

HOW TO USE THE CHECKLISTS

For each of the statements in the Checklist, compare the condition of your function to the "ideal" as described in the statement. Then:

1. If you consider the statement to be *generally true* of your function, check the YES column.

2. If you consider the statement to be *untrue* of your function, check the NO column.

3. If you consider the statement to be *less than true* (but not totally untrue) of your function, check the SOMETIMES OR PARTIAL column.

4. If the statement does not apply to your particular situation, write "Not Applicable" across the response spaces (or simply draw a line through them).

5. If you lack the data for a definite response, write in "Not Answerable" or "Don't Know."

HOW TO EVALUATE YOUR RESPONSES

When you have completed the checklist, glance over your responses, keeping these points in mind:

1. A negative answer is always unfavorable because it indicates a problem within the function: the greater the number of NOs, the more serious the situation.

2. A positive response is always a good indication. But too many YES answers could indicate that your review is not objective enough.

3. Too many SOMETIMES OR PARTIALLY answers can point to internal weaknesses or to a lack of firm direction.

4. A lot of "Not Applicable" answers could indicate that you are avoiding the issue.

5. A large number of "Not Answerable" or "Don't Know" answers could be symptomatic of inadequate records or data bases.

HOW TO RATE AND SCORE YOUR RESPONSES

When you are satisfied with your responses in general, you are ready to score the Checklist. For your convenience, a self-explanatory Scoring and Rating Block follows each Checklist. This block not only tells you whether the condition of your function is satisfactory, but it also gives you a measure of its effectiveness.

Here's how to total up the points for inclusion in the Scoring and Rating Block:

1. Total up the number of points you scored:
   a. For each YES, give yourself one point.
   b. For each NO, give yourself zero.
   c. For each SOMETIMES OR PARTIALLY, give yourself a half-point.
   d. For each "Not Applicable" answer, give yourself zero and deduct one from the number of items on the Checklist.
   e. For each "Not Answerable" or "Don't Know" answer, give yourself zero.

2. Next divide the total number of points you score by the total number of items (statements) on the Checklist (less items marked "Not Applicable"). You'll get a 1.0 for a perfect score and a fraction for anything less.

3. Multiply the result of step 2 by 100 to arrive at the percentage for your score.

What is a satisfactory rating? A rating of less than 65 percent is unacceptable and calls for an improvement program: Obviously, the lower the rating, the more drastic the action required.

A brief "how-to" example of this Scoring and Rating system follows . . .

EXAMPLE

	YES (1)	NO (0)	S/P* (½)

1. Field sale reports designed to provide information on sales progress contain data on the following topics:

   a. sales calls and sales presentations made by salespersons and sales agents,　✓

   b. bids, quotations, and proposals made,　✓

   c. new orders booked,　✓

   d. lost business, and reasons for the loss,　　✓ (NO)

   e. accomplishments toward future orders,　　　✓ (S/P)

   f. performance in filling orders, handling complaints, and otherwise servicing individual customers,　✓

   g. action taken in response to customer requests, such as sending samples, spec sheets, etc.,　✓

   h. accomplishments of significance and value to other members of the sales force.　　　✓ (S/P)

*SOMETIMES OR PARTIALLY

TOTAL POINTS　　$\boxed{5}$ + 0 + $\boxed{1}$

= $\boxed{6}$

RATING

$$\frac{\text{Enter number of points scored} \quad \boxed{6}}{\text{Enter number of items on checklist} \quad \boxed{8}} = .75 \times 100 = \boxed{75 \%}$$

10-A
ORGANIZATION, ADMINISTRATION AND OPERATION

	YES (1)	NO (0)	S/P* (½)

1. The sales analysis function is recognized on the organization charts and in managers' position descriptions as an important activity within the market research function. _____ _____ _____

2. The function is supervised and staffed by marketing professionals (who may have other responsibilities) trained in modern techniques of sales analysis and informed about the company's products and customers. _____ _____ _____

3. The market research budget has an allocation covering internal expenses for sales analysis. _____ _____ _____

4. Collection and analysis of sales data and dissemination and use of sales analyses are guided and governed by written procedures. _____ _____ _____

5. Sales analyses are treated as "company confidential" material by all personnel. _____ _____ _____

6. Consistent use is made of sales analyses by sales and marketing management in making decisions to deploy sales personnel, establish sales territories, and to increase or reduce size of sales force. _____ _____ _____

7. Consistent use is made of sales analyses by marketing people in market demand analysis and competitor evaluation. _____ _____ _____

8. Persons who conduct sales analysis:

   a. help design field sales reports, and _____ _____ _____

   b. receive field sales reports and product distribution reports on a routine basis. _____ _____ _____

9. Key account profiles are prepared and updated by the responsible salesperson and are readily accessible to the sales analysis function. _____ _____ _____

10. In all major sales analysis projects:

    a. the purpose and usefulness of each analysis is known before work is started, _____ _____ _____

    b. the method of analysis or approach is defined in advance, _____ _____ _____

    c. new product types and uses, new customer classes, and new categories of resellers introduced since the previous period are incorporated, _____ _____ _____

    d. sampling is employed where appropriate, _____ _____ _____

    e. cross-classifications are developed and analyzed for meaningful relationships, and _____ _____ _____

    f. results are tested for validity and accuracy. _____ _____ _____

11. Analyses of order input and sales are detailed: _____ _____ _____

    a. by model, size, price, etc., _____ _____ _____

    b. by customer type, _____ _____ _____

    c. by geographical area _____ _____ _____

    d. by distribution channel, and _____ _____ _____

    e. by order size, sales frequency, lead time, seasonality, use, method of sale, etc. _____ _____ _____

*SOMETIMES OR PARTIALLY

	YES (1)	NO (0)	S/P* (½)

12. Sales analyses are segmented in terms of market shares:

    a. by product line or major product,

    b. by type of customer

    c. by major distribution channel, and

    d. by geographical area.

13. Forecasts are made in sufficient detail of:

    a. order input and sales,

    b. gross profit margins,

    c. market shares, and

    d. selling expenses.

14. Sales analysis routinely analyzes performance of the sales force, in total and in detail, in terms of:

    a. order input and/or sales vs. quotas,

    b. gross profit margins,

    c. sales by type of product or service,

    d. number of sales calls,

    e. sales (or orders) per sales call,

    f. selling expenses, and

    g. other, such as sales order size, average account size, frequence of purchase, etc.

15. Analyses are routinely made of:

    a. new business by source, size, product mix, gross margins, etc.,

    b. lost business by type and by cause,

    c. key account profile information, and

    d. profit margin contribution.

16. These studies adequately identify the reasons for:

    a. new business,

    b. changes in key account activity,

    c. changes in gross margins, and

    d. lost business.

17. These studies forecast, on the basis of the foregoing, the future amount and composition of order input, sales, and gross margins.

18. These studies and reports:

    a. analyze sales into significant segments,

    b. use cross-classification to bring out meaningful relationships,

*SOMETIMES OR PARTIALLY

	YES (1)	NO (0)	S/P* (½)

    c. determine the share of market, and

    d. detect and call attention to adverse trends early enough to permit management to take effective action.

19. Sales analyses are used by sales and marketing management:

    a. as inputs to sales forecasts, budgets, and sales plans,

    b. to establish sales territories and sales quotas,

    c. in sales training,

    d. for marketing policy (minimum order size, elimination of small accounts, etc.), and

    e. to establish performance measures, such as call frequency requirements.

20. Sales analyses are used by customer service and distribution:

    a. to project product availability, and

    b. for order handling cost studies.

21. Sales analyses are used by product/market development:

    a. as inputs to the development of marketing plans and programs,

    b. as inputs to setting prices and terms of sale, and

    c. to delineate new-product/market test areas.

22. Sales analyses are used by advertising and sales promotion:

    a. to develop plans and programs, and

    b. to measure effectiveness and results.

23. Sales analyses are used by market research to identify subjects and priorities for:

    a. market demand analysis, and

    b. competitor analysis.

24. Sales analyses are used to make detailed evaluations of distribution channel cost-effectiveness.

25. The majority of recommendations made by the sales analysis function were accepted and acted upon by top management.

*SOMETIMES OR PARTIALLY

TOTAL POINTS   ☐ + 0 + ☐

= ☐

RATING

Enter number of points scored   ☐

───────────────────────────── =   × 100 = ☐ %

Enter number of items on checklist   ☐

WHAT THE RATING SIGNIFIES

A less-than-acceptable rating for the sales analysis function indicates that managers may be making critical marketing and management decisions in the absence of accurate and timely information vital to these decisions. If this conclusion is borne out by further analysis, it points to a need for intensive management attention and action.

While this deficiency is grave, its correction, fortunately, is not very difficult (unless the basic historical data records don't exist; a situation that is not likely.) The essential issues are (1) whether or not the information exists, (2) whether it is being organized and evaluated intelligently, and (3) whether it is being used effectively to make decisions.

Each of these issues represents a higher-order problem than the preceding one. The solution must begin with the third point, however, rather than the first, because the search for information and the processing requirements should be guided by the decision-maker's needs.

It has been said that "all our information is about the past, while all our decisions are about the future." Forecasting future sales is an essential task element of the sales analysis process, therefore, because without a forecast the information has little or no value for decision making, but has only historical interest.

WHAT TO DO NOW

1. First, identify what specific information is needed by the various decision makers. Start at the top. This requires that the managers responsible for sales analysis be exposed to the conditions under which the decisions are made. Perhaps the most important of these are the top-level operations review meetings conducted in most progressive organizations, often on a quarterly schedule.

2. Work back through the process to the basic data requirements, and search this out. If it doesn't exist, it will have to be obtained or derived from other data.

3. You now have two pieces of the puzzle; the need for information is defined, and you have access to base data. The next step is to design a processing system to convert data into information—to organize the data into meaningful patterns and trends, draw some conclusions from these, and then project them into the future.

4. Never start the process by collecting and manipulating a lot of data simply because it exists, in the hope that somewhere "up the line" someone may need it. Unfortunately, this is the usual approach. As a consequence many executives find themselves *deluged with data and starved for information.*

10-B
AUTHORITY, RESPONSIBILITY AND ACCOUNTABILITY

	YES (1)	NO (0)	S/P* (½)

1. Authority has been allocated to the manager of market research, through allocation of budget funds and a written position description, to expend funds and assign tasks necessary to perform internal sales analysis.   ____ ____ ____

2. The manager is responsible for detecting and reporting significant sales trends, patterns, and relationship to sales and marketing management for appropriate action.   ____ ____ ____

3. He is also responsible for making firm recommendations as to courses of action the company should follow to improve sales effectiveness.   ____ ____ ____

4. The manager is held accountable for serious losses of sales volume, or for failure to meet sales plan objectives, resulting from lack of timely sales analyses or from invalid sales analyses and projections.   ____ ____ ____

*SOMETIMES OR PARTIALLY

TOTAL POINTS [ ] + 0 + [ ]

= [ ]

RATING

Enter number of points scored [ ]
—————————————————————— = [ ] × 100 = [ ] %
Enter number of items on checklist [ ]

WHAT THE RATING SIGNIFIES

Sales analysis is not a high-cost activity, but it does require a specific allocation of budget funds and delegation of authority to spend them. It also requires firm assignment of responsibility for performance of the tasks involved. Negative answers to these points indicates that the necessary work may not get accomplished for lack of one or both of these essentials.

A negative response to point 4 is evidence that the quality of the work done may not be as high as it could be, because those performing it are not held firmly accountable for deficient output.

WHAT TO DO NOW

1. Start with *accountability*. When individuals understand clearly what are the consequences of failure, they tend either to "shape up or ship out"; either way, you're better off.

2. Work back to *responsibility*. Define tasks precisely. Define them in terms of *results*, not activities.

3. Only then delegate *authority*. To do so earlier is unfair and unproductive, because the individual may exercise authority in ways unrelated to task accomplishment and results. The manager, that is, may become "authoritarian" in behavior—this can lead to lots of activity but little results.

*SOMETIMES OR PARTIALLY

10-C
MEASUREMENTS, CONTROL REPORTS AND PERFORMANCE RECORDS

	YES (1)	NO (0)	S/P* (½)

1. The effectiveness of the sales analysis function is measured and evaluated regularly and continuously. _____ _____ _____

2. This effectiveness is measured by comparing actual performance *and results* to specific benchmarks, targets or standards, such as:

   a. accuracy of sales forecasts, _____ _____ _____

   b. actual results from following recommendations made on the basis of sales analyses, and _____ _____ _____

   c. improvement in sales and profitability of major product lines. _____ _____ _____

3. The effectiveness of the sales analysis function is also determined by:

   a. timeliness of reports, _____ _____ _____

   b. credibility of assumptions and information inputs, _____ _____ _____

   c. validity of analyses and findings, _____ _____ _____

   d. firmness of recommendations, and _____ _____ _____

   e. soundness of supporting data. _____ _____ _____

4. Comparisons are made of order input, new business, sales, and sales productivity with prior periods to measure gains:

   a. in total, _____ _____ _____

   b. by product line, _____ _____ _____

   c. by sales district, _____ _____ _____

   d. by customer class, and _____ _____ _____

   e. by individual salesperson. _____ _____ _____

5. Sales forecasts are routinely compared with actual sales after the fact, for test of accuracy. _____ _____ _____

6. Sales analysis advises other functions of its requirements for information, in terms of:

   a. types of data and information needed, and _____ _____ _____

   b. the form in which such data and information are accumulated. _____ _____ _____

7. Sales analysis routinely receives and analyzes inputs of data from:

   a. sales manager (such as sales performance records and summaries, number and frequency of calls, lost business), _____ _____ _____

   b. comptroller (such as order input, sales, shippable backlog, gross margins), _____ _____ _____

   c. customer service (such as back orders, complaints), _____ _____ _____

   d. advertising/sales promotion and other marketing functions (such as response to advertising, industry data, etc.), and _____ _____ _____

*SOMETIMES OR PARTIALLY

    e. non-marketing functions (such as product test comparisons, quality reports, service records).

8. Expenses are routinely compared with budget, and major variances analyzed for corrective action.

*SOMETIMES OR PARTIALLY

TOTAL POINTS

☐ + 0 + ☐

= ☐

RATING

Enter number of points scored ☐

─────────────────────────────── = × 100 = ☐ %

Enter number of items on checklist ☐

WHAT THE RATING SIGNIFIES

Every function that provides input—in whatever form—to another function should be treated as a separate and distinct business function. A low rating for measurements and controls may indicate that the sales analysis activity is not considered important enough to be managed and measured as a separate function.

A low rating may also signify that the function emphasizes *activity* rather than *output*, as discussed in the section on Competitor Evaluation Measurements and Controls. If this is the case, the full benefits of good sales analysis—which are considerable—will be lost to the organization.

WHAT TO DO NOW

1. As mentioned earlier, one may define *control* as measurement. This implies that whatever is not measured is not totally controlled. Be sure that performance is measured regularly.

2. Shift the emphasis from activity to results by setting goals. Every manager, technician, professional, or supervisor involved should set clear and specific objectives for his own area of responsibility. If your organization has a formal MBO program, get fully involved, because as manager of a function you will gain considerably.

10-D
OPERATING PERFORMANCE HISTORY

| | YES (1) | NO (0) | S/P* (½) |

1. A review has been made of control reports and records for the past year or more.

2. This review shows that performance has improved and all major goals have been met.

*SOMETIMES OR PARTIALLY

	YES (1)	NO (0)	S/P* (½)

3. A review of these control reports and records for the past year shows no evidence of major failures to meet Sales Plan objectives resulting from lack of timely sales analyses, or invalid sales analyses and forecasts. (Answer "yes" if true.) _____ _____ _____

4. During the past year, there has been an improving trend in:

   a. actual order input vs. forecast, _____ _____ _____

   b. actual sales vs. forecast, _____ _____ _____

   c. sales productivity, in total, by sales territory and by individual salespersons, _____ _____ _____

   d. new business gained, _____ _____ _____

   e. lost business, and _____ _____ _____

   f. order backlog. _____ _____ _____

5. During the past year, there has been an improving trend in:

   a. timeliness of reports issued, _____ _____ _____

   b. number of recommendations accepted and endorsed by management, and _____ _____ _____

   c. actual results compared to actions recommended. _____ _____ _____

6. The expense budget has essentially been met for the past year. _____ _____ _____

*SOMETIMES OR PARTIALLY

TOTAL POINTS ☐ + 0 + ☐

= ☐

RATING

Enter number of points scored ☐ = ☐ × 100 = ☐ %

Enter number of items on checklist ☐

WHAT THE RATING SIGNIFIES

Perhaps the most critical point in this appraisal checklist is point 3. If there has been a serious failure to meet the goals of the sales plan because the sales analyses and forecasts on which the action plans were based were faulty or misleading, as indicated by a negative answer to this point, then the whole process has to be questioned.

WHAT TO DO NOW

Managers responsible for sales analysis should be fully involved in sales planning, not simply with the sales forecasts that are contained in the Sales Plan. After all, a sales plan is no better than the sales forecasts on which the action plans are based, sales territories are assigned, major accounts are identified for special effort, and the sales force is manned.

There is probably no better way to impress the sales analyst with the importance of the work he or she is responsible for.

10-E
TOP-LEVEL SUPPORT AND GUIDANCE

	YES (1)	NO (0)	S/P* (½)

The executive office demonstrates active support of the sales function by providing:

a. budget approval,

b. guidance through informed comments on sales reports and analyses,

c. endorsement of sales plans and marketing plans, and the sales forecasts on which they are based,

d. guidance through participation in sales planning and market planning progess review meetings, and

e. recognition and reward for outstanding accomplishment.

*SOMETIMES OR PARTIALLY

TOTAL POINTS   ☐ + 0 + ☐

= ☐

RATING

Enter number of points scored ☐

Enter number of items on checklist ☐

= ☐ × 100 = ☐ %

WHAT THE RATING SIGNIFIES   A low rating indicates that top management tends to regard the sales analysis function as a very minor function, and shows awareness of it only at the time that sales plans and marketing plans are given executive review and approval in advance of the business year. If this is the case, some special effort is needed to raise the "consciousness level" of the executive office to the importance of the activity.

WHAT TO DO NOW
1. Sales analysis activity should be broken out in your operating budget as a separate item for executive scrutiny.
2. Prepare to defend your request for operating funds. This is your best opportunity to tell the boss how vital your activity is to the firm's market leadership.

10-F
INNOVATION IN METHODS AND TECHNIQUES

	YES (1)	NO (0)	S/P* (½)

1. There is an active search for better ways to analyze sales data and to forecast more accurately, including:

   a. participation in seminars and workshops,

*SOMETIMES OR PARTIALLY

	YES (1)	NO (0)	S/P* (½)
b. review of management literature,	_____	_____	_____
c. professional association activities,	_____	_____	_____
d. industry contacts,	_____	_____	_____
e. solicitation of ideas and suggestions from personnel at all levels, and	_____	_____	_____
f. budgets provide funds for such activities.	_____	_____	_____

2. The computer is used to store, process and display information on order input, sales, sales productivity, customer behavior (ordering patterns, etc.), order backlogs, territory sales performance.
   _____ _____ _____

3. The computer is also employed to forecast major variables for use in business plans, market plans, sales plans, and budgets.
   _____ _____ _____

*SOMETIMES OR PARTIALLY

TOTAL POINTS   ☐ + 0 + ☐

= ☐

RATING

Enter number of points scored ☐ = × 100 = ☐ %

Enter number of items on checklist ☐

WHAT THE RATING SIGNIFIES

The previous chapter—competitor evaluation—was concerned with management's knowledge about the firm's competition. This present chapter might well be entitled "customer evaluation" because it is concerned with management's knowledge about the firm's customers. Surprisingly, some otherwise progressive companies fail to use modern methods of sales analysis and forecasting. As a consequence, they know less than they should about their existing customers' buying habits, the ways in which these customers use the firm's products, their needs for other products and services, and what can be expected from these purchasers in the future.

It is important to know that marketing management is keeping up with the latest developments in sales forecasting and sales analysis—a field that is changing rapidly as computers and software become smarter and more available—so that its knowledge of customers will be up to date and valid.

A low rating is a sign that management may be failing to generate a lot of potential business from existing customers, or from prospects with similar characteristics, because its information is inadequate or out of date.

WHAT TO DO NOW

1. Make sure that your budget includes an allocation for the outside activities necessary for keeping up with state-of-the-art in sales analysis and forecasting.

2. Use the information systems specialists, either inside the firm or outside, to help you set up your sales information handling process.

3. Assign good people to this task. Never forget that sales analysis is an

intellectual activity that requires human intelligence—the computer can help, *but it can't think*.

10-G
INTERFUNCTIONAL COMMUNICATIONS AND COORDINATION

	YES (1)	NO (0)	S/P* (½)

1. The manager of market research maintains a close and continuing relationship with other functions of the business in order to facilitate sales analysis, particularly:

   a. field sales, for day-to-day information exchange,

   b. comptroller, for access to accounting data,

   c. product distribution, for information exchange,

   d. information systems, for access to data processing,

   e. customer service, for information exchange, and

   f. other marketing functions, for coordination of efforts.

2. Other functions are responsive to sales analysis information requests, both routine and special.

*SOMETIMES OR PARTIALLY

TOTAL POINTS [ ] + 0 + [ ] = [ ]

RATING

$$\frac{\text{Enter number of points scored} \quad [\quad]}{\text{Enter number of items on checklist} \quad [\quad]} = \times 100 = [\quad] \%$$

WHAT THE RATING SIGNIFIES

Sales analysis should not be done by a "green eyeshade" type off in a remote corner of the office. To be fully productive, sales analysis should involve other people and other functions. Active interchange of information and ideas keeps the sales analysis process vital and "tuned in" to the real world.

A low rating indicates that this essential intercommunication is lacking.

WHAT TO DO NOW

1. You should be assertive in initiating these contacts with others if they don't now exist in an effective way. Don't be passive about it. Make your needs known, and keep constant pressure on to get them.
2. Don't take the attitude, however, that others should give you the information you need "because they're supposed to." Recognize that they have their own job pressures and priorities.

10-H
FUNCTIONAL IMPROVEMENT PROGRAM

	YES (1)	NO (0)	S/P* (½)

1. There is an active, on-going interfunctional team effort to improve the quality and value of sales analyses, with emphasis on:

   a. improved forecasting accuracy, ___ ___ ___

   b. timeliness of information inputs, ___ ___ ___

   c. improved analytical methods, and ___ ___ ___

   d. more action-oriented reports to management. ___ ___ ___

2. The team has representation from the following functions:

   a. marketing, ___ ___ ___

   b. information systems, ___ ___ ___

   c. field sales, ___ ___ ___

   d. comptroller, ___ ___ ___

   e. customer service, and ___ ___ ___

   f. systems and procedures. ___ ___ ___

3. A special effort is underway to secure sales analysis information as a by-product of routine electronic data processing. ___ ___ ___

*SOMETIMES OR PARTIALLY

TOTAL POINTS   ☐ + 0 + ☐

= ☐

RATING

Enter number of points scored ☐

—————————————————————— = × 100 = ☐ %

Enter number of items on checklist ☐

WHAT THE RATING SIGNIFIES

This section takes the previous appraisal a step further, and seeks to know whether the relationships with other functions are focused on improvement of the sales analysis activity. A low rating indicates that a great deal of useful input to the sales analysis process may be lost because of failure to formalize the information exchange and communications with other people in the organization.

WHAT TO DO NOW

1. The kind of activity referred to in the checklist is not at all common, even in the most progressive organizations. There is enormous benefit to be gained, however, from an interfunctional program to set improvement objectives and to guide the effort toward their accomplishment.

2. Don't let the team become a committee, "a group that takes hours to

produce minutes." The team should focus on a single important objective and when that is accomplished, the team should move on to another, perhaps with a different membership.

3. Provide strong leadership. Groups do not make decisions; individuals make decisions. The group may provide concensus, but it takes a leader to articulate the decision itself.

10-1
RESOURCES

	YES (1)	NO (0)	S/P* (½)
1. The manager of market research is informed about company objectives, plans, and programs through access to appropriate business plans, marketing plans, sales plans, capital budgets and operating reports.	____	____	____
2. Based on the foregoing information, resources for sales analysis are considered to be adequate to meet the company's needs during the next 3, 6 and 12 months, in terms of:			
a. manpower,	____	____	____
b. capabilities,	____	____	____
c. budget funding,	____	____	____
d. information systems support,	____	____	____
e. computer time and capacity, and	____	____	____
f. other functional support.	____	____	____

*SOMETIMES OR PARTIALLY

TOTAL POINTS   [ ] + 0 + [ ]

= [ ]

RATING

Enter number of points scored [ ]
─────────────────────────────── = [ ] × 100 = [ ] %
Enter number of items on checklist [ ]

WHAT THE RATING SIGNIFIES

A negative response to point 1 means that point 2 can't be answered with any degree of confidence, because information is one of the important and critical resources needed for good sales analysis.

The other crucial resource is the capability to convert raw data into useful information. This requires human intelligence, not a computer. The computer is an indispensible *assistant* to the human intellect, to be sure, but it cannot do the *thinking*.

WHAT TO DO NOW

1. Look upon this activity as a vital contributor to the company's competitiveness in the marketplace, because it is. It should be assigned to your *best* analyst, not given to a junior clerk who has free time.

2. Keep the analyst informed about company goals and plans. He or she is in a unique position to discern patterns and trends that can be of enormous significance to these objectives; to contribute, in fact, to their development, given proper encouragement.

THE BOTTOM LINE:

The expression "knowledge is power" is as true today as when Francis Bacon wrote it some four centuries ago. In today's business world it could well be paraphrased as *market knowledge is marketing power.*

Bacon wrote something else that market researchers should frame and hang over their desks. It is this:

If a person begins with certainties he shall end in doubts; but if he will begin with doubts he shall end in certainties.

For experience tells us that whenever a market research project starts out with a preconceived notion of what the market wants, instead of beginning the search with an open mind, a questioning attitude, and a degree of uncertainty about the end result, the chances of arriving at an invalid conclusion are greatly increased.

THE CASE OF THE MISSING MARKET

The management of Western Union, several years ago, became entranced with the idea that people would order gifts by telephone for delivery the following day to a friend or loved one hundreds or thousands of miles away. The new venture—called Gift America—was preceded by some of the most extensive (and expensive) market research since the introduction of the Edsel. The enterprise was quietly folded many months later after the expenditure of $28 million failed to develop a groundswell of demand for the new service.

As a non-participating observer—in my capacity as marketing vice president for the telegraph company, a separate subsidiary—I became convinced that the market researchers recorded all data which favored the project, but simply ignored any information that didn't accord with their biases. In fairness, it should be mentioned that people frequently give positive responses to questionnaires, then behave quite differently when it comes to actually spending their money.

SUMMARY OF SELF-AUDIT RATINGS
AND FUNCTIONAL IMPROVEMENT GOALS

If you wish, you may summarize the ratings for each function at the end of each section, on this "Summary Rating" form. (A "function" is the equivalent of a chapter.) The rating is simply an arithmetic average of the ratings on Checklists A through I—that is, the total divided by 9. This form also provides space for listing the Improvement Goals for each function.

Under each function, enter the rating percentage for each Checklist section, A through I. "Function Number 1," for example, is the first (1st) chapter in the section, regardless of its number in the book—5, 11, or so on. The Summary Rating is the total of each column divided by 9, to give you an average rating for the total function. The lower portion of the form can be used to list your improvement goals for each function.

	FUNCTION NUMBER					
CHECKLIST	1 %	2 %	3 %	4 %	5 %	6 %
A	_____	_____	_____	_____	_____	_____
B	_____	_____	_____	_____	_____	_____
C	_____	_____	_____	_____	_____	_____
D	_____	_____	_____	_____	_____	_____
E	_____	_____	_____	_____	_____	_____
F	_____	_____	_____	_____	_____	_____
G	_____	_____	_____	_____	_____	_____
H	_____	_____	_____	_____	_____	_____
I	_____	_____	_____	_____	_____	_____
SUMMARY RATING (%)	_____	_____	_____	_____	_____	_____

IMPROVEMENT GOALS

_____

_____

_____

_____

_____

_____

_____

(Use separate sheet as required)

Section **IV**

Managing the Selling Message

Advertising, sales promotion, and product publicity are sales communication tools designed to *pre-sell* products and services. These instruments can often move goods with greater economy and speed than can be accomplished through other means. For many packaged goods, they virtually replace the salesperson at the consumer point-of-purchase. In direct response selling, advertising does the total selling job. Even where personal selling is necessary—as in the sale of most industrial products—they reinforce and support the face-to-face salesmanship involved. No matter what your product or service, advertising, sales promotion, and product publicity can significantly increase your total marketing effectiveness. Without them, you'll find it hard to get your prospect's attention.

> **I don't know your company;**
> **I don't know what you stand for;**
> **I don't know your product—**
> **now, what was it you wanted to see me about?**

A memorable series of ads in *Business Week* magazine a couple of years ago showed a prospect seated at a desk saying these words to a hypothetical salesman.

A company will achieve maximum results in the marketplace only when there is proper balance among all the elements of its marketing effort. Advertising, sales promotion, and product publicity are particularly important marketing implements—it is through these activities that products and services are most often brought to the attention of present and potential customers. The company image is established and enhanced through effective, innovative advertising, sales promotion, and product publicity, and each helps pave the way toward the ultimate objective—profitable sales. The competitive advantage of product improvements, excellent delivery performance, superior product quality, and good customer service, for example, may go unrealized if the prospective customers are not made aware of and favorably disposed toward the company and its products through advertising.

POOR ADVERTISING+ SALES PROMOTION CAN BE WORSE THAN NONE

Some businessmen believe that all advertising and sales promotion has a positive effect; therefore, any effort in this area is better than none. In effect, "Say anything you want about me as long as you spell my name correctly." These vital functions must not be approached with such a casual attitude. A poorly done program can actually have a negative effect. The only kind of program the company should undertake is one that is superior to its competition. This does not mean a more expensive or more elaborate program, but rather one that is better planned, designed, and executed. In short, a more persuasive program.

FOUR LEVELS OF RECEPTIVITY NEEDED BEFORE A PROSPECT BECOMES A CUSTOMER

The ultimate purpose of advertising, sales promotion, and product publicity is to move the prospective purchaser through several successive levels of receptivity toward the purchase of the product or service. These four levels are:

Level 1. AWARENESS of the company name, trademark, or service.
Level 2. COMPREHENSION, where the prospect is aware of and recognizes the trademark or package, and possesses some understanding of what the product is and does.
Level 3. CONVICTION—prospect now can identify the product, and is convinced of its usefulness and quality.
Level 4. ACTION—the prospect has made a positive move toward purchase, such as visiting a sales outlet, requesting literature, or requesting a sales call.

HOW REALISTIC ADVERTISING GOALS GENERATE BENEFITS

One of the most crucial aspects of managing advertising is setting goals that are at once realistic and challenging. But because advertising and sales promotion are among the most intangible of business forces, advertising objectives often tend to be broad generalizations rather than specific and measurable. Too often they are treated as window dressing, forgotten once the marketing plan is approved. When goals are carefully developed and agreed to by all concerned, they generate many benefits, the most important of which are:

1. GOALS PREVENT WASTED EFFORT. They reduce to a minimum those cases where a program or plan is later rejected because "this isn't what we want to do at all."

2. GOALS ENHANCE INDIVIDUAL PERFORMANCE. Each participant knows what is being attempted and what he is expected to do.

3. GOALS ENSURE CONCENTRATION of professional time and budget money on essential tasks. The establishment of specific goals helps avoid inefficient "supermarket" programs that appear to offer something to everyone.

4. GOALS MAKE IT POSSIBLE TO MEASURE RESULTS, and thereby enable the investment to deliver maximum results with minimum guesswork.

Managing an advertising/salespromotion/product publicity activity may vary from the part-time responsibility of one person to the direction of a department of a dozen or more persons. Yet, even for an organization of the smallest size, determining the best basic structure requires skill and experience, particularly when viewed over the longer run. Consideration of the best organization structure and staffing should include making periodic comparisons with the structure and operations of competitors. It should also include periodic "make or buy" decisions regarding whether to take on permanent personnel to do the job or to have it supplied by agency or vendor.

Without minimizing the importance of organizing, staffing and motivating the department, the typical advertising/sales promotion manager will recognize that by far the greatest amount of time is devoted to the direction and control of day-to-day operations. This includes dealing with agency personnel, meeting with marketing management, checking exhibit schedules, making plans and revising plans. In the final analysis, the successful implementation of plans and programs depends on how well the manager directs their execution. The essential need is to maintain a proper balance between short-term and long-term activities, between planning and implementation, between evaluation and control, and between action and reaction.

KEY AIM OF THE SELF-AUDIT

The principal goals of the appraisal are to ensure that the sales communication tools of advertising, sales promotion, and product publicity are effectively designed and used; that objectives are realistic and attainable; that costs are related to results, and that the function is well managed.

Generally, the firm's advertising, sales promotion, and product publicity should be equal to or superior to that of the strongest competitor in quality, creativity, impact, and cost-effectiveness.

Following are detailed checklists which cover each of the three principal elements of managing the selling message:

1. supporting salesmanship with advertising and sales promotion,

2. using product publicity, and

3. evaluating agency/company relations.

Chapter **11**

Supporting Salesmanship with Advertising and Sales Promotion

The prospective buyers of the products you make and sell are seldom able to compare your products directly with all of the competing products made by other manufacturers. They may test-drive one or two competing automobiles, look at a couple of different makes of appliances, or buy and consume several competing brands of food, liquor, or cosmetics until they find the one they like best. Even industrial users are rarely able to test all competing products before buying.

Most often, the comparison which the first-time purchaser makes is a comparison of *your advertising* with that of your several competitors. When your claims are more persuasive and credible than theirs, your product gets the vote. And when your product lives up to the claims made for it, chances are you have a repeat buyer. Should the actual performance (or appearance, or taste, or durability) of your product seriously fail to live up to its promise, however, you have assuredly lost a future customer.

Unfortunately, your one-time buyers seldom tell you that they won't buy from you again. What is worse, you may never know *why*. The first-time purchaser is putting your product on trial—when he or she is gulled into buying by inflated or false advertising claims, the product is convicted of the crime, while the guilty party, your advertising, is acquitted.

The point of this discussion is that there is a more important quality in advertising than human creativity—it is truth. Actually, the combination of the two—creativity and truth—is the most potent joining of forces in advertising.

There is persistent myth in business that portrays the creator of advertising facing a blank sheet of paper in the typewriter or a blank sheet on the drawing pad until suddenly inspiration strikes—then furiously writing the copy or sketching the layout before the thought escapes. The resulting product of this process may be inspired, but it is less likely to build a solid base of loyal customers than an advertising program which results from an intensive search for facts about the product, its markets, its likely competitors in the marketplace, and its benefits to users—coupled with the application of creative thinking to these hard facts.

When the output of the latter process is coordinated with all other functions of the business, and when the advertising is backed up with high product quality, effective selling, good product distribution, and superior customer service, nothing can stop the company from achieving market leadership.

KEY AIM OF THE SELF-AUDIT

The main purposes of the appraisal are to ensure that the firm's advertising and sales promotion activity is directed toward the accomplishment of goals that are in harmony with overall policies, strategies, and long-range objectives; that programs are based on hard information and knowledge about products, markets, competition, as well as media; and that all advertising is measured in terms of the results that really count— sales and profit to the company.

HOW TO USE THE CHECKLISTS

For each of the statements in the Checklist, compare the condition of your function to the "ideal" as described in the statement. Then:

1. If you consider the statement to be *generally true* of your function, check the YES column.

2. If you consider the statement to be *untrue* of your function, check the NO column.

3. If you consider the statement to be *less than true* (but not totally untrue) of your function, check the SOMETIMES OR PARTIAL column.

4. If the statement does not apply to your particular situation, write "Not Applicable" across the response spaces (or simply draw a line through them).

5. If you lack the data for a definite response, write in "Not Answerable" or "Don't Know."

HOW TO EVALUATE YOUR RESPONSES

When you have completed the checklist, glance over your responses, keeping these points in mind:

1. A negative answer is always unfavorable because it indicates a problem within the function: the greater the number of NOs, the more serious the situation.

2. A positive response is always a good indication. But too many YES answers could indicate that your review is not objective enough.

3. Too many SOMETIMES OR PARTIALLY answers can point to internal weaknesses or to a lack of firm direction.

4. A lot of "Not Applicable" answers could indicate that you are avoiding the issue.

5. A large number of "Not Answerable" or "Don't Know" answers could be symptomatic of inadequate records or data bases.

HOW TO RATE AND SCORE YOUR RESPONSES

When you are satisfied with your responses in general, you are ready to score the Checklist. For your convenience, a self-explanatory Scoring and Rating Block follows each Checklist. This block not only tells you whether the condition of your function is satisfactory, but it also gives you a measure of its effectiveness.

Here's how to total up the points for inclusion in the Scoring and Rating Block:

1. Total up the number of points you scored:
   a. For each YES, give yourself one point.
   b. For each NO, give yourself zero.
   c. For each SOMETIMES OR PARTIALLY, give yourself a half-point.
   d. For each "Not Applicable" answer, give yourself zero and deduct one from the number of items on the Checklist.
   e. For each "Not Answerable" or "Don't Know" answer, give yourself zero.

2. Next divide the total number of points you score by the total number of items (statements) on the Checklist (less items marked "Not Applicable"). You'll get a 1.0 for a perfect score and a fraction for anything less.

3. Multiply the result of step 2 by 100 to arrive at the percentage for your score.

What is a satisfactory rating? A rating of less than 65 percent is unacceptable and calls for an improvement program: Obviously, the lower the rating, the more drastic the action required.

A brief "how-to" example of this Scoring and Rating system follows . . .

EXAMPLE

	YES (1)	NO (0)	S/P* (½)

1. Field sale reports designed to provide information on sales progress contain data on the following topics:

	YES	NO	S/P
a. sales calls and sales presentations made by salespersons and sales agents,	✓	—	—
b. bids, quotations, and proposals made,	✓	—	—
c. new orders booked,	✓	—	—
d. lost business, and reasons for the loss,	—	✓	—
e. accomplishments toward future orders,	—	—	✓
f. performance in filling orders, handling complaints, and otherwise servicing individual customers,	✓	—	—
g. action taken in response to customer requests, such as sending samples, spec sheets, etc.,	✓	—	—
h. accomplishments of significance and value to other members of the sales force.	—	—	✓

*SOMETIMES OR PARTIALLY

TOTAL POINTS $\boxed{5}$ + 0 + $\boxed{1}$

$= \boxed{6}$

RATING

Enter number of points scored $\boxed{6}$

Enter number of items on checklist $\boxed{8}$

$= .75 \times 100 = \boxed{75\ \%}$

11-A
ORGANIZATION, ADMINISTRATION AND OPERATION

	YES (1)	NO (0)	S/P* (½)

1. Advertising/sales promotion of the company's products and services is

    a. recognized as a vital company activity, and _____ _____ _____

    b. is shown on organization charts as an important function of marketing. _____ _____ _____

2. The function has a formal budget allocation covering internal expenses of operation and fees for outside services, separate and apart from costs of media space and time. _____ _____ _____

3. The budget was developed on the basis of a review and evaluation of all tasks and activities that are critical to the department's results. _____ _____ _____

4. The manager of advertising/sales promotion reports directly to the top marketing executive or to an executive of equal or higher status. _____ _____ _____

5. All key positions on the organization chart are staffed by advertising professionals who are well-informed about the company, its products and services, and its markets. _____ _____ _____

6. The manager routinely attends top-level meetings on matters of marketing planning, sales planning, business development, new-product and new-market development, and marketing budgets. _____ _____ _____

7. The function is structured essentially as a management organization designed to guide, direct, and control activities of the company's advertising agencies and suppliers of sales promotion materials and services. _____ _____ _____

8. The function also has capability to provide marketing services internally. _____ _____ _____

9. In dealings with agencies and suppliers, personnel are guided by written procedures and standard practices governing administrative and legal aspects of the relationships. _____ _____ _____

10. Procedures and practices are written so as to stimulate, not inhibit, the creative and innovative talents of advertising and sales promotion personnel. _____ _____ _____

11. Specific goals for advertising and sales promotion are included in the marketing plan. _____ _____ _____

12. Advertising and sales promotion goals are measurable, and provision has been made for periodically checking their attainment. _____ _____ _____

13. Advertising and sales promotion goals are realistic and attainable in light of the resources that can reasonably be expected to be available. _____ _____ _____

14. Separate statements of objectives and step-by-step plans are coordinated with each other. _____ _____ _____

15. Advertising and sales promotion goals are in harmony with objectives and strategies, and company policies. _____ _____ _____

16. Goals are communicated to all marketing personnel and to all other functions involved. _____ _____ _____

*SOMETIMES OR PARTIALLY

193

17. Advertising and sales promotion personnel are kept informed about company objectives, plans, problems, and decisions that must be considered in advertising and sales promotion goals development. ___ ___

18. Advertising and sales promotion plans are developed after the goals are established, not before. ___ ___ ___

19. Step-by-step plans include a timetable for each stage of the plan. ___ ___ ___

20. The preliminary advertising and sales promotion plan is tested by reducing the annual budget by 25 percent, to see which items could be reduced or deleted without serious adverse effect on results. ___ ___

21. Plans include, for each step, a clear assignment of responsibility and an estimate of cost. ___ ___ ___

22. Position descriptions for the managers and other key employees have been formalized and discussed with the individuals concerned. ___ ___ ___

23. The advertising and sales promotion activity is correctly staffed in numbers of people, as well as their capabilities and experience. ___ ___ ___

24. The marketing manager reviews the adequacy and effectiveness of the advertising and sales promotion organization, staff, and operations at least once a year. ___ ___ ___

25. An annual review is conducted with the advertising agency of work methods, relationships, and accomplishments. ___ ___ ___

26. Where advertising and sales promotion is designed to develop sales leads or inquiries, these leads or inquiries are typically handled within three days of their receipt. ___ ___ ___

27. Employees are informed in advance about new advertising and promotional programs. ___ ___ ___

28. The firm's advertising agency has fully exploited, wherever possible, the use of tested media. ___ ___ ___

29. a. Readership, ratings, or effectiveness studies of advertising are used to develop a trendline of effectiveness over the year. ___ ___ ___

   b. This trendline indicates that advertising effectiveness is increasing. ___ ___ ___

30. The firm's advertising is regularly reviewed and compared with that of its principal competitors. ___ ___ ___

31. The firm's advertising compared well with that of its principal competitors during the past 12 months in terms of:

   a. total impact and creativity, and ___ ___ ___

   b. advertising cost relative to sales. ___ ___ ___

32. There is a regularly scheduled program to research and test advertising effectiveness via such techniques as coupons, split runs, TV and/or radio test markets. ___ ___ ___

33. The facts developed in #32 are used in developing advertising and sales promotion goals and step-by-step plans. ___ ___ ___

34. There is a regularly scheduled research program to determine the company's image and periodically update the findings. ___ ___ ___

*SOMETIMES OR PARTIALLY

	YES (1)	NO (0)	S/P* (½)

35. The facts developed in #34 are used in developing advertising and sales promotion goals and step-by-step plans. _____ _____ _____

36. Research is performed sufficiently "in-depth" to provide solid support for the conclusions. _____ _____ _____

37. Promotional materials such as catalogs, specification sheets, and similar items are compared annually with similar items from at least two principal competitors. _____ _____ _____

38. Promotional materials are competitive in cost, being neither too lavish nor too obviously cost-conscious. _____ _____ _____

39. Promotional materials are competitive in effectiveness. _____ _____ _____

40. "Traditional" programs are periodically analyzed to determine what would happen if they were discontinued or substantially revised. _____ _____ _____

41. With regard to shows and exhibits, associated company units are advised in advance so that exhibits can be combined and coordinated. _____ _____ _____

42. For each show and exhibit scheduled, the following key exhibit performance factors are taken into consideration:

    a. new products are given priority, _____ _____ _____

    b. the products selected have product and buying level interest for the show audience, and _____ _____ _____

    c. the displays are well organized. _____ _____ _____

43. Product presentations (working models, animation or live presentations) are used for exhibits. _____ _____ _____

44. Exhibit locations are adequate. _____ _____ _____

45. Exhibits are adequately manned 100 percent of the time. _____ _____ _____

46. Exhibit floor space is generally adequate. _____ _____ _____

47. A briefing session is held prior to each show opening to ensure all personnel are well-versed on the performance, availability, and price of products exhibited. _____ _____ _____

48. During the past twelve months, the company has exhibited at shows only where the potential audience was large and the quality high. _____ _____ _____

49. A semi-annual review is made of upcoming shows to determine whether to expand the schedule because of new products or the need for more distributors. _____ _____ _____

50. The company has *not participated* in shows during the past year for one or more of the following reasons:

    a. to improve the company image, _____ _____ _____

    b. because the company had always been in the show, _____ _____ _____

    c. because competition was there, and _____ _____ _____

    d. because the show deserved support. _____ _____ _____

    (Answer "yes" if true).

*SOMETIMES OR PARTIALLY

TOTAL POINTS   □ + 0 + □

︸

= □

RATING

Enter number of points scored ___ □

Enter number of items on checklist   □

= × 100 = □ %

WHAT THE RATING SIGNIFIES

When the company's advertising and sales promotion activities are conducted in a manner that channels the full innovative and creative energies of talented people into support of the organization's goals, the productivity of the function and the return on every dollar of advertising investment will be high.

Contrary to some thinking, innovation and creativity can flourish best within the framework of a disciplined organization and a structured process—provided that the organizational environment and the process are designed to foster, rather than to inhibit, creative thinking and innovative action, and provided further that the goals of the company are perceived by members of the organization to be stimulating and rewarding to them personally.

One of the keys to this situation is a full and free flow of information throughout the organization. Another is that new ideas are encouraged and are nurtured through their early stages when they are most vulnerable to criticism. A third is willingness to take calculated risk—and the courage to fail occasionally.

Because an organization is smaller in size is no reason to assume that communications between individuals and departments is good, or that the atmosphere is more receptive to new ideas. People don't always communicate well, even when they work together closely. The system has to encourage, even demand, that information must be exchanged freely and often. And regardless of the size of the firm, its policies have to encourage and reward new ideas.

A less-than-acceptable rating here indicates that the internal environment may be less hospitable to innovative action than they should be. As a consequence, the company's advertising and sales promotion expenditures are probably not producing satisfactory results, regardless of the size of the budget.

WHAT TO DO NOW

1. If advertising results are unsatisfactory, the worst possible solution is to throw additional money at the problem.
2. The second worst solution is to fire the advertising agency.
3. The best solution is probably the most difficult. It requires an honest and painstaking search for the facts—and the courage to accept these facts even when they are unpleasant, or offensive to your professional ego.
4. Rarely are agency personnel over-informed —most frequently they are kept under-informed about the company, its products, its markets, its

goals and policies. As a consequence, agency creativity is often misdirected, and time and money wasted.

5. If you regularly have to rewrite agency copy and redesign agency artwork, chances are that you're at fault, not the agency. Try bringing agency people into the picture early, during product development, when their creativity will contribute to the new product, not simply to its advertising. This also avoids the need to educate them later on about the product.

11-B
AUTHORITY, RESPONSIBILITY AND ACCOUNTABILITY

	YES (1)	NO (0)	S/P* (½)
1. Authority has been formally delegated to the manager of advertising and sales promotion, through budget allocation, position description, and title, to expend company funds, sign contracts, and assign tasks necessary to advertise and promote sales of the company's products.	———	———	———
2. The manager is responsible to:			
a. staff and manage an organization capable of planning and implementing effective advertising and sales promotion programs,	———	———	———
b. develop and administer sound operating and control procedures, and	———	———	———
c. establish and manage contractual relations with advertising agencies and suppliers of promotional materials and services.	———	———	———
3. The manager is held accountable for:			
a. serious failure to meet marketing plan and sales plan objectives resulting from ineffective advertising and sales promotion,	———	———	———
b. failure of new products to meet sales goals because of inadequate or ineffective promotion,	———	———	———
c. excessive costs of advertising or sales promotion,	———	———	———
d. serious schedule delays in completion of advertising and sales promotion projects, and	———	———	———
e. serious deterioration of the company "image" as perceived by customers and others.	———	———	———

*SOMETIMES OR PARTIALLY

TOTAL POINTS   ☐ + 0 + ☐

= ☐

RATING

Enter number of points scored ☐

Enter number of items on checklist ☐

= × 100 = ☐ %

WHAT THE RATING SIGNIFIES

Regardless of the size of the company's advertising budget, every advertising manager's responsibility is the same—it is to manage the budget in such a way as to maximize the return on every dollar invested in advertising. This requires that "return" be defined in terms of tangible results—of real *output* such as new orders, sales, new accounts gained, increase in store traffic, etc. Only when results can be quantified, measured, and compared with goals and standards of performance, can true effectiveness be determined. Unless this is done, there will be a tendency to evaluate the effectiveness of advertising in subjective terms, or the acclaim of professional colleagues—or worse, in terms of total dollars expended.

WHAT TO DO NOW

1. Define results in the terms described, and make certain that every job description specifies precise performance standards and goals as part of the job.
2. Be especially sure that agency personnel understand and work toward the same results, goals, and performance standards.
3. Be sure that the authority, title, and power of the manager are sufficient that dealings with agency executives and suppliers can be conducted on equitable terms and on the proper level.

11-C
MEASUREMENTS, CONTROL REPORTS AND PERFORMANCE RECORDS

	YES (1)	NO (0)	S/P* (½)
1. The effectiveness of the company's advertising and sales promotion activities is measured regularly and systematically.	_____	_____	_____
2. This effectiveness is measured in specific terms, by comparing actual performance of advertising and sales promotion with certain benchmarks, targets, or standards, such as:			
a. number of customer inquiries, requests for quotation, purchase orders, store traffic, etc.,	_____	_____	_____
b. shares of market,	_____	_____	_____
c. customer response per dollar of expenditures, and	_____	_____	_____
d. consumer attitudes toward the company and its offerings.	_____	_____	_____
3. Accurate records are kept of the number of inquiries, orders, and to the extent possible, sales, resulting from each advertising and sales promotion program.	_____	_____	_____
4. The response to each program is related to its cost in terms of inquiries, orders, or sales per dollar of expenditures.	_____	_____	_____
5. A survey of consumer attitudes toward the company's offerings is made periodically, at least every two years.	_____	_____	_____
6. Studies of advertising readership, program ratings, and impact are used in planning advertising expenditures, but are not considered to be final determinants of effectiveness.	_____	_____	_____

*SOMETIMES OR PARTIALLY

	YES (1)	NO (0)	S/P* (½)

7. A comparison is made at least yearly of advertising expenditures (per item sold or as a percent of sales) with those of principal competitors.* Where data is unavailable, compare use of space in key consumer and/or trade media with competition.

8. The advertising department obtains reports of all sales leads and inquiries received so that records may be kept on the relative pulling power of media used. Consideration is given to adding these reader names to the promotional mailing list.

9. Advertising budgets include adequate funds for testing and measuring advertising impact.

10. Performance measurements and controls are computerized.

*SOMETIMES OR PARTIALLY

TOTAL POINTS

$$\boxed{} + 0 + \boxed{}$$

$$= \boxed{}$$

RATING

Enter number of points scored $\dfrac{\boxed{}}{\boxed{}}$

Enter number of items on checklist

$= \quad \times 100 = \boxed{} \%$

WHAT THE RATING SIGNIFIES

Henry Ford was once advised to slash his advertising expenditures because, he was told, 90 percent of his advertising was wasted. In reply he said he couldn't do that because he didn't know *which* 90 percent was wasted. We've learned something since then, it is now possible to measure with a fair degree of accuracy each of the four levels of purchaser receptivity to advertising and sales promotion—awareness, comprehension, conviction, and action. Unless this is done, management cannot know with assurance which advertising messages are reaching their target audiences and which are not.

A less-than-satisfactory rating is evidence that these measurements are not being made regularly and systematically. As a consequence, money may be spent putting out ineffective messages—or worse, a persuasive message may be terminated even while it is still producing a satisfactory response.

WHAT TO DO NOW

1. *Test and measure* every ad campaign. Sampling techniques make it possible to do this at affordable cost.
2. Make sure that the advertising budget provides for the expenses of testing and measuring advertising impact as an integral part of the cost of the advertising.
3. When a test comes up negative, discontinue the ad—unless you have more faith in your intuition than in your test procedures (in this event, you ought to stop testing and pay yourself the money it costs).

*Defined as the principal competitors in products or product lines the advertising effort is mainly concerned with.

4. Don't strive for professional recognition and awards for advertising at the expense of results. The average consumer doesn't necessarily share your professional colleagues' opinions, any more than the typical play-goer agrees with the professional theater critic.

11-D
OPERATING PERFORMANCE HISTORY

	YES (1)	NO (0)	S/P* (½)
1. An analysis has been made of control reports and records for at least one year past.	_____	_____	_____
2. This review of records and control reports for the past year shows:			
a. no serious shortfall from Plan objectives, because of ineffective advertising,	_____	_____	_____
b. no serious failure of new-product introductions, because of inadequate promotion,	_____	_____	_____
c. no serious excess costs of advertising and sales promotion, and	_____	_____	_____
d. no serious delays in major projects and programs.	_____	_____	_____
(Answer "yes" if true).			
3. During the past year, there has been an improving trend in advertising results, as measured by inquiries, orders, and sales per dollar of expenditures.	_____	_____	_____
4. The latest customer attitude survey showed more favorable customer perceptions of the company and its products.	_____	_____	_____
5. Last year's advertising and sales promotion plan was followed in its essentials (with revisions necessitated by changed circumstances) and goals were generally met.	_____	_____	_____
6. The operating budget was essentially met during the past year.	_____	_____	_____
7. For the prior full year, sales promotion performance compares well with that of the principal competitors in terms of:			
a. sales effectiveness of promotional materials as indicated by sampling the reaction of key customers, and	_____	_____	_____
b. results from trade show presentations and exhibits.	_____	_____	_____

*SOMETIMES OR PARTIALLY

TOTAL POINTS [ ] + 0 + [ ]

= [ ]

RATING

Enter number of points scored [ ]
───────────────────────────────── =   × 100 = [ ] %
Enter number of items on checklist [ ]

WHAT THE RATING SIGNIFIES   The past is not always a reliable indicator of future performance, but it's all you've got. A history of past failures, though, can hardly generate confidence that future promises will be kept. A poor rating here is a signal that there may be some serious deficiencies in the organization or in the process by which the company's advertising and sales promotion is produced.

WHAT TO DO NOW

1. Be sure that you, your entire staff, and your agency all know where you've been before you decide where you're going. This means getting all the facts about past performance out in the open regardless of whose ego gets bruised.

2. Look for basic causes of past failures, not for excuses or scapegoats to pin the blame on.

3. If past goals were seriously missed, the fault may be that the goals were too high rather than performance too low. Better to set achievable goals that ensure success and build confidence than to risk failure (and disappointment) because the objectives are beyond reach.

11-E
TOP-LEVEL SUPPORT AND GUIDANCE

	YES (1)	NO (0)	S/P* (½)
1. The executive office demonstrates active support, guidance, and recognition of advertising and sales promotion activities, through:			
a. approval of plans and budgets,	___	___	___
b. review and approval of major advertising/sales promotion projects and programs,	___	___	___
c. participation in progress review meetings,	___	___	___
d. informed comments on departmental progress reports,	___	___	___
e. active participation at key trade shows and exhibits,	___	___	___
f. recognition and reward for outstanding accomplishment, and	___	___	___
g. appointment of the manager to key task groups.	___	___	___

*SOMETIMES OR PARTIALLY

TOTAL POINTS   [ ] + 0 + [ ]

= [ ]

RATING

Enter number of points scored [ ]
——————————————————————————— = [ ] × 100 = [ ] %
Enter number of items on checklist [ ]

WHAT THE RATING SIGNIFIES

An executive presence during the development and implementation of important advertising programs can do a lot to enhance advertising productivity, by ensuring that the new programs accord with overall corporate strategy and policy. This doesn't necessarily call for the chairman to appear in every television commercial like Frank Perdue or Frank Borman of Eastern Airlines (although in Perdue's case the results can't be disputed). Nor does it mean that the chief executive spends hours rewriting draft ad copy and revising draft ad layouts (as frequently happens).

What is needed is broad general guidance, encouragement, and support—and recognition that innovation and creativity are sometimes more important to results than the size of the advertising budget.

WHAT TO DO NOW

1. One of the most delicate issues to face is the question of *when* to get the executive office involved in a new advertising program. Too soon—and a brilliant marketing idea can be stifled by an executive mind trained in engineering logic, legal process, or financial order. Too late, and a fully executed campaign can be sent back to the drawing board because it doesn't conform to corporate desires.

2. Keep the executive office informed—but also let it be known (with discretion, of course) that you are the advertising professional. Let it be known also (again with discretion) that if the boss rewrites the copy, then you can no longer be held accountable if it fails.

11-F
INNOVATION IN METHODS AND TECHNIQUES

	YES (1)	NO (0)	S/P* (½)
1. Advertising management actively seeks better and more cost-effective ways to reach and influence people to buy the company's products, through solicitation of ideas from:			
a. agencies and suppliers,	____	____	____
b. professional associations,	____	____	____
c. seminars, workshops, and conferences,	____	____	____
d. outside specialists,	____	____	____
e. customer and industry contacts, and	____	____	____
f. company personnel at all levels and in all functions and	____	____	____
g. budgets provide funds for such activities.	____	____	____
2. The computer is used to store, process, and display information on advertising media, products and services, progress on projects under way, effectiveness and costs of advertising and sales promotion.	____	____	____
3. New media and new sales promotion schemes are tested on small scale. Results are measured and evaluated before large-scale use.	____	____	____

*SOMETIMES OR PARTIALLY

TOTAL POINTS   ☐ + 0 + ☐

= ☐

RATING

Enter number of points scored ☐

Enter number of items on checklist ☐

= × 100 = ☐ %

WHAT THE RATING SIGNIFIES

In no other function of the business is innovation more critical to productivity. No advertising department or agency, however successful, has a corner on fresh new ideas—so it is vitally important to use outside sources well and often.

A low rating here may indicate that the organization is becoming insulated from the "outside world." As a consequence the department may tend to recycle old themes rather than to generate dynamic new ones.

WHAT TO DO NOW

1. The advice to keep well informed about what others are doing may seem trite, but internal work pressures can often become so intense as to prevent attendance at important seminars, workshops, and professional association meetings.

2. Following the leader, or copying successful competitors, may produce short-term results, but at the risk of losing your most creative people.

3. Innovate with a purpose. Set firm objectives, make them known, and then turn people loose to come up with innovative ways to achieve these goals.

11-G
INTERFUNCTIONAL COMMUNICATIONS AND COORDINATION

	YES (1)	NO (0)	S/P* (½)
1. Close and harmonious working relations are maintained at several organizational levels with other company functions, including:			
a. field sales,	_____	_____	_____
b. market research,	_____	_____	_____
c. product distribution,	_____	_____	_____
d. RD&E, and	_____	_____	_____
e. customer service.	_____	_____	_____
2. Engineering, production, distribution, and marketing personnel are responsive to department requests for information and assistance.	_____	_____	_____
3. New advertising programs are reviewed during development with managers of other functions, and their viewpoints are considered.	_____	_____	_____
4. Personnel in other functions are kept informed about new programs (to the extent competitive security permits), so they can respond intelligently to customer queries.	_____	_____	_____

*SOMETIMES OR PARTIALLY

TOTAL POINTS   [   ] + 0 + [   ]

= [   ]

RATING

Enter number of points scored [   ]

Enter number of items on checklist [   ]

= × 100 = [   ] %

203

The company's advertising is often the primary interface between the firm and all of its constituents—not only customers and prospects, but investors, lenders, suppliers, government entities and the general public. Advertising, therefore, must do more than sell products—it should convey an image of substance, quality, and fair dealing. It also should represent the total organization, not just the advertising department. To this end, advertising personnel must maintain continuous communications and close contact with all other functions of the business.

A less-than-acceptable rating is a sign of danger that the advertising may be parochial in nature and narrow in orientation, because department managers are isolated from the organization's information flow.

WHAT TO DO NOW

1. Contact between the heads of functional departments is essential, but it isn't enough. Knowledge increasingly resides with specialists and technicians on lower management levels. To keep well and fully informed, therefore, you should assign individuals at several levels of the organization to set up and maintain contacts with others.

2. Information that doesn't move tends to age fast—and decisions made with outdated information are almost certain to be wrong. Action is needed to keep data up to date and flowing—and the initiative is up to you to keep open all channels of communication with other departments.

11-H
FUNCTIONAL IMPROVEMENT PROGRAM

	YES (1)	NO (0)	S/P* (½)
1. There is an active, on-going team effort to improve the effectiveness of the firm's advertising and sales promotion. Principal efforts, on a task basis, are directed toward:			
a. more timely and useful feedback on attitudes and response of customers from field to advertising personnel, and	___	___	___
b. increased involvement by advertising people throughout the development of new products and markets, especially during the formative stages.	___	___	___
2. Functions participating on the teams include, depending on the task:			
a. design engineering,	___	___	___
b. marketing,	___	___	___
c. field sales,	___	___	___
d. customer service,	___	___	___
e. information systems, and	___	___	___
f. product distribution.	___	___	___
3. Key advertising agency personnel are actively involved in these efforts.	___	___	___

*SOMETIMES OR PARTIALLY

RATING

Enter number of points scored ☐

Enter number of items on checklist ☐

= ☐ × 100 = ☐ %

WHAT THE RATING SIGNIFIES

Advertising is one of the activities that can benefit immensely from a cross-functional team or task force effort. What this does is to formalize and add structure to the internal communications and coordination effort.

To repeat, advertising should represent the entire organization—the enterprise as a whole—not just marketing. Everyone is an *advertising expert*, of course, so the effort must be controlled to prevent the advertising from becoming a "committee product."

WHAT TO DO NOW

1. Make certain to include a responsible person from the advertising agency on each improvement team, especially if the agency is expected to aid in implementation.

2. Set realistic objectives to ensure success. Repeated failure to meet goals can be demoralizing—especially when the goals are perceived to be set deliberately high to extract extra effort from people.

3. Concentrate improvement efforts on the two aspects of operation that are often deficient; direct customer feedback and early involvement of advertising personnel in new-product development.

11-I
RESOURCES

	YES (1)	NO (0)	S/P* (½)
1. Advertising and sales promotion management is kept informed about company objectives, policies, plans, and programs, through participation in key meetings and access to appropriate business plans, marketing and sales plans, capital budgets, and operating reports.	___	___	___
2. Based on this knowledge and the preceding appraisal, resources are considered to be adequate to meet the needs of the company for product advertising and sales promotion during the next 3, 6, and 12 months, in terms of:			
a. manpower,	___	___	___
b. capabilities,	___	___	___
c. budget funding,	___	___	___

*SOMETIMES OR PARTIALLY

	YES (1)	NO (0)	S/P* (½)
d. agency capabilities,	___	___	___
e. supplier capabilities,	___	___	___
f. computer time and capacity, and	___	___	___
g. support from other company functions.	___	___	___

*SOMETIMES OR PARTIALLY

TOTAL POINTS ☐ + 0 + ☐

= ☐

RATING

Enter number of points scored ☐

Enter number of items on checklist ☐

= × 100 = ☐ %

WHAT THE RATING SIGNIFIES

When assessing resources to determine whether they are adequate for the company's advertising and sales promotion needs for the near-term future, resources other than budget funding must be considered. The creative capabilities of your people are your most important resource. And of course the capabilities and resources of agencies and outside suppliers can be vital to the effectiveness of the effort.

The adequacy of resources can be determined with assurance only when advertising management is well informed about the company's overall goals, policies, and major business development strategies. The agency needs this kind of input, as well, in order to appraise its own resources to support the company (with proper regard for competitive security).

WHAT TO DO NOW

1. The task of assessing resources should be a joint effort involving the agency, and to a lesser extent, major suppliers of sales promotion materials and services.

2. Support by other company departments also can be critical to near-term programs, so their capabilities should be evaluated as well.

3. If human resources are lacking—that is, people with creative ideas and drive—chances are that your advertising dollars are not generating a high return. So providing these resources should be your first priority.

Chapter **12**

How to Use
Product Publicity Productively

When preparing publicity releases on your products or services, it is well to keep in mind that the readers of the printed material are totally self-centered creatures. All they care about is what your product will do for them. The readers, or viewers, or listeners, as the case may be, couldn't care less how much you invested in product design and development, what a superior technical staff your firm employs, or what a marvelous facility produces the product.

Your prospective customers are suspicious and skeptical, as well, with a tendency to regard your claims for the product as "interesting if true." Not only that, but they're an ungrateful lot. Even though you may have served them well in the past they need constant reassurance about your intentions. Their attitude seems to be not so much a case of "what have you done for me lately", as "what are you going to do for me now?"

FOCUS IS WHAT'S
IMPORTANT

Editors are worse. They are not even interested in your product as a product—what they want is a story that will grab their readers' attention. They're not really interested in you, either, as the producer of the product, unless you are so unique that people will want to know about you in which event we're dealing with personal, not product, publicity.

The point of all this is that when you are preparing product publicity, you should first put yourself in the place of typical users or consumers and ask yourself, how does my product meet their needs for utility and personal gratification? Next, you should put yourself in the place of a typical editor and ask yourself, how do I meet his needs for materials that attract, entertain, and satisfy his readers (or audience)?

Of course, if you ask the first question *before* the product gets out of the conceptual or design stage—which is when prospective customers' needs can be factored into the new product—then the resulting product publicity will not only write itself, but it will receive a warm welcome from editors, as well.

Product publicity is not the means to build into the product attributes it does not actually possess. Which is not to say you shouldn't weave some romance or mystique around the product in order to make the release interesting reading. What is warned against is inflated performance claims, with the consequent danger of user dissatisfaction because the product does not measure up to its promises.

KEY AIM OF THE SELF-AUDIT

The main objective of the self-audit is to ensure that product publicity is managed as an important marketing activity which can pave the way for the field salesperson or for direct sales. Also, product publicity should be prepared with the needs of both user and publication in mind. To simply broadcast a description of the product in the hope that some publication will print it, and that someone, somewhere, will read it, is not only wasteful—it is counterproductive.

HOW TO USE THE CHECKLISTS

For each of the statements in the Checklist, compare the condition of your function to the "ideal" as described in the statement. Then:

1. If you consider the statement to be *generally true* of your function, check the YES column.

2. If you consider the statement to be *untrue* of your function, check the NO column.

3. If you consider the statement to be *less than true* (but not totally untrue) of your function, check the SOMETIMES OR PARTIAL column.

4. If the statement does not apply to your particular situation, write "Not Applicable" across the response spaces (or simply draw a line through them).

5. If you lack the data for a definite response, write in "Not Answerable" or "Don't Know."

HOW TO EVALUATE YOUR RESPONSES

When you have completed the checklist, glance over your responses, keeping these points in mind:

1. A negative answer is always unfavorable because it indicates a problem within the function: the greater the number of NOs, the more serious the situation.

2. A positive response is always a good indication. But too many YES answers could indicate that your review is not objective enough.

3. Too many SOMETIMES OR PARTIALLY answers can point to internal weaknesses or to a lack of firm direction.

4. A lot of "Not Applicable" answers could indicate that you are avoiding the issue.

5. A large number of "Not Answerable" or "Don't Know" answers could be symptomatic of inadequate records or data bases.

HOW TO RATE AND SCORE YOUR RESPONSES

When you are satisfied with your responses in general, you are ready to score the Checklist. For your convenience, a self-explanatory Scoring and Rating Block follows each Checklist. This block not only tells you whether the condition of your function is satisfactory, but it also gives you a measure of its effectiveness.

Here's how to total up the points for inclusion in the Scoring and Rating Block:

1. Total up the number of points you scored:
   a. For each YES, give yourself one point.
   b. For each NO, give yourself zero.
   c. For each SOMETIMES OR PARTIALLY, give yourself a half-point.
   d. For each "Not Applicable" answer, give yourself zero and deduct one from the number of items on the Checklist.
   e. For each "Not Answerable" or "Don't Know" answer, give yourself zero.

2. Next divide the total number of points you score by the total number of items (statements) on the Checklist (less items marked "Not Applicable"). You'll get a 1.0 for a perfect score and a fraction for anything less.

3. Multiply the result of step 2 by 100 to arrive at the percentage for your score.

What is a satisfactory rating? A rating of less than 65 percent is unacceptable and calls for an improvement program: Obviously, the lower the rating, the more drastic the action required.

A brief "how-to" example of this Scoring and Rating system follows . . .

EXAMPLE

	YES (1)	NO (0)	S/P* (½)

1. Field sale reports designed to provide information on sales progress contain data on the following topics:

	YES (1)	NO (0)	S/P* (½)
a. sales calls and sales presentations made by salespersons and sales agents,	✓		
b. bids, quotations, and proposals made,	✓		
c. new orders booked,	✓		
d. lost business, and reasons for the loss,		✓	
e. accomplishments toward future orders,			✓
f. performance in filling orders, handling complaints, and otherwise servicing individual customers,	✓		
g. action taken in response to customer requests, such as sending samples, spec sheets, etc.,	✓		
h. accomplishments of significance and value to other members of the sales force.			✓

*SOMETIMES OR PARTIALLY

TOTAL POINTS $\boxed{5}$ + 0 + $\boxed{1}$

= $\boxed{6}$

RATING

$$\frac{\text{Enter number of points scored} \quad \boxed{6}}{\text{Enter number of items on checklist} \quad \boxed{8}} = .75 \times 100 = \boxed{75}\%$$

12-A
ORGANIZATION, ADMINISTRATION, AND OPERATION

	YES (1)	NO (0)	S/P* (½)

1. The use of publicity in trade and technical publications and other media is recognized by company management as an important supplement to paid advertising, and an essential part of new-product development plans and sales plans.

2. This function is shown on organization charts and in managers' position descriptions as an important function of marketing personnel.

3. The function is staffed (not necessarily full time) by experienced professionals trained in product publicity, thoroughly familiar with the company's products, markets, and competition, and knowledgeable about the various media.

4. The marketing budget has a formal allocation of funds to cover all expenses of this activity, including entertainment of media people as required, and professional outside services such as product photography and direct mail services.

5. Product publicity is conducted in a systematic and organized fashion, guided and governed by formal written procedures and standard practices.

6. An up-to-date list is maintained of publications and other media of greatest importance to the company.

7. The product publicity staff is aquainted with the key personnel in each of these media forms.

8. Editors (or reporters) are contacted regularly to check on their current editorial needs.

9. Separate versions of important publicity releases are produced to take account of differing requirements of the various media categories.

10. Product publicity on new products is tailored to the editorial format of particular publications, and the accompanying photos are in proper format.

11. The timing of new product releases is coordinated so that:

    a. there is assurance that product tests have been completed,

    b. salesmen, distributors or others with a need to know have been notified, and

    c. information will be available to answer inquiries.

12. Case histories of company products in real situations are employed whenever possible, combining the product benefit story with customer endorsement.

13. Publication of technical articles originated within the company is recognized as a sales aid and specifically considered in new-product plans.

14. The technical department is regularly checked for leads on possible product technical articles.

15. Engineers are encouraged to take advantage of opportunities for both professional and personal gain in authoring technical articles. Engineers are aware that some technical journals pay authors for published articles.

211

	YES (1)	NO (0)	S/P* (½)

16. Announcements are issued covering changes in personnel importantly concerned with particular products or lines, whenever appropriate.

17. When good coverage of a product news story is obtained, possible ways of following up are promptly explored as by arranging interviews with company engineers and management.

18. A complete and up-to-date product information and photograph file is maintained on major products.

19. A photo and biography file is maintained on unit executives and other personnel importantly concerned with particular product lines.

20. Presentations on the value and uses of product publicity are made at meetings of company management periodically.

21. All inquiries resulting from product publicity are acknowledged, and answered *promptly*, and the appropriate sales representative, distributor, or dealer is notified *promptly*.

22. Mailing lists of customers and prospects are kept up-to-date with names and position titles of key buying influences.

23. Company top management is kept informed of the results of the product publicity effort through periodic summaries and product press clips.

24. All staff members are aware that information about company activities, products and services, and personnel is sensitive—and will be read by competitors as well as prospects.

25. Reprints of product articles are used to get extra mileage out of print publicity.

*SOMETIMES OR PARTIALLY

TOTAL POINTS   ☐ + 0 + ☐

= ☐

RATING

Enter number of points scored ☐
—————————————————— = × 100 = ☐ %
Enter number of items on checklist ☐

WHAT THE RATING SIGNIFIES

Product publicity is low in cost, but it is decidedly not free. If its cost is not provided for in the annual budget, the chances are that it will not be done well. This cost should include the expenses of maintaining amicable business relations with editorial people as well as production costs such as photography, writing, reproduction and mailing.

A less-than-satisfactory rating for the product publicity function is evidence that the company may be failing to exploit an important means of communication with its customers, prospects, and other people who are important to its success. As a consequence, business may be lost to competitors, and the company's reputation as an innovator may suffer.

WHAT TO DO NOW

1. The most important essential for getting your product publicity in print is to meet the editorial needs and format specifications of the publication. Being an advertiser won't take the place of these essentials with most publications.

2. Neither will free lunch for the editor, although this is an acceptable part of maintaining a good relationship.

3. Product publicity can be a "two-edged sword." It informs not only your prospects but your competitors as well. Premature disclosure of a new product could tip them off in time to set up defenses against your play. Targeted direct mail can help avoid this danger.

4. Above all else, product publicity must be timed so that every prospect inquiry will be promptly and thoroughly followed up. This requires that all company personnel involved are kept informed about all releases in time to prepare responses.

5. Smaller firms can benefit from product publicity just as readily as large corporations. Editors don't automatically publish copy just because it came from a large well-known organization—they're seeking interesting material for their readers, regardless of source.

6. Don't assume that your product release has been seen by your prospects just because it was published in one or more media. Use reprints as a direct mail follow-up.

12-B
AUTHORITY, RESPONSIBILITY AND ACCOUNTABILITY

	YES (1)	NO (0)	S/P* (½)
1. Authority has been delegated to a specified manager to expend company funds and assign tasks necessary to ensure that the company gets the maximum benefit from product publicity.	___	___	___
2. Responsibility has been firmly assigned to this manager to staff and manage the activity (not necessarily full time).	___	___	___
3. Responsibility has been assigned to specific individuals to acknowledge and respond fully to prospect inquiries within a specified period of time.	___	___	___
4. The responsibility of other function managers (technical, personnel, etc.) to support and contribute to this activity is known and accepted—including responsibility to respond to inquiries for information in their areas of knowledge.	___	___	___
5. The specified manager is held accountable for serious failure of new products to achieve plan goals because of inadequate or ineffective product publicity, or ineffective follow-up.	___	___	___

*SOMETIMES OR PARTIALLY

TOTAL POINTS [   ] + 0 + [   ]

= [   ]

RATING

Enter number of points scored [   ]
_____ =   × 100 = [   ] %
Enter number of items on checklist [   ]

213

WHAT THE RATING SIGNIFIES

A company can do all the right things to get publicity for its products except one—and may fail to get results. The critical thing is to clearly assign to individuals responsibility for performance and accountability for results.

Product publicity should be an essential element of every new-product plan, and the plan must spell out in specific terms what must be done and who is to do it. The designated individuals must also know clearly what the consequences are for serious or repeated failure to accomplish results.

It may be too obvious to mention that sufficient authority is needed to spend the money and use the company's resources necessary to carry out the plan. Product publicity, it must be repeated, is never free.

A low rating indicates that these essentials may be lacking. As a result, the company may be missing out on important sales opportunities through failure to do a responsible job of product publicity.

WHAT TO DO NOW

1. Review the new-product planning and development procedures to ensure that product publicity is included as an essential part of the product introduction, and that responsibility for it is clearly defined.

2. Review job descriptions to ensure that individuals know and understand their personal responsibilities to carry out the product publicity function, including prompt response and follow-up; and accountability for failure to perform satisfactorily is clearly spelled out.

12-C
MEASUREMENTS, CONTROL REPORTS AND PERFORMANCE RECORDS

	YES (1)	NO (0)	S/P* (½)
1. The effectiveness of the product publicity activity is measured and evaluated regularly and continuously.	___	___	___
2. This effectiveness is measured by comparing the number and quality of actual inquiries by prospects to goals or standards.	___	___	___
3. The number of inquiries from each publicity release in each medium is recorded, in order to compare the effectiveness of the various media used.	___	___	___
4. Each inquiry is logged in and the time of acknowledgement or reply is recorded, to ensure prompt response to prospects.	___	___	___
5. Sales, engineering, and accounting progress reports are routinely analyzed for their significance to the product publicity activity.	___	___	___
6. Costs of the product publicity activity are recorded and routinely compared with budget.	___	___	___

*SOMETIMES OR PARTIALLY

RATING

Enter number of points scored [ ]
—————————————————————————————— = [ ] × 100 = [ ] %
Enter number of items on checklist [ ]

WHAT THE RATING SIGNIFIES

The results from product publicity can vary widely from one media form to another. It's fairly easy to record the inquiries and perform some simple analysis to measure their relative effectiveness. To track these further to determine which publications are most productive in terms of actual buying decisions is a bit more difficult, but is immensely more useful to decision making.

A low rating here indicates that inquiries from product publicity may be handled in a less well organized manner than they deserve. As a consequence the company may be ignoring some potential product sales, and neglecting an important means of enhancing the company image as a product innovator.

WHAT TO DO NOW

1. Inquiries resulting from product publicity can be valuable sales leads, and should be handled with proper regard to their value. This requires a *procedure* for logging-in responses, and assigning them to individuals for follow-up.

2. Set up a *tracking system* to follow the sales lead until it either is converted into a sale or is determined to have no real sales potential.

12-D
OPERATING PERFORMANCE HISTORY

	YES (1)	NO (0)	S/P* (½)
1. A review and analysis has been made of departmental control reports and records for at least one year past.	——	——	——
2. This review shows that all major functional goals were essentially met.	——	——	——
3. This review also shows that there has been a satisfactory improvement in cost-effectiveness of the company's product publicity as measured by prospect inquiries per dollar of expense.	——	——	——
4. There have been no cases of new-product failure to meet plan goals because of inadequate or ineffective product publicity. (Answer "yes" if true.)	——	——	——

5. A review of trade and technical media over the past year shows that the company's product publicity compares well with that of its strongest competitor in terms of:

    a. placement of product publicity releases,

    b. use of product photographs,

    c. number and quality of technical articles and papers authored and published, and

    d. success in reaching major prospect audiences.

6. The expense budget has essentially been met for the past year.

*SOMETIMES OR PARTIALLY

TOTAL POINTS

$$\boxed{} + 0 + \boxed{}$$

$$= \boxed{}$$

RATING

Enter number of points scored $\dfrac{\boxed{}}{\boxed{}}$ = $\boxed{} \times 100 = \boxed{}$ %

Enter number of items on checklist

WHAT THE RATING SIGNIFIES

A periodic review of past performance is an essential part of a product publicity improvement program coupled, of course, with an evaluation of the current status of all major programs. The knowledge that past trends and current progress are favorable gives confidence to set high goals for the future. Success builds on success.

If, on the other hand, a low rating indicates that performance trends and progress are unsatisfactory, improvement goals should be set with caution so as not to create over-expectations that can lead to further failure and disappointment.

WHAT TO DO NOW

1. If publicity program goals were badly missed in the past, make sure that the failure was not a result of unrealistic goal-setting rather than poor performance.

2. Quality of publicity is as important as quantity. Fuzzy photos and sloppy writing can turn off prospects, even if the editor accepts them. If you don't have a professional in-house, use a qualified outside specialist.

12-E
TOP-LEVEL SUPPORT AND GUIDANCE

	YES (1)	NO (0)	S/P* (½)

1. The executive office provides active support, guidance, and recognition of the product publicity activity, through:

	YES (1)	NO (0)	S/P* (½)
a. approval of expense budget,	___	___	___
b. availability for personal follow-up to product news releases,	___	___	___
c. review of and comments on news release summaries, and	___	___	___
d. recognition and reward for outstanding accomplishment.	___	___	___

*SOMETIMES OR PARTIALLY

TOTAL POINTS ☐ + 0 + ☐

= ☐

RATING

Enter number of points scored ☐

───────────────────────────── =   × 100 = ☐ %

Enter number of items on checklist ☐

WHAT THE RATING SIGNIFIES

There is an unfortunate tendency for top-level people to take product publicity for granted, as a kind of free step-child to the advertising and sales promotion activity.

Good product publicity, however, can sometimes outdraw paid advertising in serious prospect inquiries. Top management interest in the activity is essential to keep the people involved buoyed up and productive.

WHAT TO DO NOW

1. Make sure that every evidence of top-level interest is publicized within the department for all to see. Give credit wherever possible to individuals.
2. Make your executive summaries as attractive and interesting as possible. Always emphasize bottom-line *results*. Don't hesitate to ask for comments.

12-F
INNOVATION IN METHODS AND TECHNIQUES

	YES (1)	NO (0)	S/P* (½)

1. Advertising Management keeps actively informed about new and better ways to stimulate prospect interest in the company's products and services through product publicity.

	YES (1)	NO (0)	S/P* (½)
	___	___	___

*SOMETIMES OR PARTIALLY

	YES (1)	NO (0)	S/P* (½)

2. This is done regularly and systematically by means of:

    a. participation in seminars and workshops,

    b. use of outside specialists,

    c. customer and industry contacts,

    d. media contacts,

    e. professional associations,

    f. review of current literature,

    g. solicitation of ideas from personnel at all levels, and

    h. budgets provide funds for such activities.

3. Up-to-date communications means are used to disseminate product publicity, collect inquiries, and respond to prospects, including:

    a. WATS-service,

    b. Telex/TWX,

    c. Western Union Mailgrams,

    d. Audio and Video tapes,

    e. computer terminals,

    f. computerized letters, and

    g. facsimile.

4. The computer is used to store, process, and display information on products, prospects, media coverage and circulation, and results of product news releases.

5. Word processing and text editing equipment is utilized for preparation of publicity.

*SOMETIMES OR PARTIALLY

TOTAL POINTS   ☐   + 0 +   ☐

= ☐

RATING

Enter number of points scored ☐
———————————————————— = × 100 = ☐ %
Enter number of items on checklist ☐

WHAT THE RATING SIGNIFIES

Prospects and customers are overwhelmed by information in today's media world. At the same time they are hungry for information that will help them directly. In an age of fifteen-second TV commercials, a product story has to be told quickly and dramatically in order to get attention, hold interest, and stimulate action.

A low rating here indicates that the company may be relying too heavily on outmoded methods of preparing and disseminating product information, with the consequent danger that it will get lost in the daily blizzard of publicity that falls on your prospects' desks.

1. Dramatize the facts—but never let the drama overwhelm the facts.

2. Always emphasize *benefits* to the user. Your prospects are interested only in what your product can do for them, not how much time and money you spent on its development, or what a marvelous new factory it is produced in.

3. New developments in word processing and communications equipment can make the product publicity activity more productive—and the resulting publicity enormously more effective. Don't wait until your competitor starts using it—and make sure your media contacts know that you're using up-to-date methods (they might even publicize it.)

12-G
INTERFUNCTIONAL COMMUNICATIONS AND COORDINATION

	YES (1)	NO (0)	S/P* (½)
1. Personnel responsible for product publicity maintain close, continuous, and harmonious working relations with other functions of the business, especially new-product design and development, product distribution, and sales.	——	——	——
2. Product publicity is circulated internally *in advance* of its appearance.	——	——	——
3. Other departments cooperate fully in:			
a. preparation and dissemination of product publicity,	——	——	——
b. responding to inquiries, and	——	——	——
c. following up leads.	——	——	——
4. Technical people are all responsive to requests for journal articles.	——	——	——
5. Product publicity personnel periodically accompany field sales and/or customer service people on customer calls in order to experience customer reactions first-hand.	——	——	——
6. Product publicity personnel are involved with new-product developments at an early stage of their development.	——	——	——

*SOMETIMES OR PARTIALLY

TOTAL POINTS   [ ] + 0 + [ ]

= [ ]

RATING

Enter number of points scored [ ]

Enter number of items on checklist [ ]

= × 100 = [ ] %

Product publicity personnel perform an important data processing and coordinating function. They collect data from engineering, marketing, and other departments and process it into information designed to *create awareness, build comprehension and conviction,* and *cause action* on the part of prospective purchasers of the product.

Needless to say, prompt and thorough follow-up to product news releases is essential. Nothing is more futile than a customer inquiry that sits unanswered on the desk of an engineer or a sales manager.

To this end, close and harmonious relationships with other functions are a key ingredient for successful product publicity. A low rating in this section is an indication that these relationships may be lacking, with the result that product publicity may lack real substance and real conviction, or may lack systematic follow through.

WHAT TO DO NOW

1. It is better to issue no publicity at all than poorly written publicity that lacks solid facts and a point of view. Publicity "boilerplate" can cause a negative impression on editors, distributors, prospects, and customers. It requires more effort to overcome a bad impression than to create a good one in the first place.

2. Circulate all published product publicity widely within the organization, especially to people who contributed to it. (It doesn't hurt to attach a buckslip acknowledging the contributors, with thanks.)

12-H
FUNCTIONAL IMPROVEMENT PROGRAM

	YES (1)	NO (0)	S/P* (½)
1. There is an active, on-going team effort to improve the effectiveness of the company's product publicity. Major efforts are aimed at:			
a. faster and better response to inquiries about products,	___	___	___
b. more timely and relevant feedback from field sales, customer service, and distribution about customer reaction to publicity,	___	___	___
c. improved tracking of responses to product publicity from inquiry to action.	___	___	___
2. The team has representation from (depending on the task):			
a. field sales and service,	___	___	___
b. communications,	___	___	___
c. product distribution,	___	___	___
d. advertising and sales promotion, and	___	___	___
e. engineering and development.	___	___	___

*SOMETIMES OR PARTIALLY

TOTAL POINTS   ☐ + 0 + ☐

= ☐

RATING

Enter number of points scored ☐

─────────────────────────────   =   × 100 = ☐ %

Enter number of items on checklist ☐

WHAT THE RATING SIGNIFIES

Because of product publicity's coordinating role, an organized cross-functional team effort can pay dividends in improved results. This approach has the added benefit of harmonizing the objectives of the various functions, and focusing these goals on the all-important marketplace.

A good rating here is evidence of strong leadership by the product publicity function in harnessing the energies of people in the several departments toward making the company more competitive.

WHAT TO DO NOW

1. You must take the initiative and the lead in this effort. The kind of internal coordination and cooperation represented by this approach is not a natural function of organizations. It must be made to happen.

2. Make sure that the other participants have a voice in setting the objectives of the team. Full commitment to the goals by every member is crucial to results.

12-1
RESOURCES

	YES (1)	NO (0)	S/P* (½)
1. Personnel responsible for product publicity are kept informed about the company's objectives, policies, plans, and programs through involvement in marketing planning, sales planning, and access to appropriate internal operating reports.	———	———	———
2. Product publicity people are kept informed about the progress of new products throughout their development.	———	———	———
3. Based on this knowledge, resources for product publicity are considered adequate to meet the needs of the company for the next three, six, and twelve months, in terms of:			
a. manpower,	———	———	———
b. expense budget funding,	———	———	———
c. staff capabilities,	———	———	———
d. communications,	———	———	———
e. outside services,	———	———	———
f. computer time and capacity,	———	———	———
g. other functional support, and	———	———	———
h. access to word processing equipment, if required.	———	———	———

*SOMETIMES OR PARTIALLY

TOTAL POINTS ☐ + 0 + ☐

= ☐

RATING

Enter number of points scored ☐

——————————————————————— = ×100 = ☐ %

Enter number of items on checklist ☐

221

WHAT THE RATING SIGNIFIES

One of the resources needed for effective product publicity is data—lots of it. Data is useless, however, without the intelligence to organize it into information in a form that causes buyer action. Human resources, especially brain power, therefore are the most important.

Physical resources to handle, transmit, and receive information are less critical but still necessary for productive output. A less-than-satisfactory rating indicates a need for more productive utilization of the firm's resources in this important effort.

WHAT TO DO NOW

1. Make certain the product publicity personnel are in the company's information loop, but ensure that they know and understand that sensitive company information must be handled with discretion.

2. The capabilities of people and resources of other functions to contribute to and support the product publicity activity are important, and should be appraised as part of this evaluation.

Chapter **13**

Evaluating Agency/ Company Relations

This section is concerned with the manner in which the company manages its relations with advertising agencies and providers of sales promotional material. The appraisal is intended to cover the technical competence, creative ability, administrative efficiency, cooperativeness, and general expertise of the outside organizations employed by the firm, either contractually or on a project basis.

WHEN + WHY TO EVALUATE AGENCY/ COMPANY RELATIONS

Advertising agencies, sales promotion suppliers, exhibit suppliers, design houses, and other vendors in the promotional field typically offer both creativity and productive methods of implementing creative ideas. These providers and vendors are dynamic and changing organizations, of course, so a systematic and continuing program of evaluation is needed in order to ensure that they continually deliver maximum value to the company. Because their principal product is brain power, their value and usefulness can often change dramatically with a change in key personnel.

The first step in evaluating the agency/company relationship is to make an evaluation of the leadership, guidance, and information that the company provides to the agency. To a great extent, the quality of input by the company governs the quality of the output by the agency/supplier. To do the best job, agencies and suppliers need to know *all* the facts, not just what company personnel might think are the important ones. This implies a high degree of trust in the agency's people.

To be effective, agency/supplier relationships and performance must be assessed regularly. In practice, however, assessments tend to be made only where there has been a noticeable decline in performance. To a certain extent, the assessment is automatic; after every job, the question is asked, "How does the performance or material considered today compare with the agency's or supplier's usual standards?"

Useful as this can be, a more formal and systematic assessment is called for on a periodic basis. How often this is done will vary from one company to another, but as a general rule, it should be done at least every six months.

EVERY SIZE COMPANY CAN BENEFIT FROM AD AGENCIES

A company that is small in size and sales volume can benefit from an advertising agency relationship just as much as a giant corporation. Regardless of size, every firm needs the professionalism and creativity that a competent advertising agency can impart to the sales message. It is possible, of course, for the firm to have an in-house organization staffed to handle all of its advertising and sales promotion. Even if this can be afforded—which is unlikely for most companies—it often serves to deprive the company of the creativity that advertising agencies possess. A well-known agency head put it this way: "Many clients do their own marketing, buy their media, have superb research. But is there any advertiser with an excellent creative department? Creative people prefer an agency environment, the challenge of many products, the stimulation of other disciplines, all concerned with advertising. Advertisers need agencies for the creative product best produced by agencies."

The object for the growing small firm is to find an agency whose management is farsighted enough to invest some current time and talent to help the small firm grow faster—to forego some current income for the sake of a profitable relationship later when the firm's advertising budget may be substantial. A progressive agency should have some business development funds budgeted for such worthwhile purposes. The advertiser should not expect a free ride, of course, but the cost will probably be a good deal less than the agency's normal fees to established firms.

A northern New Jersey producer of ultrasonic testing equipment doubled its annual growth rate through such an arrangement with an area agency. The firm is now a valued and profitable account of the agency—which has also grown substantially in volume of billings.

KEY AIM OF THE SELF-AUDIT

The major objective of this appraisal of advertising agency and sales promotion supplier performance and relationships with the company is to ensure a high level of creative contribution to "in-house" efforts. This contribution should be superior in effectiveness at reasonable costs, and therefore constitute a genuine contribution to the company's success in the marketplace.

HOW TO USE THE CHECKLISTS

For each of the statements in the Checklist, compare the condition of your function to the "ideal" as described in the statement. Then:

1. If you consider the statement to be *generally true* of your function, check the YES column.

2. If you consider the statement to be *untrue* of your function, check the NO column.

3. If you consider the statement to be *less than true* (but not totally untrue) of your function, check the SOMETIMES OR PARTIAL column.

4. If the statement does not apply to your particular situation, write "Not Applicable" across the response spaces (or simply draw a line through them).

5. If you lack the data for a definite response, write in "Not Answerable" or "Don't Know."

HOW TO EVALUATE YOUR RESPONSES

When you have completed the checklist, glance over your responses, keeping these points in mind:

1. A negative answer is always unfavorable because it indicates a problem within the function: the greater the number of NOs, the more serious the situation.

2. A positive response is always a good indication. But too many YES answers could indicate that your review is not objective enough.

3. Too many SOMETIMES OR PARTIALLY answers can point to internal weaknesses or to a lack of firm direction.

4. A lot of "Not Applicable" answers could indicate that you are avoiding the issue.

5. A large number of "Not Answerable" or "Don't Know" answers could be symptomatic of inadequate records or data bases.

HOW TO RATE AND SCORE YOUR RESPONSES

When you are satisfied with your responses in general, you are ready to score the Checklist. For your convenience, a self-explanatory Scoring and Rating Block follows each Checklist. This block not only tells you whether the condition of your function is satisfactory, but it also gives you a measure of its effectiveness.

Here's how to total up the points for inclusion in the Scoring and Rating Block:

1. Total up the number of points you scored:
   a. For each YES, give yourself one point.
   b. For each NO, give yourself zero.
   c. For each SOMETIMES OR PARTIALLY, give yourself a half-point.
   d. For each "Not Applicable" answer, give yourself zero and deduct one from the number of items on the Checklist.
   e. For each "Not Answerable" or "Don't Know" answer, give yourself zero.

2. Next divide the total number of points you score by the total number of items (statements) on the Checklist (less items marked "Not Applicable"). You'll get a 1.0 for a perfect score and a fraction for anything less.

3. Multiply the result of step 2 by 100 to arrive at the percentage for your score.

What is a satisfactory rating? A rating of less than 65 percent is unacceptable and calls for an improvement program: Obviously, the lower the rating, the more drastic the action required.

A brief "how-to" example of this Scoring and Rating system follows . . .

EXAMPLE

	YES (1)	NO (0)	S/P* (½)
1. Field sale reports designed to provide information on sales progress contain data on the following topics:			
a. sales calls and sales presentations made by salespersons and sales agents,	✓		
b. bids, quotations, and proposals made,	✓		
c. new orders booked,	✓		
d. lost business, and reasons for the loss,		✓	
e. accomplishments toward future orders,			✓
f. performance in filling orders, handling complaints, and otherwise servicing individual customers,	✓		
g. action taken in response to customer requests, such as sending samples, spec sheets, etc.,	✓		
h. accomplishments of significance and value to other members of the sales force.			✓

*SOMETIMES OR PARTIALLY

TOTAL POINTS $\boxed{5}$ + 0 + $\boxed{1}$

= $\boxed{6}$

RATING

$$\frac{\text{Enter number of points scored} \quad \boxed{6}}{\text{Enter number of items on checklist} \quad \boxed{8}} = .75 \times 100 = \boxed{75}\ \%$$

226

13-A
ORGANIZATION, ADMINISTRATION, AND OPERATION

	YES (1)	NO (0)	S/P* (½)

1. The quality of the relationship between the company and its advertising agencies and providers of sales promotion materials and services is considered to be vital to the effectiveness of the advertising/sales promotion function. _____ _____ _____

2. The management of this relationship and the performance of agencies/suppliers is recognized on organization charts and in manager's position descriptions as an important function of marketing. _____ _____ _____

3. The function is organized internally to provide active and productive direction to the activities of advertising agencies and suppliers of sales promotion materials. _____ _____ _____

4. The function is staffed and supervised by advertising/sales promotion professionals who know the company, its products, and its markets. _____ _____ _____

5. The marketing budget provides an allocation of funds to cover expenses of this management function, separate from the advertising itself. _____ _____ _____

6. Relations between the company and its agencies and suppliers are guided and governed by formal written procedures and standard practices. _____ _____ _____

7. The agency is kept fully informed about the company's goals, activities, and progress, within the constraints of competitive security. _____ _____ _____

8. Meetings are held with the advertising agency on a regularly scheduled basis to review new developments concerning the company, its products and markets, and pany's account. _____ _____ _____

9. The agency issues a written conference report on all agency/client meetings within 48 hours. _____ _____ _____

10. A regularly scheduled review is made of the agency's performance during the preceding year to compare its work with that of the previous year and with current competitive efforts. _____ _____ _____

11. A responsible member of agency management is actively involved in the company's account. _____ _____ _____

12. The agency account group is staffed adequately with experienced persons. _____ _____ _____

13. The advertising agency or sales promotion supplier provides a completion date promise for each new assignment it receives. _____ _____ _____

14. The company has an effective follow-up procedure to see that the agency or supplier delivers on time. _____ _____ _____

15. The amount and variety of additional services (research, merchandising, etc.) provided by the advertising agency are considered satisfactory in relation to the amount of billings. _____ _____ _____

16. The advertising agency is generally responsive to requests for additional services, and when charges are made they are considered to be justified. _____ _____ _____

17. a. The advertising agency is invited once a year to submit an independent assessment of the company's advertising and sales promotion policies, organization, and programs. _____ _____ _____

	YES (1)	NO (0)	S/P* (½)

b. The agency's response to this request is candid and contains useful ideas for improvement.

c. The company gives sincere consideration to the agency's recommendations.

18. Advertising copy submitted by the agency is free of technical and grammatical errors at all stages of development.

19. Final art and copy submitted for approval is invariably free of errors and defects.

20. Legal and technical clearance for advertising and sales promotion art and copy is obtained without serious delay.

21. a. The firm has a long-standing association with its providers of sales promotion materials.

b. This association is based on suppliers' overall performance in meeting the company's sales promotion needs, not simply on cost factors alone (they are not always low bidder).

c. These suppliers regularly come up with unsolicited new ideas to improve the company's sales promotion efforts.

22. All agency and vendor invoices are routinely verified for accuracy, and discrepancies are brought to their attention promptly for reconciliation.

23. Cash discounts for prompt payment are routinely taken, and credit for them reflected in the annual budget.

*SOMETIMES OR PARTIALLY

TOTAL POINTS ☐ + 0 + ☐ = ☐

RATING

Enter number of points scored ☐ / Enter number of items on checklist ☐ = × 100 = ☐ %

WHAT THE RATING SIGNIFIES

The performance and effectiveness of the advertising/sales promotion activity is to a large extent a function of the quality and strength of the relationship between the company and its advertising agencies and providers of sales promotion materials and services. In situations where the advertising department is not a producer of advertising itself, but a *manager* of outside services, effectiveness can be a direct function of the relationship.

A less-than-acceptable rating on agency/company relations is an indication that the dealings between the company and its agency and suppliers are conducted on a less-than-businesslike basis. As a consequence, the company's advertising and sales promotion may be costing more than they should, or their effectiveness may be lower than they could be, or both.

In such a case, the fault seldom lies totally with one or the other, but is usually a shared accountability. Regardless of fault, it is primarily the responsibility of the company to repair the defective relationship.

WHAT TO DO NOW

1. Review the procedures and organization for keeping agency personnel informed about the company, its products and services, and its business development programs. If these are found wanting, set up a remedial program at once.

2. Review the agency/company relationship to ensure that there exists a clear understanding of exactly what each is supposed to do. This may require a memorandum of agreement supplement to the contract.

3. Review all points of contact between agency and company to ensure that personal frictions and conflicts are not impairing the effectiveness of the partnership. If there are irreparable differences, changes in personnel assignments either in company or agency may be called for.

4. A periodic round table meeting between key members of each organization can help to clear up misperceptions and disagreements. *You must control the agenda* to keep the focus on major issues. Make clear, specific action assignments and follow-up until these are completed.

5. Changing agencies seldom resolves the problem, and should be done only after all alternatives have been tried.

13-B
AUTHORITY, RESPONSIBILITY, AND ACCOUNTABILITY

	YES (1)	NO (0)	S/P* (½)
1. Authority has been delegated to the manager of advertising and sales promotion to expend company funds and enter into contacts on behalf of the company, for the purpose of carrying out an effective advertising and sales promotion program.	———	———	———
2. Responsibility has been firmly assigned to the manager to staff and manage an organization capable of directing and controlling the performance of advertising agencies and providers of sales promotion materials and services.	———	———	———
3. The manager is also responsible to select qualified, responsible agencies and suppliers, and to negotiate terms that are favorable to the company and fair to agencies and vendors.	———	———	———
4. Department personnel are responsible to keep the agencies/suppliers well informed about company matters that affect their work for the company.	———	———	———
5. The manager is held accountable for:			
a. serious failure to meet marketing plan or sales plan goals,	———	———	———
b. failure of new products to meet sales goals,	———	———	———
c. excessive costs of advertising or sales promotion, or	———	———	———
d. serious schedule delays on advertising or sales promotion projects, and	———	———	———
e. serious deterioration of the company "image."	———	———	———

Any of these problems may be caused by inadequate or ineffective performance by advertising agencies or suppliers.

□ + 0 + □

= □

RATING

Enter number of points scored □

Enter number of items on checklist □

= × 100 = □ %

WHAT THE RATING SIGNIFIES

Agencies and suppliers must be "managed" just as firmly and efficiently as the internal functions of the company. An advertising agency may, in fact, spend more of the firm's money than many internal departments. Managing the agency's work for the company calls for unique management skills—a blend of tight financial control and creative freedom in order to get the maximum value out of the relationship.

The manager of the function must have firm delegated authority to enter into contracts—and the responsibilities and accountabilities that this authority entails must be clearly defined. It almost goes without saying that the manager cannot delegate these to the agency. If the advertising programs fail, the manager alone must bear the blame—provided, it must be added, that authority was genuine and not withdrawn after it was granted through budget limitations, withheld resources, restrictions on scope of activity, or failure by higher management to honor and support his/her decisions.

A less-than-satisfactory rating indicates that one or more of these essentials is lacking, with the consequent danger of later finger-pointing in the case of failure.

WHAT TO DO NOW

1. Make certain that your authority to expend funds and sign contracts is firm, visible to all, and unequivocal—and its limits are clearly spelled out.

2. Accountability and responsibility should be defined in terms of results, not simply activity.

3. Agencies and suppliers must, on their part, demonstrate responsibility and accept accountability for failure. This clearly implies that they must do what they believe is right professionally and ethically—that one of their responsibilities is to tell you when you're wrong. The last thing you need is an agency that simply carries out orders without question, and then when trouble arises, disclaims responsibility saying, "We did what you told us to do."

13-C
MEASUREMENTS, CONTROL REPORTS, AND PERFORMANCE RECORDS

	YES (1)	NO (0)	S/P* (½)
1. The effectiveness of the company's advertising agencies and providers of sales promotion materials and services is measured and evaluated regularly and continuously.	_____	_____	_____
2. This effectiveness is measured by comparing their actual performance and results to certain benchmarks, targets, or standards, such as:			
a. response by prospective buyers,	_____	_____	_____
b. completing projects on time and within cost budgets, and	_____	_____	_____
c. meeting overall cost budgets.	_____	_____	_____
3. All advertising programs and sales promotion projects contain firm time and cost schedules.	_____	_____	_____
4. Agencies and vendors are required to report progress weekly and monthly, and to "red flag" potential problems early.	_____	_____	_____
5. Cost of outside work is periodically compared with estimates of cost if done internally.	_____	_____	_____
6. Major projects are put out for competitive bids routinely, although work is awarded on the basis of factors other than price alone.	_____	_____	_____

*SOMETIMES OR PARTIALLY

TOTAL POINTS [ ] + 0 + [ ]

= [ ]

RATING

Enter number of points scored [ ]
─────────────────────────────── = × 100 = [ ] %
Enter number of items on checklist [ ]

WHAT THE RATING SIGNIFIES

Time and cost are critical to the effectiveness of advertising and sales promotion. Every program and project should be controlled to firm time and cost schedules. This does not constrain creative thought and innovative action on the part of both members of the relationship; it can in fact, stimulate and enhance these factors.

A low rating on measurements and controls is evidence that management may have the misconception that innovation cannot be managed, and that creativity flourishes only in a permissive environment. As a consequence, market opportunities may be missed through schedule delays, or excessive costs may prevent full exploitation of these opportunities.

WHAT TO DO NOW

1. If your advertising agency or providers of sales promotion materials and services decline to work to firm cost and time schedules, or repeatedly fail to comply with them, you have grounds for terminating the

relationship, perhaps the only valid grounds for doing so aside from dishonesty or unethical dealings.

2. All measurements must be in terms of output, not activity. The true output of advertising is the volume and quality of response by prospective buyers—good sales leads, firm inquiries, new orders, sales and billings. Ratings and professional acclaim are gratifying, but they are not genuine output.

3. Stay with suppliers who perform and make sure that your account is profitable to them. If they regularly lose money on your account they may not be around when you need them. The "shopper" who buys advertising on price only will soon discover this fact.

13-D
OPERATING PERFORMANCE HISTORY

	YES (1)	NO (0)	S/P* (½)
1. A review and analysis has been made of records and control reports for at least one year past, for the purpose of assessing past performance.	___	___	___
2. This review shows that during the past year major advertising and sales promotion goals were essentially met.	___	___	___
3. The review also shows an improving trend during the past year in projects completed on time and within cost estimates.	___	___	___
4. During the past year, the effectiveness of advertising and sales promotion improved, as measured by the quantity and quality of responses by prospective purchasers.	___	___	___
5. During the past year, at least two important improvement suggestions offered by agencies/suppliers were adopted.	___	___	___
6. Cost and expense budgets were essentially met.	___	___	___
7. During the past year, the agency or supplier has met scheduled due dates for assignments better than 90 percent of the time.	___	___	___

*SOMETIMES OR PARTIALLY

TOTAL POINTS   [   ] + 0 + [   ]

= [   ]

RATING

Enter number of points scored [   ]
───────────────────────────────────── =   × 100 = [   ] %
Enter number of items on checklist [   ]

WHAT THE RATING SIGNIFIES   The validity of the measurements can be proven only in the light of past performance. And the performance of the function can be evaluated only in the same light.

A low rating indicates that the "track record" of the agency/company relationship has not been as good as it could have been. As a consequence, a record of good performance must be created before future goals will be accepted.

WHAT TO DO NOW

1. Other factors in the agency/company relationship have a bearing on performance, but this factor is perhaps the most crucial one to productivity, and really encompasses all others.

2. You need at least one year's actual performance in order to discern trends. Unfavorable trends need time to turn around—a downtrend first has to be stopped before it can turn upward.

3. Review your past goals to make sure they were realistic and achievable. Many an agency has been fired for failure to achieve impossible objectives.

13-E
TOP-LEVEL SUPPORT AND GUIDANCE

	YES (1)	NO (0)	S/P* (½)
1. The executive office provides active support and guidance to the agency/company relationship through:			
a. approval of advertising and expense budgets,	———	———	———
b. participation in review meetings of advertising program plans,	———	———	———
c. informed comments on progress reports,	———	———	———
d. recognition and reward for outstanding accomplishment, and	———	———	———
e. a personal relationship with the manager of advertising/sales promotion and the agency principal together.	———	———	———

*SOMETIMES OR PARTIALLY

TOTAL POINTS [ ] + 0 + [ ] = [ ]

RATING

Enter number of points scored [ ]

─────────────────────────────── = [ ] × 100 = [ ] %

Enter number of items on checklist [ ]

WHAT THE RATING SIGNIFIES

Regardless of the size of the advertising budget, advertising is the face of the business that is seen by the most people. Top management, therefore, should take an active role in fostering a productive relationship between the company and its advertising agencies and suppliers, one that will result in advertising that shows the best face of the company. A low rating suggests that the role of the executive office may be passive rather than active.

An over-active executive can create problems, too. When every piece of copy and every layout has to be OK'd by the top boss, productivity and creativity suffer. There's no known cure for this, but if it can't be tolerated, a move to a less stifling environment might be called for.

WHAT TO DO NOW

1. Try to strike a balance between too little and too much top-level involvement in the agency/company relationship. When schedule dates are missed because of too many people in the approval process, it's your obligation to demand a change.

2. A balance is needed, also, between too early and too late involvement. Too early, and creative ideas can be crushed before they are fully formed. Too late, and a great deal of work may have to be redone.

13-F
INNOVATION IN METHODS AND TECHNIQUES

	YES (1)	NO (0)	S/P* (½)
1. Advertising and sales promotion management actively seeks ways to improve coordination and control of the advertising and sales promotion work between the company and its agencies and suppliers.	___	___	___
2. Agency management and vendor management also participate actively in this search.	___	___	___
3. To this end, management actively keeps current on new developments through:			
a. seminars and workshops,	___	___	___
b. surveys of current literature,	___	___	___
c. industry contacts,	___	___	___
d. professional associations,	___	___	___
e. outside specialists,	___	___	___
f. solicitation of ideas from many sources, and	___	___	___
g. budgets provide funds for such activities.	___	___	___
4. The computer is used to store, process, and display information on progress of major programs and projects, advertising media, response to advertising and sales promotion, costs vs. budgets, and other performance factors.	___	___	___

*SOMETIMES OR PARTIALLY

TOTAL POINTS [ ] + 0 + [ ]

= [ ]

RATING

Enter number of points scored [ ]
——————————————————————— = × 100 = [ ] %
Enter number of items on checklist [ ]

Advertising people justifiably pride themselves on their creativity. The same passion for innovation should mark the search for ways to improve the effectiveness of the agency/company partnership.

A low rating here indicates that this search is not conducted systematically. As a result, the two-way relationship may lose its effectiveness over time for lack of new ideas.

WHAT TO DO NOW

1. The agency and suppliers should be required to participate in the search for new methods as a part of their assignment, and should be rated on their contributions in this area as well as in others.

2. The agency/company relationship is above all a set of relationships between individuals. Any idea that enhances these human relations is grist for the mill.

13-G
INTERFUNCTIONAL COMMUNICATIONS AND COORDINATION

	YES (1)	NO (0)	S/P* (½)

1. Close and harmonious working relations are maintained at several levels with other functions of the business and with agency personnel.

2. Engineering, production, distribution, legal, sales and marketing personnel are responsive to requests for information and assistance to the company's agencies and vendors of sales promotion materials.

3. Managers of other functions are invited to participate in meetings and express their views on current and proposed advertising and sales promotion programs.

*SOMETIMES OR PARTIALLY

TOTAL POINTS ☐ + 0 + ☐

= ☐

RATING

Enter number of points scored ☐
—————————————————— = × 100 = ☐ %
Enter number of items on checklist ☐

WHAT THE RATING SIGNIFIES

In a very real sense, the true role of advertising and sales promotion management is to act as a two-way liaison between the other business functions—sales, engineering, marketing, general management, etc.—and the company's agencies and suppliers. The agency's role, of course, is to process the input from these important activities into selling messages.

A less than satisfactory rating indicates that the advertising department is not organized and managed as a coordinating function, but rather is perceived to be somewhat apart, independent of other company activities. If other evidence corroborates this conclusion, then the company's advertising and sales promotion lacks input from the other functions, and thus may tend to lack genuine substance.

WHAT TO DO NOW

1. Recognize that *information* is the principal commodity you're dealing with. The better the information you provide to the agency, other things being equal, the better the advertising produced.

2. It's your responsibility to get the other functions involved. They all have other pressures on their time and energies. Make sure that their contributions of information are acknowledged and show them how these contributions are used.

13-H
FUNCTIONAL IMPROVEMENT PROGRAM

	YES (1)	NO (0)	S/P* (½)
1. There is a formal, organized cross-functional team effort to improve the quality and effectiveness of the relationship between the company and its advertising agencies and suppliers of sales promotion materials and services.	___	___	___
2. Primary efforts are directed at:			
a. earlier participation of advertising people in new-product and new-market development programs,	___	___	___
b. more effective communication between company functions and the agency, and	___	___	___
c. improved timing and coordination of advertising and sales promotion programs with other company activities.	___	___	___
3. Company functions participating in the effort are, depending on the task:			
a. product design and development,	___	___	___
b. marketing,	___	___	___
c. sales, and	___	___	___
d. product distribution.	___	___	___

*SOMETIMES OR PARTIALLY

TOTAL POINTS   [ ] + 0 + [ ]

= [ ]

RATING

Enter number of points scored [ ]

Enter number of items on checklist [ ]

= × 100 = [ ] %

WHAT THE RATING SIGNIFIES

The two most critical success factors for advertising and sales promotion are *high quality* of the selling messages and *strategic timing*. Neither is sufficient alone; both are needed. Timing is particularly important. Nothing is more futile or devastating to morale, for example, than a brilliant sales promotion program that fails because manufacturing and product distribution are unable to support it with adequate stocks in dealers' hands to meet demand.

It is far from uncommon for a new product to be announced with considerable fanfare long before it is fully debugged and ready for the market. One such case was the electric heat pump, which was brought to market in the early 1970s and failed miserably. It took about ten years to live down its bad reputation.

A team approach with representation by engineering, quality assurance, and other key interests can help prevent such occurrences.

WHAT TO DO NOW

1. Sales and product distribution should be members of the team regardless of the specific task assignment. Without their support, the chances for success of any improvement program are small.

2. The agency should always be represented on the team as a full participant.

13-1
RESOURCES

	YES (1)	NO (0)	S/P* (½)
1. Advertising management and key agency people are kept informed about major company goals, policies, plans, and programs through joint involvement in key marketing meetings, and access to appropriate marketing plans, sales plans, and operating reports (with due regard for the security of confidential information).	———	———	———
2. Based on this knowledge, resources for managing the agency/company relationship are considered adequate to meet the needs of the company during the next three, six, and twelve months, in terms of:			
a. manpower,	———	———	———
b. expense budget,	———	———	———
c. staff capabilities,	———	———	———
d. communications,	———	———	———
e. information systems,	———	———	———
f. computer time and capacity, and	———	———	———
g. support by other company functions.	———	———	———

*SOMETIMES OR PARTIALLY

TOTAL POINTS [ ] + 0 + [ ]

= [ ]

RATING

Enter number of points scored [ ]
————————————————————————— = × 100 = [ ] %
Enter number of items on checklist [ ]

WHAT THE RATING SIGNIFIES

It does not require a large investment in resources to create and maintain a productive working relationship between the company and its agencies and suppliers. The key resources needed are human resources. The next most critical requirement is communications—a full and free flow of information between company and agency.

It requires considerable courage for advertising management to permit other company functions to communicate directly with agency people, for there is always a risk that a piece of information may be used out of context, or may be mistimed in its release. Nevertheless, open channels of communication are vital to the productivity of the relationship. The task of advertising management is to ensure that appropriate safeguards are in place to prevent misuse of company data or violation of competitive security.

A "no" rating on point 1 indicates that open communications may be lacking. As a consequence, people's efforts may be uncoordinated with others in the company and with the agency.

WHAT TO DO NOW

1. Make sure that procedures for proper handling of company information are up-to-date and effective—and are known to both company and agency personnel.

2. Make sure that these procedures are not so restrictive as to inhibit creative advertising output.

3. Company liaison with the agency should be on several levels, and there should be frequent communication between these levels.

4. If resources are lacking, set up a program to get them. Good intentions are not enough—you need a plan of action with goals, deadlines, and assignment of responsibility for results.

THE BOTTOM LINE

Modern life would be pretty dull without advertising. It's probably not stretching a point to say that modern life as we know it wouldn't even exist without advertising, sales promotion, and product publicity. It is through these vital tools of communication that we, as consumers, learn about what is new and better in products and services to make our lives more interesting and easier.

For the business organization—of any size—professional advertising, sales promotion, and publicity are absolutely essential to the firm's productivity and profitability. The more professional these activities are, and the more they are coordinated with other marketing and sales activities, the higher the company's productivity and profitability will be, other things being equal.

Need for Periodic Evaluation

It is necessary, therefore, to review and appraise these activities regularly and in a systematic manner in order to ensure that they are professionally managed and conducted, as well as to expose weaknesses for corrective action.

The advertising department of an East Coast building products manufacturer has used the checklist self-appraisal with good results to solve some deep-seated problems, set new goals, and improve the department's creative output.

A review by the advertising manager of the appraisals of advertising, sales promotion, product publicity, and agency relations made it painfully clear that subordinate managers were working to different goals than those of the department head. Not only that, their various goals were often at cross purposes to each other. To compound the problem, there was a lack of clear understanding by subordinates of the corporate policies that affected the firm's advertising posture.

The department was also suffering from some rather common ailments among advertising sections of large corporations. Some of its best creative work was "nit-picked" to death by topside executives and lawyers. Strong product themes were diluted and weakened when top management added descriptions of the company's production facilities, the history of the firm, and photos of the board chairman. And the company's advertising agency seemed to be more interested in winning creative awards than in promoting the firm's products.

The department head discovered, through his own self-audit, that his authority was limited by requirements for higher level approval on relatively minor expenditures, and severe restrictions on authority to negotiate and sign contracts with outside agencies and suppliers.

One of the most forceful actions taken by the advertising manager was to insist that an advertising program, once OK'd by top management in concept and story board form, was not subject to further critique and change. This meant, of course, that he had to accept full responsibility for results and complete accountability for failure, whereas before he could always "get off the hook" by blaming the failure on the changes made by others. The manager's delegation of authority was also broadened and put in writing, to give him freedom of action and power needed to deal effectively with agencies and suppliers.

A remedial program was put into effect to define and clarify policy, coordinate objectives, and reconcile differences among managers. The agency was brought into line by setting measurable goals for each advertising and sales promotion program in terms of number and quality of prospect inquiries. One result was to provide field sales with better sales leads, which effectively increased selling productivity by over 65 percent as measured by closed sales.

SUMMARY OF SELF-AUDIT RATINGS
AND FUNCTIONAL IMPROVEMENT GOALS

If you wish, you may summarize the ratings for each function at the end of each section, on this "Summary Rating" form. (A "function" is the equivalent of a chapter.) The rating is simply an arithmetic average of the ratings on Checklists A through I—that is, the total divided by 9. This form also provides space for listing the Improvement Goals for each function.

Under each function, enter the rating percentage for each Checklist section, A through I. "Function Number 1," for example, is the first (1st) chapter in the section, regardless of its number in the book—5, 11, or so on. The Summary Rating is the total of each column divided by 9, to give you an average rating for the total function. The lower portion of the form can be used to list your improvement goals for each function.

	FUNCTION NUMBER					
CHECKLIST	**1** %	**2** %	**3** %	**4** %	**5** %	**6** %
A	_____	_____	_____	_____	_____	_____
B	_____	_____	_____	_____	_____	_____
C	_____	_____	_____	_____	_____	_____
D	_____	_____	_____	_____	_____	_____
E	_____	_____	_____	_____	_____	_____
F	_____	_____	_____	_____	_____	_____
G	_____	_____	_____	_____	_____	_____
H	_____	_____	_____	_____	_____	_____
I	_____	_____	_____	_____	_____	_____
SUMMARY RATING (%)	_____	_____	_____	_____	_____	_____

IMPROVEMENT GOALS

_____

_____

_____

_____

_____

_____

_____

(Use separate sheet as required)

Section **V**

Managing
Product Distribution

The next two chapters are concerned with the systematic appraisal and analysis of the company's distribution system in order to identify opportunities for improvement in cost-effectiveness and competitiveness. The term *distribution system* is used here in a broad sense, therefore, the evaluation must cover all aspects of company organization and operations involved in making its products available to buyers. This appraisal is a detailed examination of the methods by which the company serves its end-user markets to determine if they maximize sales at minimum cost. An effective distribution system makes it easy for the customer to buy—by ensuring that the product he wants is readily available to him where and when he wants it. In its simplest terms, *distribution is the product's route to the end-user, or consumer.*

DISTRIBUTION: THE SUM OF MANY ACTIVITIES   The effectiveness of a distribution system must be measured in terms of both costs and sales; this requires an economic comparison of existing methods of distribution with all feasible alternatives. Because of our rapidly changing market environment, this comparison should be made systematically and frequently. It goes without saying that the distribution system should be reviewed and revised when required by changed circumstances, but this is simply a reaction to events. Clearly, this is not a satisfactory substitute for a systematic, scheduled evaluation, preferably once a year. This is especially critical because of the legal complexities of marketing in today's environment, so an annual review for compliance with antitrust laws and other applicable legal and regulatory constraints should be made in any distribution evaluation.

In its broadest use, distribution encompasses virtually the entire

243

process of getting products to market—a scope that parallels much of the scope of marketing itself. In this Manual, however, the term "distribution system" is used in a less global sense; as a part of marketing, not as a substitute for it. Emphasis is placed on "system" to stress that distribution is not a separate function in itself, but the collective result of many other marketing (and non-marketing) functions. Some of the functions that make up distribution are:

1. advertising, sales promotion, and product publicity,
2. field sales,
3. applications engineering,
4. providing product information (customer communications),
5. processing orders,
6. post-sale service,
7. reporting market information, and
8. customer credit, billing, and collection.

The non-marketing functions of credit, billing, and collection are included because, to the customer, they are essential steps in the distribution process. Like advertising, these activities may be performed at least partially by resellers instead of by the company.

Assuring product availability, through product and parts storage and transporting the product to stocking points and to end-users are covered under the section on physical distribution in Volume II of this series.

The essential purpose of a distribution system is to develop the most effective combination of selling capability, product availability, and associated service that produces *maximum sales at minimum cost*; therefore, every distribution decision is basically a trade-off between its *effect on sales* and its *effect on cost*. For this reason, evaluation of the distribution system in total is the subject of the first chapter in this section. In this chapter, evaluation of the distribution system is treated in terms of (1) distribution channels employed; (2) cost-effectiveness of the total system, and (3) competitiveness of the system. The second chapter is limited to one important aspect of distribution—indirect distribution through resellers. Indirect distribution is the promotion and sale by sales representatives and sales agents to independent distributors and retailers, who purchase the products for resale to end-users. The servicing of end-users is performed primarily by the reseller. Indirect distribution is actually selling *through* resellers, rather than *to* them, since end-users buy the producer's products through the resellers. A manufacturer of a broad line of products may, of course, employ a combination of direct and indirect distribution methods.

THREE CRITERIA FOR EVALUATING DISTRIBUTION

1. Are intended end-users aware of and receptive toward the producer and its products and services? That is, do prospects know who the company is and what it has to sell?

2. Are the producer's products and services made conveniently available for purchase by intended end-users? That is, can buyers get the product where and when they want it?

3. Does the service provided by the producer, both before and after the sale, attract buyers and ensure customer satisfaction? That is, can users get help when they need it?

Chapter **14**

Keeping Distribution Attuned
To the Changing Marketplace

Distribution is as much management art as management science. After the mathematical cost-effectiveness analysis is made; after the precise competitive evaluation is completed; then marketing management must apply its intuitive and creative talents to the results to come up with the distribution system that is best for the firm. The mathematics and the analysis are only the starting point.

A neglected aspect of distribution evaluation is a degree of humility on the part of the producer. The manufacturer who believes his product is so superior, so in demand, that buyers will go out of their way to obtain it may succeed for a while—but sooner or later someone else will make his product more convenient to buy, more readily available, more appealing to the impulse buyer, or easier to afford—and producer A will see his customers switch to producer B.

Your company's engineers can dream up the most technically advanced product in the industry, but all their inventiveness may be wasted if prospective users aren't told about it in a persuasive way. Your production people can turn out widgets faster, cheaper, and better than your competitors, but all their energy and production know-how can be lost if potential buyers can't find the product where and when they are accustomed to shop.

KEEP UP WITH CHANGING CURRENTS OF DISTRIBUTION

Distribution is undergoing a virtual revolution. The distinctions between distribution channels are becoming less clear, and the conventional channels are merging and crossing. Drivers are buying cigarettes and milk at the local gas station, and buying motor oil in the food supermarket.

245

Buying cooperatives are by-passing established wholesalers in many lines. Brand names no longer command the loyalty of consumers. And franchising is rapidly changing the shape of distribution for many products and services.

Clearly, the business organization that neglects to observe and keep up with these changing currents of distribution will find itself burdened with slow-moving stocks, high distribution costs, and excess production capacity. All of these have an adverse effect on productivity—each of them reduces the firm's profitability.

KEY AIM OF THE SELF-AUDIT

The main objective of the self-audit is to ensure that the firm's distribution system is systematically and regularly reviewed and revised as required to keep it cost-effective and competitive, and suited to the markets served by the company.

Generally, the distribution system should be equal to or better than that of the company's strongest competitor.

HOW TO USE THE CHECKLISTS

For each of the statements in the Checklist, compare the condition of your function to the "ideal" as described in the statement. Then:

1. If you consider the statement to be *generally true* of your function, check the YES column.
2. If you consider the statement to be *untrue* of your function, check the NO column.
3. If you consider the statement to be *less than true* (but not totally untrue) of your function, check the SOMETIMES OR PARTIAL column.
4. If the statement does not apply to your particular situation, write "Not Applicable" across the response spaces (or simply draw a line through them).
5. If you lack the data for a definite response, write in "Not Answerable" or "Don't Know."

HOW TO EVALUATE YOUR RESPONSES

When you have completed the checklist, glance over your responses, keeping these points in mind:

1. A negative answer is always unfavorable because it indicates a problem within the function: the greater the number of NOs, the more serious the situation.
2. A positive response is always a good indication. But too many YES answers could indicate that your review is not objective enough.
3. Too many SOMETIMES OR PARTIALLY answers can point to internal weaknesses or to a lack of firm direction.
4. A lot of "Not Applicable" answers could indicate that you are avoiding the issue.
5. A large number of "Not Answerable" or "Don't Know" answers could be symptomatic of inadequate records or data bases.

HOW TO RATE AND SCORE YOUR RESPONSES

When you are satisfied with your responses in general, you are ready to score the Checklist. For your convenience, a self-explanatory Scoring and Rating Block follows each Checklist. This block not only tells you whether the condition of your function is satisfactory, but it also gives you a measure of its effectiveness.

Here's how to total up the points for inclusion in the Scoring and Rating Block:

1. Total up the number of points you scored:
   a. For each YES, give yourself one point.
   b. For each NO, give yourself zero.
   c. For each SOMETIMES OR PARTIALLY, give yourself a half-point.
   d. For each "Not Applicable" answer, give yourself zero and deduct one from the number of items on the Checklist.
   e. For each "Not Answerable" or "Don't Know" answer, give yourself zero.
2. Next divide the total number of points you score by the total number of items (statements) on the Checklist (less items marked "Not Applicable"). You'll get a 1.0 for a perfect score and a fraction for anything less.
3. Multiply the result of step 2 by 100 to arrive at the percentage for your score.

What is a satisfactory rating? A rating of less than 65 percent is unacceptable and calls for an improvement program: Obviously, the lower the rating, the more drastic the action required.

A brief "how-to" example of this Scoring and Rating system follows . . .

EXAMPLE

	YES (1)	NO (0)	S/P* (½)

1. Field sale reports designed to provide information on sales progress contain data on the following topics:

   a. sales calls and sales presentations made by salespersons and sales agents,   ✓

   b. bids, quotations, and proposals made,   ✓

   c. new orders booked,   ✓

   d. lost business, and reasons for the loss,   ✓

   e. accomplishments toward future orders,   ✓

   f. performance in filling orders, handling complaints, and otherwise servicing individual customers,   ✓

   g. action taken in response to customer requests, such as sending samples, spec sheets, etc.,   ✓

   h. accomplishments of significance and value to other members of the sales force.   ✓

*SOMETIMES OR PARTIALLY

TOTAL POINTS   5 + 0 + 1

= 6

RATING

Enter number of points scored $\dfrac{6}{8}$ Enter number of items on checklist = .75 × 100 = 75 %

248

14-A
ORGANIZATION, ADMINISTRATION, AND OPERATION

	YES (1)	NO (0)	S/P* (½)

1. The distribution system through which the firm's products reach their ultimate users and consumers is continuously and systematically evaluated and amended to keep it attuned to changing market conditions.

2. The process of evaluating and revising the distribution system is recognized:

   a. as a vital company activity, that has top management endorsement and support, and

   b. on the organization charts and in manager's position descriptions as an important function of marketing.

3. The function has a formal budget allocation covering all internal expenses of planning, collecting and analyzing data, and implementing changes in the distribution system.

4. The budget also covers costs of outside services, if required.

5. The budget was developed through:

   a. intensive review and analysis of all tasks and activities that are critical to keeping the distribution system competitive and cost-effective,

   b. elimination of all non-essential activities and tasks, and

   c. consideration of future growth and business development needs.

6. A formal comparative analysis of the cost effectiveness and competitiveness of the distribution system is made at least once a year.

7. This analysis is similar to that shown on the attached three exhibits, and is done either manually or by computer. (Exhibits I, II, and III, with instructions, follow this checklist.)

Points 8 to 14 can be answered after filling out Exhibit I.

8. The costs of *each* existing distribution channel that accounts for 10 percent of total sales have been compared with at least one alternative channel.

9. The alternative channels analyzed include channels used by important competitors but not by the company.

10. Each cost comparison has been made on a common basis (using end-user price or total end-user purchases value as 100 percent).

11. Each channel analysis identifies all reseller margins, agent commissions and/or selling expense in the channel.

12. Any significant distribution costs that are borne directly by the end-user (such as freight) are noted if they differ between the existing channel and its alternative.

13. The estimated costs of each alternative channel realistically reflect the effort that would be required to achieve the same sales volume (and mix) as that of the existing channel.

14. The preceding analysis is sufficiently accurate to be used (together with other pertinent information) in making important distribution decisions.

*SOMETIMES OR PARTIALLY

The remaining points can be answered after filling out Exhibits II and III.

15. The summary conclusions reached in Exhibit III are consistent with:

    a. over-all marketing objectives and strategies and marketing plans, and

    b. plans for offering new and improved products and services to existing and new customer classes (including plans for their distribution).

16. The projected sales and marketing expense effect of the conclusions is included in the current marketing plan and budget where appropriate.

17. The over-all competitiveness of the company's distribution system compares favorably with that of its principal competitors in terms of:

    a. end-user awareness of and receptivity toward the producer and its products,

    b. convenient availability of the producer's products and services to end-users, and

    c. pre-sale and post-sale service, including credit and billing, that satisfies customer requirements.

18. Changes from present channels of distribution are made when:

    a. there is a significant cost benefit, or

    b. there are compelling competitive reasons for making the change.

*SOMETIMES OR PARTIALLY

TOTAL POINTS   ☐ + 0 + ☐

= ☐

RATING

Enter number of points scored ☐
———————————————————— =   × 100 = ☐ %
Enter number of items on checklist ☐

WHAT THE RATING SIGNIFIES

Every significant change in the needs of end-users or consumers of the firm's products and services can have an impact on the way that these products and services are brought to market. Every major change in competitors' product lines or the distribution channels they use has an effect, as well, on the firm's distribution system. Every important change in the company's product mix, pricing or credit policies, or business development strategy can cause a change in the distribution process. Quite obviously, too, changes in the way that marketing intermediaries—such as wholesalers, jobbers, manufacturers representatives, retailers, and others —carry out their functions can have important effects on the firm's marketing methods. And new technology in communication, transportation and information handling can severely impact the system as well.

All too often, unfortunately, the separate activities that make up the distribution system operate as individual functions, without regard for

EXHIBIT I. DISTRIBUTION COMPARATIVE COST ANALYSIS

Annual dollar volume of sales through channel
(assuming current sales volume and mix) $ _____

Percent of total sales   _____

Product(s) sold   _____

End-user class   _____

	Existing Channel		Alternative Channel	
	$	Percent	$	Percent
1. Price to end-users (or total purchase value)	____	100.0%	____	100.0%
2. a. First reseller margin (if applicable)	____	____	____	____
b. Second reseller margin (if applicable)	____	____	____	____
3. Company selling price	____	____	____	____
Company distribution expense (as applicable):				
Advertising and promotion	____	____	____	____
Selling (salesmen's comp. & travel)	____	____	____	____
Commissions to agents	____	____	____	____
Sales supervision and training	____	____	____	____
Customer application engineering	____	____	____	____
Customer communications	____	____	____	____
Order handling	____	____	____	____
Warehousing (incl. branches)	____	____	____	____
Freight (to branches or customers)	____	____	____	____
Post-sale service	____	____	____	____
Credit	____	____	____	____
Billing	____	____	____	____
Other _____	____	____	____	____
4. Total Company distribution expense	____	____	____	____

	Existing Channel Distr. Cost Effectiveness Ratio	Alternative Channel Distr. Cost Effectiveness Ratio
5. Total identified distribution costs, including reseller margin(s) (lines 2 + 4)	$ ____ [%]	$ ____ [%]
6. Balance after distribution costs (lines 1-5)	$ ____ ____%	$ ____ ____%

Describe the types of distribution costs (freight, storage, credit, etc.) covered by the reseller's
margins in 2a and 2b above _____
_____

Instructions for Completing Exhibit I

1. Show for each distribution channel used at the present time the approximate sales volume and percentage of total sales moving through the channel. A separate channel should be shown for each class of end-users that is, or could logically be, served by a different method of distribution.

2. Show for *each* major existing channel, the principal *alternative* channel which might serve the same class of end-users, including any channels used by competitors but not by the company. Alternative channel possibilities include, for example, the use of agents instead of salesmen, or field warehouses instead of central storage, as well as the substitution of direct for indirect distribution or vice versa.

3. The distribution patterns within a company may vary widely, ranging from the sale of a relatively homogeneous product line through one channel of distribution to a relatively homogeneous class of end-users, to the sale of different product lines through different channels of distribution to different classes of end-users. In such cases, the full extent of the *present* distribution system should be shown, but *alternative* channels need be identified for only the most important present channels, that is, for each channel accounting for 10 percent or more of total sales.

251

EXHIBIT II. DISTRIBUTION COST-EFFECTIVENESS ANALYSIS

Summarize the distribution cost-effectiveness ratios of each existing channel and its alternative channel as developed in the preceding comparative cost analysis (line 5), and indicate any differences between them. Distribution cost effectiveness ratio is the total of distribution costs for the channel expressed as a percent of the end-user price (or total value of end-user purchases).

Channel Comparison (end-user class and channel)	Distribution Cost-Effectiveness Ratio		Cost Ratio Difference (col. 2-1)	Weighting (% of Total Sales)	Weighted Differences (col. 3x4)
	Existing (1)	Alternative (2)	(3)	(4)	(5)
1. _____	_____	_____	_____	_____	_____
Existing _____	_____	_____	_____	_____	_____
Alternative _____	_____	_____	_____	_____	_____
2. _____	_____	_____	_____	_____	_____
Existing _____	_____	_____	_____	_____	_____
Alternative _____	_____	_____	_____	_____	_____
3. _____	_____	_____	_____	_____	_____
Existing _____	_____	_____	_____	_____	_____
Alternative _____	_____	_____	_____	_____	_____
4. _____	_____	_____	_____	_____	_____
Existing _____	_____	_____	_____	_____	_____
Alternative _____	_____	_____	_____	_____	_____
5. _____	_____	_____	_____	_____	_____
Existing _____	_____	_____	_____	_____	_____
Alternative _____	_____	_____	_____	_____	_____
Total of above (use additional sheets if necessary)				_____	_____

their interdependence as elements of a system. As a result, advertising and sales promotion programs may work at cross purposes to the direct selling effort, or overly-restrictive credit practices may prevent full development of a particular customer class.

Every business enterprise, regardless of size, that has more than a single product line and has broader than local product distribution, needs a systematic and organized process of evaluation to keep its distribution system cost-effective and competitive.

A less-than-satisfactory rating indicates that company management may not recognize and treat the individual business functions as parts of an integrated distribution *system*. What is more, management may fail to recognize the need to keep the distribution system constantly and systematically attuned to changing conditions. As a consequence, the company's distribution can become obsolescent and out of phase with the realities of the marketplace. When this happens, profit margins are soon impacted by declining sales or excessive distribution costs, or both.

A well-known cosmetics manufacturer discovered this, to its sorrow. The company stayed with its long-established outlets in pharmacies and

EXHIBIT III.   SUMMARY CONCLUSIONS

List below each of the channel comparisons and its "Weighted Difference", given in Exhibit II (Distribution Cost-Effectiveness Analysis). For those comparisons with a zero or *positive* difference, indicate either that the existing channel *will continue to be used*, or state the reasons *why it should not continue to be used* (such as limited capacity for growth, changing sales mix, etc.). For those comparisons with a *negative* difference, indicate either how the existing channel *will be changed*, or state the reasons *why it should not be changed* (such as a declining cost ratio due to increased volume, the time and cost required to change to the lower-cost alternative channel, etc.).

Channel Comparison (end-user class and channel)	Weighted Difference (Ex. II, col. 5)	Conclusions (Indicate prospective continuing use of or change in existing channels
1. _____	_____	_____
Existing: _____		_____
Alternative: _____		_____
2. _____	_____	_____
Existing: _____		_____
Alternative: _____		_____
3. _____	_____	_____
Existing: _____		_____
Alternative: _____		_____
4. _____	_____	_____
Existing: _____		_____
Alternative: _____		_____
5. _____	_____	_____
Existing: _____		_____
Alternative: _____		_____

department stores long after its competitors had moved into chain super-markets and discount houses. The firm is now vainly seeking new financing to regain its lost market share.

WHAT TO DO NOW

1. Organize the distribution system as a management function with sufficient "clout" to coordinate the activities of the other departments that are part of the total system.

2. Make sure that all contributing departments know the overall goals and plans for distribution, and that their own goals are compatible.

3. Involve the other functions in the process of evaluation, so they will understand the reasons for changing methods and channels of distribution—and what is required from them.

4. Make sure that all new-product development plans consider potential impact on present distribution methods and channels.

14-B
AUTHORITY, RESPONSIBILITY, AND ACCOUNTABILITY

	YES (1)	NO (0)	S/P* (½)

1. Authority has been delegated in writing to the manager of marketing (or other senior manager) to expend company funds, enter into contracts on behalf of the company, and utilize company resources for the purpose of ensuring effective distribution of the company's products to end-users and consumers.   ___ ___ ___

2. The manager is responsible to:

   a. staff and manage an organization capable of establishing and administering a cost-effective and competitive system of distribution,   ___ ___ ___

   b. establish policies, control procedures and standard practices to guide the distribution process, and   ___ ___ ___

   c. establish and manage relations with sales agents and/or resellers of the company's products.   ___ ___ ___

3. The manager is responsible for continuous and systematic appraisal of all channels of distribution to ensure that those employed are cost-effective and competitive, and are adapted to changing conditions.   ___ ___ ___

4. The manager is responsible to develop an annual distribution plan as part of the overall marketing plan based, in part, on an in-depth appraisal of the system.   ___ ___ ___

5. Managers of functions that are elements of the total distribution system, such as advertising, sales, materials management, etc., are responsible to coordinate their individual plans and activities with the overall distribution plan.   ___ ___ ___

6. Managers of these functions are held accountable for serious failure to meet marketing plan and sales plan goals resulting from inadequate or ineffective coordination and support to the distribution system.   ___ ___ ___

7. The manager responsible for product distribution is held accountable for serious failure to meet marketing plan and sales plan goals resulting from an inadequate or ineffective system of distribution.   ___ ___ ___

8. The manager is also held accountable for serious excessive costs of distribution.

*SOMETIMES OR PARTIALLY

TOTAL POINTS   [ ] + 0 + [ ]

= [ ]

RATING

Enter number of points scored [ ]

Enter number of items on checklist [ ]

= × 100 = [ ] %

WHAT THE RATING SIGNIFIES   Above all else, product distribution has to be a fluid and dynamic process—constantly shifting to accommodate changes in the business, social and economic environments in which we function. And as the marketplace becomes more and more segmented, distribution channels become more complex to accommodate this diversity of consumer needs.

Strong authority is needed by distribution management in order that company resources can be quickly reallocated to respond to change and complexity. If it is lacking or weak, a slow or inadequate response to changing circumstances could cost the company dearly in lost business. This dynamic environment also requires firm responsibility for individual performance and well-defined accountability for individual failure to perform, but both must be administered with flexibility and judged in terms of *results*.

A low rating here indicates that responsibility and accountability are either not clearly expressed, or are defined in terms other than results. As a consequence, less essential activity will tend to take up people's time and energies.

WHAT TO DO NOW

1. Your authority must be broad enough to cover all distribution activities, regardless of functional responsibility. This may require that you have a "dotted line" authority over some non-marketing functions, such as credit and collection, insofar as their activities affect distribution.

2. Job descriptions should spell out in specific terms what is required of all managers who interact with the distribution system. You may have to define these responsibilities for other departments not under your direct jurisdiction.

3. Recognize that this may create some tensions and conflicts with other job responsibilities that will require resolution by higher management. Tensions should be minimized by advance discussion and negotiation with affected individuals.

4. It is vitally important to spell out the penalties for failure to perform assigned responsibilities, not only by members of the distribution function, but also by personnel of functions that provide support, such as order processing, billing, applications engineering, etc.

14-C
MEASUREMENTS, CONTROL REPORTS, AND PERFORMANCE RECORDS

	YES (1)	NO (0)	S/P* (½)
1. Cost-effectiveness and competitiveness of the company's distribution system are measured regularly and systematically.	___	___	___
2. Cost-effectiveness and competitiveness are measured by comparing actual performance and results of the system to certain benchmarks, standards and targets, such as:			
a. marketing plan market share objectives,	___	___	___
b. sales plan goals,	___	___	___
c. cost-effectiveness ratios by channel,	___	___	___
d. finished goods inventory ratios to sales, and	___	___	___
e. repeat orders, number of new accounts, etc.	___	___	___

*SOMETIMES OR PARTIALLY

	YES (1)	NO (0)	S/P* (½)

3. Cost-effectiveness and competitiveness are measured and evaluated by analytical comparison of existing distribution channels with all viable alternative channels.

4. Accounting reports and sales analyses are routinely analyzed for significance to the existing distribution system.

5. Competitive evaluations made by marketing are routinely analyzed for significance to existing channels of distribution.

6. Field sales reports are routinely analyzed for significance to existing channels of distribution.

7. Costs and expenses of distribution are routinely compared with budget, and major variances analyzed for corrective action.

*SOMETIMES OR PARTIALLY

TOTAL POINTS   ☐ + 0 + ☐

= ☐

RATING

Enter number of points scored / Enter number of items on checklist = ☐/☐ = ☐ × 100 = ☐ %

WHAT THE RATING SIGNIFIES

All measurements and controls should be designed to promote high productivity of the distribution system, not simply to measure costs, time spent on specific tasks, and variances from standards.

This means total emphasis on *output*. The ultimate and real output of the distribution activity is satisfied users and consumers who will buy again. This is a most difficult measurement to make, of course, in many business situations, so other interim measures of output must be used. These include sales versus sales plan, market shares versus marketing plan goals, profit margins by product line, finished goods inventory ratios to sales, distribution cost ratios to total sales—but they all should point toward the desired end-result—satisfied customers.

A less-than-satisfactory rating on the first three points is evidence that management may be more concerned with activity than results. As a consequence, the company may be failing to reach important segments of the buying population, distribution costs may be excessive, or the firm may have a disproportionate share of "one-time" users.

Every piece of data from the field has potential value to the distribution process, especially that which informs management about customer preferences in products, reaction to advertising and sales promotion programs, needs for shopping convenience, price reactions, and perceptions of the company's reputation and service.

Negative answers to points 4, 5, and 6 indicate a low level of concern for marketplace "feedback," lack of which may cause the distribution system to become outmoded by events and uncompetitive.

WHAT TO DO NOW

1. Design all control reports to report actual results, not just numbers of people, hours worked, and costs incurred.
2. Compare actual results to firm targets, "engineered" standards and past performance.
3. Analyze favorable variances from standards as well as unfavorable, in order to reward (and learn from) superior performance.
4. Budget sufficient funds for marketing intelligence. It's one of your best investments.

14-D
OPERATING PERFORMANCE ASSESSMENT

	YES (1)	NO (0)	S/P* (½)
1. A review and analysis has been made of control reports and records for at least one year past for purposes of evaluating performance of the company's distribution system.	_____	_____	_____
2. This review shows that all major goals of marketing and sales plans have essentially been met.	_____	_____	_____
3. The review shows an improving trend in cost-effectiveness of the system.	_____	_____	_____
4. The review shows an improving trend in sales volume and product profit margins by major product lines.	_____	_____	_____
5. The review shows no evidence of serious failure of new products to meet sales and profit objectives of new-product plans, resulting from ineffective product distribution (answer "yes" if true).	_____	_____	_____
6. The review shows no evidence of serious loss of market shares of major products, excessive costs of distribution, serious out of stock conditions, or losses of major customers because of inadequate or ineffective distribution (answer "yes" if true).	_____	_____	_____
7. The review shows an improving trend in finished goods inventory ratios to sales, and in inventory costs.	_____	_____	_____
8. Distribution costs are routinely compared with budget, and variances analyzed for corrective action.	_____	_____	_____

*SOMETIMES OR PARTIALLY

TOTAL POINTS [ ] + 0 + [ ]

= [ ]

RATING

Enter number of points scored [ ]
————————————————— = × 100 = [ ] %
Enter number of items on checklist [ ]

WHAT THE RATING SIGNIFIES The only real test of a distribution system's effectiveness is its actual recorded performance, past and present. All else is speculation or prophecy. To be valid, an analysis of performance requires a review of at least one year's actual performance records, together with a review of the status of all current projects and programs.

A poor rating on this section indicates that the track record of the function either is lacking or is below standard. Either way, you cannot set goals for the period ahead with any confidence.

WHAT TO DO NOW

1. Don't base your review on people's memories. They're often faulty or biased.

2. If you don't have good records, start now to build a good performance file.

3. If past goals were badly missed, review your goal-setting process to ensure that goals are not unrealistic.

14-E
TOP-LEVEL SUPPORT AND GUIDANCE

	YES (1)	NO (0)	S/P* (½)

The executive office demonstrates active support, guidance, and recognition of the need to regularly and systematically evaluate and revise the company's distribution system in order to keep it cost-effective and attuned to changing company needs and market conditions. This support is evidenced by:

a. approval of expense budgets for all elements of the system,

b. review and approval of distribution plans and programs,

c. participation in progress review meetings of major distribution programs,

d. informed comments on progress reports, and

e. recognition and reward for outstanding accomplishment.

*SOMETIMES OR PARTIALLY

TOTAL POINTS   ☐ + 0 + ☐

= ☐

RATING

Enter number of points scored ☐

――――――――――――――――――――― =   × 100 = ☐ %

Enter number of items on checklist ☐

WHAT THE RATING SIGNIFIES

Distribution is an integrated system that involves every function of the business in one way or another. Accordingly, the function needs clear and positive direction from topside, as well as support and recognition. A low rating indicates that top management may not be aware of its role and responsibility to actively oversee this vital company activity, and make sure that all elements of the system perform in harmony with one another. As a result, individual managers may not realize the value of their separate contributions to the effective functioning of the system. They may also lack the motivation to excel that comes from being part of a company process that is considered important by top management.

WHAT TO DO NOW

1. The system aspect of distribution may not be apparent to managers of functions other than marketing. Every effort should be made to educate these managers—and the executive office as well—about the need to coordinate all plans and activities that affect the company's product distribution.

2. All reports to the executive office should point up the need for top management to play an active role in the distribution process.

3. A strong corporate policy statement stressing the need for coordination of activities should be drafted.

14-F
INNOVATION IN METHODS AND TECHNIQUES

	YES (1)	NO (0)	S/P* (½)
1. Managers responsible for evaluating the company's distribution system actively seek out better methods and techniques to keep the system competitive and cost-effective, through:			
a. participation in marketing and product distribution seminars, conferences, and workshops,	___	___	___
b. trade and professional associations,	___	___	___
c. use of competent outside specialists,	___	___	___
d. customer and industry contacts,	___	___	___
e. solicitation of ideas from company personnel at all levels, and	___	___	___
f. budgets provide funds for such activities.	___	___	___
2. The computer is used to store, process and display information on sales and distribution system costs, by major distribution channels and major cost elements within each channel.	___	___	___
3. The computer is used to produce comparative cost analyses of existing channels of distribution with alternative channels, including those used by major competitors.	___	___	___
4. Changes from existing channels of distribution are tested on a small scale, and results are documented and evaluated before a major change is implemented.	___	___	___

*SOMETIMES OR PARTIALLY

TOTAL POINTS

⬜ + 0 + ⬜

‿‿‿‿‿

= ⬜

RATING

Enter number of points scored ⬜

―――――――――――――――――――――― = ⬜ × 100 = ⬜ %

Enter number of items on checklist ⬜

WHAT THE RATING SIGNIFIES

Product distribution is a rapidly changing process. New methods, new channels of distribution, and new technology are making present methods and techniques obsolete at a dizzying pace. The business enterprise that ignores these changes, and fails to keep up with the state of the art—regardless of how large or how small the business happens to be—will find itself blind-sided by the competition.

New techniques of operations research and modeling make it possible to stimulate and test new channels of distribution in the computer at low cost. This offers a firm that distributes a variety of product lines through multiple channels a low-risk way to assess changes in distribution.

A less-than-acceptable rating in this section indicates that the company is in danger of being out-smarted by competition who utilize more up-to-date methods to get their products to users and consumers.

WHAT TO DO NOW

1. Be sure to include in the annual distribution budget a sufficient amount to cover costs of keeping your managers up to date on distribution methods and techniques.

2. It's hard to imagine how a business firm of any size can compete in today's fast-moving marketplace without the use of a computer to aid its distribution activity. If you don't now use one, look into it "ASAP."

3. Keep up your contacts with trade associations, professional associations, customers and industry colleagues. They are all fertile sources of new ideas.

14-G
INTERFUNCTIONAL COMMUNICATIONS AND COORDINATION

	YES (1)	NO (0)	S/P* (½)
1. Managers responsible for the company's distribution system maintain close and continuous contact with managers of other company functions, especially:			
a. advertising and sales promotion,	――	――	――
b. field sales,	――	――	――

*SOMETIMES OR PARTIALLY

	YES (1)	NO (0)	S/P* (½)
c. customer service,	————	————	————
d. sales training,	————	————	————
e. market research,	————	————	————
f. order processing,	————	————	————
g. applications engineering,	————	————	————
h. credit and collection, and	————	————	————
i. materials management.	————	————	————

2. Managers of other company functions are kept informed about impending changes in distribution channels through the means of regular progress reports, marketing plans, meetings, personal contact.

3. Managers maintain continuous contact with intermediaries in the distribution system, including resellers of the company's products.

*SOMETIMES OR PARTIALLY

TOTAL POINTS [ ] + 0 + [ ]

= [ ]

RATING

$$\frac{\text{Enter number of points scored} \quad [\ ]}{\text{Enter number of items on checklist} \quad [\ ]} = \times 100 = [\quad] \%$$

WHAT THE RATING SIGNIFIES

A free and full flow of information among the different departments is an absolute essential for good distribution. It's difficult to think of any significant event within the organization, or any development out in the marketplace, that doesn't have some relevance to the company's distribution system.

The earlier that knowledge of the events and developments is transmitted to those responsible, the quicker and more effective the response can be. The formal information system of most organizations of any size is too slow for this purpose—what is required is constant personal contact at many levels throughout the organization.

A less-than-acceptable rating indicates that this kind of dynamic information interchange is lacking. As a consequence, important information may not reach the people who need it in time for effective action, and marketing momentum will be lost.

WHAT TO DO NOW

1. Make sure that your people maintain their contacts with others. The company's informal communication system often can bring you valuable information you can not get otherwise.

2. Don't neglect rumors. They're often the advance signals of events to come. But insist that your people not spread gossip on pain of penalty.

	YES (1)	NO (0)	S/P* (½)

1. There is an organized on-going cross-functional team effort to improve distribution of the company's products. Major efforts, on a task basis, are directed toward:

    a. making the distribution system more adaptable and responsive to changes in products and markets,

    b. improving feedback and use of information from end-users and intermediaries in the distribution system,

    c. improving coordination of all internal business functions with respect to their involvement in the distribution system, and

    d. improving cost-effectiveness of the system, and improving finished goods inventory ratios to sales.

2. Represented on the team, depending on the particular task, are the functions of:

    a. field sales,

    b. materials management,

    c. advertising and sales promotion,

    d. information systems, and

    e. market research.

*SOMETIMES OR PARTIALLY

TOTAL POINTS [ ] + 0 + [ ]

= [ ]

RATING

Enter number of points scored [ ]
—————————————————————————— = [ ] × 100 = [ ] %
Enter number of items on checklist [ ]

WHAT THE RATING SIGNIFIES

Of all business functions, the one that can benefit most from an interfunctional team effort is distribution because, in the broadest sense of the function, every member of the organization exists for the purpose of getting the firm's products to end-users and consumers. The team approach indicated here can help to focus the energies of many people on this vital purpose. It can also help to break down the artificial barriers between departments.

A low rating indicates a need to formalize and structure the communications and coordination among functions. Unless this is done, the various departments may go their separate ways, without a central purpose to their efforts.

WHAT TO DO NOW

1. Get the broadest representation possible on the team. Each of the tasks listed in 1. can benefit from many points of view.

2. Meetings are needed to keep the effort focused on results. Keep the team's objectives always in view, set a firm agenda, and control each meeting to get the most value out of it.

14-I
RESOURCES

	YES (1)	NO (0)	S/P* (½)
1. Managers responsible for the company's distribution system are kept well-informed about the company's overall objectives, policies and business development plans, through:			
a. participation in key management and planning meetings,	___	___	___
b. participation in the strategic business planning process,	___	___	___
c. intensive involvement with marketing planning, sales planning, and new-product planning, and	___	___	___
d. access to appropriate operating reports.	___	___	___
2. Based on this knowledge of forward plans, the company's resources for evaluating the distribution system and keeping it attuned to changing market circumstances are considered adequate to meet company needs for the next 3, 6 and 12 months, in terms of:			
a. budget funding,	___	___	___
b. capabilities,	___	___	___
c. manpower,	___	___	___
d. computer time and capacity, and	___	___	___
e. support of other functions.	___	___	___

*SOMETIMES OR PARTIALLY

TOTAL POINTS ☐ + 0 + ☐

= ☐

RATING

Enter number of points scored ☐
—————————————————— = ☐ × 100 = ☐ %
Enter number of items on checklist ☐

WHAT THE RATING SIGNIFIES

Resources needed for effective product distribution are, of course, extensive, and involve many functions of the business. Needless to say, the primary resources required are human. Information is a critical resource as well—both from within the organization and from the external environment.

In a world of rapid change, it is mandatory that managers responsible for effective distribution be kept extremely well informed about the company's current goals, policies, norms, values and business development plans. This requires first-hand involvement and active participation in the process through which these plans, policies and goals are developed. It will not happen if managers are only handed written directives to read and obey. Without such knowledge, distribution programs may well be out of joint with the firm's overall direction.

The other critical resource is full and enthusiastic support and cooperation of other company functions that are elements of the total distribution system, advertising, sales, applications engineering, etc. A low rating in this section indicates that one or more of these functions may be deficient, with the consequence that the distribution chain may break because of one or more weak links in the chain.

WHAT TO DO NOW

1. The resources of the entire enterprise must be evaluated in order to answer with certainty that the distribution system is adequate.

2. Make sure that the company's information systems are up to date and efficient, so that distribution can respond quickly to changes in the marketplace. This doesn't necessarily require electronic data processing, although the computer can make it possible to evaluate many alternatives quickly, thereby giving you the speed of response needed to be competitive in today's markets.

Chapter **15**

Selling Through Resellers— Indirect Distribution

Distribution through resellers, or resale distribution, means indirect distribution of the company's products through intermediate business enterprises—wholesalers, distributors, jobbers, retailers, dealers, etc.— who purchase and take title to the company's products for resale to end-users and consumers, or to other resellers.

The purpose of distribution through resellers is to maximize the profitable sale of products through distribution channels that most effectively serve end-users and consumers. For many products, typically those requiring localized sales and service, distribution through resellers is the only practical way of securing the exposure to end-users needed for volume sales. But even where this is not the case, resellers can often be helpful in supplementing direct methods of distribution.

THREE BASIC FACTORS VITAL TO SUCCESSFUL RESELLER DISTRIBUTION

The factors that determine the requirements for successful distribution through resellers are many and they vary; there are, however, three basic and universal requisites: (1) acceptance of the product by end-users and consumers, (2) selling where end-users like to buy, and (3) a positive attitude toward resellers by the producer.

GOOD MANAGEMENT IS THE KEY

In many respects, resale distribution is a different business than selling directly to end-users. It is more a matter of management than sales; as evidenced by the principal activities required for implementing indirect distribution—namely, the selection, training, motivation, servicing, and evaluation of resellers. It must be recognized that resellers are independent businesspersons with their own interests, customers, priorities, and problems, and the producer who sells through such intermediaries should have a positive and constructive attitude in his or her relationships with them. From the point of view of society in general, and of the consumer in particular, resellers serve a vital economic role. Successful distribution through resellers requires that producers recognize the mutual interdependence of all elements in an indirect channel of distribution. If managers respect resellers as equals in the distribution system, they will have made their most important single move toward "getting good distribution." Above all, the reseller is a customer, and should be treated accordingly.

KEY AIM OF THE SELF-AUDIT

The overriding objective of the appraisal is to assure that the indirect distribution scheme is structured and managed effectively, so that products reach end-users and consumers in the most cost-effective manner.

Generally, the system should be equal to or better than that employed by the strongest competitor.

Note: In this appraisal, sales agents are not considered resellers because they represent the producer under agency agreements, and do not take title to the products they sell. Original equipment manufacturers (OEM's) are not considered as resellers either, even though these businesses technically "resell" products they purchase as a part of their product.

HOW TO USE THE CHECKLISTS

For each of the statements in the Checklist, compare the condition of your function to the "ideal" as described in the statement. Then:

1. If you consider the statement to be *generally true* of your function, check the YES column.

2. If you consider the statement to be *untrue* of your function, check the NO column.

3. If you consider the statement to be *less than true* (but not totally untrue) of your function, check the SOMETIMES OR PARTIAL column.

4. If the statement does not apply to your particular situation, write "Not Applicable" across the response spaces (or simply draw a line through them).

5. If you lack the data for a definite response, write in "Not Answerable" or "Don't Know."

HOW TO EVALUATE YOUR RESPONSES

When you have completed the checklist, glance over your responses, keeping these points in mind:

1. A negative answer is always unfavorable because it indicates a problem within the function: the greater the number of NOs, the more serious the situation.

2. A positive response is always a good indication. But too many YES answers could indicate that your review is not objective enough.

3. Too many SOMETIMES OR PARTIALLY answers can point to internal weaknesses or to a lack of firm direction.

4. A lot of "Not Applicable" answers could indicate that you are avoiding the issue.

5. A large number of "Not Answerable" or "Don't Know" answers could be symptomatic of inadequate records or data bases.

HOW TO RATE AND SCORE YOUR RESPONSES

When you are satisfied with your responses in general, you are ready to score the Checklist. For your convenience, a self-explanatory Scoring and Rating Block follows each Checklist. This block not only tells you whether the condition of your function is satisfactory, but it also gives you a measure of its effectiveness.

Here's how to total up the points for inclusion in the Scoring and Rating Block:

1. Total up the number of points you scored:
   a. For each YES, give yourself one point.
   b. For each NO, give yourself zero.
   c. For each SOMETIMES OR PARTIALLY, give yourself a half-point.
   d. For each "Not Applicable" answer, give yourself zero and deduct one from the number of items on the Checklist.
   e. For each "Not Answerable" or "Don't Know" answer, give yourself zero.

2. Next divide the total number of points you score by the total number of items (statements) on the Checklist (less items marked "Not Applicable"). You'll get a 1.0 for a perfect score and a fraction for anything less.

3. Multiply the result of step 2 by 100 to arrive at the percentage for your score.

What is a satisfactory rating? A rating of less than 65 percent is unacceptable and calls for an improvement program: Obviously, the lower the rating, the more drastic the action required.

A brief "how-to" example of this Scoring and Rating system follows . . .

EXAMPLE

	YES (1)	NO (0)	S/P* (½)
1. Field sale reports designed to provide information on sales progress contain data on the following topics:			
a. sales calls and sales presentations made by salespersons and sales agents,	✓		
b. bids, quotations, and proposals made,	✓		
c. new orders booked,	✓		
d. lost business, and reasons for the loss,		✓	
e. accomplishments toward future orders,			✓
f. performance in filling orders, handling complaints, and otherwise servicing individual customers,	✓		
g. action taken in response to customer requests, such as sending samples, spec sheets, etc.,	✓		
h. accomplishments of significance and value to other members of the sales force.			✓

*SOMETIMES OR PARTIALLY

TOTAL POINTS $\boxed{5}$ + 0 + $\boxed{1}$

$= \boxed{6}$

RATING

$$\frac{\text{Enter number of points scored} \quad \boxed{6}}{\text{Enter number of items on checklist} \quad \boxed{8}} = .75 \times 100 = \boxed{75} \%$$

15-A
ORGANIZATION, ADMINISTRATION, AND OPERATION

	YES (1)	NO (0)	S/P* (½)

1. The company's system of product distribution through resellers is recognized on the organization charts as a vital company activity and an important function of marketing.

2. The function has a formal budget allocation covering all expenses of setting up and operating the distribution system.

3. The budget is based upon a critical review and evaluation of all tasks and activities involved in managing a contemporary *indirect* product distribution system.

4. The function is managed and staffed by experienced marketing professionals who:

   a. are trained in selling through and managing a reseller organization, and

   b. know the company's products, customers, competitors, distributors, and dealers.

5. The manager of the function reports to the top marketing executive, or an executive of equal rank.

6. The manager routinely attends top-level meetings on matters of customer policy, marketing and sales planning, new-product/market planning, advertising/sales promotion planning, inventory and accounts receivable policy, credit and collection policy, and other matters affecting distribution of the company's products.

7. The function is structured essentially as a management organization, designed to expedite and control the flow of product to end-users through a system of independent distributors and dealers who buy and resell the company's products.

8. Personnel of the *indirect* distribution function are guided in their day-to-day work by written procedures and standard practices governing the bulk of their activities.

9. A recent analysis of the company's total distribution system (covered in the preceding section) has confirmed that the *indirect* distribution system in effect is both cost-effective and competitive.

10. Firm goals, plans, and programs have been established to improve operational and sales productivity of the *indirect* distribution system during the current year.

11. The company has a written policy or form of reseller agreement that spells out:

    a. minimum requirements for reseller selection, expressed in terms of marketing, financial, and other qualifications,

    b. assignment of geographic area,

    c. responsibilities of the company to independent resellers, and

    d. responsibilities of independent resellers to the company.

12. Prospective resellers are screened against a uniform checklist of qualifications.

13. Evaluation of prospective resellers considers *business competence* in terms of:

    a. adequacy of financing,

*SOMETIMES OR PARTIALLY

		YES (1)	NO (0)	S/P* (½)

b. management competence, _____ _____ _____

c. customer service practices, _____ _____ _____

d. credit standing and reputation, _____ _____ _____

e. adequacy of facilities, _____ _____ _____

f. profitability, and _____ _____ _____

g. growth prospects. _____ _____ _____

14. Evaluation of prospective resellers considers *marketing effectiveness*, including:

   a. conflicting lines or products, _____ _____ _____

   b. complementary lines or products, _____ _____ _____

   c. number of salespersons, product/sales knowledge, and sales training, _____ _____ _____

   d. territorial coverage, _____ _____ _____

   e. coverage of end-users and others who influence purchase (architects, designers, etc.), _____ _____ _____

   f. management attention to the company's products, _____ _____ _____

   g. commitment to a specific volume or business, _____ _____ _____

   h. accepting and meeting quotas, and _____ _____ _____

   i. maintaining adequate inventories. _____ _____ _____

15. The company provides all new resellers with sales training that covers:

   a. product knowledge, _____ _____ _____

   b. product applications, _____ _____ _____

   c. competitive benefits and features, and _____ _____ _____

   d. selling techniques. _____ _____ _____

16. Refresher sales training is given to existing resellers:

   a. at least once a year, _____ _____ _____

   b. through product bulletins, _____ _____ _____

   c. by company sales personnel at reseller sales offices, and with reseller salesmen in the field, and _____ _____ _____

   d. by company sales trainers or other specialists. _____ _____ _____

17. Company sales personnel are competent and available to assist resellers with their business problems. _____ _____ _____

18. Reseller inventories of company products are reported regularly in sufficient detail for analysis. _____ _____ _____

19. The company keeps reseller inventories restocked promptly. _____ _____ _____

20. The company maintains a reseller council, advisory committee, or other formal means by which resellers can communicate their suggestions and complaints to the unit. _____ _____ _____

21. The council meets on a fixed schedule, works to a prepared agenda, and issues minutes in the form of action assignments.

22. The company is represented at important reseller conventions by means of product displays, booths, etc.

23. Resellers are invited, when appropriate, to participate in sales meetings held by the company.

24. Communications and contact are maintained with reseller management by several levels of company management; sales or distribution manager, marketing manager, and general manager.

25. Orders or inquiries for resellers are acknowledged immediately, and processed within a specific time.

26. Reseller sales results are monitored by sales management through regular sales reports.

27. Performance evaluations are made of all key resellers at least annually by the sales or distribution manager.

28. These annual evaluations are used:

    a. to improve reseller effectiveness and performance,

    b. in reviewing the company's methods of reseller selection, choice of distribution channels, and

    c. in changing and replacing resellers.

29. Annual evaluations include review of reseller effectiveness in terms of:

    a. sales goals and sales plans,

    b. credit review and approval policies and practices,

    c. maintenance of adequate inventories,

    d. promptness in filling orders,

    e. sales organizations,

    f. assignment of salespersons to the company's product lines, and

    g. customer service and complaint handling.

30. The annual evaluation of resellers also covers:

    a. actual sales vs. quotas, forecasts,

    b. actual sales vs. prior period,

    c. comparison with performance of similar resellers,

    d. credit losses, and

    e. payment history to the company.

31. The company's sales plan covers reseller activities, such as:

    a. plan for increasing reseller sales where warranted,

    b. reseller sales targets or quotas where appropriate, and

271

	YES (1)	NO (0)	S/P* (½)

c. reseller sales meetings, training reseller salespersons, reseller promotions, etc. ____ ____ ____

32. The company provides sales incentives for reseller's salespersons. ____ ____ ____

33. The company's resellers are kept informed about the company's trade show planning, promotions, etc. ____ ____ ____

34. Reseller profit margins are considered to be competitive and sufficient to provide a high level of service for the company's products. ____ ____ ____

35. Dealings with resellers reflect understanding of their needs, obligations, and costs, and their independent status. ____ ____ ____

36. Resellers regularly provide the company with:

    a. sales figures, by customer category, and ____ ____ ____

    b. general information. ____ ____ ____

37. The company regularly provides major resellers with:

    a. catalogs and product literature, ____ ____ ____

    b. promotional material, ____ ____ ____

    c. advertising and/or publicity, and ____ ____ ____

    d. exhibit material where needed. ____ ____ ____

38. Resellers are periodically surveyed for their sales promotion needs. ____ ____ ____

39. Services of company salespersons, application specialists, or others, is provided to:

    a. organize or assist in reseller sales meetings, ____ ____ ____

    b. help in reseller sales presentations, ____ ____ ____

    c. assist reseller sales force recruiting where practical, ____ ____ ____

    d. assist in reseller market appraisals and sales analyses, and ____ ____ ____

    e. solve customer problems. ____ ____ ____

40. The company promptly refers to resellers:

    a. product inquiries (or orders) received from the reseller's territory, and ____ ____ ____

    b. leads and other pertinent sales information uncovered or developed by the company. ____ ____ ____

*SOMETIMES OR PARTIALLY

TOTAL POINTS [ ] + 0 + [ ]

= [ ]

RATING

Enter number of points scored [ ]
⎯⎯⎯⎯⎯⎯⎯⎯⎯⎯⎯⎯⎯⎯⎯⎯⎯⎯⎯⎯ = × 100 = [ ] %
Enter number of items on checklist [ ]

WHAT THE RATING SIGNIFIES

A less-than-acceptable rating for indirect distribution indicates that company management may underrate the value to the firm's growth and profitability of its established independent distributors and dealers. As a consequence, the company's sales may be lower than they should be, or its distribution costs may be greater than they ought to be. Either way, the firm's profit margins are probably less than they potentially could be.

The finest, most desirable product in the world can become a market disappointment if the process for delivering it to the prospective user is not well organized, efficiently administered, competently managed and staffed, and strongly supported by the resources of the entire organization. Conversely, when a product is readily accessible and available to the buyer, when it is merchandised and displayed attractively by the retail dealer, when its benefits are known and extolled by the dealer's sales staff, and when the dealer backs up the sale with reputation, strong warranties, and good service, high sales volume and profit will accrue to the firm—even when that product has less-than-superior features.

A contemporary case in point is the market battle for the new videodisc between the Philips-MCA laser-operated disc and the more conventional stylus-played disc made by RCA. It is generally conceded that the Philips disc is far and away the most superior and advanced technologically. RCA, however, is betting on its superb distribution and customer service system to put its product into millions of U.S. homes, and is putting its full resources behind its distributors and dealers. It's too early to pick a winner at this point, but it's probably safe to say that the RCA product will do very well in the marketplace.

A company need not be as large and long-established as RCA in order to benefit and prosper through the use of an efficient reseller organization. A smaller firm, in fact, can sometimes use established resellers to gain a marketing advantage over larger competitors who sell direct. The trick is to make it profitable for independent distributors and dealers to stock and resell the product, and to back them up with superior product benefit information, innovative merchandising assistance, adequate stocks, and an honest warranty they can stand behind.

WHAT TO DO NOW

1. It all starts with an enlightened company policy and attitude that recognizes independent resellers as valued members of the organization and important contributors to the firm's profitability and growth.

2. The policy must be backed up with strong and visible commitment by management to support the distribution organization with money, management time, and company resources.

3. Commitment and support must be made visible to your resellers. They've heard all the promises before, and only real action by company personnel will make believers out of them.

4. Make it easy—and worthwhile—for your dealers to feedback information about customer reaction to your products and merchandising programs—and customer perceptions of your company. They can be an invaluable source of such information, provided you keep the communication channels open.

5. In return, keep your resellers informed about your plans and programs as fully as possible consistent with competitive security. Chances are that you are telling them too little rather than too much.

15-B
AUTHORITY, RESPONSIBILITY, AND ACCOUNTABILITY

	YES (1)	NO (0)	S/P* (½)

1. Authority has been delegated to the manager of product distribution through written delegation of authority, budget allocation, and position description, to expend company funds and enter into contracts on behalf of the firm, as necessary to ensure the effective distribution of company's products through independent resellers.

2. The manager is responsible for:

   a. staffing and managing an organization capable of administering a competitive and cost-effective product distribution system,

   b. establishing and managing a network of sales representatives, distributors, dealers, and

   c. setting up and administering procedures and controls on inventories, sales, and costs.

3. Responsibilities are firmly assigned to individuals for selection, training, servicing, and evaluation of resellers.

4. Responsibility is firmly assigned to an individual for control of inventories in the distribution system.

5. The manager is held accountable for:

   a. serious failure to meet sales plan objectives,

   b. loss of major distributors or dealers, and

   c. excessive distribution costs
   resulting from an ineffective distribution system or ineffective administration of the system.

6. Resellers are held accountable for serious or repeated failure to meet sales goals and quotas caused by their failure to use company merchandising aids, sales training, or to stock adequate inventories.

*SOMETIMES OR PARTIALLY

TOTAL POINTS ☐ + 0 + ☐

= ☐

RATING

Enter number of points scored ☐

Enter number of items on checklist ☐

= ☐ × 100 = ☐ %

A product distribution system will work well only when all participants clearly understand their respective responsibilities for performance, and accept accountability for failure to perform—not only company employees but reseller personnel as well. It is almost too obvious to mention that the manager of the function must have firm delegation of authority to expend company funds and sign binding contracts; lacking this authority, the system cannot operate effectively.

Discipline is needed, as well, if the system is to function properly, and resellers, although independent businesspersons, must accept the company's right and obligation to monitor their activities in relation to the firm's products. Serious or repeated shortfalls from quotas and sales goals by resellers resulting from improper use of selling aids and merchandising programs, failure to use available sales and product training, or failure to keep adequate stocks of merchandise on hand should be penalized, in the extreme, by loss of franchise.

WHAT TO DO NOW

1. An effective distribution system doesn't just happen—it must be planned. If the system isn't functioning well, go back to the annual sales plan to determine what is not happening that was planned to happen— or what may be happening that was not anticipated to happen.

2. If the plan does not spell out very clearly and specifically who was supposed to do what, then the plan is deficient and you have a planning problem. If on the other hand, individuals are doing other things than were specified in the plan, then you have an operating or an organizational problem.

3. While recognizing that distributors and dealers are independent businessmen, the company must reserve the right to refuse to sell to any reseller who knowingly violates the firm's code of ethical business conduct, or who fails to move appropriate quantities of product.

15-C
MEASUREMENTS, CONTROL REPORTS AND PERFORMANCE RECORDS

	YES (1)	NO (0)	S/P* (½)
1. The effectiveness of the indirect distribution system is measured regularly and continuously.	___	___	___
2. Effectiveness is measured by comparing actual performance and results with certain benchmarks, standards, or targets, such as			
a. dollar volume of product moved through the system to the end-user,	___	___	___
b. profit margins on product sold,	___	___	___
c. cost per unit of product sold, and	___	___	___
d. meeting sales plan goals.	___	___	___

*SOMETIMES OR PARTIALLY

	YES (1)	NO (0)	S/P* (½)

3. Records are kept, and reports are made, of reseller performance, in terms of:

    a. sales, in units and dollars, vs. quotas and sales plans,

    b. inventories and inventory ratios,

    c. credit and payment performance,

    d. reorder frequency and order size,

    e. reseller turnover, and

    f. problems and complaints.

4. Records are kept of indirect distribution costs and expenses, in total, by geographic district, and by major reseller; detailed by cost element including warranty costs.

5. Cost and expenses are routinely compared with budget, and major variances analyzed for corrective action.

*SOMETIMES OR PARTIALLY

TOTAL POINTS ☐ + 0 + ☐

= ☐

RATING

Enter number of points scored ☐ / Enter number of items on checklist ☐ = × 100 = ☐ %

WHAT THE RATING SIGNIFIES

A product should not be considered as *sold* until it is purchased by the ultimate end-user or consumer, even though the company may have received payment from the distributor or dealer. Ideally, measurements and controls should track products all the way through the distribution chain to their final destination. Only, when the journey is complete—and the consumer is satisfied with his purchase—can the company be assured that the product is really sold. Company management has an obligation to help every member of the chain move the product.

The book publishing industry is presently going through turmoil as booksellers return great amounts of unsold books to publishers for credit. One publisher, in fact, has issued a policy prohibiting returns, but is forced to grant substantial discounts from list price in return. The book business is not typical, to be sure, but it is not entirely unique for producers to find themselves deluged with products returned by wholesalers and dealers long after they had recorded the sales and taken up the profit in the company ledgers.

Ideally, your product should never stop moving, but should flow continuously from production floor to the ultimate user or consumer. This seldom happens in real life, of course, but it represents an ideal condition to strive for.

Reseller performance should be monitored and measured frequently, and in the same terms as that of the firm's own selling employees; that is to say, their effectiveness should be determined by the contributions they make to the firm's gross profit margins in the order book and billings. Sales volume alone is an inadequate measure of real effectiveness because dealers may be moving the lower-margin, low end of the line products that are easier to sell.

A low rating indicates that reseller performance may not be systematically measured, or else may be measured in terms other than genuine results. As a consequence, the profit contribution of resellers may be below its real potential.

WHAT TO DO NOW

1. Make sure that records and control reports are detailed enough to pinpoint trouble spots fast, not just by area but right down to the specific distributor and dealer.

2. The age of inventories at stocking distributors and in dealer's hands is the critical thing to watch; even more critical than the amount. A product that stops moving, and sits on a warehouse shelf or in a showroom is a potential problem, not only for the reseller but the company as well.

3. Educate every member of the distribution chain to the importance of selling the high-margin items in the line. Selling low-margin products and loss leaders is only swapping dollars.

4. Make it easy for your resellers to keep you informed by providing them with a reporting and communication system that is simple to use. Ideally, the system should give distributors and dealers the information *they* need for their own control at the same time.

5. Pay particular attention to problems and complaints, lest they turn into grievances and loss of good resellers.

6. Costs of indirect distribution are important, of course, but they always should be related to performance and results. This means they must be reported as *ratios* as well as absolute dollars.

15-D
OPERATING HISTORY ASSESSMENT

	YES (1)	NO (0)	S/P* (½)
1. A review of records and control reports for the past year shows:			
a. no serious failures to meet objectives of the sales plan,	———	———	———
b. no losses of major distributors or dealers,	———	———	———
c. no major credit losses,	———	———	———
d. no serious inventory buildup or losses, and	———	———	———
e. no excessive cost overruns from budgets resulting from ineffective indirect distribution. (Answer "yes" if true).	———	———	———

	YES (1)	NO (0)	S/P* (½)

2. During the past year there has been an improving trend in:

    a. distribution cost ratio to sales, in total and by major reseller, ___ ___ ___

    b. reseller inventory ratio to sales, ___ ___ ___

    c. reseller turnover, ___ ___ ___

    d. warranty costs, ___ ___ ___

    e. unresolved reseller problems and grievances, ___ ___ ___

    f. size of average reseller order, and ___ ___ ___

    g. credit and collection performance. ___ ___ ___

3. Cost and expense budgets have essentially been met for the past year. ___ ___ ___

*SOMETIMES OR PARTIALLY

TOTAL POINTS [ ] + 0 + [ ]

= [ ]

RATING

Enter number of points scored [ ]
_____ = [ ] × 100 = [ ] %
Enter number of items on checklist [ ]

WHAT THE RATING SIGNIFIES

If this review shows that performance trends and ratios during the past 12 months have not been improving, but are flat or unfavorable, this is a signal that your distribution organization or your procedures need tightening up (or both). Performance that is not getting better may actually be deteriorating in relation to competition, because at least one of your competitors is certain to be improving in performance.

WHAT TO DO NOW

1. It can be risky to wait until year-end to review performance of your reseller organization, because a lot can happen in the meantime. An in-depth analysis, however, based on twelve months of performance reports, can reveal important trends and relationships that are often hidden in interim reports.

2. A set of simple graphs can make the review easier. Plot only one or two factors on each graph—more than this makes them confusing.

15-E
TOP-LEVEL SUPPORT AND GUIDANCE

	YES (1)	NO (0)	S/P* (½)

1. The executive office actively demonstrates support, guidance, and recognition of the indirect distribution function as a major management activity, through:

    a. budget approval, ___ ___ ___

*SOMETIMES OR PARTIALLY

	YES (1)	NO (0)	S/P* (½)

b. periodic review of progress, and ____ ____ ____

c. review and comments on progress reports. ____ ____ ____

2. Top management recognizes the company's resellers as important contributors to the firm's growth and profitability, through:

    a. active participation in reseller council meetings, on occasion, and ____ ____ ____

    b. personal visits to key distributors and dealers. ____ ____ ____

TOTAL POINTS ☐ + 0 + ☐

= ☐

RATING

$$\frac{\text{Enter number of points scored}}{\text{Enter number of items on checklist}} \quad \boxed{} = \boxed{} \times 100 = \boxed{} \%$$

WHAT THE RATING SIGNIFIES

When a substantial portion of the company's output moves to market through independent resellers, top management should provide active and visible endorsement to the organization that manages the distribution process. Top executives must also demonstrate genuine interest and strong support to key distributors and dealers in their work for the company.

A low rating here indicates a low level of concern for the activity by the executive office. As a consequence, company personnel and resellers both may lose motivation to put out their best efforts—leading in the extreme, to failure of the firm's products in the marketplace.

WHAT TO DO NOW

1. In every report to topside, stress the value and the contribution to profit made by the reseller organization, and point out the need for top-level recognition for superior reselling performance.
2. Pareto's Law, also known as the 80/20 rule, says that normally 80 percent of your product is sold by about 20 percent of your resellers. Identify these key resellers and concentrate top management attention on them.

15-F
INNOVATION IN METHODS AND TECHNIQUES

	YES (1)	NO (0)	S/P* (½)

1. An active search is conducted by management for ways to improve the overall effectiveness of the indirect distribution system, through:

    a. reseller committees or councils, ____ ____ ____

	YES (1)	NO (0)	S/P* (½)

b. participation in seminars, workshops, conferences,

c. review of management literature,

d. professional association activities,

e. solicitation of ideas and suggestions from dealers and distributors,

f. industry contacts, and

g. budgets include funds for such activities.

2. The most cost-effective communications means are utilized for two-way communications between home office and the distributor organization in the field, such as:

a. WATS-lines or private wire system,

b. data phone,

c. Telex or TWX,

d. computer terminals,

e. mailgrams,

f. facsimile.

3. The computer is used to store, process, and display information on the indirect distribution organization, including:

a. reseller financial and operating profiles,

b. sales performance,

c. credit limits and collection record,

d. inventories,

e. costs and expenses, and

f. ordering history.

*SOMETIMES OR PARTIALLY

TOTAL POINTS ☐ + 0 + ☐

= ☐

RATING

Enter number of points scored ☐
——————————————————— = ☐ × 100 = ☐ %
Enter number of items on checklist ☐

WHAT THE RATING SIGNIFIES

Any organization made up of independent businesspersons, such as an indirect distribution system, is among the most difficult of organizations to manage. For one thing, the goals and values of the resellers are not always in harmony with those of the company—and sometimes are in conflict. Accordingly, it is essential that distribution management actively seek better ways to control, direct, and motivate the organization.

A less-than-acceptable rating here indicates that the information processing and communication systems between company and resellers may be outmoded and inefficient. As a consequence, reseller productivity may be low and sales opportunities may be missed.

WHAT TO DO NOW

1. Enlist your key distributors and dealers in the search for better methods. Reward them with recognition in company information bulletins, letters from top executives, money, or special terms (if permitted legally).

2. If your reseller organization is more than just local and is made up of more than just a few members, you need a computer to track sales, inventories, and costs. This doesn't necessarily require that you buy your own machine, although the new microprocessors are getting cheaper every day. Actually, the software is more critical than the hardware and it will pay you to get the best.

3. An investment in a modern electronic communication network tying in your resellers can pay dividends in the form of faster-moving and lower inventories, and quicker market feedback on merchandising programs. This can be combined with a computerized control system to give you virtual total control over product distribution.

15-G
INTERFUNCTIONAL COMMUNICATIONS AND COORDINATION

	YES (1)	NO (0)	S/P* (½)
1. The manager of indirect distribution maintains close and continuing contact with managers of other functions of the organization, especially:			
a. legal, on matters relating to trade practices, regulation, and reseller relations,	___	___	___
b. marketing, on matters relative to market demand, sales analysis, new-product plans, competition,	___	___	___
c. production, on matters relating to product quality and availability,	___	___	___
d. comptroller, on matters of credit, collection, and cost controls,	___	___	___
e. advertising and sales promotion, on matters relating to sales support, trade shows, literature,	___	___	___
f. sales training, on matters relating to training assistance to resellers,	___	___	___
g. engineering, on matters relating to product specifications and performance.	___	___	___

*SOMETIMES OR PARTIALLY

TOTAL POINTS □ + 0 + □

= □

RATING

Enter number of points scored   □
—————————————————— =   × 100 = □ %
Enter number of items on checklist □

All functions of the business are involved to an extent with product distribution, even though their involvement may be rather indirect. It is important, therefore, that distribution management maintains good communication with these functions. A low rating here indicates that this vital communication may be less effective than it should be—as a result, important product information may be denied to resellers who need it, and sales may be lost to competitors.

WHAT TO DO NOW

1. There are advantages to allowing direct communications between your resellers and key company departments, but make sure that you are always in the information loop.

2. It is possible to tell your resellers too much, but it rarely happens in practice. More often they are given too little too late.

15-H
INTERFUNCTIONAL IMPROVEMENT PROGRAM

	YES (1)	NO (0)	S/P* (½)
1. There is an active, on-going interfunctional team effort to improve the company's indirect distribution. Major efforts are directed toward:			
a. improved communications between the reseller organization and company personnel,	___	___	___
b. better inventory control,	___	___	___
c. improved incentives and rewards for outstanding reseller sales performance, and	___	___	___
d. improved sales training and sales aids.	___	___	___
2. The team has representation from the following functions, depending on the task:			
a. marketing,	___	___	___
b. information systems,	___	___	___
c. advertising and sales promotion,	___	___	___
d. sales training, and	___	___	___
e. production.	___	___	___
3. The group includes representatives from your independent reseller organization.	___	___	___

*SOMETIMES OR PARTIALLY

TOTAL POINTS   ☐ + 0 + ☐

= ☐

RATING

Enter number of points scored   ☐
———————————————————————   =   ☐ × 100 =   ☐ %
Enter number of items on checklist   ☐

WHAT THE RATING SIGNIFIES

A good rating here indicates that the search for better ways to operate the indirect distribution system is sincere and well organized. There is probably no better way to ensure productive reseller relations than to include one or more of your most progressive resellers on a task force to improve the distribution process.

WHAT TO DO NOW

1. A worthwhile project to tackle using the team approach could be to improve communications between company people and resellers. These are invariably less effective than they could be. This can benefit both immensely, and you can learn a great deal from the team effort.
2. Be sure to record all progress made and document the results. This can benefit subsequent projects.

15-1
RESOURCES

	YES (1)	NO (0)	S/P* (½)
1. The manager of indirect distribution is kept informed about company objectives, policies, plans, and programs, through attendance at key meetings and access to appropriate business plans, marketing and sales plans, capital budgets, and operating reports.	___	___	___
2. Based on the above knowledge, company resources to manage the indirect distribution function are judged to be adequate to meet the needs of the company during the next three, six, and twelve months, in terms of:			
a. manpower,	___	___	___
b. capabilities,	___	___	___
c. facilities,	___	___	___
d. budget funding,	___	___	___
e. communications,	___	___	___
f. computer time and capacity, and	___	___	___
g. other functional support.	___	___	___
3. Resources of the reseller organization are adequate to meet the needs of the company during this same period in terms of:			
a. number of distributors and dealers,	___	___	___
b. reseller facilities for stocking, display, and delivery,	___	___	___
c. reseller sales staffs,	___	___	___
d. geographic coverage,	___	___	___
e. market segment coverage, and	___	___	___
f. reseller financial and management capabilities.	___	___	___

*SOMETIMES OR PARTIALLY

$$\boxed{} + 0 + \boxed{}$$

$$= \boxed{}$$

RATING

Enter number of points scored $\boxed{}$

Enter number of items on checklist $\boxed{}$ $=$ $\boxed{}$ $\times 100 =$ $\boxed{}$ %

WHAT THE RATING SIGNIFIES

Resources must always be evaluated in terms of future needs—in this case, the three, six, and twelve months ahead. Resources are of two kinds, (1) company resources needed to *manage* a distribution network, and (2) reseller resources needed to stock the product, transport it, display it, sell it, and deliver it to the buyer (as well as to install and service the product in some cases).

A low rating here calls for immediate action to obtain the needed resources, at the risk of losing sales and share of market.

WHAT TO DO NOW

1. If resources are lacking you need a *plan* to get them, and your plan should be a selling document. If it requires a reallocation of existing physical resources—computer capacity, for example—you may have to build a case for diverting them from some other purpose.

2. If new resources are needed, your task may be more difficult, because it may require additional funding outside the current budget.

3. In any case, your plan should express benefits in hard dollar terms, preferably as "bottom line" enhancement. This is not always easy, but it is almost always necessary to quantify benefits this way in order to gain top management support.

THE BOTTOM LINE

Distribution is undergoing so much change in so short a time that many marketing managers are bewildered or disoriented. New types of middlemen are appearing, older ones are becoming less effective, distribution channels are becoming more complex, and the marketplace itself is increasingly segmented.

No other function of the business, however, is so crucial to the company's profitability and growth.

More than ever it is essential for management to keep ahead of the distribution power curve, and continually adapt the company's distribution system to the changing realities and complexities of the marketplace. This is particularly true of the smaller, rapidly growing enterprise. As markets become more and more segmented and selective, and as distribution costs become one of the firm's largest cost factors, management must ensure that the activity is regularly and systematically reviewed so that the most cost-effective and competitive channels of distribution are used. Often this requires innovative new combinations of direct and indirect channels, and controlled experimentation with new methods for reaching the consumer or end-user, such as through franchising, rack jobbers, or vending.

One fact is clear; a producer that clings to outmoded distribution systems and fails to adapt to changes in user buying patterns takes a chance of losing not only share of market, but profitability as well.

Distribution in a Service Organization

Providers of services as well as producers of products must constantly evaluate and change their distribution methods. Western Union, for instance, has been forced to make a massive change in the way it distributes its basic product, the telegram. Not too long ago, Western Union owned and operated telegraph offices could be found in every city, town, and hamlet in the country—today few of these offices remain.

As telegram volume declined in recent years, the costs of staffing and maintaining thousands of offices became a heavy burden on the company. The first change was to shift message and money order traffic to commission agents as offices were closed. As telegram volume continued to drop, however, the strategy was to shift delivery of most messages to the U.S. Postal Service which has offices everywhere. Thus the Western Union Mailgram—a form of electronic mail—was born. Slower than the telegram, but a whole lot cheaper, the volume of Mailgrams grew as the number of telegrams diminished. By now, the telegram has almost vanished from the American scene, a victim of low-cost long distance telephone rates and a massive change in population demographics.

SUMMARY OF SELF-AUDIT RATINGS
AND FUNCTIONAL IMPROVEMENT GOALS

If you wish, you may summarize the ratings for each function at the end of each section, on this "Summary Rating" form. (A "function" is the equivalent of a chapter.) The rating is simply an arithmetic average of the ratings on Checklists A through I—that is, the total divided by 9. This form also provides space for listing the Improvement Goals for each function.

Under each function, enter the rating percentage for each Checklist section, A through I. "Function Number 1," for example, is the first (1st) chapter in the section, regardless of its number in the book—5, 11, or so on. The Summary Rating is the total of each column divided by 9, to give you an average rating for the total function. The lower portion of the form can be used to list your improvement goals for each function.

	FUNCTION NUMBER					
CHECKLIST	1 %	2 %	3 %	4 %	5 %	6 %
A	_____	_____	_____	_____	_____	_____
B	_____	_____	_____	_____	_____	_____
C	_____	_____	_____	_____	_____	_____
D	_____	_____	_____	_____	_____	_____
E	_____	_____	_____	_____	_____	_____
F	_____	_____	_____	_____	_____	_____
G	_____	_____	_____	_____	_____	_____
H	_____	_____	_____	_____	_____	_____
I	_____	_____	_____	_____	_____	_____
SUMMARY RATING (%)	_____	_____	_____	_____	_____	_____

IMPROVEMENT GOALS

_____

_____

_____

_____

_____

_____

_____

(Use separate sheet as required)

Section **VI**

Managing the Selling Effort

Sales management is not a single function but rather encompasses a wide range of organized activities which add up to the efficient direction of the company's field selling organization. As defined here for purposes of appraisal, the sales management section will cover six separate but interrelated functions. They are:

1. *Training the Sales Force*—The combination of formal classroom training and on-the-job (OJT) training in the field.
2. *Improving Sales Productivity*—Sharpening up the basic skills that sales representatives exercise when actually making sales, from preparing for the call to the post-order wrap-up.
3. *Controlling Sales Activities*—The combination of formalized controls used by the sales manager to direct the activities of the sales force as it carries out the Sales Plan, together with the "self controls" used by individual sales representatives to manage their own activities efficiently. In effect, sales control is the implementation of the annual sales plan.
4. *Preparing the Sales Plan*—The annual development of a formal sales plan intended to guide the selling activities productively throughout the year. An important element of the sales plan is a set of goals or objectives that are realistic and achievable, yet "stretch the capabilities" of every individual.
5. *Supervising the Field Sales Force*—The direct first-level supervision of sales representatives in the field.

287

6. *Reporting Sales Activities*—The formalized system of two-way communications between field and home offices designed to keep both well-informed.

Obviously, in large business firms these activities tend to become highly specialized, while in smaller firms people often have responsibility for two or more of these activities. Nevertheless, every one of these functions must be performed by a selling organization that has more than local market coverage and is made up of more than just a few individuals.

It must be recognized, of course, that these activities cost money and take time of both management and field sales people. It is probable, however, that no other investment will pay such high dividends in growth and profitability.

The field sales force is out on the competitive firing line every day of the week. When it is made up of well-trained individuals who are skilled in the techniques of professional salesmanship and knowledgeable about the company, its products, and its competition—and intelligently supervised by first-level managers skilled in human relations—the company's order book and billings will be healthy. When the sales force and its individual members are further motivated by goals and plans that emphasize personal development as well as company profit, remarkable things can be accomplished.

EVERY BUSINESS FIRM WAS SMALL ONCE

Those that survived the perilous early stages, and grew into strong, profitable organizations with well-balanced product lines, did so because they developed the ability to meet the changing needs of customers. This was done largely by fielding sales forces superior in skill and dedication to their competitors, and backing them up with strong support and intelligent sales management. Those that failed did so largely because they failed to build a personal relationship with customers and prospects through the selling organization, or else they lost touch with their customers by neglecting their needs once they were sold.

SALES MANAGEMENT— WHAT IT IS AND ISN'T

Both literally and in practice, sales management means the management of selling; that is, to persuade prospective buyers through personal contact to purchase the company's products and services. Sales management covers selling *directly* to end-users through company salesmen or sales agents, and also *indirectly* through distributors, wholesalers, and retailers. (Product distribution is covered in two separate sections of this manual.)

Selling is, of course, one of the three fundamental line operations of a business; the other two being designing the product and producing it. With recognition that marketing is an integrated series of activities, it can be said that selling (at a profit) is the end objective and ultimate test of effective marketing—and its most important single activity.

Although in some usage the term "sales management" may cover other marketing activities (such as order handling, warehouse control or sales analysis, sometimes even covering the full scope of marketing itself), this broader interpretation can only lead to confusion and should be discouraged. The fact that a "sales manager" in a particular situation may be responsible for activities outside the scope of sales management as defined here does not change the basic functional content of sales management.

TWO KEY IDEAS   The term "sales management" encompasses two ideas. The first, *sales*, emphasizes the vital role of personal selling; of getting the order and making the sale. Three of the functions covered by this section of the manual—Sales Training, Salesmanship, and Sales Control—concentrate primarily on this aspect. The other word and concept, *management*, refers to the "planning, organization, and direction" aspect, which is particularly evident on the sections in Sales Planning, Field Sales Supervision and Sales Reporting. The reason for emphasizing this distinction between selling and management is to stress the point that successful sales management requires a skillful mix and balancing of both elements.

A thorough and searching review should be made of the six functions comprising sales management. The review and appraisal should focus on measurements of actual sales department performance and *results*—sales productivity, sales and new order input, new accounts gained, product profit margins and other measures of real output.

Each of these is covered in detail in the six sections that follow. (Note: The terms "salesman," "salesperson," and "sales representative" are used interchangeably with full awareness of the increasing role of women in sales work and sales management.)

KEY AIM OF THE SELF-AUDIT   The overall objective of the appraisal is to ensure that the company has a professional sales management competence and effectiveness equal to or better than that of its strongest competitor.

Other specific goals of the appraisal are to assure that sales management has demonstrated a high degree of capability to plan, organize, direct, and control all sales activities, so that market opportunities are converted economically and efficiently into firm orders and sales.

Chapter **16**

How to Train
The Sales Force

Sales training is an organized activity designed to develop, improve, and maintain the selling skills, knowledge, and attitudes of personnel responsible for selling the firm's products and services. It includes initial training for new salespersons and sales agents, continuous retraining for experienced sales personnel, and special training for sales support (e.g., order handling) personnel.

The principal purpose of sales training is to make new sales personnel effective and productive in the field quickly, and to keep experienced sales representatives and sales agents functioning with ever-improving skill and competitive effectiveness.

TRAINING IS NO PLACE FOR AMATEURS

Sales training, in one form or another, is performed by every sales organization. Whether it is done well depends to a great extent on whether it is conducted by a competent trainer on a formal, organized basis. This does not necessarily mean that a full-time sales training professional be employed (which smaller companies frequently cannot afford), but it does mean that responsibility for developing and implementing sales training should be assigned (even though part-time) to someone who has been trained in sales training. *An unskilled sales trainer can do more harm than good.*

WHO SHOULD ATTEND SALES TRAINING

Participation in sales training should not be limited to direct sales representatives and sales agents, but should include all employees who are regularly in contact with prospects or customers. Marketing and sales support personnel, such as those involved in sales promotion, advertising, customer service, and proposal preparation, should also be provided with appropriate sales training in order to support the direct selling effort productively.

Training of customers in the use of the company's products is part of customer service,* so is not included under sales training. Training may also be provided to distributor and dealer sales personnel, but that is covered in the section on Product Distribution.

THE FOUR BASIC ASPECTS OF SALES TRAINING:

1. *quality* of the sales training,
2. *content* of sales training programs,
3. the extent of *participation in* training and retraining,
4. *use of* effective sales training facilities, techniques, and materials.

KEY AIM OF THE SELF-AUDIT

The principal goals of the appraisal are to assure that every direct salesperson is thoroughly trained in basic selling techniques, principles of professional salesmanship, and the features and benefits of the company's products before confronting a prospect on his or her own; every salesperson is continually retrained in order to keep his or her selling competence and sales productivity high; and all sales support people are exposed to sales training in order to perform their support roles more effectively.

A basic criterion is that the sales training produce a sales force that is equal to or better than that of the company's strongest competitors in selling skill and product knowledge.

*See Section VII—"Managing Customer Service."

HOW TO USE THE CHECKLISTS

For each of the statements in the Checklist, compare the condition of your function to the "ideal" as described in the statement. Then:

1. If you consider the statement to be *generally true* of your function, check the YES column.
2. If you consider the statement to be *untrue* of your function, check the NO column.
3. If you consider the statement to be *less than true* (but not totally untrue) of your function, check the SOMETIMES OR PARTIAL column.
4. If the statement does not apply to your particular situation, write "Not Applicable" across the response spaces (or simply draw a line through them).
5. If you lack the data for a definite response, write in "Not Answerable" or "Don't Know."

HOW TO EVALUATE YOUR RESPONSES

When you have completed the checklist, glance over your responses, keeping these points in mind:

1. A negative answer is always unfavorable because it indicates a problem within the function: the greater the number of NOs, the more serious the situation.
2. A positive response is always a good indication. But too many YES answers could indicate that your review is not objective enough.
3. Too many SOMETIMES OR PARTIALLY answers can point to internal weaknesses or to a lack of firm direction.
4. A lot of "Not Applicable" answers could indicate that you are avoiding the issue.
5. A large number of "Not Answerable" or "Don't Know" answers could be symptomatic of inadequate records or data bases.

HOW TO RATE AND SCORE YOUR RESPONSES

When you are satisfied with your responses in general, you are ready to score the Checklist. For your convenience, a self-explanatory Scoring and Rating Block follows each Checklist. This block not only tells you whether the condition of your function is satisfactory, but it also gives you a measure of its effectiveness.

Here's how to total up the points for inclusion in the Scoring and Rating Block:

1. Total up the number of points you scored:
   a. For each YES, give yourself one point.
   b. For each NO, give yourself zero.
   c. For each SOMETIMES OR PARTIALLY, give yourself a half-point.
   d. For each "Not Applicable" answer, give yourself zero and deduct one from the number of items on the Checklist.
   e. For each "Not Answerable" or "Don't Know" answer, give yourself zero.
2. Next divide the total number of points you score by the total number of items (statements) on the Checklist (less items marked "Not Applicable"). You'll get a 1.0 for a perfect score and a fraction for anything less.
3. Multiply the result of step 2 by 100 to arrive at the percentage for your score.

What is a satisfactory rating? A rating of less than 65 percent is unacceptable and calls for an improvement program: Obviously, the lower the rating, the more drastic the action required.

A brief "how-to" example of this Scoring and Rating system follows . . .

EXAMPLE

	YES (1)	NO (0)	S/P* (½)
1. Field sale reports designed to provide information on sales progress contain data on the following topics:			
a. sales calls and sales presentations made by salespersons and sales agents,	✓		
b. bids, quotations, and proposals made,	✓		
c. new orders booked,	✓		
d. lost business, and reasons for the loss,		✓	
e. accomplishments toward future orders,			✓
f. performance in filling orders, handling complaints, and otherwise servicing individual customers,	✓		
g. action taken in response to customer requests, such as sending samples, spec sheets, etc.,	✓		
h. accomplishments of significance and value to other members of the sales force.			✓

*SOMETIMES OR PARTIALLY

TOTAL POINTS $\boxed{5}$ + 0 + $\boxed{1}$

= $\boxed{6}$

RATING

$$\frac{\text{Enter number of points scored} \quad \boxed{6}}{\text{Enter number of items on checklist} \quad \boxed{8}} = .75 \times 100 = \boxed{75}\%$$

16-A
ORGANIZATION, ADMINISTRATION, AND OPERATION

	YES (1)	NO (0)	S/P* (½)
1. Sales training is recognized as a vital company activity that has top management endorsement and support, and an important function of the sales department.	_____	_____	_____
2. The activity is recognized on the organization charts as a discrete function (even though part-time) reporting to the sales manager.	_____	_____	_____
3. The function is managed and staffed by training professionals who are informed about the company's products, markets, and sales organization (or if the sales force is small, by a sales manager trained in sales training).	_____	_____	_____
4. The activity has a formal budget allocation covering internal expenses and outside services if required, including housing and transportation of trainees.	_____	_____	_____
5. Sales training procedures and course materials are professionally prepared and documented in writing.	_____	_____	_____
6. Every newly hired salesperson is given formal classroom sales training before going into the field, *regardless of his experience*.	_____	_____	_____
7. All direct sales personnel and sales supervisors participate in formal retraining sessions on a regular scheduled basis.	_____	_____	_____
8. Sales supervisors and managers are given specialized training in sales management, either in-house or by outside specialists.	_____	_____	_____
9. Sales support personnel regularly participate in formal sales training classes.	_____	_____	_____
10. The manager of sales training routinely attends top-level meetings on matters of sales planning, sales control, sales productivity, and field sales reporting.	_____	_____	_____
11. The sales training function effectively conducts both formal classroom and on-the-job-training.	_____	_____	_____
12. Field sales supervisors who train salespersons are given training in sales training.	_____	_____	_____
13. The sales training function follows through to ensure that established standards are maintained by sales supervisors when conducting field training.	_____	_____	_____
14. The progress of sales trainees in the field is closely followed for three to six months after their initial training is completed.	_____	_____	_____
15. Sales training programs are tailored to the company's needs in terms of content and amount of training.	_____	_____	_____
16. The sales training function responds quickly to changes in the company's needs; that is, to changes in products and markets.	_____	_____	_____
17. Salespersons' performance during sales training is recorded and included in their performance evaluations.	_____	_____	_____
18. Training facilities are adequate in size and ammenities.	_____	_____	_____
19. All candidates for sales positions are given company indoctrination by working in key departments, such as customer service, order processing, or installation, prior to going into the field.	_____	_____	_____

*SOMETIMES OR PARTIALLY

	YES (1)	NO (0)	S/P* (½)

20. Sales training is comprehensive, covering:

    a. the job of the salesperson,

    b. knowledge of the company's history, policies, procedures and objectives,

    c. knowledge of the company's products and services,

    d. knowledge of competitive products,

    e. the psychology of selling,

    f. selling techniques, and

    g. principles of professional salesmanship.

21. Sales training courses emphasize the practical side of selling, such as:

    a. how to prospect for new business,

    b. how to use time efficiently,

    c. how to complete field sales reports,

    d. how to control expenses,

    e. how to use the telephone to sell,

    f. how to use sales aids and visual aids,

    g. how to improve customer relations and communications,

    h. how to forecast sales, and

    i. product quality as a sales tool.

22. Sales training covers important policy matters, such as:

    a. pricing policies,

    b. credit policies,

    c. cancellation and return policies,

    d. delivery procedures and problems, and

    e. service policies.

23. Sales training strongly emphasizes self-control, self-appraisal, and personal development.

24. Training program goals are expressed in terms that can be monitored and measured.

25. Trainers employ up-to-date teaching methods, equipment, materials, and training aids.

26. Sales training is included on the agenda of all sales meetings.

27. An important part of training is the close and continuous exchange of ideas and experience among field sales people.

28. Sales training personnel are aware of training methods used by other firms in the industry, and by competitors.

29. Last but not least, all sales training emphasizes *how to close the sale.*

*SOMETIMES OR PARTIALLY

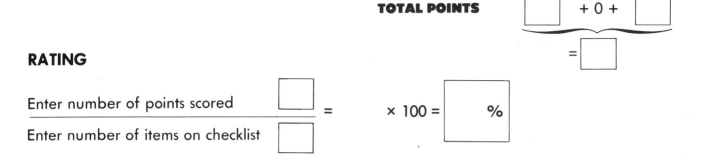

TOTAL POINTS   ☐ + 0 + ☐

= ☐

RATING

Enter number of points scored ☐
―――――――――――――――――――――――――――――   =   × 100 = ☐ %
Enter number of items on checklist ☐

WHAT THE RATING   **Sales Training Is a Critical Part**
SIGNIFIES   **Of the Sales Force Selection Process**

Despite the claims of some sales recruiting people, no one really knows with certainty what the profile is of an ideal salesperson, or whether a candidate for a selling job will be successful. A good training program can help immeasurably by weeding out the unfit before they are put into the field where they might cause great harm to the company.

Sales Training Is Never Finished

Products change, customer needs change, competitors change, and companies change—so sales people need constant training and retraining to keep current with these changes. Simply to send out periodic notices and bulletins to the sales force is not enough. What is needed is assurance that the significance of these changes is understood, and that sales people factor their understanding into their selling efforts when they are face-to-face with customers.

If the appraisal discloses deficiencies in *formal initial training*, such as lack of professionalism by the training staff, ineffective training programs, or outmoded training methods and equipment, you may be creating problems by fielding salespeople inadequately informed about the company, its products, and its customer policies. It doesn't matter that the new people may have been selling for twenty years, they still need this training, perhaps even more so!

Never forget that a sales representative commits the company to a specific course of action every time a new customer order is written up. If the sales person unknowingly violates credit policy or pricing policy, or commits the company to an impossible delivery date, the situation is set up for at minimum a customer complaint and at worst, a legal action.

On-the-job training (OJT) is a necessary part of a good sales training program, but it does not take the place of formal training. All too often, trainers in the field are overworked sales supervisors with insufficient time to spend training new sales reps. Or worse, the supervisor pairs up the new arrivals with experienced sales reps who promptly pass on all their bad habits to the newcomers.

No company is so small that it does not need to train its salespeople. Many small firms, in fact, have thrived by fielding a better trained and motivated sales force than their larger competitors—some of whom had become fat, dumb, and happy over the years, and had neglected to keep their selling organization trained to meet their customers' changing needs.

A less-than-satisfactory rating is evidence of management failure to recognize that sales training can be one of the most important contributors to the firm's sales success. Good salespeople are not born; they're *made*. The raw material has to be there to begin with, to be sure, but raw material always has to be processed to make it into a finished product.

WHAT TO DO NOW

1. You *must* have a sales training program—it is not an option. If you can't sell management on the need, then you have failed the test as a salesperson yourself.

2. While you're creating the program, put your new sales candidates to work for a day or two in several key departments, such as customer service, credit and collection, order processing, warehousing, etc. Ask a responsible person in each department to coach the newcomers, and make sure they do "hands-on" work. This is a good test; a candidate who refuses doesn't belong on your sales team.

3. If candidates lack training in professional salesmanship, utilize one of the professional outside resources for this until you can provide it in-house.

4. Send each trainee out on joint sales calls with your *best* salesperson and meet with them jointly to discuss results of each call.

16-B
AUTHORITY, RESPONSIBILITY AND ACCOUNTABILITY

	YES (1)	NO (0)	S/P* (½)
1. Authority has been delegated, through budget allocation and position description, to the manager of sales training to expend company funds and assign tasks necessary to train the company's sales force.	___	___	___
2. The manager is responsible for staffing and managing an organization capable of training the sales force to a high order of selling effectiveness.	___	___	___
3. The manager is also responsible for establishing and administering effective sales training programs and courses.	___	___	___
4. Sales supervisors are responsible for scheduling training for all newly hired sales representatives, and for periodic retraining of all sales representatives.	___	___	___
5. The manager of sales training is held accountable for serious failure to meet sales plan objectives caused by inadequate or ineffective training of the sales force.	___	___	___
6. Sales supervisors likewise are held accountable for failure to meet sales plan objectives in their respective districts or territories, because of inadequate on-the-job training.	___	___	___

*SOMETIMES OR PARTIALLY

TOTAL POINTS   ☐ + 0 + ☐

☐

= ☐

RATING

Enter number of points scored ☐

——————————————— = × 100 = ☐ %

Enter number of items on checklist ☐

WHAT THE RATING SIGNIFIES

Accountability is the key factor here. Personnel responsible for sales training should be held accountable for results in terms of performance by the people they train. The output of a sales training program is not numbers of trainees put through the program—*it is the value of new business booked by these people in the field.*

It's not unlike our educational system which is doing a good job if measured by the numbers of individuals graduated by the nation's high schools. Unfortunately, it has been found that many of these who go on to college have to be given remedial training before they can cope with college-level material, and those who enter the job market are found to lack needed skills.

Before people can be held accountable for results, of course, they must know what results they're responsible for, and they must have a measure of authority in order to accomplish these results.

A low rating indicates that one or more of these factors are not clearly defined. As a consequence, sales training may tend to be a "numbers game" rather than a quality development program.

WHAT TO DO NOW

1. Start by defining precisely what each sales trainer is accountable for, beginning with yourself.

2. Recognize that there is a natural tendency to avoid liability for failure to meet the goals of the sales plan by blaming the failure on factors other than training—such as tough competition, poor product quality, the recession, high prices, the weather, or just plain bad luck! Don't fall into this trap. The purpose of training is to equip your salespeople to cope with these adversities; if they can't, *it's your fault, not theirs.*

3. To define responsibility, turn these definitions of accountability around into positive statements of results for each individual, again starting with yourself.

4. Finally, make sure you have adequate authority to do the job. Not just a job title, but money, resources, and power to reward accomplishment and penalize failure. Training is an easy target for cost-cutting because there's an immediate favorable impact on the bottom line. It's only later that new orders slow down, customers defect to competitors, production capacity becomes idle, overhead costs per unit go through the roof, and profits disappear—starting a new cycle of cost-cutting that can spiral the company downward into insolvency.

	YES (1)	NO (0)	S/P* (½)

1. The effectiveness of sales training is determined by:

   a. the effectiveness (productivity) of the new hires in the field,

   b. continued improvement in productivity of the total sales force, and

   c. in the final analysis, by the ability of the sales force to meet sales plan objectives.

   (It is recognized that other factors have an influence on performance, but sales training is a major determinant of sales success.)

2. Records of key sales productivity measures by individual and by group, such as percent of quota achieved, sales to call ratio, and ratio of repeat orders to new orders are used to evaluate training effectiveness.

3. Monthly reports are prepared by sales training covering number of persons trained, expenses vs. budget, and cost per trainee.

*SOMETIMES OR PARTIALLY

TOTAL POINTS   ☐ + 0 + ☐

= ☐

RATING

Enter number of points scored ☐
─────────────────────────────── = × 100 = ☐ %
Enter number of items on checklist ☐

WHAT THE RATING SIGNIFIES

All performance measurements should be designed to measure actual selling productivity, nothing else. Internal reports on numbers of individuals trained, cost per trainee, and the like are necessary of course, but these are measures of training *efficiency*, not effectiveness. (*Efficiency* has been defined as "doing something right;" *effectiveness* as "doing the right something.")

A low rating here indicates that the effectiveness of the sales training function may not be measured in terms of genuine *results*, that is, the performance of trained sales people in the field.

WHAT TO DO NOW

What is needed is a four-step process to:

1. Define the specific results you desire from the training program.
2. Identify the standards, benchmarks, targets, or goals by which these results should be measured.
3. Set up control reports to capture actual results and compare these with your standards.
4. Flag sub-standard performance by individuals and groups for corrective action, as well as to highlight above-standard performers for commendation (and incentive for others).

16-D
OPERATING PERFORMANCE HISTORY

	YES (1)	NO (0)	S/P* (½)
1. A review of records and control reports for the past year shows no serious failures to meet sales plan goals resulting from inadequate training programs, or inadequately trained sales personnel. (Answer "yes" if true.)	———	———	———
2. A review of control reports and performance records for the past year shows:			
a. an improving trend in sales productivity for the sales force in total,	———	———	———
b. improved selling effectiveness of new salespersons during their first three months in the field,	———	———	———
c. an increase in the number of persons receiving routine retraining.	———	———	———
3. The function essentially met its expense budget for the past year.	———	———	———

*SOMETIMES OR PARTIALLY

TOTAL POINTS ☐ + 0 + ☐

= ☐

RATING

Enter number of points scored ☐

―――――――――――――――――――――― = × 100 = ☐ %

Enter number of items on checklist ☐

WHAT THE RATING SIGNIFIES

A periodic review—at least once a year—of past performance is essential in order to know with any certainty what deficiencies and weaknesses may exist within the sales training function. Data for a period of at least one full year is needed to show whether trends are favorable or unfavorable. This requires an analysis of actual records, not just someone's recollection of what may have happened. This may be hazy or inaccurate.

Remember that it is said that all our knowledge is about the past, yet all our decisions are about the future. A less-than-acceptable rating here is a signal that our only real knowledge is being ignored.

WHAT TO DO NOW

1. One of the best ways to analyze trends is through simple time-series graphs. Assign a responsible person the task to set up and maintain such a graph for each key performance factor, going back as far as your records allow. This is good training in management.

2. Recognize that unfavorable trends cannot be reversed overnight. Set a reasonable time schedule to bring each unfavorable factor up to standard.

16-E
TOP-LEVEL SUPPORT AND GUIDANCE

	YES (1)	NO (0)	S/P* (½)

1. The executive office demonstrates active support of sales training by:

    a. approval of capital and expense budgets for sales training, _____ _____ _____

    b. endorsement of sales training as company policy, _____ _____ _____

    c. recognition of outstanding trainees, and _____ _____ _____

    d. talks to training classes. _____ _____ _____

*SOMETIMES OR PARTIALLY

TOTAL POINTS [ ] + 0 + [ ]

= [ ]

RATING

Enter number of points scored [ ]
——————————————————————— = × 100 = [ ] %
Enter number of items on checklist [ ]

WHAT THE RATING SIGNIFIES

The more aware top management is of the value of sales training, the better the chances are that the company has an effective program. What's more, the chances are better that the program will not be thrown overboard at the first sign of stormy weather.

A poor rating in this section is a warning that the "awareness level" of the executive office may be dangerously low. As a consequence, the training activity may be starved for funding or other resources.

WHAT TO DO NOW

1. Sell the value of your function to top management at every opportunity, even if you have to create the opportunity. Play up the achievements of your trainees in the field in your progress reports.

2. Stress results in terms of the bottom line whenever possible in reports to top management.

3. Get top-level managers *involved*. Invite them to address graduation classes and present awards to the outstanding students.

16-F
INNOVATION IN METHODS AND TECHNIQUES

	YES (1)	NO (0)	S/P* (½)

1. New and more effective training methods are actively sought through participation by training managers in:

    a. sales training seminars and conferences,

    b. professional associations,

    c. industry contacts,

    d. supplier demos and trade shows,

    e. review of current literature,

    f. solicitation of ideas from personnel at all levels, especially field sales, and

    g. budgets include funds for such activities.

2. Sales training personnel use up-to-date training methods and materials, including:

    a. role playing,

    b. case studies,

    c. demonstrations,

    d. sales meetings,

    e. field coaching and counseling,

    f. samples and models,

    g. sales manuals,

    h. tests (written and performance),

    i. textbooks on salesmanship,

    j. sales bulletins,

    k. product catalogs, and

    l. training manuals.

3. Training programs also utilize such methods as:

    a. live presentations and skits,

    b. motion pictures, closed circuit TV, video tape,

    c. tape recorders,

    d. slides, flipcharts, transparencies,

    e. exhibits and displays, and

    f. joint sales calls.

4. When appropriate, training programs include:

    a. branch office training,

    b. programmed learning courses,

*SOMETIMES OR PARTIALLY

	YES (1)	NO (0)	S/P* (½)
c. public speaking courses,	___	___	___
d. correspondence courses,	___	___	___
e. headquarters schools,	___	___	___
f. industry training courses, and	___	___	___
g. trade journals.	___	___	___

5. The computer is used for training, as well as to store, process, and display information on productivity of sales personnel.

TOTAL POINTS [ ] + 0 + [ ]

= [ ]

RATING

Enter number of points scored [ ]
———————————————————— = [ ] × 100 = [ ] %
Enter number of items on checklist [ ]

WHAT THE RATING SIGNIFIES

A less-than-satisfactory rating indicates that the company's sales training may be out of step with the times. Training methods constantly change. To use old-fashioned, unproductive methods to teach people how to sell productively in the 1980's is like using a quill pen to write a computer program.

WHAT TO DO NOW

1. Make sure that training people stay up with the latest state of the art, by taking periodic refresher courses and by keeping informed about what others are doing. This costs money, of course, but it can pay a high return in better trained sales personnel who produce more sales sooner.

2. If you're not using most of the methods and materials listed under point 2, consider them for future use. Practically every one has a place in a good sales training program at one time or another.

3. New developments such as microprocessors, satellite communications, and videodiscs will make it possible to train people quicker and at less cost in the future. Keep up with the literature on these.

16-G
INTERFUNCTIONAL COMMUNICATIONS AND COORDINATION

	YES (1)	NO (0)	S/P* (½)

1. Managers responsible for sales training maintain close and continuing contact with managers of other business functions, especially:

    a. field sales, to assure that training is relevant to the "real world," _____ _____ _____

    b. customer service, to keep informed about consumer attitudes and changing needs, _____ _____ _____

    c. marketing, to be informed about new product and new market developments, _____ _____ _____

    d. production, to keep informed about product quality and output problems, _____ _____ _____

    e. product distribution, to keep informed about product availability, and distributor/dealer attitudes, and _____ _____ _____

    f. legal, for advice on legal aspects of selling and consumer rights. _____ _____ _____

2. Communication with other functions is achieved through personal contact and:

    a. exchange of progress reports, and _____ _____ _____

    b. reciprocal attendance privileges at departmental meetings. _____ _____ _____

3. Other functions—engineering, production, quality assurance, marketing, etc.—make a positive contribution to sales training. _____ _____ _____

*SOMETIMES OR PARTIALLY

TOTAL POINTS [ ] + 0 + [ ]

= [ ]

RATING

Enter number of points scored [ ]
──────────────────────────────── = × 100 = [ ] %
Enter number of items on checklist [ ]

WHAT THE RATING SIGNIFIES
The field salesperson is the chief means through which all business functions communicate directly with customers. Sales training is an important part of this communication process, so every business function needs to be involved in the training.

A low rating here is an indication that the sales trainers may be failing to serve this communication purpose, by not factoring trends and developments in other functions into the training.

WHAT TO DO NOW
1. Make sure that those responsible for sales training, including field sales supervisors who do on-the-job training, are wired in to what's happening in other company departments. This takes time, of course, but it's a worthwhile expenditure of their time.

2. Persuade managers from other departments to give sales trainees firsthand information about the goings-on in their functions. This can build a useful, productive, and beneficial bridge between these functions and the field sales force.

16-H
FUNCTIONAL IMPROVEMENT PROGRAM

	YES (1)	NO (0)	S/P* (½)

1. There is an active on-going interfunctional team effort to improve sales training, specifically to:

   a. convert product features into benefits to customers,

   b. make programs more responsive to changing customer needs,

   c. enhance the professionalism of sales personnel,

   d. relate training to company objectives, and

   e. emphasize self-control, self-appraisal, and personal development of all sales personnel.

2. The team includes representatives from the following functions, depending on the task:

   a. field sales,

   b. customer service,

   c. marketing,

   d. personnel and organizational development, and

   e. product distribution.

*SOMETIMES OR PARTIALLY

TOTAL POINTS   ☐ + 0 + ☐

= ☐

RATING

Enter number of points scored ☐
────────────────────────────── = ☐ × 100 = ☐ %
Enter number of items on checklist ☐

WHAT THE RATING SIGNIFIES

This section is an extension of the previous one. It is intended to measure the extent to which the various functions work together on an organized basis to improve sales training operations.

Few organizations have an organized process of the kind indicated here, but those that do are highly productive. If yours is one of these, consider yourself lucky. If not, as evidenced by a low rating here, you could probably benefit by setting one up.

1. Start by identifying the single aspect of sales training that needs improving most; let's say item 1(a) which places emphasis on customer benefits.
2. Decide what other functions are involved, or could contribute to the improvement task; for example, quality assurance, market research, and customer service.
3. Persuade, cajole, or otherwise induce a member of each of these functions to meet together with you to jointly develop a training program to stress *customer benefits* from the use of the company's product; in particular, how to convert product features into user benefits.
4. Make sure that participants are rewarded, at least with public credit, for their contributions.

16-1
RESOURCES

	YES (1)	NO (0)	S/P* (½)
1. The manager of sales training is kept informed about major new developments, objectives, and forward plans of the company, by means of participation in marketing meetings, and access to appropriate business plans, capital budgets, new-product plans, and operating reports.	———	———	———
2. Based on knowledge of the company's plans and objectives, resources are considered adequate to meet company needs for sales training for the next three, six, and twelve months, in terms of:			
a. manpower,	———	———	———
b. capabilities,	———	———	———
c. budget funding,	———	———	———
d. facilities and equipment,	———	———	———
e. outside services, and	———	———	———
f. support from other functions.	———	———	———

*SOMETIMES OR PARTIALLY

TOTAL POINTS $\boxed{} + 0 + \boxed{}$

$= \boxed{}$

RATING

Enter number of points scored $\boxed{}$

Enter number of items on checklist $\boxed{}$

$= \times 100 = \boxed{}\ \%$

A sales trainer who is ill-informed about the company's direction and its progress can't possibly do an effective job of training sales people. This is a clear case of the "blind leading the blind!" What is more, without knowledge of the company's needs, the trainer has no way of knowing whether the resources of the function are adequate to meet those needs during the period ahead.

A low rating in this final section is a strong signal that the sales training function may be isolated from the company's information network. This poses a risk that the training will be out of joint with the company's goals, policies, standards, norms, and values. It also leads to the danger that its resources may be inadequate to meet future training needs—or to the lesser danger that resources could be excessive to needs and therefore more costly than they should be.

WHAT TO DO NOW

1. Make sure that all sales training people are in the mainstream of information about the company, its product lines, its markets, and competitors. This will ensure that the sales personnel are trained by well-informed people.

2. It must be recognized that there is an element of risk that sensitive plans for market development or new products might leak to competitors. This risk can never be eliminated, but you can minimize it by ensuring that the department has clear specific policies and standard practices relating to the handling and distribution of company confidential material.

17

How to Improve Productivity
Of the Individual Salesperson

Salesmanship is the ability, based on knowledge, training and skill, of a representative personally to persuade a prospective buyer to make a favorable buying decision.

The success of the company in meeting its marketing objectives (indeed, its ultimate survival) depends largely on the selling performance of its sales representatives, whether direct sales personnel, sales agents, or distributors and dealers. Sales productivity improvement is concerned with activities designed to upgrade the personal selling skills of persons responsible for face-to-face contact with prospects. These skills must be reviewed constantly by sales and marketing management to ensure sales productivity.

Despite the variations in product characteristics, customer needs, and nature of competition that exist among companies, successful selling requires certain basic skills common to all sales groups.

SIX BASIC SKILLS: ESSENTIAL ELEMENTS OF SALESMANSHIP

1. preparation for making the call,
2. approach to the prospect or customer,
3. presentation or sales message,
4. overcoming objections,
5. closing the sale, and
6. post-order performance.

SUPERIOR SALESMANSHIP AND HIGH SALES PRODUCTIVITY GO HAND-IN-HAND.

Both these attributes are direct functions of superior sales training and superior sales management, and manifest themselves by meeting and exceeding the objectives of the sales plan.

Note: Although salesmanship is not a discrete and tangible organizational function in the same sense as sales training, it is nonetheless possible and necessary to appraise it as a business activity. This is done by reviewing your appraisals of *sales training*, *sales control*, and *sales supervision*. Deficiencies in these functions are evidence of deficiencies in salesmanship—these should then be further defined by responding to the specific Salesmanship Checklist "A" attached. Checklists "B" through "I" do not apply to this particular activity.

HOW TO USE THE CHECKLISTS

For each of the statements in the Checklist, compare the condition of your function to the "ideal" as described in the statement. Then:

1. If you consider the statement to be *generally true* of your function, check the YES column.

2. If you consider the statement to be *untrue* of your function, check the NO column.

3. If you consider the statement to be *less than true* (but not totally untrue) of your function, check the SOMETIMES OR PARTIAL column.

4. If the statement does not apply to your particular situation, write "Not Applicable" across the response spaces (or simply draw a line through them).

5. If you lack the data for a definite response, write in "Not Answerable" or "Don't Know."

HOW TO EVALUATE YOUR RESPONSES

When you have completed the checklist, glance over your responses, keeping these points in mind:

1. A negative answer is always unfavorable because it indicates a problem within the function: the greater the number of NOs, the more serious the situation.

2. A positive response is always a good indication. But too many YES answers could indicate that your review is not objective enough.

3. Too many SOMETIMES OR PARTIALLY answers can point to internal weaknesses or to a lack of firm direction.

4. A lot of "Not Applicable" answers could indicate that you are avoiding the issue.

5. A large number of "Not Answerable" or "Don't Know" answers could be symptomatic of inadequate records or data bases.

HOW TO RATE AND SCORE YOUR RESPONSES

When you are satisfied with your responses in general, you are ready to score the Checklist. For your convenience, a self-explanatory Scoring and Rating Block follows each Checklist. This block not only tells you whether the condition of your function is satisfactory, but it also gives you a measure of its effectiveness.

Here's how to total up the points for inclusion in the Scoring and Rating Block:

1. Total up the number of points you scored:
   a. For each YES, give yourself one point.
   b. For each NO, give yourself zero.
   c. For each SOMETIMES OR PARTIALLY, give yourself a half-point.
   d. For each "Not Applicable" answer, give yourself zero and deduct one from the number of items on the Checklist.
   e. For each "Not Answerable" or "Don't Know" answer, give yourself zero.

2. Next divide the total number of points you score by the total number of items (statements) on the Checklist (less items marked "Not Applicable"). You'll get a 1.0 for a perfect score and a fraction for anything less.

3. Multiply the result of step 2 by 100 to arrive at the percentage for your score.

What is a satisfactory rating? A rating of less than 65 percent is unacceptable and calls for an improvement program: Obviously, the lower the rating, the more drastic the action required.

A brief "how-to" example of this Scoring and Rating system follows . . .

EXAMPLE

	YES (1)	NO (0)	S/P* (½)

1. Field sale reports designed to provide information on sales progress contain data on the following topics:

	YES (1)	NO (0)	S/P* (½)
a. sales calls and sales presentations made by salespersons and sales agents,	✓		
b. bids, quotations, and proposals made,	✓		
c. new orders booked,	✓		
d. lost business, and reasons for the loss,		✓	
e. accomplishments toward future orders,			✓
f. performance in filling orders, handling complaints, and otherwise servicing individual customers,	✓		
g. action taken in response to customer requests, such as sending samples, spec sheets, etc.,	✓		
h. accomplishments of significance and value to other members of the sales force.			✓

*SOMETIMES OR PARTIALLY

TOTAL POINTS $\boxed{5}$ + 0 + $\boxed{1}$

= $\boxed{6}$

RATING

$$\frac{\text{Enter number of points scored} \quad \boxed{6}}{\text{Enter number of items on checklist} \quad \boxed{8}} = .75 \times 100 = \boxed{75}\%$$

	YES (1)	NO (0)	S/P* (½)

1. The sales department takes an organized approach to maintaining and upgrading the personal selling skills of sales personnel through training, retraining, personal development, intelligent supervision in the field, and constant review.   _____ _____ _____

2. All approaches to improving salesmanship stress the fundamentals of preparation, approach, presentation, overcoming objections, and closing.   _____ _____ _____

3. Post-order performance, or "customer keeping" is also emphasized as a key element of salesmanship.   _____ _____ _____

   The following appraisal points should be answered in terms of the typical or representative member of the sales organization—that is, the *majority* of the sales force.

4. The typical sales representative (or sales agent) is a sales professional, experienced and trained in the essentials of selling.   _____ _____ _____

5. In preparing for the sales call, salespersons:

   a. know their specific objective before making a call,   _____ _____ _____

   b. have pertinent facts about the prospect or customer they are calling on,   _____ _____ _____

   c. know the best time to call,   _____ _____ _____

   d. know the important features and benefits of their own and their competitive products,   _____ _____ _____

   e. know the price and terms of sale of each product they may sell,   _____ _____ _____

   f. know who the competitors are,   _____ _____ _____

   g. plan their use of sales promotion aids, manuals, and similar materials, and   _____ _____ _____

   h. practice their presentation, sales demonstration, and use of sales aids.   _____ _____ _____

6. In approaching the prospect, typical salespersons:

   a. think out their opening statement or question to be sure it is appropriate to the nature of the sales interview,   _____ _____ _____

   b. gain the interest of prospects quickly and put them at ease,   _____ _____ _____

   c. convey sincere interest in prospects and their problems,   _____ _____ _____

   d. speak intelligently about new products and new ideas affecting the industry,   _____ _____ _____

   e. induce prospects to talk and to reveal needed facts about their business,   _____ _____ _____

   f. question prospects skillfully,   _____ _____ _____

   g. determine the needs of prospects that the product may satisfy, and   _____ _____ _____

   h. probe prospects' interest in competitive products.   _____ _____ _____

7. In making a presentation, salespersons:

   a. identify the current problems and interests of the prospect,   _____ _____ _____

   b. maintain control of the discussion during the presentation,   _____ _____ _____

*SOMETIMES OR PARTIALLY

	YES (1)	NO (0)	S/P* (½)

c. use visuals or sample products to make salient points, ____ ____ ____

d. point out product advantages and benefits step-by-step, ____ ____ ____

e. use case histories and user testimonials, ____ ____ ____

f. show imagination in solving customers' problems, ____ ____ ____

g. have the ability to make a sales presentation to buying committees or other groups, ____ ____ ____

h. use demonstrations to show how the product will benefit the buyer, and ____ ____ ____

i. ask questions to find out to what degree the prospect is convinced. ____ ____ ____

8. In overcoming objections, salespersons:

a. listen to objections without interrupting, ____ ____ ____

b. handle objections without showing stress, ____ ____ ____

c. prove, not argue, reasons to buy, ____ ____ ____

d. tactfully correct a prospect's misinformation, ____ ____ ____

e. discuss competitive products knowledgeably, ____ ____ ____

f. know how to overcome objections regarding price, ____ ____ ____

g. intelligently defend sales policies and procedures, ____ ____ ____

h. understand and explain clearly the credit terms offered, ____ ____ ____

i. show dramatically what prospects or customers will miss if they do not make a favorable buying decision, ____ ____ ____

j. use the technique of rephrasing the objection to lessen its impact, ____ ____ ____

k. distinguish between excuses/put-offs and true objections, ____ ____ ____

l. use sound questioning techniques to get at the cause of the objection, and ____ ____ ____

m. seek help when particular objections present unusual difficulties. ____ ____ ____

9. In closing, salespersons:

a. ask for the order more than once, ____ ____ ____

b. make more than one attempt to close the sale, ____ ____ ____

c. know and use several different closes, as appropriate to the situation, ____ ____ ____

d. use alternatives (e.g., "Which do you prefer?"), when appropriate, as a closing technique, ____ ____ ____

e. review benefits and try to close after summarizing them, and ____ ____ ____

f. ask for the order in sufficient product quantities. ____ ____ ____

10. Salespersons:

a. practice a "customer-keeping" philosophy, ____ ____ ____

b. promise no more than can be reasonably delivered, ____ ____ ____

c. contact customers as required to service their needs, ____ ____ ____

*SOMETIMES OR PARTIALLY

	YES (1)	NO (0)	S/P* (½)

d. monitor performance in filling customer orders,

e. check on deliveries,

f. handle complaints promptly,

g. know who to approach in the company to get good customer service,

h. set up a procedure to keep informed on problems affecting customers,

i. contact the customer before the customer contacts the firm when they know something has gone wrong,

j. explain customer requirements and problems to management so that maximum service may be offered to the customer, and

k. convey the impression to the customer that a lasting, meaningful relationship with the firm is established *after* the sale is made.

11. The typical salesperson—and the sales force in total—is productive in terms of:

a. meeting sales quotas consistently,

b. making bonus points by selling the high-margin products,

c. booking a high proportion of repeat business, and

d. maintaining a high sales value per dollar of selling expense.

12. The productivity of the firm's salespersons and/or sales agents compares favorably with that of its principal competitors.

*SOMETIMES OR PARTIALLY

TOTAL POINTS   ☐ + 0 + ☐

= ☐

RATING

Enter number of points scored ☐
——————————————————— =   × 100 = ☐ %
Enter number of items on checklist ☐

WHAT THE RATING SIGNIFIES

The most difficult problem posed by this appraisal is when a satisfactory rating is given to the salesperson's basic skills of preparation, approach, presentation, overcoming objections, and after-sale performance—yet the rating is low on the two "pay off" sections, *Closing the Sale* (point #9) and *Sales Productivity* (points #11 and #12).

When this happens, and there is confirming evidence in the form of shortfalls from the sales plan, high selling expenses vs. budget, and poor profit margins, it calls for a review of all other factors affecting sales productivity, including compensation.

Compensation is especially critical, and should be based on profit margin contribution, not on sales volume alone. A small Midwestern manufacturer of building products was floundering despite its high order backlog and billings because its sales force was selling the older low-margin products in the line, while the new high-margin products weren't moving. A change to commissions based on profit margins turned the firm around.

WHAT TO DO NOW

1. First, make an intensive review of the sales training programs. Sales people should not be permitted to go into the field lacking the six basic skills covered in this appraisal. It is not safe to assume that an experienced salesperson has them.

2. If sales training is found to be satisfactory in coverage and quality—and all salespeople are required to participate—then the entire recruiting, screening, and selection process should be examined to ensure that the quality of new sales candidates is up to standard.

3. If this process is found not to be deficient, then the company's sales compensation and incentive policies should be questioned, and the quality of sales supervision should be re-evaluated.

4. Finally, if after all this, sales productivity remains low, then serious questions must be raised about the company's product lines, pricing policies, credit policies, distribution and stocking practices, customer service, and product quality.

Chapter **18**

Controlling
Sales Activities

Sales control is an organized and continuous process of monitoring and measuring actual results against those planned, and taking corrective action where necessary, either to bring performance up to planned levels, or to revise the sales plan itself. Sales control applies to outside sales agents as well as the company's own selling employees; both are "salespersons" or "sales representatives" in manual terminology. Control of agents must, of course, be performed with allowance for their contractually independent (non-employee) status.

The essential purpose of sales control is to ensure achievement of the company's sales objectives. Normally, this is done by implementing the programs and actions in the annual sales plan. Changes in the marketplace, however, frequently require revision of the plan in order to meet the original objectives. Revisions must be made at two levels—the local level of the individual salesperson, and the level of the total sales force.

PLANNING AND CONTROL—TWO SIDES OF THE SAME COIN

Annual sales planning and sales control are separated in the Manual in order to facilitate their appraisal, even though they are interrelated in practice. Tactical sales planning—the kind that is done on a week-by-week and day-by-day basis by the individual salesperson or agent—is included in this section because it is not practical to separate planning of localized short-term activities from their actual control. Sales control, therefore, covers both the *tactical planning and control* of the individual salesperson or agent, and the *overall control* of the sales force as an integrated unit.

Accordingly, two aspects of sales control should be considered in this appraisal:

1. control of the salesperson (local planning and self-control), and
2. control of the total sales force through the sales manager's control system.

KEY AIM OF THE SELF-AUDIT

The main objective of the appraisal is to ensure that the procedures and practices for control of the field sales forces are effectively designed, clearly expressed, thoroughly understood, and followed by all personnel involved, so that objectives of the sales plan will be met.

HOW TO USE THE CHECKLISTS

For each of the statements in the Checklist, compare the condition of your function to the "ideal" as described in the statement. Then:

1. If you consider the statement to be *generally true* of your function, check the YES column.

2. If you consider the statement to be *untrue* of your function, check the NO column.

3. If you consider the statement to be *less than true* (but not totally untrue) of your function, check the SOMETIMES OR PARTIAL column.

4. If the statement does not apply to your particular situation, write "Not Applicable" across the response spaces (or simply draw a line through them).

5. If you lack the data for a definite response, write in "Not Answerable" or "Don't Know."

HOW TO EVALUATE YOUR RESPONSES

When you have completed the checklist, glance over your responses, keeping these points in mind:

1. A negative answer is always unfavorable because it indicates a problem within the function: the greater the number of NOs, the more serious the situation.

2. A positive response is always a good indication. But too many YES answers could indicate that your review is not objective enough.

3. Too many SOMETIMES OR PARTIALLY answers can point to internal weaknesses or to a lack of firm direction.

4. A lot of "Not Applicable" answers could indicate that you are avoiding the issue.

5. A large number of "Not Answerable" or "Don't Know" answers could be symptomatic of inadequate records or data bases.

HOW TO RATE AND SCORE YOUR RESPONSES

When you are satisfied with your responses in general, you are ready to score the Checklist. For your convenience, a self-explanatory Scoring and Rating Block follows each Checklist. This block not only tells you whether the condition of your function is satisfactory, but it also gives you a measure of its effectiveness.

Here's how to total up the points for inclusion in the Scoring and Rating Block:

1. Total up the number of points you scored:
    a. For each YES, give yourself one point.
    b. For each NO, give yourself zero.
    c. For each SOMETIMES OR PARTIALLY, give yourself a half-point.
    d. For each "Not Applicable" answer, give yourself zero and deduct one from the number of items on the Checklist.
    e. For each "Not Answerable" or "Don't Know" answer, give yourself zero.

2. Next divide the total number of points you score by the total number of items (statements) on the Checklist (less items marked "Not Applicable"). You'll get a 1.0 for a perfect score and a fraction for anything less.

3. Multiply the result of step 2 by 100 to arrive at the percentage for your score.

What is a satisfactory rating? A rating of less than 65 percent is unacceptable and calls for an improvement program: Obviously, the lower the rating, the more drastic the action required.

A brief "how-to" example of this Scoring and Rating system follows . . .

EXAMPLE

	YES (1)	NO (0)	S/P* (½)

1. Field sale reports designed to provide information on sales progress contain data on the following topics:

   a. sales calls and sales presentations made by salespersons and sales agents,   ✓

   b. bids, quotations, and proposals made,   ✓

   c. new orders booked,   ✓

   d. lost business, and reasons for the loss,   ✓ (NO)

   e. accomplishments toward future orders,   ✓ (S/P)

   f. performance in filling orders, handling complaints, and otherwise servicing individual customers,   ✓

   g. action taken in response to customer requests, such as sending samples, spec sheets, etc.,   ✓

   h. accomplishments of significance and value to other members of the sales force.   ✓ (S/P)

*SOMETIMES OR PARTIALLY

TOTAL POINTS $\boxed{5}$ + 0 + $\boxed{1}$

= $\boxed{6}$

RATING

Enter number of points scored $\boxed{6}$

Enter number of items on checklist $\boxed{8}$

= .75 × 100 = $\boxed{75}$ %

	YES (1)	NO (0)	S/P* (½)
1. Day-to-day control of all sales activities is recognized in managers' position descriptions as an important function of sales management.	_____	_____	_____
2. The sales manager personally devotes an adequate portion of his or her time to sales control activities.	_____	_____	_____
3. The sales department budget includes an allocation covering expenses of this activity.	_____	_____	_____
4. The sales department has an organized and cohesive structure of management, control systems, written procedures and standard practices that governs the implementation of the sales plan.	_____	_____	_____
5. The firm has an effective set of local controls, or "self-controls," governing the activities of the individual salesperson in the field.	_____	_____	_____
6. The firm also has a formal written system of controls over the activities of the sales force as a whole.	_____	_____	_____
7. Sales control involves all sales managers, sales supervisors, sales support, and sales representatives.	_____	_____	_____
8. All personnel receive training in sales control methods and techniques.	_____	_____	_____
9. The sales plan is the principal guide to managers for sales control.	_____	_____	_____
10. Self-control is encouraged to the maximum extent consistent with the need for top-level direction.	_____	_____	_____
11. A work plan is prepared by each salesperson:			
a. in writing,	_____	_____	_____
b. at least every two weeks, and	_____	_____	_____
c. on a day-by-day basis.	_____	_____	_____
12. The work plan for the typical salesperson contains:			
a. month-by-month quotas with performance to date,	_____	_____	_____
b. a routing plan,	_____	_____	_____
c. prospects or customers to be called on (with indication of when they were last called on),	_____	_____	_____
d. results expected from each call,	_____	_____	_____
e. provision for recording results,	_____	_____	_____
f. new business targeted, and	_____	_____	_____
g. time for travel, meetings, etc.	_____	_____	_____
13. Salespersons are provided with guidelines derived from experience that tell them:			
a. how to identify decision-makers,	_____	_____	_____
b. the best sequence in which to call on them,	_____	_____	_____

*SOMETIMES OR PARTIALLY

	YES (1)	NO (0)	S/P* (½)

c. how to determine the size of order that serves customer needs best at optimum profit,

d. how to secure reorders,

e. how to contact customers when inperson calls cannot be made, and

f. how to handle complaints.

14. The typical salesperson:

   a. records sales results achieved vs. those targeted,

   b. submits required call and other reports on time, and in appropriate detail,

   c. makes his or her own analysis of sales made and sales lost,

   d. has alternatives planned, and uses them effectively, and

   e. is able to point to sales made which were not targeted.

15. Typical salespersons:

   a. initiate corrective action themselves, checking with their supervisors only when necessary,

   b. keep their expense records in writing on a day-by-day basis, and

   c. submit their expense records at least monthly.

16. Typical sales representatives know that their supervisors:

   a. monitor reports for problems or deviations from course,

   b. redirect their salespersons' efforts when they are off course, and

   c. evaluate salespersons' results and help them to adjust their standards or to re-plan their work.

17. The sales representative knows his or her assigned contact at the sales office who will:

   a. provide needed information on prices, shipping dates, etc., and

   b. initiate required action on complaints, requests for catalogs, etc.

18. The salesperson needing help on a problem is able to reach his or her supervisor promptly.

19. The company has a system of automatic controls, including:

   a. order minimums, standard pricing practices, and expense guides, and

   b. procedures for maintaining "account profiles," introducing new salespersons in established territories, etc.

20. Automatic controls are checked periodically for compliance, effectiveness, and need for revision.

21. The firm has an organized system of operating sales controls based on:

   a. field sales reports that are reliable, complete, timely, and comprehensive; and are used regularly by sales management, and

*SOMETIMES OR PARTIALLY

322

	YES (1)	NO (0)	S/P* (½)

b. sales analyses that organize order input, sales, and sales expense data into meaningful patterns.

22. Operating sales controls are reviewed periodically and revised as required.

23. The sales manager utilizes field sales reports:

    a. to monitor salesperson call frequency,

    b. to keep abreast of sales and product approaches used by sales representatives,

    c. to monitor time allocation and expense,

    d. to advise the sales force of:

        (1) needed changes in selling approach or selling emphasis, and

        (2) action taken by sales management in response to field reports or requests.

    e. to evaluate reported sales progress in terms of established standards,

    f. to take action on problems noted in reports, and

    g. to make sure that significant data contained in field sales reports are used in sales analyses.

24. The sales manager uses analyses of sales to determine:

    a. specific products sold, in what volume, at what price,

    b. to whom, for what use or application,

    c. method of distribution used, and

    d. applicable selling expenses.

25. The sales manager maintains current charts:

    a. relating sales to order input, amount of shippable backlog, back orders, etc.,

    b. showing progress vs. budget and sales plan, and

    c. evaluating and ranking salesperson's performance.

26. The sales analysis system identifies specific areas of sales strength and weakness.

27. Rolling forecasts are made of order input, sales, and sales expense:

    a. by each salesperson and/or sales supervisor,

    b. by the sales manager,

    c. by other marketing functions, and

    d. for each major product/customer category.

28. Rolling forecasts are made of shippable backlog, if appropriate.

29. The sales manager:

    a. distributes rolling order input and sales forecasts to production, financial control, and other marketing functions, and

*SOMETIMES OR PARTIALLY

323

	YES (1)	NO (0)	S/P* (½)

b. advises manufacturing promptly of sales problems affecting production planning.

30. The sales manager periodically checks forecasts for accuracy, and takes action to improve their accuracy.

31. The sales manager personally evaluates how well sales supervisors and salespersons:

    a. understand sales plan objectives,

    b. follow through on sales plan changes,

    c. monitor their own progress,

    d. report problems promptly, and

    e. take corrective action promptly.

32. The sales manager personally evaluates the effectiveness of his sales control system.

33. The sales manager personally recognizes and commends:

    a. effective local control by supervisors, and

    b. effective self-corrective action by salespersons.

34. The sales manager personally investigates lost business for action to salvage loss.

*SOMETIMES OR PARTIALLY

TOTAL POINTS ☐ + 0 + ☐

= ☐

RATING

Enter number of points scored ☐ / Enter number of items on checklist ☐ = ☐ × 100 = ☐ %

WHAT THE RATING SIGNIFIES

A less-than-acceptable rating for sales control indicates that the field sales force may be going after new business on an opportunistic or "hit or miss" basis, rather than in a disciplined, planned, systematic manner. Going after unanticipated opportunities is a necessary part of any sales program, of course, but this should represent only a minor portion of the selling effort. In order to be really productive, the major portion of the selling effort should be carefully planned and the plan should be followed. The old cliche, "Plan your work and work your plan," is still good advice for sales personnel, not only in large firms but in small organizations as well.

Some sales people consider time spent on planning to be time taken away from the actual selling. Others believe that selling cannot be planned; apparently in the belief that personal charm, a smooth line of talk, and good luck are the main ingredients of successful salesmanship. These qualities have no lasting value, however. The salesperson who diligently lays out and follows a weekly plan of sales calls, the route to be traveled, a listing of alternative prospects when appointments are broken—and carefully records the results of each call—will book more (and better) business in the long run. And the company, however small, that sets up and follows good control procedures will always get the jump on its larger competitors who fail to do so.

WHAT TO DO NOW

1. If the selling effort is less organized and disciplined than it should be, a review first of the sales planning effort is called for. This is where it starts. If the sales plan lacks firm and specific tasks, schedule dates, and assignments of responsibility, you can't possibly have good sales control.

2. Make sure that all salespersons have sufficient time to prepare their individual work plans, and provide them with forms and procedures to make the task easier.

3. Make sure that the sales training gives enough attention to planning and control procedures. These are important elements of salesmanship, just as important as the sales presentation itself.

4. An important part of good field sales supervision is making sure that each salesperson prepares a regular work plan, keeps good "account profiles," and follows standard procedures and practices. The average salesperson who does these well will outsell supersalesman "Joe Charisma" every time.

18-B
AUTHORITY, RESPONSIBILITY, AND ACCOUNTABILITY

	YES (1)	NO (0)	S/P* (½)
1. Authority has been delegated to the sales manager, through budget allocation and position description, to expend company funds and assign tasks necessary to assure control of the sales plan during implementation.	———	———	———
2. The sales manager is responsible to staff and manage an organization capable of controlling all sales activities effectively and economically.	———	———	———
3. Authority is redelegated to field sales supervisors to control the activities of sales personnel in the field.	———	———	———
4. Responsibilities are firmly assigned:			
a. to the sales manager for establishing and maintaining an effective system of sales controls,	———	———	———
b. to sales supervisors for applying and using these controls, and	———	———	———
c. to all sales personnel for adhering to the system in their day-to-day work.	———	———	———

5. The sales Manager is held accountable for serious failure to meet sales plan

*SOMETIMES OR PARTIALLY

	YES (1)	NO (0)	S/P* (½)

objectives (including for selling expenses) resulting from inadequate and ineffective sales controls, or from loss of control of the field sales forces.

6. Sales supervisors similarly are held accountable for serious failure to meet sales plan objectives in their respective districts or territories.

7. Sales representatives or sales agents are held accountable for serious failure to meet sales quotas in the sales plan, and for excessive sales expenses.

*SOMETIMES OR PARTIALLY

TOTAL POINTS ☐ + 0 + ☐

= ☐

RATING

Enter number of points scored ☐

Enter number of items on checklist ☐

= ☐ × 100 = ☐ %

WHAT THE RATING SIGNIFIES

Control of the company's selling effort is a responsibility of every member of the sales force, not just the sales manager alone. And every member should know that he or she is accountable for results as well as for failure to produce these results in his or her specific area or territory.

The other side of the coin is that each person must have adequate time and resources to carry out the assigned responsibility. *Control takes time and costs money*—it doesn't come free. Every task in the plan has a cost implication in terms of its control.

A low rating in this section indicates that sales control may not be considered important enough to be managed and budgeted as a separate activity and responsibility of all personnel. As a result, the goals of the sales plan are less likely to be achieved.

WHAT TO DO NOW

1. Go back to the sales plan and make sure that each major task has a price tag on it in terms of its cost to control during the period covered by the plan. The cost of a new sales district, for example, is more than just the cost of setting up and staffing a district sales office—it involves an allocation of time and travel expense by management to monitor and measure actual performance, especially during its early stages.

2. Make sure that each individual knows and understands his or her self-control responsibilities and accountabilities, and that each one has sufficient time to carry them out. This should be regarded not as a distraction from actual selling, but as a necessary part of the sales job.

18-C

MEASUREMENTS, CONTROL REPORTS, AND PERFORMANCE RECORDS

	YES (1)	NO (0)	S/P* (½)

1. The effectiveness of sales control is determined by its ability to control sales activities to the objectives, action plans, costs, and schedules in the approved sales plan (and approved up-dates of the plan).   _____ _____ _____

2. Field sales reports and expense reports are logged-in upon receipt, and a record kept of timeliness and completeness.   _____ _____ _____

3. Salespersons' expense reports are reviewed regularly for compliance with expense allowances.   _____ _____ _____

4. Salesperson's sales plans are reviewed periodically by supervisors for adherence to procedures.   _____ _____ _____

5. Sales and order input reports are routinely compared with the plan, and major variances are analyzed for cause and corrective action.   _____ _____ _____

6. Selling expenses are routinely compared with the plan, and major variances are analyzed for cause and corrective action.   _____ _____ _____

7. Progress review meetings are held quarterly to review all sales activities vs. the sales plan; major deviations are assigned for corrective action.   _____ _____ _____

8. Progress review meetings:

    a. are held on a fixed schedule,   _____ _____ _____

    b. work to a prepared agenda,   _____ _____ _____

    c. include all other functions involved, and   _____ _____ _____

    d. issue action assignments.   _____ _____ _____

9. The agenda allows sufficient time for discussion of sales strategies and tactics, in addition to review of the numbers.   _____ _____ _____

10. Monthly progress reports from all sales managers and supervisors record progress against sales plan, major problems, and action taken.   _____ _____ _____

11. Expenses are routinely compared with budget, and variances analyzed for correction.   _____ _____ _____

*SOMETIMES OR PARTIALLY

TOTAL POINTS   [   ] + 0 + [   ]

= [   ]

RATING

Enter number of points scored [   ] = × 100 = [   ] %

Enter number of items on checklist [   ]

WHAT THE RATING SIGNIFIES   Control is *measurement*. A less-than-satisfactory rating in this section indicates that the company may lack the measurements needed for good sales control.

327

Effective sales control—like control of any other activity—requires that the performance of every task and every person be measured, regularly and continuously. Mature, self-assured people don't mind being measured; only the incompetent resent it, because their failures are exposed for others to see.

WHAT TO DO NOW

1. Let everyone know what they're being measured against, and why.
2. Make the measurements highly visible to all. The high performers will like it, and the good newcomers will strive to get on top.
3. Give the sub-standard performers another chance. First determine who is at fault. If poor training or supervision is the cause, correct this first.
4. No need to fire the real incompetents; they'll go away soon enough when their continued incompetence is made visible to their peers.

18-D
OPERATING PERFORMANCE HISTORY

	YES (1)	NO (0)	S/P* (½)
1. A review of control reports and records for the past year shows no serious failures to meet Sales Plan objectives or budgets as a result of ineffective sales controls or loss of control of the field sales forces. (Answer "yes" if true.)	____	____	____
2. During the past year, there has been an improving trend in:			
a. actual performance vs. sales plan,	____	____	____
b. individual salesperson's productivity,	____	____	____
c. selling expenses vs. budget, and	____	____	____
d. timeliness and quality of field sales reports.	____	____	____

*SOMETIMES OR PARTIALLY

TOTAL POINTS ☐ + 0 + ☐

= ☐

RATING

Enter number of points scored ☐

───────────────────────── = ☐ × 100 = ☐ %

Enter number of items on checklist ☐

WHAT THE RATING SIGNIFIES

The true measure of sales control effectiveness is *selling results*; that is, meeting all of the sales goals and new order input forecasts in the sales plan. Controlling selling expenses and reporting on time are important, of course, but these are only means to an end—they are not the primary purpose of control. If the appraisal reveals past failure to meet sales goals and targets, it doesn't matter how well expense budgets were met, or how good the sales reports were.

WHAT TO DO NOW

1. Review the sales plan to make sure that the sales and new order input goals and forecasts are realistic, not just in total, but by district, territory, and individual salesperson.

2. Watch the trends. A good trend during the past gives confidence that future performance will be satisfactory, while an unfavorable trend means that corrective action is needed, and this takes time.

18-E
TOP-LEVEL SUPPORT AND GUIDANCE

	YES (1)	NO (0)	S/P* (½)

The executive office demonstrates active guidance and support during implementation of the sales plan through:

a. periodic reviews of progress toward the plan objectives,

b. active participation in "executive sales" programs,

c. contacts with key customers,

d. periodic visits to field sales offices,

e. informed comments on executive sales reports, and

f. frequent direct communication with the sales manager.

*SOMETIMES OR PARTIALLY

TOTAL POINTS ☐ + 0 + ☐

= ☐

RATING

Enter number of points scored ☐

Enter number of items on checklist ☐

= ☐ × 100 = ☐ %

WHAT THE RATING SIGNIFIES

Control of sales activity is not a highly visible function as such. Top management support is needed, however, in order to ensure successful implementation of the sales plan. The executive office can and should provide this by taking an aggressive part in the selling effort, and maintaining close and supportive contact with the sales department.

A low rating here indicates that the front office may not be aware that top level executives should be out in the forefront of the firm's sales effort. They should be selling the company and its reputation to everyone they come in contact with—including elected and appointive government officials and consumer bodies, as well as key customers and prospects.

WHAT TO DO NOW

1. Make sure that the sales plan includes top level executives as active contributors. If the plan makes sense, and the demands on their time are not excessive, you'll probably get their cooperation—plus a better understanding and appreciation on their part of the sales manager's job.

2. Nothing will improve the caliber of salesmens' work plans and call reports like the knowledge that they are seen by top level executives on occasion. Send up the best of these periodically and ask for written comments that you can pass on to the salesperson.

3. Participation by top executives in sales meetings can sharpen up the discussions and sales force morale immeasurably. Just make sure that you control the agenda and timing of the visits.

18-F
INNOVATION IN METHODS AND TECHNIQUES

	YES (1)	NO (0)	S/P* (½)
1. There is a continuing active search for better methods of controlling sales activities, including:			
a. participation in seminars and workshops,	____	____	____
b. review of management literature,	____	____	____
c. professional associations,	____	____	____
d. industry contacts,	____	____	____
e. outside specialists,	____	____	____
f. solicitation of ideas and improvement suggestions from personnel at all levels, especially field sales, and	____	____	____
g. budgets include funds for such activities.	____	____	____
2. The computer is used to store, process, and display data on actual progress vs. the plan and prior periods, for all major plan variables.	____	____	____
3. The most effective and timely communications means are employed for transmission and dissemination of control reports between field and home office, including:			
a. Data-Phone,	____	____	____
b. Telex/TWX,	____	____	____
c. facsimile,	____	____	____
d. computer terminal, and	____	____	____
e. tape cassettes.	____	____	____

*SOMETIMES OR PARTIALLY

TOTAL POINTS ☐ + 0 + ☐

= ☐

RATING

Enter number of points scored ☐

――――――――――――――――――――――― = × 100 = ☐ %

Enter number of items on checklist ☐

330

Good sales control requires information—accurate, up-to-date information, and lots of it. What's more, it demands that information move quickly. Even more important, good control requires that information trigger *action*.

A low rating here indicates that sales management people may not be taking advantage of new developments in information systems and technology. Only by getting out and learning about what others are doing can management be aware of new equipment and new techniques for improving information flow and control. This takes time and money. *Not* doing it, however, can cost a good deal more, through loss of effective control of sales activities.

WHAT TO DO NOW

1. No single individual is responsible for sales control, of course—control involves every member of the sales force. You can, however, assign a responsible manager to be your key advisor on new developments; your "innovation manager," so to speak.

2. All members of the department should contribute by channeling information to this individual everytime they attend a seminar, or learn about a new development through personal contacts or reading.

18-G
INTERFUNCTIONAL COMMUNICATIONS AND COORDINATION

	YES (1)	NO (0)	S/P* (½)

1. Individuals responsible for implementation and control of sales plans maintain close and continuing contact with:

   a. production, on matters relating to product quality, _____ _____ _____

   b. product distribution, on matters relating to product availability, _____ _____ _____

   c. engineering, on matters relating to product performance, _____ _____ _____

   d. accounting, on matters relating to product profit margins and accounting reports, and _____ _____ _____

   e. marketing, on matters relating to product pricing, sales analysis and new product/market planning. _____ _____ _____

2. Communication with other functions is achieved through personal contact and:

   a. exchange of progress reports, _____ _____ _____

   b. quarterly progress review meetings, and _____ _____ _____

   c. participation in cross-functional task groups. _____ _____ _____

*SOMETIMES OR PARTIALLY

TOTAL POINTS [ ] + 0 + [ ]

= [ ]

RATING

Enter number of points scored [ ]

───────────────────────────────────── = × 100 = [ ] %

Enter number of items on checklist [ ]

331

WHAT THE RATING SIGNIFIES

It was stated earlier that control is measurement, and that measurement requires information. Good sales control also requires productive two-way communication and coordination with all of the other departments of the business. Every function of an organization contributes to the selling effort—even though indirectly or remotely.

To neglect and fail to use the contributions that the other functions can make to selling productivity is a great waste. A less-than-satisfactory rating here is an indication that this may be taking place.

WHAT TO DO NOW

1. You should take the initiative in establishing and nurturing this kind of interfunctional coordination, if it doesn't presently exist. You have the most to gain by it.

2. Start by *giving*. Set up an internal procedure to disseminate information about sales and new orders to the other department heads. Invite others to your sales meetings. Consult them about your sales plan early, while it is in development.

3. Set up contacts with the other departments at several organization levels. You may be surprised how much more your subordinates can learn about what is really going on than you can by talking only to the other department heads.

18-H
FUNCTIONAL IMPROVEMENT PROGRAM

	YES (1)	NO (0)	S/P* (½)
1. An active, organized team effort to improve sales control employs personnel from:			
a. marketing,	___	___	___
b. information systems,	___	___	___
c. sales training,	___	___	___
d. field sales, and	___	___	___
e. other functions as required by task.	___	___	___
2. Improvement efforts are directed toward:			
a. better communications between home office and field sales,	___	___	___
b. improved "self-control" for sales representatives in the field,	___	___	___
c. a higher proportion of "automatic" controls and programmed responses, and	___	___	___
d. more effective and timely sales analysis and forecasting.	___	___	___

*SOMETIMES OR PARTIALLY

TOTAL POINTS [ ] + 0 + [ ]

= [ ]

RATING

Enter number of points scored [ ]

Enter number of items on checklist [ ] = × 100 = [ ] %

WHAT THE RATING SIGNIFIES

A unified team effort to improve sales control can often produce substantial benefits. One of these could be better self-control by sales personnel in the field. Another, better communications between field and home office. The first requires the participation of people from sales training and personnel; the second by the company's information systems people and an office procedures specialist.

Almost any aspect of sales control can benefit from a team approach, by bringing many varied points of view to bear on the problem.

WHAT TO DO NOW

1. Initiate a trial team effort on a single task. It may take some salesmanship to get people in other functions to participate in such a project, but once the benefits are demonstrated, they often become converts.

2. First step is to jointly set the objectives for the task. It's important that the others contribute to this—don't call them in only after the goals have been set.

3. Be certain to give credit for all contributions made. You can, of course, take all the credit yourself; after all, it was your idea. However, if you want to use the team idea again, you might find it difficult to enlist any helpers.

18-I
RESOURCES

	YES (1)	NO (0)	S/P* (½)
1. Sales management is kept informed about company objectives and matters affecting implementation of the sales plan, through access to appropriate capital budgets, business plans, new product/marketing plans, operating reports, and participation in key management meetings.	___	___	___
2. Based on knowledge of the company's objectives and forward planning, resources for effective implementation and control of the sales plan are considered adequate to meet the company's needs for the next three, six, and twelve months, in terms of:			
a. supervisory and support personnel,	___	___	___
b. capabilities,	___	___	___
c. budget funding,	___	___	___
d. computer time and capacity,	___	___	___
e. communications equipment,	___	___	___
f. other functional support, and	___	___	___
g. facilities and equipment.	___	___	___

*SOMETIMES OR PARTIALLY

TOTAL POINTS   ☐ + 0 + ☐ = ☐

RATING

Enter number of points scored ☐
_____   =   × 100 = ☐ %
Enter number of items on checklist ☐

333

When sales management is kept in the dark about the company's overall strategic goal and long-range plans—perhaps because top management thinks that the selling activity should be concerned only with short-term, tactical matters—not only is immediate sales productivity reduced, but the future of the firm is jeopardized.

Only when the annual sales plan is viewed as the first year of the firm's long-range plan, and the goals of the sales plan are in harmony with long-range objectives, will sales control be effective. A negative answer to the first point, therefore, means that point 2 can't be answered with confidence.

Negative answers to the other points—that is, to a lack either of experienced and support personnel, of good communications facilities for sales reporting, or of adequate facilities for sales meetings—mean that you run the risk of failing to meet the goals of the sales plan for lack of resources to control plan implementation.

WHAT TO DO NOW

1. Make sure that your knowledge of the company's goals, plans and policies is up to date and complete. If not, you need to get yourself into the company's information loop quickly.

2. If physical resources are lacking, you need a program to get them. This requires, first, a credible plan with benefits to the company clearly spelled out. Second, you had better get the backing of your direct supervisor for the plan.

3. It's a good idea to enlist the support of your functional colleagues for your plan—especially if it involves a contest for shares of limited resources. Without their support, your chances for success are greatly reduced.

19

How to Prepare
The Sales Plan

The product of any planning activity, whether corporate long-range strategic planning, five-year marketing planning, annual sales planning, or even weekly sales call planning by the individual salesperson in the field, is not the *plan*—it is the planning process itself. The output of the process is not a bound document with the word "PLAN" embossed on the cover. It is the knowledge and insight gained by the individuals who participate in the process.

One of the most persistent management myths is that planning helps managers predict the future. The fact is, the future cannot be predicted. We know three things about the future for sure: (1) it will be different from the past, (2) it will be different from what we think it will be, and (3) it will be here sooner than we expect.

WHAT SALES PLANNING CAN DO

Having said what planning can*not* do, we need to know what it *can* do. What will sales planning do for us? What, in short, is sales planning?

Sales planning is an organized management process of identifying specific courses of action that offer the best chance of achieving sales objectives. Sales planning comes in two types and sizes. The first is medium-range and somewhat strategic in nature, and involves all managers with sales responsibilities (as well as some managers of other company functions). This kind of planning is the principal concern of this section, the preparation of the company's annual sales plan.

The second kind of sales planning is done by the individual salesperson in the field—the preparation of daily and weekly plans for his or her own guidance. This kind of sales planning is very short-term and tactical in nature, and goes on all the time. You will find this discussed in Chapter 18 as part of Controlling Sales Activities.

THE PURPOSE OF SALES PLANNING

The principal purpose of annual sales planning is to ensure the productive deployment and administration of the firm's sales organization in its pursuit of sales goals. Without planning, the individual sales districts, territories, and individual sales representatives would tend to go their own separate ways, doing their own thing without regard to the other members of the organization. (Try to picture the Dallas Cowboys meeting the Green Bay Packers on Sunday afternoon without a game plan!) The annual sales plan serves to guide these individual parts of the organization toward common goals, and provides benchmarks and standards by which to measure progress.

SIX STEPS IN THE SALES PLANNING PROCESS

The annual sales plan is prepared through a systematic and organized six-step process, as follows:

1. collect and analyze data on past sales performance and the current status of major sales programs,

2. evaluate the company's selling strengths and weaknesses (physical, financial, human),

3. isolate the really serious problems and deficiencies for attention,

4. identify the most promising sales opportunities, and determine which ones best fit the company's strengths and available resources,

5. set sales goals that are challenging—yet realistic and potentially achievable, and

6. program the specific tasks that must be done to accomplish these goals. (This involves setting time-tables for results and assigning firm responsibility for each task to an individual.)

KEY AIM OF THE SELF-AUDIT

The main objective of the self-audit is to provide assurance to management that a realistic sales plan is prepared before the start of the business year; that this plan is developed through a systematic process with active participation by all managers with sales responsibilities; and that the plan is kept current as conditions change throughout the year.

HOW TO USE THE CHECKLISTS

For each of the statements in the Checklist, compare the condition of your function to the "ideal" as described in the statement. Then:

1. If you consider the statement to be *generally true* of your function, check the YES column.
2. If you consider the statement to be *untrue* of your function, check the NO column.
3. If you consider the statement to be *less than true* (but not totally untrue) of your function, check the SOMETIMES OR PARTIAL column.
4. If the statement does not apply to your particular situation, write "Not Applicable" across the response spaces (or simply draw a line through them).
5. If you lack the data for a definite response, write in "Not Answerable" or "Don't Know."

HOW TO EVALUATE YOUR RESPONSES

When you have completed the checklist, glance over your responses, keeping these points in mind:

1. A negative answer is always unfavorable because it indicates a problem within the function: the greater the number of NOs, the more serious the situation.
2. A positive response is always a good indication. But too many YES answers could indicate that your review is not objective enough.
3. Too many SOMETIMES OR PARTIALLY answers can point to internal weaknesses or to a lack of firm direction.
4. A lot of "Not Applicable" answers could indicate that you are avoiding the issue.
5. A large number of "Not Answerable" or "Don't Know" answers could be symptomatic of inadequate records or data bases.

HOW TO RATE AND SCORE YOUR RESPONSES

When you are satisfied with your responses in general, you are ready to score the Checklist. For your convenience, a self-explanatory Scoring and Rating Block follows each Checklist. This block not only tells you whether the condition of your function is satisfactory, but it also gives you a measure of its effectiveness.

Here's how to total up the points for inclusion in the Scoring and Rating Block:

1. Total up the number of points you scored:
    a. For each YES, give yourself one point.
    b. For each NO, give yourself zero.
    c. For each SOMETIMES OR PARTIALLY, give yourself a half-point.
    d. For each "Not Applicable" answer, give yourself zero and deduct one from the number of items on the Checklist.
    e. For each "Not Answerable" or "Don't Know" answer, give yourself zero.
2. Next divide the total number of points you score by the total number of items (statements) on the Checklist (less items marked "Not Applicable"). You'll get a 1.0 for a perfect score and a fraction for anything less.
3. Multiply the result of step 2 by 100 to arrive at the percentage for your score.

What is a satisfactory rating? A rating of less than 65 percent is unacceptable and calls for an improvement program: Obviously, the lower the rating, the more drastic the action required.

A brief "how-to" example of this Scoring and Rating system follows . . .

EXAMPLE

	YES (1)	NO (0)	S/P* (½)

1. Field sale reports designed to provide information on sales progress contain data on the following topics:

    a. sales calls and sales presentations made by salespersons and sales agents, ✓

    b. bids, quotations, and proposals made, ✓

    c. new orders booked, ✓

    d. lost business, and reasons for the loss, ✓ (NO)

    e. accomplishments toward future orders, ✓ (S/P)

    f. performance in filling orders, handling complaints, and otherwise servicing individual customers, ✓

    g. action taken in response to customer requests, such as sending samples, spec sheets, etc., ✓

    h. accomplishments of significance and value to other members of the sales force. ✓ (S/P)

*SOMETIMES OR PARTIALLY

TOTAL POINTS $\boxed{5}$ + 0 + $\boxed{1}$

= $\boxed{6}$

RATING

$$\frac{\text{Enter number of points scored} \quad \boxed{6}}{\text{Enter number of items on checklist} \quad \boxed{8}} = .75 \times 100 = \boxed{75 \%}$$

19-A
ORGANIZATION, ADMINISTRATION, AND OPERATION

	YES (1)	NO (0)	S/P* (½)
1. Sales planning and preparation of an annual sales plan are recognized as vital company activities that have top management endorsement and support.	___	___	___
2. Sales planning is recognized on the organization charts and in managers' position descriptions as an important function of sales management.	___	___	___
3. The work is done under the personal direction of the sales manager.	___	___	___
4. The sales manager allocates a substantial portion of his time to the sales planning activity.	___	___	___
5. The sales department budget includes an allocation covering expenses of sales planning and publication of an annual sales plan.	___	___	___
6. Key managers involved are trained in sales planning and are well-informed about the company's products, customers, and competitors.	___	___	___
7. Development of the annual sales plan is conducted as an organized process, guided and governed by written procedures and standard practices and a firm time schedule.	___	___	___
8. Sales planning involves active participation by sales managers and supervisors at all levels, and to the maximum extent possible, sales representatives.	___	___	___
9. Policy requires executive review and approval of the sales plan before implementation.	___	___	___
10. Sales plan are treated as "company confidential" material by all personnel.	___	___	___
11. In developing and evaluating sales planning inputs, valid historical data on order input, sales, and sales expenses are used.	___	___	___
12. As input to the sales planning process, marketing provides market demand projections:			
a. by quarters for the year ahead,	___	___	___
b. by product line or product group, and	___	___	___
c. by customer class.	___	___	___
13. Marketing also provides overall planning guidance on:			
a. growth and profit goals,	___	___	___
b. products and markets and distribution channels to be emphasized, and	___	___	___
c. advertising, service, and other support to be provided.	___	___	___
14. Price forecasts are furnished by marketing in terms of average prices and timing of anticipated price changes.	___	___	___
15. Order input/sales forecasts are provided by marketing:			
a. for the total year and by quarter,	___	___	___
b. by product or product group, by customer or customer class, by sales territory, and	___	___	___

*SOMETIMES OR PARTIALLY

339

	YES (1)	NO (0)	S/P* (½)

c. with commentary, including competitive outlook. _____ _____ _____

16. Planning guidance is provided by the sales manager on:

    a. the outlook and opportunities for securing order input/sales, _____ _____ _____

    b. the desired product mix, _____ _____ _____

    c. time to be apportioned to current selling effort, post-order performance, and developing future business, and _____ _____ _____

    d. limits on sales expenses. _____ _____ _____

17. The sales manager makes forecasts of selling expenses:

    a. for the total year and by quarter, and _____ _____ _____

    b. with supporting commentary, including identification of territory changes and shifts in key account responsibilities. _____ _____ _____

18. The sales manager:

    a. makes own sales projections and forecasts, _____ _____ _____

    b. collects all planning inputs in one place for comparison, _____ _____ _____

    c. analyzes and reconciles differences within the sales force, and _____ _____ _____

    d. presents to management a set of projections and forecasts that can be supported. _____ _____ _____

19. The sales plan provides month-by-month:

    a. order input/sales forecasts by product and/or customer category, reconciling any changes in the totals from previous submissions, and _____ _____ _____

    b. selling expense forecasts, reconciling any changes from previous submissions. _____ _____ _____

20. The selling expense plan includes provision for all expenses related to the selling activity, including:

    a. sales training, _____ _____ _____

    b. sales meetings, _____ _____ _____

    c. sales contests, _____ _____ _____

    d. field sales office operation, and _____ _____ _____

    e. sales management. _____ _____ _____

21. a. Sales territories are reviewed for possible re-alignment annually, at time of developing the sales plan. _____ _____ _____

    b. Territory guidelines are clearly defined and are known and understood. _____ _____ _____

22. a. Sales territories are determined and assigned in an analytical and systematic manner, not simply by hunch or habit. _____ _____ _____

    b. Territory assignments give adequate consideration to sales potential, sales-persons' capabilities, types of customers served, distribution channels used, costs of serving the territory, and income needs of the salesperson. _____ _____ _____

*SOMETIMES OR PARTIALLY

	YES (1)	NO (0)	S/P* (½)

23. Sales territory assignments are reviewed whenever events or competitive circumstances require, such as:

   a. increases in sales potential that require dividing territories,

   b. decreases in sales potential that involve combining territories, reassigning the territory to a junior salesman, or assigning to an agent, and

   c. changes in salesperson's capabilities, level of experience and aspirations, etc.

24. Sales quotas established at time of sales planning:

   a. are set for each salesperson, agent, or reseller,

   b. encourage sale of the desired "sales mix",

   c. are related to incentive compensation, and

   d. are set at or above budgeted order input of sales levels.

25. Sales quotas reflect consideration of:

   a. individual performance records,

   b. individual capabilities, and

   c. other benchmarks, such as industry growth or competitors' performance.

26. As the end product of sales planning, the sales manager has a documented sales plan containing:

   a. identification and quantification of market served and share targeted,

   b. marketing objectives, with planning assumptions and guidelines,

   c. strategies to be followed on product emphasis, pricing, etc.,

   d. the order input/sales budget, and

   e. the sales expense budget.

27. The sales plan contains:

   a. major programs and schedules, including new product introductions, sales meetings, contests, training,

   b. territorial sales plans, covering for each territory:

     (1) monthly order input/sales and sales expense budgets by major product group and major customer class,

     (2) monthly quotas for each salesperson,

     (3) performance standards,

     (4) targeted markets, market share, profit objectives, and

     (5) strategies, programs and schedules specifically related to the territory.

28. The sales manager distributes *appropriate portions* of the approved sales plan to:

   a. district managers and sales supervisors,

   b. each salesperson or agent, and

*SOMETIMES OR PARTIALLY

341

	YES (1)	NO (0)	S/P* (½)

c. other marketing functions. ___ ___ ___

29. Before the start of the year, the sales plan is introduced and launched:

    a. first to top-level sales management, ___ ___ ___

    b. next, at general sales meetings in each region or area, attended by:

        (1) every salesperson, ___ ___ ___

        (2) every sales supervisor, and ___ ___ ___

        (3) sales support personnel. ___ ___ ___

    c. With participation by:

        (1) marketing management, ___ ___ ___

        (2) top management, and ___ ___ ___

        (3) other company functions, such as advertising customer service, etc. ___ ___ ___

30. The sales plan is kept current during the year:

    a. through supplements to the plan issued to all holders, ___ ___ ___

    b. the nature and basis for changes is communicated to each salesperson by his sales manager, and ___ ___ ___

    c. follow-up is made to assure compliance with the changes. ___ ___ ___

31. The sales plan is used by sales supervisors as a basis for developing weekly sales plans for each territory. ___ ___ ___

32. The company's sales incentive plan* is revised annually to reflect changes in products, markets and competition. ___ ___ ___

33. The system of sales incentive compensation is designed to:

    a. be competitive with the industry, ___ ___ ___

    b. motivate every salesperson to do his part in reaching objectives, ___ ___ ___

    c. provide incentives for above-average performance, ___ ___

    d. enable the company to attract and hold qualified personnel, and ___ ___ ___

    e. be flexible to permit changes during the budget year. ___ ___ ___

*SOMETIMES OR PARTIALLY

TOTAL POINTS [ ] + 0 + [ ]

= [ ]

RATING

Enter number of points scored [ ]

────────────────────────────── = × 100 = [ ] %

Enter number of items on checklist [ ]

*Because of the sensitive nature of incentive plans, they should not be part of the Sales Plan, but should be covered separately.

WHAT THE RATING SIGNIFIES

The real output of sales planning is not the printed document with the words "SALES PLAN" on the binding—it is the knowledge, insight, and understanding that managers, supervisors, and individual salespersons gain through their involvement in the planning process.

When the annual sales planning is done on an organized basis, guided by written procedures and schedules, and with participation by all levels of the organization, the company benefits enormously—because the goals and plans of individuals are brought into harmony with the overall objectives of the company.

Managers in many small to medium size firms consider sales planning to be something that only a large corporation like IBM or General Foods can afford to do. On the contrary, sales planning is not expensive. Mostly, it requires brain-power, and the large corporations have no monopoly on that. In fact, one of the most important benefits a small company can gain from planning is to identify "market niches" where the large companies are not filling customer needs, and moving aggressively into these. Large corporations tend to react slowly, and by the time they do, the smaller company can have a secure hold on this segment of the market.

A less-than-satisfactory rating for sales planning indicates that the company may be forgoing these important benefits and gains through failure to provide sufficient time or money for the sales planning activity. As a consequence, the skills and energies of competent people may be misdirected into nonproductive activities.

WHAT TO DO NOW

1. Make sure that every sales job description includes sales planning as an essential part of the job.

2. When scheduling the department's activities, allow sufficient time for the planning, including at least one meeting away from the daily distractions of the office.

3. It's essential to get the field sales people involved as much as possible. Their intimate knowledge of customer needs, wants, and perceptions of the company are vital to sales planning. Sell them on the benefits of training for future management work.

4. Base the plan on *hard* data—on facts, not supposition. Digging out the facts and analyzing them is the hardest part of planning, but unless it is done, the plan may be out of touch with reality.

5. Be sure to get top management blessing for the plan. Don't expect this purely on the plan's merits. Here's an opportunity to demonstrate your own selling skills.

19-B
AUTHORITY, RESPONSIBILITY, AND ACCOUNTABILITY

	YES (1)	NO (0)	S/P* (½)
1. Authority has been delegated to the sales manager, through budget allocation and position description, to expend company funds and assign tasks necessary to prepare and publish an annual sales plan.	___	___	___
2. The sales manager is responsible for staffing and managing an organization capable of planning sales activities effectively and economically.	___	___	___
3. Responsibilities are clearly assigned to individuals for all needed information inputs to the annual sales plan.	___	___	___
4. Responsibility is firmly assigned to an individual to coordinate all sales planning activities, and to integrate the total sales plan.	___	___	___
5. The sales manager is held accountable for serious failure of the sales plan to work, i.e., for invalid assumptions, poor data input, inaccurate forecasting, and failure to anticipate predictable events and developments.	___	___	___

*SOMETIMES OR PARTIALLY

TOTAL POINTS   [ ] + 0 + [ ]

= [ ]

RATING

Enter number of points scored [ ]
─────────────────────────────── = [ ] × 100 = [ ] %
Enter number of items on checklist [ ]

WHAT THE RATING SIGNIFIES

A low rating here confirms that sales planning is not regarded as an activity essential to the company's success. Unless the sales manager has firm authority to spend money for sales planning, the chances are that it won't be done properly. And unless planning responsibilities of individuals are clearly spelled out, people will accede to other pressures on their time and the planning tasks won't get done.

Most importantly, if the accountability of management for *failure to plan* is not defined, other less critical work will take up the time.

WHAT TO DO NOW

1. Put all responsibilities and accountabilities in writing and make sure that they are understood and accepted by individuals as part of their jobs.

2. If adequate authority is lacking, a determined campaign must be mounted to get it from higher management. This is a selling job on your part, and you should prepare for it just as you would prepare a sales presentation to your best prospect.

	YES (1)	NO (0)	S/P* (½)
1. The effectiveness of the sales planning activity is measured by the closeness of actual results with the annual, quarterly, and monthly forecasts of order input shipments, etc. contained in the approved sales plan.	⸺	⸺	⸺
2. Monthly reports are prepared showing actual results vs. forecasts for month and year-to-date, and major variances are analyzed for causes.	⸺	⸺	⸺
3. Performance reports are made available to persons who participate in sales planning.	⸺	⸺	⸺
4. Records of actual performance vs. plan are maintained for several years, or are summarized to show past two to three year's performance, for reference at next sales planning iteration.	⸺	⸺	⸺
5. A record is kept of external and internal events and developments having an impact on sales plans, with an assessment of their effects on plans.	⸺	⸺	⸺
6. Monthly data are available for sales planning in detail for at least the past year;			
a. For order input and billings:			
(1) by product or product group,	⸺	⸺	⸺
(2) by customer or customer class,	⸺	⸺	⸺
(3) by sales territory, and	⸺	⸺	⸺
(4) by territory by product and/or customer.	⸺	⸺	⸺
b. For selling expenses:			
(1) by sales territory, covering selling expense/agent commissions, and other sales expense.	⸺	⸺	⸺
(2) by product or product group, and customer or customer class.	⸺	⸺	⸺
7. Expenses of the sales planning activity are routinely compared with budget and major variances are analyzed for correction.	⸺	⸺	⸺

*SOMETIMES OR PARTIALLY

TOTAL POINTS $\boxed{}$ + 0 + $\boxed{}$

= $\boxed{}$

RATING

Enter number of points scored $\boxed{}$ = $\quad$ × 100 = $\boxed{}$ %

Enter number of items on checklist $\boxed{}$

WHAT THE RATING SIGNIFIES Unless good performance measurements and control reports are maintained, management has no way to evaluate the effectiveness of the company's sales planning activity. And unless the effectiveness is measured and evaluated regularly and systematically by comparing actual results with what has been planned and forecasted, management will not know where to put its efforts to improve the planning.

A less-than-satisfactory rating is evidence that controls and measurements may be inadequate for this purpose. A possible consequence is that the company's sales planning will deteriorate over time—and so, eventually, will the effectiveness of the entire selling effort.

WHAT TO DO NOW

1. Set up a program to improve the quality of the department's sales planning records, measurements, and controls. Assign firm responsibility for this program to an individual whom you want to develop—you'll realize a two-fold benefit.

2. Be sure to record non-controllable events and occurrences that can impact your plans, such as internal reorganizations, government actions, strikes, etc. Your plans, of course, cannot always anticipate such events.

19-D
OPERATING PERFORMANCE HISTORY

	YES (1)	NO (0)	S/P* (½)
1. A review of control reports and performance records for the past year shows vs. prior years:			
a. an improved "track record" of actual vs. forecasted sales, order input, selling expenses and profit contribution for the year,	___	___	___
b. better forecasting by quarter and month, and	___	___	___
c. better forecasting by sales territory.	___	___	___
2. During the past year, there have been fewer changes to the sales plan as a consequence of faulty or weak plan assumptions, invalid data, or unanticipated events.	___	___	___
3. The expense budget has essentially been met for the past year.	___	___	___

*SOMETIMES OR PARTIALLY

TOTAL POINTS [ ] + 0 + [ ]

= [ ]

RATING

Enter number of points scored [ ]
_____ = [ ] × 100 = [ ] %
Enter number of items on checklist [ ]

WHAT THE RATING SIGNIFIES

A healthy and dynamic business should show a record of improving performance every year, not only in profit, but in every phase of operation. A low rating here is evidence of weaknesses or shortcomings in the sales planning process or organization.

WHAT TO DO NOW

1. A critical review of the sales planning activity is in order if the rating is poor. Look first at the process to determine whether the planning suffers from one of these common faults:

    a. false assumptions,

    b. invalid historical data, or

    c. overly-optimistic forecasting.

2. Next, review the organization to ascertain whether the planning activity involves *all* people who should participate in it, including those in other functions who should contribute information.

19-E
TOP-LEVEL SUPPORT AND GUIDANCE

	YES (1)	NO (0)	S/P* (½)

Sales planning is recognized by the executive office as an important function of the sales organization, and as a vital contributor to business planning and budgeting. Recognition, guidance, and support are manifested by:

a. budget approval,

b. executive review and approval of annual sales plans,

c. participation in the introduction (launching) of the annual sales plan to the sales force,

d. periodic reviews of progress vs. plan, and

e. recognition and reward for outstanding accomplishment.

*SOMETIMES OR PARTIALLY

TOTAL POINTS ☐ + 0 + ☐

= ☐

RATING

Enter number of points scored ☐

Enter number of items on checklist ☐

= ☐ × 100 = ☐ %

WHAT THE RATING SIGNIFIES

Sales planning is one of the most crucial functions of every business, and top management cannot disavow its responsibility for the results. The company's top executives should do more than merely support the sales planning activity; they should take an active part in the process. If they fail to do so, for lack of time or interest, they have no one to blame but themselves should plans not work out.

WHAT TO DO NOW

1. If top management is not actively participating in sales planning while it is in process, it's your fault, not theirs. If you wait until the plan is wrapped up before getting the executive office involved, you're not

only risking rejection but you're failing to incorporate in the plan some vitally important input—top-level intelligence and experience.

2. Build into every sales plan an active selling role for top management, by assigning certain key prospects to a specific executive for development. "Executive selling" should be an important part of your plan.

3. It goes without saying that it should not come as a surprise to said executive that he or she is expected to "do a number" on the president of XYZ Company—conversely, it is good practice to keep your own contacts in XYZ Company informed in advance of such a visit.

19-F
INNOVATION IN METHODS AND TECHNIQUES

	YES (1)	NO (0)	S/P* (½)
1. Sales management actively seeks better ways to plan sales activities, through:			
a. seminars, workshops, conferences,	___	___	___
b. outside specialists,	___	___	___
c. professional associations,	___	___	___
d. industry contacts,	___	___	___
e. review of current literature,	___	___	___
f. solicitation of ideas from personnel at all levels, esp. field sales, and	___	___	___
g. budgets include funds for such activities.	___	___	___
2. Up-to-date analytical techniques are used to identify, classify, and assign sales territories on the most productive basis.	___	___	___
3. The computer is used to store, process, and display:			
a. order input and shipments by product line, customer class, major account, and sales territory,	___	___	___
b. forecasts of major variables,	___	___	___
c. actual performance vs. the plan of the major plan variables.	___	___	___

*SOMETIMES OR PARTIALLY

TOTAL POINTS   [ ] + 0 + [ ]

= [ ]

RATING

Enter number of points scored [ ] = × 100 = [ ] %
Enter number of items on checklist [ ]

WHAT THE RATING SIGNIFIES   If the computer is not now being used to prepare the annual sales plan and to keep it current with changing market conditions, then the planning probably takes too much of your people's time. The computer can't do the thinking that goes into the plan, but it can relieve people of the detailed "number crunching" that computers do so well (and most people dislike).

The new word processing equipment can also make text preparation easy and fast. Some new equipment even combines word and number processing.

WHAT TO DO NOW

1. Look into the new equipment that can take the drudgery out of plan preparation. Most people don't like to plan—anything that can be done to make it more pleasant will benefit you.

2. Make sure that your managers and supervisors keep up with the state-of-the-art in sales planning, territory assignments, sales incentive plans, and forecasting. The more they know about these, the easier your job will be.

19-G
INTERFUNCTIONAL COMMUNICATIONS AND COORDINATION

	YES (1)	NO (0)	S/P* (½)

1. Sales personnel with responsibility for sales planning maintain close and continuing contact with personnel in other functions who contribute to development of the plan, or are users of information contained in the plan, including:

   a. comptroller, _____ _____ _____

   b. field sales, _____ _____ _____

   c. marketing, _____ _____ _____

   d. information systems, and _____ _____ _____

   e. customer service. _____ _____ _____

2. Communication with other functions is achieved through personal contact, and:

   a. exchange of progress reports, _____ _____ _____

   b. planning meetings, and _____ _____ _____

   c. quarterly progress review meetings. _____ _____ _____

*SOMETIMES OR PARTIALLY

TOTAL POINTS ☐ + 0 + ☐ = ☐

RATING

Enter number of points scored ☐ / Enter number of items on checklist ☐ = × 100 = ☐ %

WHAT THE RATING SIGNIFIES Good sales planning requires information inputs from other functions, not just at planning time, but during the entire year, in order to keep the plan current.

It pays to have your contacts with other functions in good repair at all times, so they will make their contribution willingly and in good spirit. Make them understand that sales planning serves the whole organization, not just the sales department.

WHAT TO DO NOW

You have the right to *demand* that other departments provide the information you need for sales planning—but don't do it. You'll get better results with persuasion, appeals to self-interest, or horse-trading.

19-H
FUNCTIONAL IMPROVEMENT PROGRAM

	YES (1)	NO (0)	S/P* (½)
1. There is an active, on-going interfunctional team effort to improve the quality of sales planning. Efforts, on a project basis, are directed specifically toward:			
a. better integration of sales planning with budgeting, business planning, marketing planning, and production planning,	_____	_____	_____
b. improved forecasting of profit contribution by product, and selling expenses in sales plans,	_____	_____	_____
c. better integration of advertising and sales promotion planning with field sales, and	_____	_____	_____
d. improved two-way communications between field sales and home office staff to assure good data input to planning and effective dissemination of plans.	_____	_____	_____
2. The following functions, in addition to sales, are represented on the team, depending on the project:			
a. marketing,	_____	_____	_____
b. product distribution,	_____	_____	_____
c. advertising and promotion,	_____	_____	_____
d. financial control,	_____	_____	_____
e. market research and analysis,	_____	_____	_____
f. information systems, and	_____	_____	_____
g. production.	_____	_____	_____

*SOMETIMES OR PARTIALLY

TOTAL POINTS   [ ] + 0 + [ ]

= [ ]

RATING

Enter number of points scored [ ]
─────────────────────────────── = × 100 = [ ] %
Enter number of items on checklist [ ]

Every function of the business benefits from good sales planning. Every function, therefore, should make a willing contribution to better planning. A multi-functional team effort can accomplish a great deal to improve the sales planning, properly motivated and directed. The trick is to make the effort worthwhile to the other participants.

A low rating here is not an indication that the function has operating problems, but it does indicate that the company could well benefit from a team approach to improvement.

WHAT TO DO NOW

1. Try the team approach on an informal basis and on a limited scope. Select a project that is not likely to be controversial to insure against failure.

2. Be sure that the first task of the team is to set project goals. Once all members of the team are committed to the same goals, the rest is easy.

19-1
RESOURCES

	YES (1)	NO (0)	S/P* (½)
1. Sales management is kept informed about company objectives, policies, plans, and programs, through participation in key management meetings, and access to appropriate marketing plans, business plans, and operating reports.	_____	_____	_____
2. Sales management is informed about new-product plans sufficiently in advance of their introduction to factor them into sales planning.	_____	_____	_____
3. Based on these forward projections, internal resources are judged to be effective and adequate to meet the company's needs for sales planning during the next three, six, and twelve months, in terms of:			
a. manpower/management,	_____	_____	_____
b. capabilities,	_____	_____	_____
c. budget funding,	_____	_____	_____
d. historical and forecast information,	_____	_____	_____
e. computer time and capacity,	_____	_____	_____
f. other functional support, and	_____	_____	_____
g. outside services.	_____	_____	_____

*SOMETIMES OR PARTIALLY

TOTAL POINTS   ☐ + 0 + ☐

= ☐

RATING

Enter number of points scored ☐
───────────────────────────────── =   × 100 = ☐ %
Enter number of items on checklist ☐

WHAT THE RATING SIGNIFIES

If the answer to points 1 and 2 is negative, then the rest of the checklist is academic. Sales planning cannot be done in the absence of knowledge about the overall direction of the company and the status of new products in the pipeline. Neither can sales management know with any certainty whether its resources are adequate to do the amount and kind of sales planning that the company needs to do in order to remain competitive.

WHAT TO DO NOW

1. Don't wait until planning time to seek out the information you need. Take the time and make the effort to keep informed constantly and fully throughout the year.

2. If you are not presently invited to attend top-level meetings where marketing and sales matters are discussed and important decisions affecting sales planning are made, you should insist on your need and right to do so, as part of your responsibility to plan the company's sales activity.

Chapter **20**

Supervising the
Field Sales Force

SALES SUPERVISION IS THE DIRECT FIRST-HAND LEADERSHIP OF THE SELLING EFFORT.

It involves the selection, field training, motivation, direction, evaluation and control of individual sales representatives and sales agents in the performance of their selling activities. The supervision of agents must consider their contractually independent, that is, non-employee, status.

This appraisal is intended to include the skills and attitudes of supervisors, as well as the structure and system of supervision. It concentrates on the personal interface between salespersons and their direct supervisors. These may be local field supervisors or district managers, or the general sales manager in small organizations. Persons responsible for sales supervision in smaller companies often have other duties, of course, but these must not interfere with the primary task of all sales supervisors which is to motivate and enable every salesperson to maximize his or her selling effectiveness.

Accordingly, the term "sales supervisor," as used here, means the *individual*, regardless of title or organizational level, *to whom sales representatives report directly.*

WHAT IS THE MAIN FUNCTION OF A SALES SUPERVISOR?

The primary purpose of sales supervision is to maximize the selling effectiveness and productivity of sales representatives in order to meet established objectives of the sales plan. To this end, sales supervisors must first develop the capabilities of individual salespersons, and then ensure that full use of these capabilities is made. Sales supervisors are responsible for meeting current sales objectives, of course, but their primary duty is to

353

help their sales personnel get orders—not to get orders through their own direct selling effort.

THREE NECESSARY APPROACHES TO EFFECTIVE SALES SUPERVISION

In an office or factory, a supervisor is able continuously to supervise the work of subordinates and take corrective action as required. In many selling situations, however, the person supervised is typically on his or her own—usually alone, frequently in unfamiliar surroundings, and without ready access to supervisory guidance if help is needed. Because of this unique characteristic of sales representatives' working conditions, effective sales supervision requires a different approach; a combination of (1) working with groups in periodic meetings, (2) working with and coaching individual salespersons on actual sales calls, and (3) intelligent use of telephone and written communication with individuals.

Through the proper balance of these activities sales supervisors are enabled to maximize the productivity of the sales force, whether large or small.

KEY AIM OF THE SELF-AUDIT

The main goals of the appraisal are to ensure that field sales supervision is adequate in size and competence, well trained in handling people, and adequately compensated—so that field sales forces are deployed for maximum market coverage and sales capabilities are fully concentrated on effective selling.

In general, field supervision of the sales force should be equal to or better than that of the strongest competitor.

HOW TO USE THE CHECKLISTS

For each of the statements in the Checklist, compare the condition of your function to the "ideal" as described in the statement. Then:

1. If you consider the statement to be *generally true* of your function, check the YES column.

2. If you consider the statement to be *untrue* of your function, check the NO column.

3. If you consider the statement to be *less than true* (but not totally untrue) of your function, check the SOMETIMES OR PARTIAL column.

4. If the statement does not apply to your particular situation, write "Not Applicable" across the response spaces (or simply draw a line through them).

5. If you lack the data for a definite response, write in "Not Answerable" or "Don't Know."

HOW TO EVALUATE YOUR RESPONSES

When you have completed the checklist, glance over your responses, keeping these points in mind:

1. A negative answer is always unfavorable because it indicates a problem within the function: the greater the number of NOs, the more serious the situation.

2. A positive response is always a good indication. But too many YES answers could indicate that your review is not objective enough.

3. Too many SOMETIMES OR PARTIALLY answers can point to internal weaknesses or to a lack of firm direction.

4. A lot of "Not Applicable" answers could indicate that you are avoiding the issue.

5. A large number of "Not Answerable" or "Don't Know" answers could be symptomatic of inadequate records or data bases.

HOW TO RATE AND SCORE YOUR RESPONSES

When you are satisfied with your responses in general, you are ready to score the Checklist. For your convenience, a self-explanatory Scoring and Rating Block follows each Checklist. This block not only tells you whether the condition of your function is satisfactory, but it also gives you a measure of its effectiveness.

Here's how to total up the points for inclusion in the Scoring and Rating Block:

1. Total up the number of points you scored:
   a. For each YES, give yourself one point.
   b. For each NO, give yourself zero.
   c. For each SOMETIMES OR PARTIALLY, give yourself a half-point.
   d. For each "Not Applicable" answer, give yourself zero and deduct one from the number of items on the Checklist.
   e. For each "Not Answerable" or "Don't Know" answer, give yourself zero.

2. Next divide the total number of points you score by the total number of items (statements) on the Checklist (less items marked "Not Applicable"). You'll get a 1.0 for a perfect score and a fraction for anything less.

3. Multiply the result of step 2 by 100 to arrive at the percentage for your score.

What is a satisfactory rating? A rating of less than 65 percent is unacceptable and calls for an improvement program: Obviously, the lower the rating, the more drastic the action required.

A brief "how-to" example of this Scoring and Rating system follows . . .

EXAMPLE

	YES (1)	NO (0)	S/P* (½)
1. Field sale reports designed to provide information on sales progress contain data on the following topics:			
a. sales calls and sales presentations made by salespersons and sales agents,	✓		
b. bids, quotations, and proposals made,	✓		
c. new orders booked,	✓		
d. lost business, and reasons for the loss,		✓	
e. accomplishments toward future orders,			✓
f. performance in filling orders, handling complaints, and otherwise servicing individual customers,	✓		
g. action taken in response to customer requests, such as sending samples, spec sheets, etc.,	✓		
h. accomplishments of significance and value to other members of the sales force.			✓

*SOMETIMES OR PARTIALLY

TOTAL POINTS $\boxed{5}$ + 0 + $\boxed{1}$

$$= \boxed{6}$$

RATING

Enter number of points scored $\boxed{6}$

Enter number of items on checklist $\boxed{8}$ = .75 × 100 = $\boxed{75}$ %

20-A
ORGANIZATION, ADMINISTRATION, AND OPERATION

	YES (1)	NO (0)	S/P* (½)

1. Field sales supervision is recognized on the organization charts and in position descriptions as an important function of sales management.

2. Field sales supervisors report directly to the sales manager, not to a coordinator or administrator.

3. The function is staffed by professional salespersons who:

   a. are trained in supervisory skills, and

   b. know the company's customers and products.

4. The function has a formal budget allocation covering all expenses of operation.

5. Field sales supervisors are guided in their everyday direction of the field sales force by written procedures which cover the majority of their activities.

6. Compensation of sales supervisors compares with industry and competition.

7. Compensation of supervisors is satisfactory in relation to the earnings of those they supervise.

8. The ratio of supervisors to direct selling personnel is within the normal range for the industry and principal competitors.

9. Field sales supervisors routinely attend top-level sales meetings on matters of sales policy, procedures, sales planning, personnel policy (time and distance permitting).

10. The selling ability of the typical field sales supervisor compares favorably with that of salespersons supervised with regard to the five basic selling skills:

    a. preparation for the sales call,

    b. sales approach and presentation,

    c. overcoming objections,

    d. closing the sale, and

    e. post-order performance.

11. The typical sales supervisor maintains selling proficiency by:

    a. hands-on instruction to new hires,

    b. helping experienced sales representatives in difficult selling situations,

    c. substituting for salesmen in emergencies, and

    d. personally trying out new selling techniques.

12. The typical sales supervisor:

    a. has adequate sales records and statistics for effective sales control,

    b. checks all salespersons' progress weekly or more often,

    c. regularly spot checks salesmens' performance in actual selling situations.

*SOMETIMES OR PARTIALLY

	YES (1)	NO (0)	S/P* (½)

13. The typical sales supervisor spends more than 75 percent of time on the following activities:

    a. direct sales supervision, _____ _____ _____

    b. coaching sales personnel, and _____ _____ _____

    c. calling on customers and prospects with salespersons. _____ _____ _____

14. Sales supervisors are free of excessive paperwork and administrative detail. _____ _____ _____

15. Ten to 15 percent of the total time of the typical salesperson is spent in the field with the supervisor. _____ _____ _____

16. In the field, the typical sales supervisor:

    a. makes maximum use of travel time (doing reports, for example), _____ _____ _____

    b. uses these occasions to teach the salesperson how to maximize time, such as by:

        (1) verifying appointments by phone, etc., during breaks and waiting time, and _____ _____ _____

        (2) using tape recorder to dictate notes while driving. _____ _____ _____

17. The typical sales supervisor:

    a. has a clear understanding of the specific job duties, _____ _____ _____

    b. executes plans promptly and with initiative, _____ _____ _____

    c. makes routine decisions without continually checking with superiors, _____ _____ _____

    d. utilizes marketing staff assistance when available, _____ _____ _____

    e. develops and uses a work schedule, and _____ _____ _____

    f. ties this schedule in with those of sales personnel and keeps them informed of plans. _____ _____ _____

18. Sales supervisors are assured of the sales manager's support when they find it necessary to discipline a salesperson for breach of company regulations or procedures, or for repeated failure to perform. _____ _____ _____

19. In controlling field sales activities, the typical supervisor takes advantage of the communications media available, such as:

    a. telephone/Telex/TWX, _____ _____ _____

    b. reports to or from field, _____ _____ _____

    c. group meetings, and _____ _____ _____

    d. personal contact. _____ _____ _____

20. The typical sales supervisor:

    a. keeps a record of prospective salespersons to serve as a reservoir for possible manpower needs, _____ _____ _____

    b. knows current hiring practices, _____ _____ _____

    c. follows a definite program for upgrading the sales organization including weeding out the weak performers, _____ _____ _____

*SOMETIMES OR PARTIALLY

	YES (1)	NO (0)	S/P* (½)
d. participates in separation interviews, and	———	———	———
e. has "profiles" of the types of salespersons who will and will not succeed.	———	———	———
21. Salespersons and sales agents actively encourage worthwhile selling candidates to apply for employment.	———	———	———
22. The typical sales supervisor has identified and is training a possible successor.	———	———	———
23. The annual rate of sales turnover during the past year has been less than 20 percent.	———	———	———
24. The typical sales supervisor:			
a. has been through the company's formal sales training program,	———	———	———
b. participates in periodic sales training sessions with sales representatives, and	———	———	———
c. conducts on-the-job training with each salesperson.	———	———	———
25. The typical sales supervisor ensures that all salespersons:			
a. attend sales meetings,	———	———	———
b. educate customers regarding the benefits of the company's products and services, and	———	———	———
c. utilize training productively.	———	———	———
26. The typical field sales supervisor takes advantage of opportunities for off-the-job studies for self-improvement.	———	———	———
27. The typical supervisor encourages salesmen to take self-development courses of study.	———	———	———
28. The sales supervisor regularly measures new sales people against standards for:			
a. knowledge of company's products,	———	———	———
b. knowledge of competitor's products,	———	———	———
c. knowledge of customers and prospects,	———	———	———
d. selling proficiency, and	———	———	———
e. time management.	———	———	———
29. The typical sales supervisor has been trained in the use of basic tools for motivating sales people, such as:			
a. building enthusiasm at meetings,	———	———	———
b. capitalizing on sales incentives, and	———	———	———
c. featuring success stories and recognition of achievement in communications.	———	———	———
30. The typical supervisor is capable of:			
a. understanding individual's motivations, strengths, weaknesses,	———	———	———
b. conveying significant problems of sales representatives to management,	———	———	———
c. getting the support of the salesperson's spouse,	———	———	———

*SOMETIMES OR PARTIALLY

	YES (1)	NO (0)	S/P* (½)

d. ensuring the salesperson's understanding of the sales compensation plan, incentives, quotas, etc.,

e. explaining the criteria for assigning territories, and

f. explaining the sales compensation plan.

31. The typical supervisor:

    a. participates in developing sales plans,

    b. understands the sales plan,

    c. ensures that salespersons understand the sales plan,

    d. when the sales plan is changed explains the changes, and

    e. keeps salespersons informed on company policies, procedures and practices.

32. In day-to-day direction of salesmen, the typical supervisor:

    a. points out new sales opportunities,

    b. identifies alternative ways to capitalize on opportunities,

    c. spotlights problems and guides the salesperson in solving them (but does not solve them himself), and

    d. sets an example consistent with what is asked of the sales representatives.

33. The typical supervisor relies on suggestions, guidance and encouragement as opposed to commands and reprimands.

34. The typical supervisor's ability is rated as good to excellent by sales representatives.

35. In making personnel evaluations, the typical sales supervisor:

    a. informally reviews each salesperson's performance monthly or more often,

    b. uses established performance standards,

    c. makes a *formal* performance evaluation of each salesperson quarterly or semi-annually, and

    d. discusses these evaluations with each salesperson, with improvement suggestions.

36. The supervisor keeps a written summary of each formal performance evaluation and refers to it in the next one.

37. The typical supervisor demonstrates flexibility by adjusting his schedule to that of the salesperson being worked with.

*SOMETIMES OR PARTIALLY

TOTAL POINTS   ☐ + 0 + ☐

                   = ☐

RATING

Enter number of points scored   ☐
————————————————————————— =   × 100 = ☐ %
Enter number of items on checklist   ☐

WHAT THE RATING SIGNIFIES

In sales work, as in other fields of endeavor, productivity is almost a direct function of the quality of first-level supervision. The difference is that field salespersons may be out of direct touch with their supervisors for extensive periods of time; thus, supervisors must rely more on motivation, encouragement and recognition, rather than direct hands-on instruction and continuous close supervision. Supervisors, too, may be out of contact with their sales manager much of the time, so they must be self-reliant, self-motivated types.

A less than satisfactory rating indicates that the company may not fully appreciate the need for and value of high quality field supervision of the sales force. This is particularly true if supervisory compensation is low relative to the industry, or is inadequate in relation to the earnings of personnel supervised. As a consequence, the field sales force may be substantially less productive than it could be.

WHAT TO DO NOW

1. When selecting sales supervisors, keep in mind that the top salesperson is not necessarily the best sales supervisor, although actual selling experience is a must. Supervision requires a different set of capabilities than selling, plus an even higher degree of skill in dealing with people. Make certain that all new supervisors receive training in "how to supervise" before they go into the field.

2. Make sure that sales supervisors are not so overloaded with administrative paper work that they can't carry out the real purpose of the job—training, motivating, and coaching sales representatives.

3. Set up your sales compensation to ensure that your sales supervisors share in the rewards of sales success, through some form of incentive compensation. This is just as important for small firms as it is for large organizations.

4. Assure your sales supervisors that they have your support in the event of serious disputes with supervised personnel—and back up your assurance with your actions.

5. In all but the smallest sales organizations, it is not good practice to have supervisors who do actual selling themselves, especially if their compensation is based on their own sales production.

20-B
AUTHORITY, RESPONSIBILITY, AND ACCOUNTABILITY

	YES (1)	NO (0)	S/P* (½)
1. Authority has been delegated to the sales manager, through budget allocation and position description, to expend company funds and assign tasks necessary to assure adequate supervision of field sales personnel and activities.	———	———	———
2. Authority has been re-delegated, through budget allocation and supervisors' position descriptions, to field sales supervisors to expend funds and assign tasks necessary to direct and control field sales personnel.	———	———	———

*SOMETIMES OR PARTIALLY

3. The sales manager is responsible for:

   a. staffing and managing an effective organization of field sales management, and

   b. full development of the company's sales potential.

4. Field sales supervisors are responsible for:

   a. staffing and managing an effective sales force, and

   b. full development of the sales potential in their particular areas.

5. Field sales supervisors are responsible for:

   a. the actions and activities of sales personnel reporting to them,

   b. maximizing individual and collective sales productivity, and

   c. meeting the objectives of the sales plan.

6. The sales manager is held accountable for:

   a. serious failure to meet sales plan objectives,

   b. losses of key customers,

   c. losses of critical orders, bids, contracts,

   d. losses of capable sales supervisors, and

   e. failure to exploit sales opportunities resulting from an ineffective sales supervisory organization.

7. Field sales supervisors are held accountable in their particular areas for:

   a. failure to meet sales plan objectives,

   b. losses of customers, orders, contracts,

   c. losses of capable salespersons,

   d. failure to cover important sales territories resulting from lack of supervision, and ineffective direction, motivation, or control of sales personnel.

*SOMETIMES OR PARTIALLY

TOTAL POINTS ☐ + 0 + ☐

= ☐

RATING

Enter number of points scored ☐

Enter number of items on checklist ☐

= × 100 = ☐ %

WHAT THE RATING SIGNIFIES   When sales supervisors are physically remote from the home office, as they frequently are, it is vitally important that considerable authority be delegated downward to them. It is equally important that supervised sales people *know* that the supervisor has this authority. Supervisors must have the power to reward accomplishments without going up through channels.

They must also have the authority to discipline individuals for serious or repeated failure to perform, without having to consult a superior.

Obviously, authority such as this implies a high degree of responsibility for results, and also requires that supervisors be mature enough to accept accountability for *their* own failures, such as serious losses of business or excessive turnover of personnel.

A low rating here indicates that these three factors of authority, responsibility, and accountability may not be as clearly prescribed as they should be for effective sales supervision.

WHAT TO DO NOW

1. Make sure that the authority limits of field sales supervisors are clearly spelled out for all to see. This means putting them in writing. Supervisors have a right to know, for example, that they can hire new salespersons up to a stated maximum compensation without checking with home office on each occasion.

2. Define the responsibilities of sales supervisors in terms of *results*, not activity alone.

3. Relate results to potential. No two sales territories are alike, so sales goals have to be realistic in terms of market potential.

4. Spell out exactly what each sales supervisor is accountable for, so there is no misunderstanding when he or she fails to perform. When an individual doesn't know what is expected of him, criticism for failure to act can be demoralizing.

20-C
MEASUREMENTS, CONTROL REPORTS AND PERFORMANCE RECORDS

	YES (1)	NO (0)	S/P* (½)
1. The effectiveness of sales supervision is measured regularly and continuously.	——	——	——
2. The effectiveness of field sales supervision is measured in the aggregate and for each supervisor by comparing actual performance to standards such as:			
a. sales productivity gains,	——	——	——
b. sales plan objectives,	——	——	——
c. employee turnover,	——	——	——
d. selling expense vs. budgets.	——	——	——
3. Records are kept of key sales productivity statistics by individual supervisor:			
a. order input and sales in units and dollars vs. sales plan and prior periods,	——	——	——
b. selling expense ratio to sales, or per unit,	——	——	——
c. sales to calls ratio, or similar ratio of results to efforts, and	——	——	——
d. turnover of sales personnel, by reason.	——	——	——
4. Expenses are routinely compared with budget and major variances analyzed for correction.	——	——	——

*SOMETIMES OR PARTIALLY

$$\boxed{} + 0 + \boxed{}$$

$$= \boxed{}$$

RATING

Enter number of points scored $\dfrac{\boxed{}}{\boxed{}}$ $=$ $\boxed{} \times 100 = \boxed{\%}$

Enter number of items on checklist

WHAT THE RATING SIGNIFIES

Supervisory effectiveness should be measured by sales *results,* not by the "happiness level" of sales representatives or low selling expenses. Supervisory effectiveness is the sum total of the results of salespersons supervised. Sales results are affected by other factors, of course—advertising and sales promotion, and territory potential among them—but it is the quality of first-level supervision, in the final analysis, that determines results.

A low rating here indicates that supervision either is not measured regularly, or is measured by factors other than selling results. Either way, productivity suffers.

WHAT TO DO NOW

1. To compare performance of supervisors with each other can be unfair, even counterproductive, because of the other factors noted. Better to compare with goals that supervisors have had a hand in setting for themselves. Comparison with their own performance in a prior period is always useful, provided allowance is made for changes in circumstances.

20-D
OPERATING PERFORMANCE HISTORY

	YES (1)	NO (0)	S/P* (½)
1. During the past year, there have been no serious failures to meet sales plan objectives as a consequence of inadequate field sales supervision. (Answer "yes" if true.)	——	——	——
2. During the past year, there were no losses of important customers or cancellations of major orders resulting from poor supervision. (Answer "yes" if true.)	——	——	——
3. During the past year, there has been an improving trend in most sales districts in:			
a. sales productivity in total, i. e., per supervisor,	——	——	——
b. productivity per salesperson,	——	——	——
c. selling expense in total,	——	——	——

*SOMETIMES OR PARTIALLY

   d. selling expense per dollar of sales, _____ _____ _____

   e. on-time sales reporting, _____ _____ _____

   f. employee turnover, and _____ _____ _____

   g. retention of key employees. _____ _____ _____

4. Costs and expenses of sales supervision have been essentially on budget for the past year.

*SOMETIMES OR PARTIALLY

TOTAL POINTS ☐ + 0 + ☐ = ☐

RATING

Enter number of points scored ☐ / Enter number of items on checklist ☐ = ☐ × 100 = ☐ %

WHAT THE RATING SIGNIFIES

Performance of sales supervison in the recent past is the only valid clue to the kind of performance that can be expected in the future. If the rating here is low, then all the forecasts of high productivity are only "promises, promises." Furthermore, if the trends for the past year or so are unfavorable, then it is unrealistic to expect superior performance in the near future. A down-trend first has to be stopped before it can turn up.

WHAT TO DO NOW

1. Identify the areas of sub-standard past performance in sales supervision, in terms of:
   a. what performance factors are unsatisfactory, and
   b. who the sub-standard performers are.
2. First, make sure that the poor performance is not caused by factors not in the supervisor's control, such as lack of good sales literature, inadequate sales training, poor support by the home office, or the like.
3. Next, make sure that the sub-standard performance was not a result of unrealistically high performance standards.
4. Then, let the supervisors participate in setting their own improvement goals. Make sure they don't *over-promise*, because this could lead to further failure.

	YES (1)	NO (0)	S/P* (½)

The executive office demonstrates active guidance and support of field sales supervision as an important management function by:

a. budget approval for the activity,

b. visits to district sales offices,

c. reading and commenting on reports of district sales activities,

d. attending key sales meetings,

e. recognition and reward for outstanding accomplishment.

*SOMETIMES OR PARTIALLY

TOTAL POINTS ☐ + 0 + ☐

= ☐

RATING

Enter number of points scored ☐

Enter number of items on checklist ☐

= × 100 = ☐ %

WHAT THE RATING SIGNIFIES

Recognition by top management of sales supervision as a vital company activity, and recognition of field sales supervisors as key members of management, can contribute substantially to high sales productivity. People invariably perform better when they know that they are regarded as important contributors to the company's progress.

Recognition by the executive office has to be genuine and tangible—not just lip service. This doesn't come naturally; you have to earn it through performance.

WHAT TO DO NOW

1. Make sure that your sales summary reports get executive attention by making them readable. Use interesting and colorful charts and graphs to bring the statistics to life. Always interpret the data and comment on its significance. A well-written executive summary can help.

2. Take advantage of the travel schedules of top execs, by arranging visits to your field sales offices. These can be a great morale booster to sales supervisors who may seldom see the company's top brass. Also, make sure that your sales people know who is coming and when.

3. Don't hide bad news. The boss is sure to hear about it from another source, then your credibility goes down. It's better to report problems when they're small, rather than cover them up while they grow into large problems.

	YES (1)	NO (0)	S/P* (½)
1. An active search is made for better methods for supervising day-to-day field sales activities. As part of this search, managers:			
a. attend sales seminars, workshops, conferences,	———	———	———
b. read current management literature,	———	———	———
c. participate in professional association activities,	———	———	———
d. maintain industry contacts,	———	———	———
e. solicit ideas and improvement suggestions from personnel at all levels, especially field sales, and	———	———	———
f. budgets include funds for such activities.	———	———	———
2. The computer is used to store, process, analyze, and display information on field sales performance by district, territory, supervisor, and sales representative.	———	———	———
3. Up-to-date communications media are used to facilitate the flow of information between supervisors and their direct reports, and between supervisors and the home office, such as:			
a. Data-Phone,	———	———	———
b. Telex/TWX,	———	———	———
c. facsimile, and	———	———	———
d. WATS-lines or tie-lines.	———	———	———

*SOMETIMES OR PARTIALLY

TOTAL POINTS $\boxed{} + 0 + \boxed{}$

$= \boxed{}$

RATING

Enter number of points scored $\boxed{}$

Enter number of items on checklist $\boxed{}$

$= \quad \times 100 = \boxed{} \%$

WHAT THE RATING SIGNIFIES

A less-than-satisfactory rating can indicate that sales management and sales supervisors are complacent, and content to do business the same old way. Meanwhile, your competitors may be adopting new methods and new communications tools that increase their competitive edge.

The problem may not be complacency, but failure of sales management to provide funds and time for supervisors to take refresher training and keep up with changes in the state of the art.

1. Insist that your sales supervisors get away once in a while to catch up with development in the outside world. Your budget should provide for this activity.

2. Supervisors should use these occasions to delegate authority to a subordinate, as part of his or her training to move up in the organization.

3. Information is the key to effective supervision in a widespread field sales organization. Make sure that the most rapid and cost effective communications media are used to transmit and receive information.

20-G
INTERFUNCTIONAL COMMUNICATIONS AND COORDINATION

	YES (1)	NO (0)	S/P* (½)

Field sales supervisors maintain close working relationships with other functions, including:

a. employee relations, on personnel recruiting matters,

b. marketing, for market and sales analysis data,

c. sales training, on new-hire training and retraining for sub-standard performers,

d. product distribution, on product availability problems,

e. production, on product quality problems, and

f. customer service, on in-service product problems.

*SOMETIES OR PARTIALLY

TOTAL POINTS   ☐ + 0 + ☐

= ☐

RATING

Enter number of points scored ☐
—————————————————————— =   × 100 = ☐ %
Enter number of items on checklist ☐

Every event and development within the company has some significance to field sales. Similarly, events in the field have importance to other company functions.

A low rating here indicates that sales supervisors may be insulated from the rest of the organization. As a consequence, field sales personnel and corporate personnel both may be poorly informed about events and developments that can severely impact the business.

1. Supervisors should be encouraged to maintain informal contacts with other functional people on their own organizational level. In this way, they can keep abreast of new developments within the organization as

they are developing. The supervisor who depends only on "top-down" communication for his information is certain to be poorly informed.

2. Communication should be two-way. Sales supervisors are important "sensors" of the marketplace, and their feedback to people in engineering, product quality assurance, sales training, marketing, and other departments, can be a vital input to the work of these individuals.

3. Make sure that the sales supervision budget contains an allocation for this kind of information exchange between functions.

20-H
FUNCTIONAL IMPROVEMENT PROGRAM

	YES (1)	NO (0)	S/P* (½)
1. An interfunctional team has been established for the purpose of improving field sales supervision. The team includes representatives of:			
a. employee relations,	____	____	____
b. marketing,	____	____	____
c. sales training, and	____	____	____
d. field sales force.	____	____	____
2. Improvement efforts are concentrated, on a task basis, upon:			
a. better identification and selection of potential field sales supervisors,	____	____	____
b. improved training in supervisory techniques,	____	____	____
c. improved incentive compensation for supervisors, and	____	____	____
d. management by objectives.	____	____	____

*SOMETIMES OR PARTIALLY

TOTAL POINTS [ ] + 0 + [ ]

= [ ]

RATING

Enter number of points scored [ ]
—————————————————————— = [ ] × 100 = [ ] %
Enter number of items on checklist [ ]

WHAT THE RATING SIGNIFIES

First-level supervision is often the neglected level of management, not only in a sales situation, but throughout many business organizations. Yet, this is where the action is, in terms of getting real results.

A way to revitalize this important part of management in the sales area is to create an interfunctional team, or task force, with the task of improving the effectiveness of field supervision. This approach can pay big dividends in improved productivity, if only by assuring your sales supervisors that they are important to the organization.

WHAT TO DO NOW

1. One aspect of the function that can benefit greatly from this kind of approach is training in supervisory practices. Another is compensation. Both of these are critical to sales supervision effectiveness; both require help from human resources people.

2. Try the approach on an informal basis first. Select a task with a low controversy level to insure success.

3. Use your success to build a concensus for formalizing the team approach. Obviously, your direct superior is the first one to sell, but it pays to have the support of your colleagues in the effort.

20-1
RESOURCES

	YES (1)	NO (0)	S/P* (½)
1. Sales management is kept informed about company objectives, policies, plans, and programs, through access to appropriate business plans, marketing plans, and operating reports—and participation in key management meetings.	___	___	___
2. Based on knowledge of company objectives, sales plans, and budgets, resources for field sales supervision are considered adequate to meet the company's needs during the next three, six, and twelve months, in terms of:			
a. manpower,	___	___	___
b. capabilities,	___	___	___
c. budget funding,	___	___	___
d. facilities,	___	___	___
e. computer time and capacity,	___	___	___
f. communications, and	___	___	___
g. functional support.	___	___	___

*SOMETIMES OR PARTIALLY

TOTAL POINTS [ ] + 0 + [ ] = [ ]

RATING

$$\frac{\text{Enter number of points scored } \boxed{}}{\text{Enter number of items on checklist } \boxed{}} = \boxed{} \times 100 = \boxed{} \%$$

WHAT THE RATING SIGNIFIES

The number of supervisors you need is not always a direct function of the size of the sales force, although it is a rough guide. Other factors enter into the work load calculation. The quality of your sales force is an important factor, for example. Well trained, highly motivated sales people are capable of managing their own activities—too much supervision could actually be a deterrent to high productivity in their case. The quality of supervision is a major factor, of course; a highly skilled supervisor can manage more people than a mediocre one.

In any case, if the answer to point 1 is negative, you probably can't respond to point 2 with confidence. If this is the case, your problem is not lack of resources but lack of information.

WHAT TO DO NOW

1. It's probably better to have too few supervisors than too many. The danger of over-supervision is that your weaker sales people tend to become too dependent on their supervisors, while your strong ones resent being controlled too closely.

2. Support your sales supervisors with adequate resources, especially home-office support. It's a lonely job out there sometimes, and a supervisor needs backup.

3. The field sales supervisor is your principal link between the home office and the customer. Keep him well-informed. There is some risk involved, but it is far less than the danger that field management will be uninformed about important matters that affect customers.

Chapter **21**

How to Report
Sales Activities

Sales reporting is the formalized system of two-way communications between field sales representatives and sales management concerning activities, sales progress, problems, opportunities, and other developments in the marketplace. Its primary purpose is to control and direct the selling activity; an equally important function is to provide marketing and top management with up-to-date intelligence on markets and competition.

WHY WRITTEN SALES REPORTS ARE IMPORTANT

Written sales reports are the principal channel of communication in all but the smallest of sales organizations. They are the means by which sales representatives who are dispersed throughout the marketplace communicate with sales management, which is necessarily concentrated in fewer places, and vice versa. Other forms of field-home office contact, such as personal conferences and sales meetings, are an essential part of the communication process, but it is the routine field sales reporting that provides the organization with the constant information flow required for effective operation.

All too often field sales reports are regarded by field sales people as impositions on their time—"necessary nuisances," so to speak—and are therefore subject to a negative attitude from the outset. These reports, however, are a vital link in the marketing feedback loop, so it is essential to educate sales personnel about their importance during training, to constantly remind sales people about the need for accurate, timely and honest reporting.

KEEP IT SIMPLE, KEEP IT CLEAN, KEEP IT A TWO-WAY FLOW.

This appraisal deals with the *two-way flow* of information between field and office. It goes without saying that the inward flow of data is essential for sales management control. What is sometimes neglected is the *feeding back* to the sales representative of information to which he or she has contributed. The biggest deterrent to quality reporting from the field has been found to be skepticism by sales representatives that the information is being read and put to worthwhile use.

Field sales reporting includes both oral and written reports; most reports, however, are in written form. The key word is *formalized*; reporting is effective only when it is done under an established system with prescribed formats, clear procedures, and discipline. Field sales reports must be *reliable, complete, clear* and *timely*. Reporting should be done at the lowest possible cost consistent with these quality standards. Telephone and postage expense is important, of course, but it is the *time* required for the preparation and use of these reports that is by far the largest element of cost. Salespersons like to say, "I can't sell while I'm writing reports." Accordingly, sales management (especially in smaller organizations) should design and administer the *simplest system of field sales reports* that will provide the required information.

Related to the sales information interchange itself is the dissemination of market information to other company functions. The field sales force constitutes the company's principal "window on the world," so to speak, and sales management must make sure that the vital information it obtains reaches those who need it promptly. Sales management is responsible not only for collecting, analyzing and evaluating these inputs, but also for ensuring their timely referral to other marketing functions such as customer service and marketing research; to non-marketing functions such as manufacturing (for product quality), engineering (for design), and personnel (for competitive hiring); and, of course, to top management (for guidance in setting customer relations policies and establishing corporate strategies.)

Appraisal of field sales reporting is concerned with:

1. *quality* of reports,
2. *use* of reports,
3. *frequency* and *timeliness* of reporting,
4. *form* of reports, and
5. *cost* of reporting.

KEY AIM OF THE SELF-AUDIT

The principal purpose of the appraisal is to assure that all essential information is communicated between field sales and sales management on a timely basis, so as to maximize the competitive effectiveness of the overall marketing and sales effort.

HOW TO USE THE CHECKLISTS

For each of the statements in the Checklist, compare the condition of your function to the "ideal" as described in the statement. Then:

1. If you consider the statement to be *generally true* of your function, check the YES column.

2. If you consider the statement to be *untrue* of your function, check the NO column.

3. If you consider the statement to be *less than true* (but not totally untrue) of your function, check the SOMETIMES OR PARTIAL column.

4. If the statement does not apply to your particular situation, write "Not Applicable" across the response spaces (or simply draw a line through them).

5. If you lack the data for a definite response, write in "Not Answerable" or "Don't Know."

HOW TO EVALUATE YOUR RESPONSES

When you have completed the checklist, glance over your responses, keeping these points in mind:

1. A negative answer is always unfavorable because it indicates a problem within the function: the greater the number of NOs, the more serious the situation.

2. A positive response is always a good indication. But too many YES answers could indicate that your review is not objective enough.

3. Too many SOMETIMES OR PARTIALLY answers can point to internal weaknesses or to a lack of firm direction.

4. A lot of "Not Applicable" answers could indicate that you are avoiding the issue.

5. A large number of "Not Answerable" or "Don't Know" answers could be symptomatic of inadequate records or data bases.

HOW TO RATE AND SCORE YOUR RESPONSES

When you are satisfied with your responses in general, you are ready to score the Checklist. For your convenience, a self-explanatory Scoring and Rating Block follows each Checklist. This block not only tells you whether the condition of your function is satisfactory, but it also gives you a measure of its effectiveness.

Here's how to total up the points for inclusion in the Scoring and Rating Block:

1. Total up the number of points you scored:
   a. For each YES, give yourself one point.
   b. For each NO, give yourself zero.
   c. For each SOMETIMES OR PARTIALLY, give yourself a half-point.
   d. For each "Not Applicable" answer, give yourself zero and deduct one from the number of items on the Checklist.
   e. For each "Not Answerable" or "Don't Know" answer, give yourself zero.

2. Next divide the total number of points you score by the total number of items (statements) on the Checklist (less items marked "Not Applicable"). You'll get a 1.0 for a perfect score and a fraction for anything less.

3. Multiply the result of step 2 by 100 to arrive at the percentage for your score.

What is a satisfactory rating? A rating of less than 65 percent is unacceptable and calls for an improvement program: Obviously, the lower the rating, the more drastic the action required.

A brief "how-to" example of this Scoring and Rating system follows . . .

374

EXAMPLE

	YES (1)	NO (0)	S/P* (½)

1. Field sale reports designed to provide information on sales progress contain data on the following topics:

    a. sales calls and sales presentations made by salespersons and sales agents,   ✓

    b. bids, quotations, and proposals made,   ✓

    c. new orders booked,   ✓

    d. lost business, and reasons for the loss,   ✓ (NO)

    e. accomplishments toward future orders,   ✓ (S/P)

    f. performance in filling orders, handling complaints, and otherwise servicing individual customers,   ✓

    g. action taken in response to customer requests, such as sending samples, spec sheets, etc.,   ✓

    h. accomplishments of significance and value to other members of the sales force.   ✓ (S/P)

*SOMETIMES OR PARTIALLY

TOTAL POINTS $5 + 0 + 1$

$= 6$

RATING

$$\frac{\text{Enter number of points scored} \quad 6}{\text{Enter number of items on checklist} \quad 8} = .75 \times 100 = \boxed{75 \%}$$

375

	YES (1)	NO (0)	S/P* (½)
1. Field sales reporting is recognized in manager's positions descriptions as a vital marketing activity, and an important function of sales management.	_____	_____	_____
2. The sales department budget includes an allocation covering expenses of this function.	_____	_____	_____
3. The firm has an organized and cohesive set of systems and procedures for field sales reporting, documented in writing, that guides and governs information flow between field sales and home office.	_____	_____	_____
4. All sales and marketing personnel receive training in preparation and use of field sales reports.	_____	_____	_____
5. All field sales personnel are informed that sales reporting is an essential part of the sales job.	_____	_____	_____
6. Sales reports from the field are read, analyzed, and summarized on an organized basis.			
a. Delinquent reporters are followed-up.	_____	_____	_____
b. Essential summary data is sent back to the field at regular intervals.	_____	_____	_____
c. Essential market data is extracted and sent to marketing, manufacturing, and technical departments on a regular basis.	_____	_____	_____
d. Critical news and competitive information is handled on a "flash" basis.	_____	_____	_____
7. Directives to the field are read and heeded. Reports containing product information and other semi-permanent information are retained by field personnel in an indexed record for ready access.	_____	_____	_____
8. Submission of sales reports from the field is required only as frequently as needed for expense control, performance measurement, and market intelligence. Routine reports to the field are sent on a fixed schedule.	_____	_____	_____
9. Reports from and to the field contain only information that is essential to the proper functioning of both the field sales force and sales management. Personnel both in field and at home office generally have a favorable attitude toward the reporting.	_____	_____	_____
10. All reports are designed to convey essential information as rapidly as possible, with an absolute minimum of extraneous, irrelevant and unnecessary data.			
a. Urgent information is conveyed in written form by Telex, TWX, or data phone.	_____	_____	_____
b. Phone reports are verified in writing.	_____	_____	_____
11. A cost analysis has been made during the past year of the reporting system, including time for preparation and time for use.	_____	_____	_____
12. Procedures for the preparation and distribution of field sales reports:			
a. are prepared in written form,	_____	_____	_____
b. are available to the field sales force and other affected personnel,	_____	_____	_____

*SOMETIMES OR PARTIALLY

	YES (1)	NO (0)	S/P* (½)

c. are clear and readily understandable,

d. are current with existing practices, and

e. are reviewed at least once a year with field and office preparers and users.

13. Field sales reports are specifically designed for:

    a. reliability (by requiring sources of information),

    b. completeness (by suggesting topics to be covered and providing adequate space),

    c. clarity (by defining terms used and giving examples), and

    d. timeliness (by stating due dates).

14. Field sales reports have been reviewed for format, adequacy, and redundancy.

15. The following types of reports or report information are submitted or issued from the sales force:

    a. call report,

    b. order/sales report,

    c. expense report,

    d. customer report, and

    e. market outlook report.

16. The following types of reports are issued to the sales force:

    a. sales manager's letter,

    b. product bulletin,

    c. customer service report, and

    d. sales bulletin.

17. A survey of users indicates that field sales reports issued from home office to field:

    a. are used to plan and make sales calls, and

    b. could not be significantly reduced in number, length or frequency.

18. Field sales reports from field to home office contain information:

    a. useful to sales management,

    b. useful to customer service, and

    c. useful to marketing.

19. Sales reports from field to home office are designed to convey the following information:

    a. information about customers' and prospects' expansion plans, personnel changes, new products, etc.,

    b. information about competitors' price changes, new products, personnel changes, etc., (including the source of such information), and

*SOMETIMES OR PARTIALLY

c. information about other market influences such as government action, crop failure, housing starts, etc.

20. Sales reports from home office to field cover the following kinds of information:

    a. changes in products, services, policies, or other actions by the company,

    b. the effect of such changes, and

    c. other timely information useful in day-to-day selling.

21. Sales reports from field to home office are designed to provide the following types of information:

    a. the outlook for major customers or prospects, and

    b. the outlook for principal competitors.

22. Sales reports from home office to field cover the following kinds of information:

    a. the outlook for the market, and

    b. the likely effect of the market outlook on the company's sales.

23. Field sales reports from field to home office are designed to provide the following types of information:

    a. sales calls and presentations made,

    b. bids, quotations, and proposals,

    c. orders secured and lost,

    d. accomplishments toward future orders,

    e. performance in filling specific orders, handling complaints, and servicing individual customers,

    f. problems and opportunities that need home office attention, and

    g. accomplishments of significance and use to the sales force.

24. Sales reports from field to home office are designed to facilitate control of the salesperson's activities and performance by reporting information that:

    a. provides sales management with specific call frequency and other market coverage data,

    b. provides sales management with information on sales and product approaches used, and

    c. provides sales management with sufficient time and expense data to permit analysis.

25. Sales reports from home office to field contain information that:

    a. guides sales reps toward more effective use of their time,

    b. makes constructive suggestions to sales personnel for handling individual customers or sales problems,

    c. gives recognition to good work.

*SOMETIMES OR PARTIALLY

378

	YES (1)	NO (0)	S/P* (½)
26. Field sales reports are filed for ready reference where needed, by both field and office.	_____	_____	_____
27. An evaluation of the adequacy of sales representatives' reports is included in their performance ratings.	_____	_____	_____
28. Sales supervisors discuss adequacy of reports with salespersons during performance reviews.	_____	_____	_____
29. The importance of field sales reporting is stressed in all training programs.	_____	_____	_____
30. Field sales reporting is included on the agenda of sales meetings.	_____	_____	_____

*SOMETIMES OR PARTIALLY

TOTAL POINTS ☐ + 0 + ☐

= ☐

RATING

$$\frac{\text{Enter number of points scored} \quad ☐}{\text{Enter number of items on checklist} \quad ☐} = \quad \times\ 100 = \boxed{\quad \%}$$

WHAT THE RATING SIGNIFIES

A less-than-acceptable rating indicates that management may not fully appreciate that the effectiveness of the selling activity is virtually a direct function of the company's sales information system. In a fast-changing market and competitive situation, an organized two-way flow of accurate and timely sales reports can be the essential difference between sales success and failure. This is particularly true in sales organizations that are decentralized over a large geographic area, in which sales representatives are isolated from their managers and remote from the home office.

Obviously, a sales reporting system costs money and takes time. The cost to the company of failure to capitalize on a sales opportunity because it wasn't properly reported, however, can be immensely greater.

WHAT TO DO NOW

1. Good field sales reporting starts with *sales training*. This is the time to educate sales people about the need for and value (to them) of good reporting. Once they're out in the field, it's too late. Make sure that this activity is emphasized in the initial training.

2. Well-designed reporting forms are another key to good reporting. Good design makes it easier for the field salesperson to report, reports are quicker to read and understand, and they lend themselves better to summarizing. A good systems and procedures specialist should be consulted. (Above all, don't let each salesperson design his or her own reports, although the field should be consulted during design.)

3. It is absolutely essential to let those who prepare reports know that the reports are read and used. (If they're not used, of course, they should be discontinued and the company should go back into the buggy whip business!) One of the best ways to ensure this is to periodically write comments on a report and send a photocopy back to the originator.

4. Your field sales supervisors are critical to the reporting. They are the information interface between the field salesperson and the home office. It's particularly important that they understand, appreciate, and *use* field sales reports.

5. Every single report should stimulate someone, somewhere, to take action. If it doesn't do this, eliminate it. What is more, if a report doesn't tell a person something he didn't know before, eliminate it (or delete that person from the distribution list).

6. Small-to-medium size companies need a good reporting system just as much as a large corporation. The only real difference is in the *amount* of information carried by the system; the *kind* of information is pretty much the same regardless of company size.

21-B
AUTHORITY, RESPONSIBILITY, AND ACCOUNTABILITY

	YES (1)	NO (0)	S/P* (½)
1. Authority has been delegated, through budget allocation and position description, to the sales manager to expend funds and assign tasks necessary to assure a full flow of sales information between field sales and home office.	___	___	___
2. The sales manager is responsible for:			
a. staffing and managing an organization to prepare, transmit, evaluate, and use field sales reports, and	___	___	___
b. establishing and administering a system of field sales reports.	___	___	___
3. Sales supervisors are responsible for:			
a. preparation and timely submission to home office of reports from the field sales representatives reporting to them,	___	___	___
b. timely dissemination of information contained in reports from the home office to sales representatives, and	___	___	___
c. action on these reports.	___	___	___
4. Responsibilities are clearly assigned to sales representatives for information inputs to sales reports from the field, and to individuals in the home office for information inputs to sales reports to the field.	___	___	___
5. The sales manager is held accountable for serious failure to meet sales plan objectives resulting from inadequate or ineffective sales reporting.	___	___	___
6. Sales supervisors similarly are held accountable for serious failure to meet sales plan objectives in their respective districts or territories.	___	___	___

*SOMETIMES OR PARTIALLY

TOTAL POINTS ☐ + 0 + ☐

= ☐

RATING

Enter number of points scored ☐
———————————————————————————— = × 100 = ☐ %
Enter number of items on checklist ☐

WHAT THE RATING SIGNIFIES

In our fast-moving competitive environment, the consequences of failure to report vital information on time can be extremely costly to the company. All sales personnel should know that they will be held accountable for loss of business resulting from late, inaccurate, or incomplete reports.

All too often, sales reporting is looked upon as a distraction from the real selling effort, rather than a crucial contributor to the effort. A low rating in this section indicates that sales reporting may not be regarded as an important separate activity that must be *managed*, and for which responsibilities must be clearly assigned and authority delegated. As a consequence, sales opportunities may be overlooked or missed because of inadequate reporting.

WHAT TO DO NOW

1. Clearly spell out what each individual is responsible and accountable for, and what the penalties are for gross failure to perform. The duty to report essential information should be written into every job description.
2. Make sure that the sales department budget has adequate provision for the costs of reporting. To ensure this, the budget should have a separate line item for the activity.

21-C
MEASUREMENTS, CONTROL REPORTS, AND PERFORMANCE RECORDS

	YES (1)	NO (0)	S/P* (½)
1. The effectiveness of the field sales reporting is measured and evaluated regularly and continuously.	_____	_____	_____
2. This effectiveness is measured by comparing actual performance and results with certain benchmarks or standards, such as:			
a. meeting budgets for sales and new order input,	_____	_____	_____
b. number of new accounts,	_____	_____	_____
c. retention of old accounts, and	_____	_____	_____
d. improvement in product profit margins.	_____	_____	_____
3. Effectiveness of the sales reporting process is also determined by the value of the reports to sales and marketing personnel in controlling sales activities. Accordingly, field sales reports are:			
a. logged in on receipt, and a record made of lateness,	_____	_____	_____
b. reports are reviewed periodically for completeness and compliance with standard practice (all information required is given, without padding or "boiler plate"),	_____	_____	_____
c. on a sampling basis, the quality of reports is rated on a scale of 0 to 10 in terms of value of information content,	_____	_____	_____

*SOMETIMES OR PARTIALLY

	YES (1)	NO (0)	S/P* (½)

d. on a sampling basis, a survey is made (annually) of time required to prepare reports, and time required to read, analyze, summarize, and disseminate information, and

——— ——— ———

e. a survey is made periodically of the reporting system by a systems and procedures professional.

——— ——— ———

4. Expenses are routinely compared with budget and variances analyzed for correction.

——— ——— ———

*SOMETIMES OR PARTIALLY

TOTAL POINTS ☐ + 0 + ☐

= ☐

RATING

Enter number of points scored ☐
——————————————————— = ☐ × 100 = ☐ %
Enter number of items on checklist ☐

WHAT THE RATING SIGNIFIES   A low rating here indicates that the real purpose of field sales reporting may not be understood. This purpose should be made clear and simple—it is to ensure that all sales plan goals and tasks are achieved; nothing else. If the reporting ever becomes more important than the selling activity itself, it's time to review the process and change it.

WHAT TO DO NOW
1. Make sure that every report has a defined purpose and is used for that purpose.
2. Assign responsibility to an individual to monitor all reporting for timeliness, accuracy and adherence to standard practice. This should be done on a periodic sampling basis.
3. Follow up delinquent reporters and discipline repeaters or else the system will fall into disuse.

21-D
OPERATING PERFORMANCE HISTORY

	YES (1)	NO (0)	S/P* (½)

1. A review and analysis has been made of sales reporting activities for at least one year past. This review was based on actual records and reports.

——— ——— ———

2. Based on this review, all major goals have been essentially met.

——— ——— ———

*SOMETIMES OR PARTIALLY

	YES (1)	NO (0)	S/P* (½)

3. During the past year, there has been an improvement in:

   a. on-time receipt of sales reports,

   b. completeness of reports,

   c. content of reports, and

   d. cost of reporting.

4. The review of records and control reports for the past year shows that there has been:

   a. no serious failure to meet sales plan objectives,

   b. no loss of important customers or prospects,

   c. no loss of critical orders, bids, or contracts,

   d. no failure to resolve serious customer complaints or to provide information,

   e. no serious delays in submitting price and delivery proposals,

   f. no serious overstock or out-of-stock situations, and

   g. no serious delays in customer shipments caused by ineffective sales reporting. (Answer "yes" if true.)

5. The expense budget has essentially been met for the past year.

*SOMETIMES OR PARTIALLY

TOTAL POINTS [ ] + 0 + [ ]

= [ ]

RATING

$$\frac{\text{Enter number of points scored} \quad [\ ]}{\text{Enter number of items on checklist} \quad [\ ]} = \quad \times 100 = \boxed{\quad \%}$$

WHAT THE RATING SIGNIFIES

If the appraisal shows that during the past year there have been cases of failure to capitalize on major sales opportunities, losses of customers to competitors, or losses of business because of out-of-stock conditions, the field sales reporting may be at fault. No matter what else may have contributed to these losses, the reporting should have provided early warning that (1) the opportunity was opening up, (2) competitors were romancing the customer, and (3) the business was in danger of being lost unless action was taken.

WHAT TO DO NOW

1. Review the field reports to make sure that field salespersons and supervisors are reporting problems and opportunities *early*, while they are developing—and while there is still time for the home office to help.

2. Getting people to report problems is not easy. People need reassurance, first of all, that they won't be penalized for the problems they report. Instead, penalties should be made for *failure to report* problems.

383

	YES (1)	NO (0)	S/P* (½)

The executive office demonstrates recognition, guidance, and support of field sales reporting as an essential management tool by:

a. informed comments on key reports or executive summaries of reports,

b. budget approval for communications equipment and operating expenses, and

c. recognition and reward for outstanding accomplishment, such as personal commendation to a salesperson for exceptional reporting.

*SOMETIMES OR PARTIALLY

TOTAL POINTS   ☐ + 0 + ☐

= ☐

RATING

Enter number of points scored ☐

───────────────────────────── = × 100 = ☐ %

Enter number of items on checklist ☐

WHAT THE RATING SIGNIFIES

A poor rating here indicates that the executive office fails to recognize that reports from field sales personnel are much more than sales reports—they can be one of the most valuable inputs to top management decision-making. Good field reporting can have an important influence on the company's new-product efforts, service policies, new capital investment program, product quality; even the firm's long-range strategic planning.

WHAT TO DO NOW

1. See that your field sales reports regularly reach the company's top-level decision makers.

2. Make sure that valuable information is not lost when summarizing the reports for executive review.

3. Let your field people know that the information they report is going up to the higher echelons for use in setting policy and strategy. Nothing improves the quality of the reports so much as the knowledge that they will be read by the top brass.

	YES (1)	NO (0)	S/P* (½)
1. A systematic search is made for better methods of information exchange between field sales and home office, through:			
a. sales management seminars, workshops, and conferences,	_____	_____	_____
b. professional associations,	_____	_____	_____
c. industry contacts,	_____	_____	_____
d. literature search,	_____	_____	_____
e. solicitation of new ideas and improvement suggestions from personnel at all levels, especially field sales, and	_____	_____	_____
f. budgets provide funds for such activities.	_____	_____	_____
2. The computer is used to store, process, and print-out information:			
a. for distribution to the field, and	_____	_____	_____
b. analyzing and summarizing quantifiable information received from the field.	_____	_____	_____
3. The most effective and timely communications means are employed to transmit and disseminate sales reports to and from the field, such as:			
a. facsimile,	_____	_____	_____
b. Telex or TWX,	_____	_____	_____
c. mailgrams,	_____	_____	_____
d. computer data entry terminals,	_____	_____	_____
e. data-phone,	_____	_____	_____
f. word processing equipment, and	_____	_____	_____
g. tape cassettes.	_____	_____	_____

*SOMETIMES OR PARTIALLY

TOTAL POINTS ☐ + 0 + ☐ = ☐

RATING

Enter number of points scored ☐
———————————————————— = × 100 = ☐ %
Enter number of items on checklist ☐

WHAT THE RATING SIGNIFIES   Electronics is rapidly replacing paper as a communications means. The company that fails to keep up with these new developments in information handling may find itself out-maneuvered by competitors who move their information faster. A low rating here is a warning that sales management may not be keeping up to date in this important respect. As a consequence, information may be out-of-date by the time it reaches the persons who should act on it.

WHAT TO DO NOW

1. Assign a responsible individual to be the sales department's "technology watcher," with authority to seek out and test new equipment and techniques for handling information.
2. Look at developments in the fast-moving fields of word processing and remote copying. Here is where there could be a high payoff in time saved by field and home office personnel both.
3. If yours is a high-volume business, consider equipping sales people with portable order entry and sales data entry terminals linked to the home office computer.

21-G
INTERFUNCTIONAL COMMUNICATIONS AND COORDINATION

	YES (1)	NO (0)	S/P* (½)
1. Sales management maintains close and continuing contact with marketing and other functional managers who furnish day-to-day support to sales reporting, including:			
a. communications,	___	___	___
b. controller's department,	___	___	___
c. information systems,	___	___	___
d. systems and procedures, and	___	___	___
e. product distribution.	___	___	___
2. Sales reports from the field are routinely distributed to other departments.	___	___	___
3. Other functional departments routinely furnish information to the sales department for dissemination to the field.	___	___	___
4. Sales management maintains regular contact with other functional departments, including			
a. engineering,	___	___	___
b. quality assurance,	___	___	___
c. product distribution,	___	___	___
d. production, and	___	___	___
e. controller.	___	___	___

*SOMETIMES OR PARTIALLY

TOTAL POINTS   [ ] + 0 + [ ]

= [ ]

RATING

Enter number of points scored   [ ]
————————————————————————   =   × 100 = [ ] %
Enter number of items on checklist [ ]

WHAT THE RATING SIGNIFIES

It is almost axiomatic that a sales department operates on information. The better this information is, the more complete and current it is, the better the job sales people can do, other things being equal.

Conversely, the more that other company functions know about customers' wants, needs, and perceptions of the company, the more effective they can be in designing new products, providing services, distributing products, producing advertising that sells, and developing competitive strategies.

A less-than-acceptable rating indicates that sales and market information may not be flowing between company functions as freely as it should. The result is that some company activities may be working at cross-purposes with market needs.

WHAT TO DO NOW

1. Start by *giving*—make sure that your field sales reports are distributed to other function managers, with pertinent information highlighted for their convenience.

2. Set up contacts at *several organization levels* with the other key functions. You may be surprised at the amount of information you will gain through these lower-level contacts.

3. Be sure to clear all information with the appropriate department head before issuing it to the field: If you fail to do this you might find your contacts cut off from their sources of information.

21-H
FUNCTIONAL IMPROVEMENT PROGRAM

	YES (1)	NO (0)	S/P* (½)
1. There is an organized, on-going interfunctional team effort to improve sales reporting. Major efforts are directed toward improving the "inward" reporting of:			
a. field activities for control purposes,	___	___	___
b. customer wants and needs for products not in the present line,	___	___	___
c. customer needs for improvements to present products, and	___	___	___
d. customer needs for services.			
2. Efforts are also aimed at improving "outward" reporting of:			
a. company policies, procedures, and objectives, and	___	___	___
b. changes that affect field sales.	___	___	___
3. The following functions are variously represented on the improvement team, depending on the specific task:			
a. market research and analysis,	___	___	___
b. engineering and design,	___	___	___
c. customer service,	___	___	___
d. systems and procedures, and	___	___	___
e. product distribution.	___	___	___

*SOMETIMES OR PARTIALLY

$$\boxed{} + 0 + \boxed{}$$

$$= \boxed{}$$

RATING

Enter number of points scored $\dfrac{\boxed{}}{\boxed{}}$ = $\boxed{} \times 100 = \boxed{}$ %

Enter number of items on checklist

WHAT THE RATING SIGNIFIES

An organized approach to improving the field sales reporting can pay large dividends. This has to be undertaken in two phases: the *inward* reporting to home office of events and developments in the marketplace; and the *outward* dissemination of information, advice, and change notifications to field sales reps and supervisors.

There are few business organizations that could not benefit from improvement in these two areas, the first in particular. Most firms fail to take full advantage of the market knowledge and competitive information that their field sales people gain through their close, day-to-day contact with customers. If yours is one that does, consider yourself fortunate. If not, you should take steps to improve the field sales reporting through a team effort involving the other functions that can benefit from this kind of information.

WHAT TO DO NOW

1. Concentrate first on the inward flow of reporting on customer and competitor activities. Identify what information is needed by each of the functions—engineering, product distribution, advertising and sales promotion, et al.—and determine what is feasible and practicable to include in the sales reports without burying the salesperson in paper.

2. Make the reporting an integral part of every field salesperson's job, for which sufficient time and training has to be provided. And make sure that the quality of reporting is a part of every salesperson's performance evaluation. Recognition and reward are important motivators.

21-I
RESOURCES

	YES (1)	NO (0)	S/P* (½)
1. Sales management is kept informed about company objectives, policies, plans, and programs, through participation in key management meetings and access to appropriate business plans, marketing plans, capital budgets, and operating reports.	___	___	___
2. Based on informed knowledge of the company's objectives, sales plans, and			

*SOMETIMES OR PARTIALLY

	YES (1)	NO (0)	S/P* (½)

budgets, resources for effective sales reporting are considered adequate to meet company needs for the next three, six, and twelve months, in terms of:

a. manpower,

b. capabilities,

c. budget support,

d. communications,

e. computer time and capacity, and

f. other functional support.

*SOMETIMES OR PARTIALLY

TOTAL POINTS   ☐ + 0 + ☐

= ☐

RATING

Enter number of points scored ☐
—————————————————————————— = ☐ × 100 = ☐ %
Enter number of items on checklist ☐

WHAT THE RATING SIGNIFIES

Back in 1910, the "traveling salesman" could mail a sales report back to the home office once a month on the back of an envelope. Today's fast-changing competitive environment demands enormous amounts of information from the field salesperson, every day in some cases. Budgets must provide for the costs of this activity.

This requires physical resources, in the form of communications facilities such as Telex or TWX, telephone WATS-lines, or computer terminals in some instances. It also requires money for telephone and postage expense, and time to prepare and issue reports.

A low rating indicates that resources may be deficient to support effective sales reporting. As a consequence, other activities will tend to be done at the expense of the reporting, and sales may be lost for lack of up-to-date knowledge of what is going on in the marketplace.

WHAT TO DO NOW

1. When forecasting sales manpower requirements, be sure to allow for the time that individual reps and supervisors must spend on field sales reporting. This can take 10 to 20 percent of a person's time, and it's unfair to expect your sales people to give up their weekends to write sales reports.

2. Make sure that facilities for word processing, reproduction, and communications are available and adequate for fast, accurate reporting.

THE BOTTOM LINE

The company's sales force can no longer be managed as a separate function of the business independent of the other functions—production, engineering, advertising, marketing, and the others. In today's complex and highly-charged competitive environment, the selling organization must be viewed as a key element of the total distribution system. Sales is the function that brings together all the other organized activities of the business and focusses them on the customer or prospect.

It is here that profit is made or lost. Profit is made when the sales department books orders that contain a high profit margin—profit is lost when salesmen accept orders with insufficient markup over cost to cover the other expenses of running the business plus a profit.

In this view, the sales manager is one of the most important individuals in the whole distribution system. Whether the company's sales force sells to retailers, to wholesalers, to other manufacturers, or directly to the consumer, its profitability—even its success or failure—is a function of the management competence or the person in charge. The day is long past when a company could simply tap a high-performing salesperson on the shoulder and say, "Now you're the sales manager—go manage." Today's sales manager must know how to sell, of course, but he or she must know a great deal more.

Today's sales manager must know how to recruit promising sales talent, how to train people, how to manage sales supervisors, how to motivate salesmen, how to plan and control work, how to establish sales territories and quotas that are challenging yet realistic, and how to measure performance of people.

Today's sales manager, in short, must be a professional manager—not just a good salesperson.

SOMETIMES IT TAKES FRESH BLOOD

A regulated communications services organization suddenly found itself playing in a new ball game when deregulation allowed other companies to offer competing services. Up to this time the company's franchise had given it virtually a monopoly position in the market. As a result, the firm had no sales capability to speak of. The sales force was composed mostly of service technicians rewarded for their years of service by promotion to selling positions.

There was a certain amount of panic when these untrained "order-takers" found themselves confronted by competitor's well-trained, professional sales representatives equipped with colorful selling aids and a high-powered sales pitch.

An in-depth appraisal of the firm's marketing capabilities revealed serious deficiencies in almost every marketing function; not only field sales, but market research, new-service planning and development, marketing planning, etc. A decision was made to concentrate initally on the sales function, with the others to be done later, on the very realistic assumption that it was necessary first *to survive* before investing in long-range marketing development.

Efforts to convert the existing sales force into a competitive selling organization turned out to be a hopeless task. So the company imported a new sales manager with heavy experience in the business machine field, and a reputation as a first-class sales trainer. He totally rebuilt the sales force, initiated the first incentive compensation plan (with potential for such high commissions that top management was aghast), and set up professional sales training programs that were the finest in the industry.

It took a couple of years, but a professional sales force was literally created out of nothing. It's not stretching a point too far to claim that it may have saved the company. Some time later, the sales manager moved on to become president of a firm in the office machine market, but he left behind a legacy of professional sales management and a strong sales organization.

SUMMARY OF SELF-AUDIT RATINGS AND FUNCTIONAL IMPROVEMENT GOALS

If you wish, you may summarize the ratings for each function at the end of each section, on this "Summary Rating" form. (A "function" is the equivalent of a chapter.) The rating is simply an arithmetic average of the ratings on Checklists A through I—that is, the total divided by 9. This form also provides space for listing the Improvement Goals for each function.

Under each function, enter the rating percentage for each Checklist section, A through I. "Function Number 1," for example, is the first (1st) chapter in the section, regardless of its number in the book—5, 11, or so on. The Summary Rating is the total of each column divided by 9, to give you an average rating for the total function. The lower portion of the form can be used to list your improvement goals for each function.

	FUNCTION NUMBER					
CHECKLIST	**1** %	**2** %	**3** %	**4** %	**5** %	**6** %
A	___	___	___	___	___	___
B	___	___	___	___	___	___
C	___	___	___	___	___	___
D	___	___	___	___	___	___
E	___	___	___	___	___	___
F	___	___	___	___	___	___
G	___	___	___	___	___	___
H	___	___	___	___	___	___
I	___	___	___	___	___	___
SUMMARY RATING (%)	___	___	___	___	___	___

IMPROVEMENT GOALS

_____

_____

_____

_____

_____

_____

_____

(Use separate sheet as required)

Section **VII**

Managing Customer Service

Customer service is the sum total of all dealings with present and potential users of the company's products and services. It covers the full range of contacts with customers and prospects. It begins with the initial inquiry from a prospective user, perhaps in response to a product advertisement, to the handling of a complaint or call for service long after the customer has purchased the product.

Customer service covers much more than the formalized activities of the sales and service departments. The contacts that engineering people have with the customer's engineers are just as critical to the company's reputation as the attitudes of sales personnel. The manner in which the billing department answers a customer's question about an invoice can either build good will or damage it. It follows that good customer service is the concern and responsibility of virtually every department or business function.

**SERVICE—
THE DIFFERENCE BETWEEN
PRODUCT SUCCESS AND
FAILURE**

Good customer service is important to the growth and profitability of the business. In cases where two or more companies produce an almost identical product, such as a commodity, the quality and amount of service given to the customer before, during, and after the sale may be *more important* that the product itself.

Even in cases where the company has a superior product, failure to install or service it properly can drive the customer to a competitor. So can failure to answer customer inquiries promptly, to keep customers informed about delays, or to handle complaints tactfully and efficiently.

393

A manufacturer must never lose sight of the needs and desires of the end-user of the product, the "consumer," regardless of how long and involved the chain of distribution may be. Its distribution system must be constructed and operated on this principle. Its concern for the user must be transmitted through the distribution chain intact and unadulterated, through the medium of enlightened customer service policies. The firm must also be sensitive and responsive to the needs of each link in the chain, in addition to those of its primary customer.

It has been said that consumers do not buy products, they buy utility—they pay a producer to fill a particular need or want. In this sense, then, what they buy is *service*. A home owner does not buy insulation. He buys comfort and protection from extremes of temperature—more recently he buys insurance against the high and increasing costs of energy. A buyer of roofing products is purchasing twenty or more years of protection against the elements for his house, his possessions, and his family.

If these concepts can be accepted throughout the organization, attitudes toward the customer will be so favorably influenced that the company's products will become the choice of more customers.

QUALITY OF SERVICE IS THE KEY ELEMENT IN CUSTOMER SATISFACTION

The main objective of the appraisal is to assure that prospects and customers are given the proper and necessary quality of service, before the order, during the processing and production cycle, and after delivery of the product.

In cases where competitive differences in the product are small, the level of customer service provided should be superior to that offered by the competition. In cases where the product is clearly superior in performance, quality, or price, then the quality of service should be at least equal to that of the strongest competitor.

Activities falling under the general category of "customer services" can be classified under the three broad headings of customer communications, order handling, and post-sale service.

A key activity of customer service involves making the product available to users through distributors and dealers. This activity is considered to be the responsibility of the "distribution" function, and is covered in that section rather than in this.

Appraisal of customer service should start from the customer's viewpoint, never from that of the producer. Customers' needs are totally different, and they have options and alternatives. Treat customers badly, neglect them, fail to answer their inquiries promptly, fail to take their complaints seriously—and see how quickly they can find another supplier to fill their needs.

ASK YOUR CUSTOMERS HOW THEY THINK YOU'RE DOING

The best way to approach this appraisal is to survey customers to determine how they perceive the service the company is providing. It may come as a shock to find that service thought to be good is often viewed by the customer as unsatisfactory. All too often, customers are taken for granted, especially those who have been around for a long time. It is all-too-common for the manufacturer to take the position that the product is everything—and fail to make it easy and pleasant for the customer to find it, buy it, use it, and live with it.

A well-designed survey can often reveal situations where poor service is preventing repeat buying, even when the product itself is superior. Failure to respond promptly to requests for information, technical data, prices, and deliveries, or failure to acknowledge and settle complaints, are often as serious as failure to send a service representative in response to a trouble call. An inefficient order-processing system that requires many retypings of the information can easily result in transcription errors that lead to producing and shipping wrong quantities, incorrect billing, and other errors that cause customer dissatisfaction.

Above all, the manner in which a customer is treated by those he comes in contact with is vitally important. If his problem or complaint, whether justified or not in the eyes of the seller, is not handled with tact and sensitivity, the producer's reputation suffers.

The checklists that follow provide the means to conduct a searching self-appraisal of each of the principal elements of customer service:

- Customer communications,
- Order handling, and
- Post-sale service.

Chapter **22**

Improving
Customer Communications

EVERY MANAGER IS INVOLVED

Customer communications in the contemporary business organization is a pervasive activity that involves, either directly or indirectly, every member of management. It is an activity that begins when the first contact is made with a prospective purchaser—*and never ends*.

Some (but decidedly not all) of the tasks included under the general heading of customer communications are:

1. responding to prospect inquiries,
2. furnishing product information/literature,
3. quoting prices and deliveries,
4. furnishing engineering data,
5. keeping customers informed about order status,
6. keeping sales representatives or sales agents informed,
7. acknowledging and handling complaints to conclusion,
8. explaining warrantees and service policies,
9. maintaining records related to all of these, and
10. resolving billing errors.

KEY AIM OF THE SELF-AUDIT

The main purpose of the self-audit is to ensure that every person who has contact with customers and prospects, whether directly or indirectly, knows what his or her tasks and responsibilities are, and performs these in a manner that promotes customer goodwill. Ideally, every single contact should cause the prospect or customer *to want to do business* with the company.

HOW TO USE THE CHECKLISTS

For each of the statements in the Checklist, compare the condition of your function to the "ideal" as described in the statement. Then:

1. If you consider the statement to be *generally true* of your function, check the YES column.

2. If you consider the statement to be *untrue* of your function, check the NO column.

3. If you consider the statement to be *less than true* (but not totally untrue) of your function, check the SOMETIMES OR PARTIAL column.

4. If the statement does not apply to your particular situation, write "Not Applicable" across the response spaces (or simply draw a line through them).

5. If you lack the data for a definite response, write in "Not Answerable" or "Don't Know."

HOW TO EVALUATE YOUR RESPONSES

When you have completed the checklist, glance over your responses, keeping these points in mind:

1. A negative answer is always unfavorable because it indicates a problem within the function: the greater the number of NOs, the more serious the situation.

2. A positive response is always a good indication. But too many YES answers could indicate that your review is not objective enough.

3. Too many SOMETIMES OR PARTIALLY answers can point to internal weaknesses or to a lack of firm direction.

4. A lot of "Not Applicable" answers could indicate that you are avoiding the issue.

5. A large number of "Not Answerable" or "Don't Know" answers could be symptomatic of inadequate records or data bases.

HOW TO RATE AND SCORE YOUR RESPONSES

When you are satisfied with your responses in general, you are ready to score the Checklist. For your convenience, a self-explanatory Scoring and Rating Block follows each Checklist. This block not only tells you whether the condition of your function is satisfactory, but it also gives you a measure of its effectiveness.

Here's how to total up the points for inclusion in the Scoring and Rating Block:

1. Total up the number of points you scored:
   a. For each YES, give yourself one point.
   b. For each NO, give yourself zero.
   c. For each SOMETIMES OR PARTIALLY, give yourself a half-point.
   d. For each "Not Applicable" answer, give yourself zero and deduct one from the number of items on the Checklist.
   e. For each "Not Answerable" or "Don't Know" answer, give yourself zero.

2. Next divide the total number of points you score by the total number of items (statements) on the Checklist (less items marked "Not Applicable"). You'll get a 1.0 for a perfect score and a fraction for anything less.

3. Multiply the result of step 2 by 100 to arrive at the percentage for your score.

What is a satisfactory rating? A rating of less than 65 percent is unacceptable and calls for an improvement program: Obviously, the lower the rating, the more drastic the action required.

A brief "how-to" example of this Scoring and Rating system follows . . .

EXAMPLE

	YES (1)	NO (0)	S/P* (½)

1. Field sale reports designed to provide information on sales progress contain data on the following topics:

   a. sales calls and sales presentations made by salespersons and sales agents, ✓

   b. bids, quotations, and proposals made, ✓

   c. new orders booked, ✓

   d. lost business, and reasons for the loss, ✓ (NO)

   e. accomplishments toward future orders, ✓ (S/P)

   f. performance in filling orders, handling complaints, and otherwise servicing individual customers, ✓ (YES)

   g. action taken in response to customer requests, such as sending samples, spec sheets, etc., ✓ (YES)

   h. accomplishments of significance and value to other members of the sales force. ✓ (S/P)

*SOMETIMES OR PARTIALLY

TOTAL POINTS $\boxed{5}$ + 0 + $\boxed{1}$

= $\boxed{6}$

RATING

$$\frac{\text{Enter number of points scored} \quad \boxed{6}}{\text{Enter number of items on checklist} \quad \boxed{8}} = .75 \times 100 = \boxed{75}\ \%$$

	YES (1)	NO (0)	S/P* (½)
1. Good customer communications is recognized as a vital company activity that has top management endorsement and support and in managers' position description as an important function of marketing and sales. (Note: As used here, the term "customer" includes *prospective or potential* customers.)	___	___	___
2. The sales department has a budget allocation covering expenses of customer communications activities (even though many activities are dispersed throughout the organization).	___	___	___
3. The accounting system tracks actual expenditures for customer communications and compares them with budgets, by responsibility center and in total, for control.	___	___	___
4. All personnel who communicate directly with customers, whether in person, in writing, or by telephone, are trained in proper conduct, attitude, and manners.	___	___	___
5. The actions and behavior of personnel who communicate with customers are guided by written procedures and standard practices.	___	___	___
6. Customer communications activities are directed and coordinated by one or more persons (not necessarily full-time) in the sales support group, trained in customer communications and well-informed about the company's products and customers.	___	___	___
7. All customer communications are channeled through the appropriate sales representative, or the sales representative is copied or advised immediately as to the nature of the communication	___	___	___
8. Inquiries that cannot be handled locally are promptly referred to a central point staffed by a specialist(s) trained and equipped to handle customer communications.	___	___	___
9. Customer problems and complaints are handled by the person who received the call or letter; the customer is not "bucked" to other company personnel or departments.	___	___	___
10. Complaints addressed to the president are acknowledged in his or her name, with reference to how and by whom the complaint will be handled.	___	___	___
11. Procedures for handling customer problems and complaints have been reviewed within the past year.	___	___	___
12. The handling of major customer complaints is "audited" on a random basis to assure proper resolution of problems, adherence to standard practices, and need for changes in procedures.	___	___	___
13. Catalogs and product information bulletins are up-to-date, complete, and available.	___	___	___
14. Price lists are up-to-date and available.	___	___	___
15. Policies covering pricing, warranties, and terms of sale are clear and understood by sales personnel.	___	___	___

*SOMETIMES OR PARTIALLY

	YES (1)	NO (0)	S/P* (½)

16. Information on availability of products and delivery times is issued to sales personnel regularly. _____ _____ _____

17. Technical assistance—design, specifications, applications—is readily available. _____ _____ _____

18. Requests for proposals are responded to quickly and effectively. _____ _____ _____

*SOMETIMES OR PARTIALLY

TOTAL POINTS [ ] + 0 + [ ]

= [ ]

RATING

Enter number of points scored [ ]

Enter number of items on checklist [ ]

= × 100 = [ ] %

WHAT THE RATING SIGNIFIES

A less-than-acceptable rating for this section is indicative of unsatisfactory attitudes and behavior within the organization toward customers. Effective customer communications starts in the office of the chief executive of the company—because the attitudes and behavior of people throughout an organization tend to reflect the attitude and behavior of the boss. If the CEO sincerely believes the customer is important, and reinforces this attitude through his every action, then people who have direct dealings with customers will treat customers with consideration and respect, and the business will prosper.

Good customer communications costs money. Unless this money is provided through a formal budget allocation, it is unlikely that the money will be spent. Customer communications involves almost every function of the business so it requires some central direction, control, and measurement of performance. It's almost impossible to achieve this unless the accounting system has the ability to record expenditures and compare them with budget estimates, both in the aggregate and by department.

WHAT TO DO NOW

1. Attitudes are often difficult to change, but behavior can be altered through training. The important thing is to insure that employee behavior toward customers is proper. To this end, every person who deals with customers should receive initial training and periodic re-training.

2. Employee's behavior toward customers should be monitored periodically. You have not only the right to do this, but the responsibility. Unless this is done—and unless your people *know* it is being done—behavior toward customers can degrade, and you won't be aware of it until the unresolved complaint file builds up, or customers change their buying habits.

3. You should welcome customer complaints—not discourage them. Instead of trying to reduce the number of complaints, you should be *encouraging* consumers to express any dissatisfaction they may feel. There is no better way to learn how your products and services are perceived and used in the marketplace—no cheaper way to learn what customers really think about your company.

401

22-B
AUTHORITY, RESPONSIBILITY, AND ACCOUNTABILITY

	YES (1)	NO (0)	S/P* (½)

1. Authority has been delegated to the sales manager (or sales support manager) to expend company funds and assign tasks necessary to assure a free and complete flow of information between the company and its customers and prospects. _____ _____ _____

2. The manager is responsible for:

   a. staffing, training, and managing an organization designed for this purpose, and _____ _____ _____

   b. establishing and administering procedures for customer communications throughout the organization. _____ _____ _____

3. Responsibility has been clearly assigned to individual managers for:

   a. availability of product and price information, _____ _____ _____

   b. expeditious handling of customer inquiries, _____ _____ _____

   c. training of personnel in proper customer dealings, _____ _____ _____

   d. effective complaint-handling, and _____ _____ _____

   e. keeping related procedures up-to-date. _____ _____ _____

4. The manager is held accountable for:

   a. loss of important customers, _____ _____ _____

   b. cancellation of major orders, _____ _____ _____

   c. escalation of complaints to executive office, and _____ _____ _____

   d. failure to obtain contracts or orders resulting from ineffective or inadequate customer communications. _____ _____ _____

5. Individual managers are held accountable for:

   a. loss of customers, _____ _____ _____

   b. cancellation of orders, or _____ _____ _____

   c. failure to book new business resulting from failure to handle customer complaints or inquiries properly. _____ _____ _____

*SOMETIMES OR PARTIALLY

TOTAL POINTS [ ] + 0 + [ ]

= [ ]

RATING

Enter number of points scored [ ]
——————————————————— = [ ] × 100 = [ ] %
Enter number of items on checklist [ ]

WHAT THE RATING SIGNIFIES

A less-than-satisfactory rating indicates that the responsibilities of people to ensure good customer communications are not clearly and precisely defined, or their accountability for results may not be understood and accepted. In the first situation, some important customer relations tasks can "fall through the cracks" and remain undone. Other tasks may be claimed by two or more people thus leading to uncertainty as to who is really responsible. In the second situation, if accountability for failure to perform is not clearly specified, it can lead to "finger-pointing" when things go wrong.

WHAT TO DO NOW

1. It's better to assign responsibility to the wrong person than not to assign it all. And be sure that each individual knows and accepts that he or she is accountable for failure to do the assigned task.

2. If an individual refuses to accept this accountability then put that person in a job remote from customers, because sooner or later you're going to lose a customer through his or her failure to perform.

22-C
MEASUREMENTS, CONTROL REPORTS, AND PERFORMANCE RECORDS

	YES (1)	NO (0)	S/P* (½)
1. The effectiveness of customer communications is measured and evaluated periodically, preferably monthly.	___	___	___
2. This effectiveness is measured by comparing actual performance and results to certain standards, benchmarks, or budgets, such as:			
a. response time to inquiries,	___	___	___
b. number of unresolved complaints on hand,	___	___	___
c. number of complaints escalated to president's office,	___	___	___
d. number of unresolved billing errors, and	___	___	___
e. costs of customer communications.	___	___	___
3. All customer correspondence and inquiries are logged in, and records are kept of response times.	___	___	___
4. A complaint record is kept, showing nature and sources of problems and complaints and the time taken to resolve them.	___	___	___
5. Inquiries and complaints not answered within a prescribed time period are automatically "flagged" for corrective action or management attention.	___	___	___
6. The logs are periodically reviewed by management for the purpose of improving performance in customer-handling and correcting deficiencies in products and services.	___	___	___
7. Expenses of the customer communication activity are routinely compared with budget, and major variances analyzed for corrective action.	___	___	___

*SOMETIMES OR PARTIALLY

TOTAL POINTS [ ] + 0 + [ ]

= [ ]

RATING

Enter number of points scored [ ]

Enter number of items on checklist [ ]

= × 100 = [ ] %

WHAT THE RATING SIGNIFIES

A negative answer to point 1 or 2 means that the company can have poor communications with its customers and management won't even know it—because it doesn't have the facts it needs to make a judgment. If the rest of the appraisal rating is low, it indicates that the organization may lack a mechanism for automatically correcting unsatisfactory performance before it becomes a serious problem.

As a consequence, it may take a crisis, such as defection of a major customer or cancellation of an important order or contract, to make management aware that it has been giving a good customer shabby treatment.

In such a case, it is not unusual for top management to over-react; to look around for a scapegoat, or fall guy, to blame for its own neglect. This does nothing, of course, to correct the problem, but only makes matters worse.

WHAT TO DO NOW

1. As the manager responsible for customer communications, it's to your advantage to prevent this from happening—especially because *you* may be the one selected to be the "whipping boy."

2. It's not difficult to set up a good customer communications program. The first requirement is a set of goals, such as to reduce the number of "executive complaints" by a certain percentage or to a specific number. (Executive complaints are customer letters of complaint addressed to the president after failure to get satisfaction from lower levels.) Next, it takes a set of simple control reports to record actual performance and compare it with targets. Then it requires follow-through in the form of reward for good performance and penalty for failure to meet goals.

3. Before any of this can be done, there has to be an admission that the company has a problem. To cure an alcoholic, it is said, the first requirement is an admission that the person drinks.

22-D
OPERATING PERFORMANCE HISTORY

	YES (1)	NO (0)	S/P* (½)
1. A review of control reports and performance records has been made for the past year.	___	___	___
2. An analysis of these documents shows that, for the past year:			
a. the proportion of inquiries handled within standard time is improving,	___	___	___
b. the number of unresolved complaints on hand shows a downward trend,	___	___	___
c. fewer complaints have been escalated to the executive office,	___	___	___
d. periodic audits of complaint-handling shows satisfactory adherence to procedures, and	___	___	___
e. there have been no cases where an important customer or a major order was lost because of failure to handle an inquiry or complaint satisfactorily. (Answer "Yes" if true.)	___	___	___
3. The function had met its expense budget for the past year.	___	___	___

*SOMETIMES OR PARTIALLY

404

TOTAL POINTS   ⬜ + 0 + ⬜

⎰ = ⬜

RATING

Enter number of points scored ⬜

─────────────────────────────── = ⬜ × 100 = ⬜ %

Enter number of items on checklist ⬜

<table>
<tr><td>**WHAT THE RATING SIGNIFIES**</td><td>If this appraisal shows an unsatisfactory history of performance, it's a good bet that procedures need tightening up, or people who deal with customers need some attention. (This assumes that the product quality is good—obviously, if quality has deteriorated the company has a different problem.)</td></tr>
</table>

WHAT TO DO NOW

1. First make sure that the records are complete and accurate. An analysis of these should provide clues to the basic problem—whether it's people or procedures.
2. If procedures are loose and lax, get some help from the professional systems and procedures people.
3. If it's a people problem, isolate the poor performers. Usually, it's only a few—often only one or two—who cause the majority of the complaints.
4. If people aren't following procedures—try retraining. If the cause of poor performance is a deep-seated attitudinal problem, however, the only solution may be job transfers for the offenders.

22-E
TOP-LEVEL SUPPORT AND GUIDANCE

	YES (1)	NO (0)	S/P* (½)

The executive office actively promotes good customer communications throughout the organization by means of:

a. published policy statements,

b. endorsement of standard practices,

c. letters to employees,

d. talks to groups of employees and managers,

e. approval of budgets for customer service activities,

f. genuine interest in serious customer complaints, and

g. personal response to complaints addressed to the chief executive.

h. recognition and reward for outstanding service performance, through management incentive programs, etc.

TOTAL POINTS [ ] + 0 + [ ]

{ } = [ ]

RATING

Enter number of points scored [ ]
———————————————————————————— = [ ] × 100 = [ ] %
Enter number of items on checklist [ ]

WHAT THE RATING SIGNIFIES
A lack of concern about customer communications at the highest levels of the organization is invariably reflected by the attitudes and behavior of employees who interface with customers. Unless the executive office displays genuine concern for customers in a highly visible way, employees who deal with customers tend to treat them with indifference and insensitivity. A low rating here is a serious danger signal that requires immediate attention. Customers may not always be right, *but they are always customers*!

WHAT TO DO NOW
1. As the manager responsible for customer service, you have to build a case for the top-level support you need. Your case should be based on a hard-headed approach that good customer communication can improve the bottom line.

2. You should be able, for example, to compare the relatively low cost of keeping a present customer with the high cost of securing a new customer; the savings can fall right through to the bottom line.

3. Every complaint addressed to the president should be answered over the president's signature—preferably in his own words. A form letter from a customer relations clerk can only add fuel to the complaint fire.

22-F
INNOVATION IN METHODS AND TECHNIQUES

	YES (1)	NO (0)	S/P* (½)
1. Up-to-date methods are used to communicate with customers and with field sales, such as:			
a. Telex/TWX,	___	___	___
b. data-phone,	___	___	___
c. mailgrams,	___	___	___
d. facsimile, and	___	___	___
e. computer terminals.	___	___	___

*SOMETIMES OR PARTIALLY

	YES (1)	NO (0)	S/P* (½)

2. The computer is used to store, process, and display information on:

   a. prices,

   b. deliveries,

   c. product availability,

   d. product specifications,

   e. customer data, and

   f. complaints.

3. Management keeps informed about better ways to communicate with customers, through:

   a. seminars and workshops,

   b. outside specialists,

   c. professional associations,

   d. industry contacts,

   e. solicitation of ideas from personnel at all levels, especially field sales and customer service, and

   f. budgets include funds for such activities.

*SOMETIMES OR PARTIALLY

TOTAL POINTS ⬜ + 0 + ⬜

= ⬜

RATING

Enter number of points scored ⬜

Enter number of items on checklist ⬜

= × 100 = ⬜ %

WHAT THE RATING SIGNIFIES

Speed of communication is often as important as the content. If the methods used to communicate with customers—or with field sales reps who deal with customers—are old-fashioned, slow, and inaccurate, then customers will be dissatisfied despite the best efforts of employees. The computer is absolutely essential for fast customer communication in every organization of any size. A low rating here is evidence that the company may be failing to respond quickly to customer inquiries or complaints; as a consequence, orders may be lost to more responsive competitors.

WHAT TO DO NOW

1. Consider putting a Telex or TWX terminal right on the premises of your largest customers, for virtually instantaneous record communication.

2. Make sure you're using the computer as fully as you can. But don't talk to the computer technicians before your *information* problem is well-defined by information specialists. Call in the company's information systems people, or an outside information specialist with good credentials.

3. Listen well to your field sales and product service people—and pay attention when they tell you a customer is unhappy with the treatment he's getting. If you don't, the next thing you may hear is that the customer has gone over to your competitor.

4. Always confirm *in writing* the substance of a telephone discussion with a customer. People's memories are unreliable, and the understanding you think you have reached may vanish in time.

22-G
INTERFUNCTIONAL COMMUNICATIONS AND COORDINATION

	YES (1)	NO (0)	S/P* (½)
1. Persons directly responsible for customer communications maintain close and continuing contact with:			
a. field sales, for direct customer contact,	___	___	___
b. engineering, for technical inquiries and resolution of product-design problems,	___	___	___
c. production, for help in delivery or product quality complaints,	___	___	___
d. accounting, for resolution of billing problems,	___	___	___
e. product distribution, for help on product availability problems,	___	___	___
f. customer service, for help on installation or warranty problems,	___	___	___
g. advertising and sales promotion, for coordination of activities, and	___	___	___
h. legal, for assistance on product liability problems.	___	___	___
2. Sales support people periodically take part in joint sales calls on customers.	___	___	___
3. Service management is kept informed about planned changes in organization, moves, price changes, product discontinuances, and other matters that will affect customers.	___	___	___

*SOMETIMES OR PARTIALLY

TOTAL POINTS [ ] + 0 + [ ]

= [ ]

RATING

Enter number of points scored [ ]
——————————————————— = [ ] × 100 = [ ] %
Enter number of items on checklist [ ]

WHAT THE RATING SIGNIFIES

Almost every function of the business gets directly involved with customers at one time or another. Every function is *indirectly* involved with customers at all times. It's important to have a central "clearing house" for customer matters. It's also important—vitally important—for the sales representative who is responsible for the account to be kept fully informed about all transactions with the customer by other functions. There is nothing worse than a sales rep being caught flat-footed by a customer by not knowing about a serious billing problem, a shipping delay, or a product quality problem. (There *is* one thing worse—that's a sales rep responding to a customer's question, "I don't know, the home office never tells me anything!")

WHAT TO DO NOW

1. There's no way to guarantee that you will have every answer to every question from every customer, instantly. The ideal system that would give you that capability would cost too much. The handling of most routine inquiries can be mechanized at affordable cost. And you can maintain good relations with other functions, so they will help you resolve customer complaints and problems promptly.

2. Tell your customer about potential delays and other problems early, before he learns about them the worst way—through your failure to deliver critical parts for assembly line, or delivery of products with serious flaws in quality.

22-H
FUNCTIONAL IMPROVEMENT PROGRAM

	YES (1)	NO (0)	S/P* (½)
1. There is an organized, active, on-going, interfunctional team effort to improve the quality of customer communications. Specific efforts on a project basis are directed toward:			
a. speeding up response times,	——	——	——
b. personalizing communications,	——	——	——
c. reducing the number of "executive" complaints (letters to the president),	——	——	——
d. eliminating billing errors,	——	——	——
e. providing better technical assistance to prospects and customers,	——	——	——
f. clarifying customer-relations policies.	——	——	——
2. The following functional representatives are actively participating in this program, depending upon the specific project:			
a. field sales,	——	——	——
b. marketing,	——	——	——
c. advertising and sales promotion,	——	——	——
d. product distribution,	——	——	——
e. engineering,	——	——	——
f. production, and	——	——	——
g. accounting.	——	——	——

*SOMETIMES OR PARTIALLY

□ + 0 + □

= □

RATING

Enter number of points scored □

Enter number of items on checklist □

= × 100 = □ %

WHAT THE RATING SIGNIFIES

A cross-functional team approach to setting objectives and working on improvement plans can often accomplish exceptional results by bringing varied experiences and insights together on customer communications problems. This approach formalizes the coordination among functions, and ensures that all points of view are considered in the solutions.

A low rating indicates that the company may be overlooking a very effective way to improve the quality and speed of customer communications. As a consequence, business may be lost to more responsive competitors.

WHAT TO DO NOW

1. Try a team approach on a single objective. Start with a relatively straight-forward uncontroversial project that has better than average chances for success, such as speeding up response time on customer inquiries.

2. Be sure to establish firm leadership of the team. *Control* the agenda of every meeting. *Control* the issuance of "action assignments" made. *Control* the follow-up of action assignments until they are completed.

3. Don't use teams merely to resolve problems. Set them up to produce positive and constructive improvements in specific areas of company operation that affect two or more functions.

22-I
RESOURCES

	YES (1)	NO (0)	S/P* (½)
1. Managers with direct responsibility for customer communications are kept informed about those aspects of business plans, budgets, and sales plans that will permit them to estimate their work loads and required resources for the next three, six, and twelve months.	___	___	___
2. Based on these projections of company activity, internal resources for handling customer communications have been judged to be adequate to meet the company's needs during the next three, six, and twelve months in terms of:			
a. manpower,	___	___	___

*SOMETIMES OR PARTIALLY

410

	YES (1)	NO (0)	S/P* (½)
b. budget support,	____	____	____
c. capabilities,	____	____	____
d. facilities and equipment,	____	____	____
e. communications,	____	____	____
f. computer time and capacity,	____	____	____
g. training support, and	____	____	____
h. other functional support.	____	____	____

*SOMETIMES OR PARTIALLY

TOTAL POINTS ☐ + 0 + ☐

= ☐

RATING

$$\frac{\text{Enter number of points scored } \boxed{}}{\text{Enter number of items on checklist } \boxed{}} = \boxed{} \times 100 = \boxed{\quad \%}$$

WHAT THE RATING SIGNIFIES

The work load for the customer communications function does not vary directly with sales volume, of course, because it is affected by many other factors. But new order input and sales volume forecasts are important quantitative inputs to the work load estimates. The number of customers, the size of the sales force, and the number of inquiries and complaints handled in the past are other needed inputs to the work load calculation. A low rating indicates that either future needs for customer communication are not known, or else resources to meet these needs are not adequate.

WHAT TO DO NOW

1. If resources are short, you need a firm program to obtain them. High on the critical list of resources needed are physical communications, of course—telephone, Telex or TWX, etc. Access to technical and other support functions, employee training, and data processing are also important to good customer communications.

2. If your business is growing rapidly, your customer communications capability should be kept ahead of the growth curve. If not, then customer and prospect inquiries can pile up, and business will be lost to competition for lack of prompt response.

Chapter **23**

Handling Customer Orders

Every business organization is unique and different from every other. Each has its own culture and customs. Very often, each one has a language—a terminology—of its own. When two organizations communicate with one another, the language barrier can sometimes get in the way of good understanding.

IT'S IMPORTANT TO "SPEAK THE LANGUAGE"

This can even happen when one organization wants to procure materials or services from another. The procuring organization may express its needs in a language that is foreign to the supplying organization, so there is a need for a function within the vendor's organization that "translates" the customer's order into the terminology of the factory or warehouse. Even when the buyer orders from a vendor's catalog there is a need for an order processing function to convert selling terms into terms used by the production department, and to check the purchase order for completeness, accuracy, and compliance with the vendor's price list and terms of sale. Prices may have to be calculated on non-standard items, and delivery times may have to be determined and conveyed to the customer.

The speed and accuracy of this order processing and conversion function is an important factor to the productivity and profitability of a company.

ACTIVITIES INCLUDED IN ORDER PROCESSING

1. receive, record, and acknowledge customer orders,
2. process customer orders for manufacturing,
3. add or verify prices and delivery times,

4. process order changes,

5. maintain contact with salesperson and/or distributor, and

6. keep records of orders and order status.

KEY AIM OF THE SELF-AUDIT   The principal purposes of the appraisal are to ensure that (1) customer orders are filled with accuracy and dispatch, (2) products, prices, and delivery times are advantageous to the supplier, and (3) customers are informed promptly of any difference between what they expect and what they will be given, in order to prevent any later dispute.

HOW TO USE THE CHECKLISTS

For each of the statements in the Checklist, compare the condition of your function to the "ideal" as described in the statement. Then:

1. If you consider the statement to be *generally true* of your function, check the YES column.
2. If you consider the statement to be *untrue* of your function, check the NO column.
3. If you consider the statement to be *less than true* (but not totally untrue) of your function, check the SOMETIMES OR PARTIAL column.
4. If the statement does not apply to your particular situation, write "Not Applicable" across the response spaces (or simply draw a line through them).
5. If you lack the data for a definite response, write in "Not Answerable" or "Don't Know."

HOW TO EVALUATE YOUR RESPONSES

When you have completed the checklist, glance over your responses, keeping these points in mind:

1. A negative answer is always unfavorable because it indicates a problem within the function: the greater the number of NOs, the more serious the situation.
2. A positive response is always a good indication. But too many YES answers could indicate that your review is not objective enough.
3. Too many SOMETIMES OR PARTIALLY answers can point to internal weaknesses or to a lack of firm direction.
4. A lot of "Not Applicable" answers could indicate that you are avoiding the issue.
5. A large number of "Not Answerable" or "Don't Know" answers could be symptomatic of inadequate records or data bases.

HOW TO RATE AND SCORE YOUR RESPONSES

When you are satisfied with your responses in general, you are ready to score the Checklist. For your convenience, a self-explanatory Scoring and Rating Block follows each Checklist. This block not only tells you whether the condition of your function is satisfactory, but it also gives you a measure of its effectiveness.

Here's how to total up the points for inclusion in the Scoring and Rating Block:

1. Total up the number of points you scored:
   a. For each YES, give yourself one point.
   b. For each NO, give yourself zero.
   c. For each SOMETIMES OR PARTIALLY, give yourself a half-point.
   d. For each "Not Applicable" answer, give yourself zero and deduct one from the number of items on the Checklist.
   e. For each "Not Answerable" or "Don't Know" answer, give yourself zero.
2. Next divide the total number of points you score by the total number of items (statements) on the Checklist (less items marked "Not Applicable"). You'll get a 1.0 for a perfect score and a fraction for anything less.
3. Multiply the result of step 2 by 100 to arrive at the percentage for your score.

What is a satisfactory rating? A rating of less than 65 percent is unacceptable and calls for an improvement program: Obviously, the lower the rating, the more drastic the action required.

A brief "how-to" example of this Scoring and Rating system follows . . .

EXAMPLE

	YES (1)	NO (0)	S/P* (½)

1. Field sale reports designed to provide information on sales progress contain data on the following topics:

   a. sales calls and sales presentations made by salespersons and sales agents,   ✓

   b. bids, quotations, and proposals made,   ✓

   c. new orders booked,   ✓

   d. lost business, and reasons for the loss,   ✓ (NO)

   e. accomplishments toward future orders,   ✓ (S/P)

   f. performance in filling orders, handling complaints, and otherwise servicing individual customers,   ✓

   g. action taken in response to customer requests, such as sending samples, spec sheets, etc.,   ✓

   h. accomplishments of significance and value to other members of the sales force.   ✓ (S/P)

*SOMETIMES OR PARTIALLY

TOTAL POINTS $\boxed{5}$ + 0 + $\boxed{1}$

= $\boxed{6}$

RATING

$$\frac{\text{Enter number of points scored} \quad \boxed{6}}{\text{Enter number of items on checklist} \quad \boxed{8}} = .75 \times 100 = \boxed{75}\%$$

	YES (1)	NO (0)	S/P* (½)
1. The handling and processing of customer's purchase orders is recognized on the organization charts and in managers' position descriptions as an important function of the sales department.	___	___	___
2. The function is supervised and staffed by responsible personnel trained in order processing and informed about the company's products and customers.	___	___	___
3. The function has a formal budget allocation covering all costs and expenses of operation.	___	___	___
4. The supervisor of the function reports to a manager high enough in the organization to assure that the importance of the activity is recognized.	___	___	___
5. The function is organized internally so as to minimize transcriptions of the orders, and to speed flow of the paper work.	___	___	___
6. Customer order processing procedures and practices are up-to-date and documented in writing.	___	___	___
7. Personnel processing customer orders are encouraged to look for possible new sales opportunities and pass them on to the sales representative.	___	___	___
8. Customer purchase orders and change orders are acknowledged within 24 hours of receipt.	___	___	___
9. Orders are processed the same day as received.	___	___	___
10. Customers are promptly notified of any changes in order status.	___	___	___
11. Delivery times promised are:			
a. based on factual data from production or distribution departments, and	___	___	___
b. are known to be reliable.	___	___	___
12. Salespersons are kept informed of order status at all times.	___	___	___
13. The order processing procedure has been reviewed during the past year.	___	___	___

*SOMETIMES OR PARTIALLY

TOTAL POINTS [ ] + 0 + [ ]

= [ ]

RATING

Enter number of points scored [ ] / Enter number of items on checklist [ ] = × 100 = [ ] %

WHAT THE RATING SIGNIFIES   The process of converting customer purchase orders into sales orders on the factory or warehouse is an important contributor to the overall productivity of the business. A less-than-satisfactory rating here indicates that the process may not be structured or administered as effectively as it could be.

Obviously, slow processing of orders can result in delayed shipments to customers. Errors can slow the billing process, and thus payment for the goods. Every time the company's cash flow is slowed down, it reduces the firm's ability—however slightly—to pay for the goods and services it needs to conduct business.

This function also makes a significant contribution to the overall return on investment (ROI) of the enterprise. When customer orders are not processed efficiently—that is, quickly and accurately—ROI can suffer. An an example, if a single item on the customer's order is priced incorrectly, the customer could hold payment of the entire invoice. The unpaid account inflates the company's open accounts receivable balance, thereby reducing turnover of assets, a factor of the ROI equation. Slower turnover has the effect of reducing the percentage return on investment. The effect of a single error is very small, of course, but the cumulative effect of many errors and delays can seriously impact ROI.

The process begins with the field salesperson. When the order form is complete, accurate, and transmitted quickly and accurately to the home office, factory, or warehouse, the process is off to a good start. The ideal system is one in which this initial form goes all the way through the process to final billing, without the need for transcription at any point. Every transcription is an opportunity for errors.

Failure to acknowledge orders quickly can also lead to customer dissatisfaction—even in the extreme to cancellation of an order. Failure to keep the customer fully informed about the status of his order can cause serious customer displeasure.

WHAT TO DO NOW

1. Review and tighten up the whole process, starting with the order form used by the field salesperson.

2. Keep responsibility intact throughout the process. Every change of responsibility is a chance for "finger-pointing" when things go wrong. The fact that the order may require some engineering is not an excuse for the sales manager to disclaim responsibility for getting the customer's order filled as expeditiously as possible.

3. Look upon every order as a sales opportunity for additional business. Train your order processing people to spot these and pass them on to the appropriate salesperson. *Pay them* when it leads to a sale—maybe through a commission split with the sales rep.

23-B
AUTHORITY, RESPONSIBILITY, AND ACCOUNTABILITY

	YES (1)	NO (0)	S/P* (½)
1. Authority has been delegated, through budget allocation and position description, to the manager of sales to expend company funds and assign tasks necessary to convert customers' purchase orders into company shop or warehouse orders. (This position title should be changed as required.)	———	———	———

*SOMETIMES OR PARTIALLY

	YES (1)	NO (0)	S/P* (½)

2. The manager is responsible for:

    a. staffing and managing an organization to process customer orders, and _____ _____ _____

    b. establishing and administering procedures for processing orders. _____ _____ _____

3. The manager is responsible for prompt and accurate processing of all customer orders. _____ _____ _____

4. Responsibility for handling customer orders is firmly assigned, covering:

    a. receipt and recording of orders, _____ _____ _____

    b. checking for errors, _____ _____ _____

    c. transcribing customer orders into shop or warehouse orders, _____ _____ _____

    d. handling customer inquiries about orders, and _____ _____ _____

    e. assuring that customer orders are filled without delay. _____ _____ _____

5. The manager is held accountable for:

    a. loss of customer purchase orders in processing, _____ _____ _____

    b. serious delays in processing, and _____ _____ _____

    c. serious errors on shop or warehouse orders. _____ _____ _____

*SOMETIMES OR PARTIALLY

TOTAL POINTS ☐ + 0 + ☐

= ☐

RATING

Enter number of points scored ☐

Enter number of items on checklist ☐

= × 100 = ☐ %

WHAT THE RATING SIGNIFIES

A low rating can indicate that authority and responsibility for getting customer orders translated into shop or warehouse orders are not clearly defined or assigned. If so, then orders may be lost, delayed, or seriously errored—despite the sincere efforts of hard-working people—simply because of misunderstandings ("*I* didn't know that!"), failure to assign important tasks ("It's not *my* job"), or inadequate resources ("You *know* I'm short-handed . . . !")

WHAT TO DO NOW

1. Make sure that every customer order is tracked through the process from the incoming mail room, either until the material and the invoice are in the customer's hands, or until there is a clear hand-off of responsibility to another function, such as to production and material control or product distribution.

2. Make sure each individual knows his or her responsibility and task assignment and understands its role in the total process. This requires a

set of clearly written job descriptions with specific standards for quantity and quality of output.

3. Make sure that definite and precise procedures and standard practices are documented and are followed. The order processing department is no place for creativity.

4. Last but not least, make sure that your resources are adequate to get the job done. It pays to train each employee to do two or more tasks, so that absenteeism doesn't put you out of business.

23-C
MEASUREMENTS, CONTROL REPORTS, AND PERFORMANCE RECORDS

	YES (1)	NO (0)	S/P* (½)
1. The effectiveness of the order handling process is measured periodically, at least monthly.	___	___	___
2. This effectiveness is measured by comparing actual performance to benchmarks, standards, or targets such as:			
a. backlog of unprocessed new orders,	___	___	___
b. number of orders processed within standard time,	___	___	___
c. number of errored orders passed, and	___	___	___
d. productivity per processing employee.	___	___	___
3. A "log" of customer orders is kept, cross-referenced to shop or warehouse order number.	___	___	___
4. A record of customer orders is kept showing date received, and other key dates.	___	___	___
5. Orders not passed on to shop or warehouse within a prescribed time period are automatically "flagged" for management attention.	___	___	___
6. When backlog of unprocessed orders reaches a predetermined number or ratio, management is automatically alerted to the need for overtime, increased staff, or other corrective action.	___	___	___
7. Individual employees work to written standards of productivity and quality, and they know without being told when their performance is below standard.	___	___	___
8. Sub-standard producers are given training, retraining, or re-assignment.	___	___	___

*SOMETIMES OR PARTIALLY

TOTAL POINTS [ ] + 0 + [ ]

= [ ]

RATING

Enter number of points scored [ ]

Enter number of items on checklist [ ]

= × 100 = [ ] %

Unless actual performance in processing customer orders is measured regularly, it is almost certain to get worse. The more frequently it is measured, the more likely it is to be efficient. It is not inconceivable that this measurement be weekly or even *daily* for good control. The processing work load can vary widely and almost unpredictably—the important thing is to be flexible enough to keep up with the flow of incoming orders. A low rating indicates that measurements and controls are not adequate; as a consequence, delays in processing customer orders may cause customer dissatisfaction—even cancellations of orders.

WHAT TO DO NOW

1. Set up "automatic" controls to the maximum extent; the kind that trigger a pre-set response, for example, a graph showing the number of unprocessed orders carried over to the next work day.

2. Emphasize "self-control" by individuals throughout the process. This requires frequent feedback on performance direct to the employee, without intervention by the boss. Not every employee is capable of this, but for the more mature and responsible individual, it is a more productive and rewarding way to work.

3. Set high quality standards and measure quality often. High output at the expense of quality is counter-productive.

23-D
OPERATING PERFORMANCE HISTORY

	YES (1)	NO (0)	S/P* (½)
1. A review and analysis of records and control reports for the past year has been made.	____	____	____
2. This review of records and control reports for the past year shows no serious complaints or order cancellations because of delays, lost paperwork, or errors in order processing. (Answer "Yes" if true.)	____	____	____
3. Employee productivity, measured by orders processed per employee/day (or week) has improved during the past year.	____	____	____
4. Quality of output has met or exceeded standards.	____	____	____
5. Overtime has not exceeded a predetermined percent of straight time.	____	____	____
6. Employee turnover has been acceptable.	____	____	____
7. Expense budget has been met for the past year.	____	____	____

*SOMETIMES OR PARTIALLY

TOTAL POINTS ☐ + 0 + ☐

= ☐

RATING

Enter number of points scored ☐

───────────────────────────── =   × 100 = ☐ %

Enter number of items on checklist ☐

If this rating is low, the problem could be in procedures or in people; neither should be changed until the underlying basic causes are understood, because nothing is more futile than trying to solve a problem that hasn't been defined.

WHAT TO DO NOW

1. Take no remedial action until an in-depth analysis has been made to determine the real reasons for sub-standard performance.

2. If the problem is found to be poor procedures, trace them all the way back to the forms and procedures used by the field sales force at the point of contact with the customer. If the process doesn't start off right, all the efforts of hard working people might be in vain.

3. If the analysis indicates a "people-problem," first try retraining. If there has been high employee turnover, new people might have been hurriedly and inadequately trained by the departing employees, or by an overworked supervisor.

4. Never compromise on quality. This is the first step in meeting the customer's needs—errors at this point can follow the order all the way through the production process and can cost the company not only money but customers.

23-E
TOP-LEVEL SUPPORT AND GUIDANCE

	YES (1)	NO (0)	S/P* (½)

The executive office demonstrates active guidance and support through:

a. budget approval

b. commenting on summary reports of departmental activity

c. recognition and reward for outstanding accomplishment.

*SOMETIMES OR PARTIALLY

TOTAL POINTS   ☐ + 0 + ☐

= ☐

RATING

Enter number of points scored   ☐

Enter number of items on checklist   ☐   =   × 100 = ☐ %

Negative answers indicate that top management may consider the order processing function as just a routine overhead clerical activity that adds nothing to the company's productivity or profitability. If this is the case, then it is very likely that the people in the group have a poor self-image and low morale—in which case poor productivity and high employee turnover will follow.

421

1. It was noted earlier that this function is an important contributor to the firm's productivity and return on investment. *Get this message across* to your people—and to top management.

2. Take every opportunity to get added new business through your people's familiarity with customers and your products. Every customer order contains the seeds of a new sale—for supporting services, for ancillary products, for larger quantities, and for repeat business. Set up an incentive program that rewards your people when they pass the sales lead on to the sales representative. There is no better way to make your function visible to the front office.

23-F
INNOVATION IN METHODS AND TECHNIQUES

	YES (1)	NO (0)	S/P* (½)
1. Orders are transmitted from field sales to processing by Telex/TWX, facsimile, data phone, or other fast record communications medium.	___	___	___
2. The computer is used to process orders, and to store and display all key information on order progress, including billing data.	___	___	___
3. The computer program has error-checking capability.	___	___	___
4. The department manager keeps informed about new techniques and equipment for handling orders, and actively seeks methods to improve productivity, through:			
a. seminars and workshops,	___	___	___
b. industry contacts,	___	___	___
c. review of management literature, and	___	___	___
d. solicitation of ideas from other functions and	___	___	___
e. budgets provide funds for such activities.	___	___	___

*SOMETIMES OR PARTIALLY

TOTAL POINTS [ ] + 0 + [ ]

= [ ]

RATING

Enter number of points scored [ ]
_____ = × 100 = [ ] %
Enter number of items on checklist [ ]

It's important to keep on the lookout for ways to speed up the order processing process, and to make it more effective. New computer hardware and software are rapidly replacing people—and reducing costs and improving quality in the process. Ultimately the whole computer-controlled production process may be driven by the data punched in to the process by the order processing clerk—who, at this point, becomes the most important person in the entire process!

WHAT TO DO NOW
1. Don't wait for this millenium—but make sure that you are utilizing the computer as fully and effectively as possible.
2. Of equal importance, make sure you are utilizing your human resources as productively as possible. Use incentives, recognition, sincere praise, and all the other good motivating practices that a good manager must employ.

23-G
INTERFUNCTIONAL COMMUNICATION AND COORDINATION

	YES (1)	NO (0)	S/P* (½)

1. The department manager meets regularly with managers of production, engineering, and distribution to resolve problems involving the flow of information between departments. _____ _____ _____

2. The manager routinely is kept informed by marketing and production about changes in product descriptions, prices, delivery times, new products, etc. _____ _____ _____

*SOMETIMES OR PARTIALLY

TOTAL POINTS ☐ + 0 + ☐

= ☐

RATING

Enter number of points scored ☐
———————————————————— = × 100 = ☐ %
Enter number of items on checklist ☐

WHAT THE RATING SIGNIFIES

Customer order processing often involves other key functions of the organization; product distribution, production, and engineering. The manager responsible for order processing should establish and maintain close and continuing contact and good working relations with managers in these departments.

There is an important two-way flow of information involved here. The managers of production, distribution, and engineering possess knowledge and current information about products and processes that is important to the handling of customer orders. The order processing manager is usually the first person in the organization to see the total new order input—therefore, he can, in return, impart valuable information to each of them about the trends in new orders being processed. Negative answers to these appraisal points is an indication that this essential intercommunication is lacking.

1. As manager of order processing it's up to you to initiate and develop these important contacts. They are essential to the effective performance of your job. Don't wait for a crisis or problem situation to arise—start the information flow by inviting them into review meetings and by circulating your summary reports to them.

2. Once you get the information flow going, it's time to insist on a *quid pro quo*—a sharing with you of their knowledge about new products and processes, technical developments, and other information useful to you in your work.

23-H
FUNCTIONAL IMPROVEMENT PROGRAM

	YES (1)	NO (0)	S/P* (½)
1. There is an active, on-going interfunctional team effort to improve customer order processing. Principal efforts are directed toward improving, on a project basis:			
a. accuracy and speed of transmission of orders and change orders from field,	___	___	___
b. order processing accuracy, by eliminating transcription of orders,	___	___	___
c. speed of acknowledgement to customer,	___	___	___
d. status reports to salesperson,	___	___	___
e. accuracy of delivery promises to customer, and	___	___	___
f. elapsed time from order receipt by salesman to entry by warehouse or shop.	___	___	___
2. Members of the team, depending on the product, include:			
a. field sales,	___	___	___
b. information systems,	___	___	___
c. production,	___	___	___
d. communications, and	___	___	___
e. marketing.	___	___	___

*SOMETIMES OR PARTIALLY

TOTAL POINTS   [ ] + 0 + [ ]

= [ ]

RATING

Enter number of points scored [ ]
———————————————————— = [ ] × 100 = [ ] %
Enter number of items on checklist [ ]

The speed and accuracy of order processing is an important contributor to company productivity and profitability. Because it is a process that involves many people and even some functions not under the control of the sales manager, a team approach is an effective way to improve the activity.

A group with representatives from all functions involved can often accomplish in a few hours what could take days or even weeks otherwise, because people become committed to the outcome as a result of their direct participation.

A less-than-satisfactory rating on this and other checklists in this chapter indicates the need for a team approach to productivity improvement in order processing.

WHAT TO DO NOW

1. Before you make a significant change in any part of the process, be sure to appraise the effect on other transactions in the chain. The best way to ensure this is to get the other functional people involved in the change at the beginning. (The worse way is to unilaterally make a change, then wait for the problems to surface so you can show how good a problem-solver you are!)

2. Give full credit to other people who contribute constructive ideas for improving your function. If you fail to do so and take all the credit yourself, the next helpful suggestion you'll get may be to "go jump in the lake!"

3. Don't overlook the potential contributions from lower-level people, where the actual work is done. It's often difficult to get them to open up, especially if the organization is somewhat autocratic in style—but when you do, they can be a gold mine of ideas for improvement. Again, be sure to give recognition to the person who contributes.

23-1
RESOURCES

	YES (1)	NO (0)	S/P* (½)
1. The manager of the order processing function is informed about order input forecasts contained in budgets and sales plans, in order to estimate the department workload for the next three, six, and twelve months.	___	___	___
2. Based on these projections, resources for handling orders are judged to be adequate to meet the company's needs, in terms of:			
a. manpower,	___	___	___
b. capabilities,	___	___	___
c. budget support,	___	___	___
d. computer time and capacity,	___	___	___
e. facilities and equipment,	___	___	___
f. communications, and	___	___	___
g. other functional support.	___	___	___

*SOMETIMES OR PARTIALLY

RATING

Enter number of points scored ⬚

—————————————————————— = × 100 = ⬚ %

Enter number of items on checklist ⬚

WHAT THE RATING SIGNIFIES

The functional workload of customer orders to be processed is dependent, of course, on the productivity of the sales force. Its output—new orders booked—is the input to the order processing function. To the extent this factor is known for the months ahead—and is accurate—the work load estimate is valid.

In the absence of a good projection or forecast of new order input, it is not possible to estimate with certainty the size of the functional staff needed during the months ahead. It follows, then, that any judgment about the adequacy of resources may be faulty.

WHAT TO DO NOW

1. The annual sales plan should be the starting point for your workload projections and staffing requirements, which could vary widely throughout the year if the firm's customers are in seasonal businesses.

2. Insist that new order input forecasts in the sales plan are specific in terms of major order types and sizes, and are broken out by months.

3. Run your work load estimates by the managers of the supporting functions like data processing and communications to ensure that their capacity is adequate for your needs. Better to identify potential bottlenecks early, so you can line up other sources.

Chapter **24**

How to Ensure
Customer Satisfaction—
After-Sale Service

**AFTER-SALE SERVICE
SHOULD BE TREATED
AS A PROFIT CENTER**
This section of the self-audit is concerned with post-sale service on those products that perform a function, such as machines, appliances, tools, vehicles, instruments, structures—and the many, many other products that are classified as "durable goods." Virtually every one of these products requires a measure of service after delivery to the user. Some of the service is performed under product warranties, in which case the cost is comprehended in the selling price of the product. Other service is performed out-of-warranty, or after the warranty period has expired; this is performed at a cost to the owner.

It is to the advantage of the producer to provide after-sale service because:

1. The availability and quality of after-sale service is frequently a major consideration to the purchase decision.

2. The quality of service can be controlled better.

3. Much valuable information is gained that can be beneficial to engineering, production, and quality control.

4. It can be an important source of revenue and profit.

After-sale service of the firm's products is a critical element of its overall customer service. The product itself can have every quality for customer acceptance, but if it is not backed up in use by prompt, effective, and economical service, people will turn to others for their needs. This is especially true of products used in the production of other goods, because every hour that the machine is idle costs the user money.

It is important that this function is managed as though it were producing a *product*. The product is an important one to customers, and can be defined as precisely as any other. What you are providing to customers is *utility*—by keeping their appliances operating, by keeping their machines producing goods, by keeping their vehicles on the road, or by keeping their airplanes in the air—in short, by keeping the products producing the utility the customers invested their money in when they bought the company's product.

ACTIVITIES COVERED UNDER POST-SALE SERVICE

1. Repairing or replacing product under warranty,
2. handling out-of-warranty repairs and service,
3. handling product recalls,
4. furnishing replacement parts or spares,
5. operating service centers,
6. maintaining inventories of parts and supplies, and
7. providing maintenance services under contract.
8. Install product (if appropriate)

KEY AIM OF THE SELF-AUDIT

The principle purpose of the appraisal is to provide assurance to the manager that the level and quality of after-sale service is adequate to customer needs, and is equal to or better than that provided by the strongest competition. Additionally, it should ensure that after-sale service is profitable to the company, in terms of both current earnings and return on investment.

HOW TO USE THE CHECKLISTS

For each of the statements in the Checklist, compare the condition of your function to the "ideal" as described in the statement. Then:

1. If you consider the statement to be *generally true* of your function, check the YES column.

2. If you consider the statement to be *untrue* of your function, check the NO column.

3. If you consider the statement to be *less than true* (but not totally untrue) of your function, check the SOMETIMES OR PARTIAL column.

4. If the statement does not apply to your particular situation, write "Not Applicable" across the response spaces (or simply draw a line through them).

5. If you lack the data for a definite response, write in "Not Answerable" or "Don't Know."

HOW TO EVALUATE YOUR RESPONSES

When you have completed the checklist, glance over your responses, keeping these points in mind:

1. A negative answer is always unfavorable because it indicates a problem within the function: the greater the number of NOs, the more serious the situation.

2. A positive response is always a good indication. But too many YES answers could indicate that your review is not objective enough.

3. Too many SOMETIMES OR PARTIALLY answers can point to internal weaknesses or to a lack of firm direction.

4. A lot of "Not Applicable" answers could indicate that you are avoiding the issue.

5. A large number of "Not Answerable" or "Don't Know" answers could be symptomatic of inadequate records or data bases.

HOW TO RATE AND SCORE YOUR RESPONSES

When you are satisfied with your responses in general, you are ready to score the Checklist. For your convenience, a self-explanatory Scoring and Rating Block follows each Checklist. This block not only tells you whether the condition of your function is satisfactory, but it also gives you a measure of its effectiveness.

Here's how to total up the points for inclusion in the Scoring and Rating Block:

1. Total up the number of points you scored:
   a. For each YES, give yourself one point.
   b. For each NO, give yourself zero.
   c. For each SOMETIMES OR PARTIALLY, give yourself a half-point.
   d. For each "Not Applicable" answer, give yourself zero and deduct one from the number of items on the Checklist.
   e. For each "Not Answerable" or "Don't Know" answer, give yourself zero.

2. Next divide the total number of points you score by the total number of items (statements) on the Checklist (less items marked "Not Applicable"). You'll get a 1.0 for a perfect score and a fraction for anything less.

3. Multiply the result of step 2 by 100 to arrive at the percentage for your score.

What is a satisfactory rating? A rating of less than 65 percent is unacceptable and calls for an improvement program: Obviously, the lower the rating, the more drastic the action required.

A brief "how-to" example of this Scoring and Rating system follows . . .

EXAMPLE

	YES (1)	NO (0)	S/P* (½)

1. Field sale reports designed to provide information on sales progress contain data on the following topics:

   a. sales calls and sales presentations made by salespersons and sales agents, — ✓ (YES)

   b. bids, quotations, and proposals made, — ✓ (YES)

   c. new orders booked, — ✓ (YES)

   d. lost business, and reasons for the loss, — ✓ (NO)

   e. accomplishments toward future orders, — ✓ (S/P)

   f. performance in filling orders, handling complaints, and otherwise servicing individual customers, — ✓ (YES)

   g. action taken in response to customer requests, such as sending samples, spec sheets, etc., — ✓ (YES)

   h. accomplishments of significance and value to other members of the sales force. — ✓ (S/P)

*SOMETIMES OR PARTIALLY

TOTAL POINTS $\boxed{5}$ + 0 + $\boxed{1}$

= $\boxed{6}$

RATING

$$\frac{\text{Enter number of points scored} \quad \boxed{6}}{\text{Enter number of items on checklist} \quad \boxed{8}} = .75 \times 100 = \boxed{75} \%$$

24-A
ORGANIZATION, ADMINISTRATION, AND OPERATION

	YES (1)	NO (0)	S/P* (½)

1. After-sale service is recognized as a vital company activity that has top management endorsement and support, and an essential element to the satisfaction of customer needs and company success. ____ ____ ____

2. The selling function has access to an organization (either internal or external) competent to provide post-sale service on the Unit's products, including installation and maintenance where appropriate. ____ ____ ____

3. The service organization is responsive to and is controlled by the selling function. ____ ____ ____

4. The function has a formal budget allocation covering operating expenses and capital equipment if required. ____ ____ ____

5. The manager of the service organization is considered to be a member of upper management, and has direct access to managers of other departments. ____ ____ ____

6. The service department is staffed by trained service personnel who are informed about the company's products and customers. ____ ____ ____

7. The department is well-equipped with vehicles, spare parts, tools, instruction manuals, and test equipment. ____ ____ ____

8. After-sale service is as good or better than that provided by the strongest competitor in terms of:

   a. availability (location, hours of service, and geographic coverage), ____ ____ ____

   b. quality and speed of service, and ____ ____ ____

   c. price. ____ ____ ____

9. Warranties and guarantees are competitive in terms of completeness and duration. ____ ____ ____

10. Warranties are known to be honored in all important respects. ____ ____ ____

11. Warranties and guarantees are in writing, and are clear and understandable. ____ ____ ____

12. a. Cost of honoring warranties and guarantees is known. ____ ____ ____

    b. Cost is acceptable as a percent of product cost, and ____ ____ ____

    c. is covered by selling price. ____ ____ ____

13. Service contracts (if applicable) are available to customers, either on a T&M (time and material) basis, or on a monthly flat rate basis. ____ ____ ____

14. Trouble calls are acknowledged immediately, and answered promptly. ____ ____ ____

15. Follow-up contact is made by sales department after all major sales. ____ ____ ____

16. Adequate stocks of replacement parts are maintained at service centers convenient to customers. ____ ____ ____

17. All new hires receive formal training on the company's products. ____ ____ ____

18. Service personnel are given training on new products before they are sold. ____ ____ ____

*SOMETIMES OR PARTIALLY

$$\boxed{} + 0 + \boxed{}$$

$$= \boxed{}$$

RATING

Enter number of points scored $\boxed{}$

—————————————————————————— = $\boxed{}$ × 100 = $\boxed{}$ %

Enter number of items on checklist $\boxed{}$

WHAT THE RATING SIGNIFIES

A less-than-satisfactory rating here can indicate that the company's after-sale service is not organized and operated on a business-like basis, but may be considered as a kind of "necessary nuisance," and a cost center. If this is so, then it very likely is costing money rather than earning its way.

Regarding after-sale service as a profit center can have a remarkably beneficial effect on product quality. The service department will demand high quality because it will reduce the number of service calls and costs. The department is also more likely to feed back information on quality problems in the field, so they can be redesigned or corrected in production.

There is a danger in this however. If a service department systematically overcharges customers in order to make a profit, customers will turn away from the company's products, no matter how attractive they are otherwise.

WHAT TO DO NOW

1. Organize the function on a profit center basis, but with controls to ensure efficient business operation, honest pricing, responsiveness, and competent work.
2. Price services competitively—word gets around.
3. Honor all warranties to the letter—nothing enrages an owner like being misled by the "small type" on the warranty.
4. Make it easy for the owner to get service. Many companies use an "800-area code" hot line.

24-B
AUTHORITY, RESPONSIBILITY, AND ACCOUNTABILITY

	YES (1)	NO (0)	S/P* (½)
1. Authority has been delegated, through budget allocation and manager's position description, to the customer service manager to expend company funds and assign tasks necessary to service the company's products after the sale.	_____	_____	_____
2. Authority has been delegated in writing to the manager to invest capital funds in facilities, up to a prescribed limit, for the purpose of providing after-sale service to customers, on a profit basis.	_____	_____	_____

*SOMETIMES OR PARTIALLY

	YES (1)	NO (0)	S/P* (½)

3. The manager is responsible for staffing and managing a profit-oriented organization capable of providing a competitive level of after-sale service.

4. Responsibility for all post-sale service and cost of service is firmly assigned, and includes both in-warranty and out-of-warranty repair and replacement, and installation and maintenance where appropriate.

5. The manager is held accountable for:

   a. loss of important customers,

   b. cancellation of orders,

   c. an unacceptable level of customer complaints,

   d. excessive costs of service, or

   e. serious citations from consumer agencies or lawsuits resulting from inadequate or ineffective after-sale service.

6. The manager is accountable for losses resulting from inefficient administration and operation.

*SOMETIMES OR PARTIALLY

TOTAL POINTS   ☐ + 0 + ☐

= ☐

RATING

Enter number of points scored ☐ / Enter number of items on checklist ☐ = × 100 = ☐ %

WHAT THE RATING SIGNIFIES

After-sale service has only two purposes: one, customer satisfaction that will lead to repeat and referral business and two, a beneficial effect on the company's bottom line. Any other assumed purpose is irrelevant and can only result in cost to the company.

The efficient achievement of both purposes requires firm delegation of authority to expend company funds for expenses and capital improvements. It also requires that accountability be clearly spelled out for failure to satisfy customers and failure to make a profit.

A low rating indicates that the authority, responsibility, and accountability of the manager may not be clear and explicit. This activity all too often is treated as an unwanted step-child of the organization. If the function is to be managed as a money-making operation, the manager needs a clear mission and the power to get the job done.

WHAT TO DO NOW

1. If the function is presently a drain on earnings, you should develop a *plan* to generate a respectable return on the company's investment in the operation. The plan should include these elements:

   a. a clear statement of business mission,

   b. a set of objectives, both quantitative and qualitative,

433

    c. assumptions on which the plan is based,

    d. detailed action steps, with assignment of responsibility for each, schedule completion dates, estimated costs, and estimated benefits,

    e. new capital investment required, and

    f. other resources and support required.

2. Build a base of support by discussing your plan with managers of other functions whose support you will need. Make them parties to the project by incorporating their recommendations into the plan.

3. Sell your direct superior on the benefits he will derive from your program.

4. With a sound plan showing that the function can be converted to a profit-making operation, and a firm base of agreement by your peers and your boss, you should make a pitch to the executive office for the go-ahead and the authority to draw upon company resources.

24-C
MEASUREMENTS, CONTROL REPORTS, AND PERFORMANCE RECORDS

	YES (1)	NO (0)	S/P* (½)
1. The effectiveness of after-sale service is regularly and continuously measured by comparing actual performance and results to benchmarks or standards, such as:			
a. the number and seriousness of customer complaints about service,	___	___	___
b. customer attitudes toward the company, as reflected in periodic surveys,	___	___	___
c. profit on contract service (if applicable),	___	___	___
d. costs of after-sale service vs. budgets and industry norms.	___	___	___
2. After-sale service is measured and controlled in the accounts as a separate profit-making product line.	___	___	___
3. A record is kept of all service calls and response times.	___	___	___
4. Costs of service labor, material, and travel are recorded for each service call.	___	___	___
5. Cost of the service department is compared with budget monthly, in total and by service center, and major variances are analyzed for corrective action.	___	___	___
6. Cost of in-warranty service is recorded separately for comparison with pricing coverage.	___	___	___
7. When records show a build up in backlog of unfilled service calls, a stretchout in response times, or an unfavorable cost trend, a predetermined set of corrective actions is automatically set in motion.	___	___	___
8. Regular reports are made to production and engineering on service problems.	___	___	___

*SOMETIMES OR PARTIALLY

TOTAL POINTS [ ] + 0 + [ ]

= [ ]

RATING

Enter number of points scored [ ]
—————————————————————— = × 100 = [   ] %
Enter number of items on checklist [ ]

WHAT THE RATING SIGNIFIES

Cost control is key to profitability of a service operation. Actual costs for after-sale service must be lower than the costs factored into the sales price. Cost control requires a set of cost standards and budgets, and good recording of actual performance against them.

A low rating in this section of the self-appraisal is evidence that this essential control may be lacking.

WHAT TO DO NOW

1. Set up your accounting and operating controls for after-sale service as though you were producing a product.

2. Variances from standard costs should be highlighted and analyzed for corrective action, the same as a manufacturing cost variance.

3. When costs for after-sale service are excessive despite good performance by your people, the design reliability or the product quality may be at fault. Work closely with reliability engineering and quality assurance—the information you can feed back to them on use of the product under actual field conditions can be invaluable to them.

4. Make sure that actual cost experience is recorded by cost accounting and fed back to the pricing section so that selling prices will reflect realistic after-sale service costs.

24-D
OPERATING PERFORMANCE HISTORY

	YES (1)	NO (0)	S/P* (½)
1. A review of records and control reports has been made for at least the past year.	——	——	——
2. This analysis shows that during the past year there were no serious losses of customers or orders caused by poor after-sale service. (Answer "Yes" if true.)	——	——	——
3. During the past year there were no serious legal actions brought against the company because of poor after-sale service. (Answer "Yes" if true.)	——	——	——
4. Records show an *improving trend* during the past year in			
a. service response times,	——	——	——

*SOMETIMES OR PARTIALLY

435

	YES (1)	NO (0)	S/P* (½)
b. backlog of held-over service calls,	___	___	___
c. service re-calls,	___	___	___
d. complaints about service or product performance,	___	___	___
e. complaints about failure to honor warranties,	___	___	___
f. costs of service, and	___	___	___
g. profit on service contract business (if applicable).	___	___	___
5. Revenue, expense, and profit budgets have been met.	___	___	___

*SOMETIMES OR PARTIALLY

TOTAL POINTS ☐ + 0 + ☐

= ☐

RATING

Enter number of points scored ☐
———————————————————————————————— = × 100 = ☐ %
Enter number of items on checklist ☐

WHAT THE RATING SIGNIFIES

A low rating on past performance is an important warning signal that business will be lost to competitors that provide better service. This is especially true if the *trend* in service response time is unfavorable. Surveys have shown that customers place a high value on promptness of response. If the trend in "service response time" is unfavorable, however, it may not be entirely a result of poor performance by service personnel—there may be other important causes. The dispatching system may be inefficient; the facilities and equipment may be inadequate; the staff may be poorly trained; or the response time standards themselves may be unrealistic.

WHAT TO DO NOW

1. Before making personnel changes, look at the process and the facilities for providing post-sale service.
2. Next, review procedures to ensure that your service people are not bogged-down by excessive paperwork.
3. Use incentives, not threats or penalties, to improve customer service performance.

TOP-LEVEL SUPPORT AND GUIDANCE

	YES (1)	NO (0)	S/P* (½)

The executive office demonstrates active guidance and support for the after-sale service activity through:

a. budget approval for expenses of operations and capital facilities,

b. personal visits to major service centers,

c. informed comments on progress reports, and

d. recognition and reward for outstanding accomplishment.

*SOMETIMES OR PARTIALLY

TOTAL POINTS ☐ + 0 + ☐

= ☐

RATING

Enter number of points scored ☐
————————————————————— = × 100 = ☐ %
Enter number of items on checklist ☐

WHAT THE RATING SIGNIFIES

The after-sale service function needs and deserves the same support and recognition from the front office as other functions. In some industries, in which there is little product differentiation, quality of service may be the deciding factor in the customer's purchase decision. In the telephone industry, a number of new companies are offering excellent products, but are seriously hampered in their efforts to take customers away from AT&T by their inability to match the Bell System's superb after-sale service.

A low rating indicates the need for the function to improve its visibility to the executive office.

WHAT TO DO NOW

1. The best kind of recognition and support is that which is *earned* by good performance. Repeat business is evidence of satisfaction by existing customers with the firm's service. Referral business also attests to good service.

2. Point out that repeat and referral business are more profitable because their selling costs are lower—and make sure that you share in the credit for this most valuable kind of business.

3. Take credit for product improvements that result from your feedback to reliability engineering, quality assurance, and production.

24-F
INNOVATION IN METHODS AND TECHNIQUES

	YES (1)	NO (0)	S/P* (½)
1. The computer is used to control, record, and display service data and costs.	____	____	____
2. The computer is used to schedule preventive maintenance and dispatch service personnel.	____	____	____
3. Telex/TWX, facsimile, WATS-service, data phone, mobile radio, or other fast communications media are used to speed up service response.	____	____	____
4. Management actively keeps informed about new ways to improve after-sale service, through:			
a. seminars and workshops,	____	____	____
b. industry contacts,	____	____	____
c. technical/professional groups,	____	____	____
d. use of outside specialists,	____	____	____
e. review of current literature,	____	____	____
f. solicitation of ideas from people in all functions and on all levels; particularly field sales, quality assurance, and reliability engineering, and	____	____	____
g. budgets provide funds for such activities.	____	____	____

*SOMETIMES OR PARTIALLY

TOTAL POINTS ☐ + 0 + ☐

= ☐

RATING

Enter number of points scored ☐ / Enter number of items on checklist ☐ = ☐ × 100 = ☐ %

WHAT THE RATING SIGNIFIES

A less than acceptable rating reflects a low level of concern by service management with the *competitiveness* of the company's service. If managers don't actively keep up with new developments in the management of after-sale service, they can be blind-sided by a competitor who does—one who will offer better, faster, and more economical service to *your* customers.

WHAT TO DO NOW

1. Make sure that your operating budget recognizes that one of the costs of providing quality after-sale service is the cost of keeping in contact with the "outside world"—of keeping abreast of new developments in the state-of-the-art.

2. Part of this effort is learning what your competition is doing that may be better than what you have to offer. This doesn't involve spying—it just requires observation, asking questions, and collecting information.

3. Make it worth while for your service reps to keep you informed about what they see and hear about competitors while on the customers' premises.

4. The computer is an indispensable tool for controlling after-sale service operations and costs if your activity covers a wide area and a sizable number of accounts.

5. Look into the new developments in mobile radio and paging systems. They can save a great deal of money in these days of high vehicle operating costs.

24-G
INTERFUNCTIONAL COMMUNICATION AND COORDINATION

	YES (1)	NO (0)	S/P* (½)

1. Service management maintains close and continuing contact with managers of value analysis, production, QA, and design engineering to discuss service problems and ways to reduce them by improved design, manufacture, reliability engineering and quality assurance.

2. Engineering and production are responsive to requests for service assistance.

3. Service management is promptly advised about pending changes in products and processes.

4. Good working relations are maintained with other company functions so that service problems can be solved with minimum inconvenience to the customer.

5. People from other functions (marketing, quality control, advertising, engineering, etc.) are encouraged to join service personnel on service calls to learn at firsthand about product problems and user attitudes toward service.

*SOMETIMES OR PARTIALLY

TOTAL POINTS ☐ + 0 + ☐

= ☐

RATING

Enter number of points scored ☐

───────────────────────────── = ☐ × 100 = ☐ %

Enter number of items on checklist ☐

WHAT THE RATING SIGNIFIES

Every function of the business is involved with after-sale service, to the degree that each contributes to product reliability and quality, or is involved with customer communications. Good service depends on a good two-way flow of information between service management and the other functions.

This kind of intercommunication can't be set up instantly, whenever a crisis occurs. It must be established and maintained on a continuous, day-by-day basis, so that when it's needed it is already in place. People have to work at it constantly, as part of their jobs.

WHAT TO DO NOW

1. Make each manager and supervisor responsible to maintain close and continuous contact with specific individuals in the other functions.
2. Circulate your summary progress reports to the other functional managers, and ask them to reciprocate.
3. Invite key people from other functions to attend your meetings, participate in progress reviews, and accompany your service reps on customer calls.

24-H
FUNCTIONAL IMPROVEMENT PROGRAM

	YES (1)	NO (0)	S/P* (½)
1. There is an active, on-going interfunctional team effort to improve after-sale service. Major efforts are directed toward:			
a. increasing the degree of preventive maintenance in order to reduce the number of breakdowns,	——	——	——
b. improving communications between owners and the company,	——	——	——
c. more understandable warranties, and	——	——	——
d. improved feedback on product problems to production, design, reliability engineering and quality assurance.	——	——	——
2. The following functions are represented on the team, depending on the task:			
a. RD&E,	——	——	——
b. reliability engineering,	——	——	——
c. quality assurance,	——	——	——
d. production,	——	——	——
e. information systems,	——	——	——
f. communications,	——	——	——
g. field sales,	——	——	——
h. legal,	——	——	——
i. marketing, and	——	——	——
j. value analysis.	——	——	——

*SOMETIMES OR PARTIALLY

TOTAL POINTS   ☐ + 0 + ☐

= ☐

RATING

Enter number of points scored ☐
——————————————————— = × 100 = ☐ %
Enter number of items on checklist ☐

440

This section is an extension of the previous one. A low rating here indicates lack of a *formalized and structured* approach to functional improvement.

WHAT TO DO NOW

1. A review of the appraisal up to this point should have helped you to set some priorities for improvement. Now you should organize a program to carry out the most critical tasks, on a project by project basis, calling on other functional people who have a stake in quality improvement and customer relations to participate.

2. Consider establishing a council or panel of users to meet periodically with company representatives to discuss quality and reliability problems with your products. You should control the agenda for these meetings—for they can easily degenerate into a shouting match without a strong leader in charge.

A major computer manufacturer neglected to do this. When service problems mounted, unhappy owners banded together *against* the company—and now the firm faces huge lawsuits.

24-1
RESOURCES

	YES (1)	NO (0)	S/P* (½)
1. Service management is kept informed about forecasts of sales volume by product line, in order to determine departmental workload, and need for possible additional resources.	———	———	———
2. Service management is kept informed about the status of new products, in order to train personnel to service them.	———	———	———
3. Based on these inputs, resources are considered to be adequate to meet the company's needs for after-sale service during the next three, six, and twelve months, in terms of:			
a. manpower,	———	———	———
b. capabilities,	———	———	———
c. budget funding,	———	———	———
d. tools, test equipment, shop facilities,	———	———	———
e. vehicles,	———	———	———
f. training support,	———	———	———
g. computer support, and	———	———	———
h. communications equipment and support.	———	———	———

*SOMETIMES OR PARTIALLY

TOTAL POINTS ☐ + 0 + ☐

⟞⟍ = ☐

RATING

Enter number of points scored ☐

――――――――――――――――――――――――― = × 100 = ☐ %

Enter number of items on checklist ☐

WHAT THE RATING SIGNIFIES

Past experience is probably the more important factor in the calculation of the department's workload, because the product service activity is often related to the age of the product in use. But a good forecast of new sales volume is a necessary input, as well, inasmuch as the service needs of many types of products can be high during the first few months of their operation.

Service management should also be alerted early about new products in development, in order to gear up for potential service problems when the products get out in the field.

WHAT TO DO NOW

1. If resources are lacking, base your proposal for needed resources on profit considerations, or even better, on a "return on investment" case.

2. The accountants may claim they can't break out the costs for aftersale service that you need for these calculations (they're in general overhead in some firms). You have an obligation to insist that this be done—meanwhile you'll have to work with best estimates.

THE BOTTOM LINE

Many businessmen, unfortunately, regard customer service only as a *cost*, rather than a profit opportunity. This can lead to a situation in which service is cut back in the mistaken notion that it will benefit the bottom line.

This is almost as bad as lowering the quality of the product to save money. Both lead to customer dissatisfaction, loss of business to competition, reduced profitability—and in the extreme, a downward spiral into business failure.

The Case of the Auto Industry

It's fashionable to blame the Japanese for the problems of the American automobile manufacturers. However, one of the major reasons Detroit got into deep trouble was the poor reputation for quality it acquired as a result of massive product recalls for manufacturing defects in the late 1970s. Another reason was the shabby treatment that dealers gave to car owners when they came in for service. The manufacturers brushed off the complaints by saying that their dealers were independent businessmen over whom they had no control. The dealers claimed they lost money on service and blamed the manufacturers for putting out a defective product. While dealers and producers pointed fingers at one another, Americans turned to Japanese imports by the millions—and Ford, GM, and Chrysler bathed in red ink.

Customer Service Begins Early

A strong case can be made that good customer communications and service contributes to profit and cash flow. A prompt and courteous response to an inquiry can often convert a prospect into a customer. The quicker a customer order is processed and entered into the factory or warehouse, the sooner the shipment can be made and billed. And the earlier a customer is informed about a potential delay on his order the more time he has to adjust his own schedule, and the less chance he will cancel the order.

After-Sale Service Can Be Profitable

Several well-known companies have found that servicing the products they make can be quite rewarding. Black & Decker claims its repair business on the tools it makes for craftsmen and homeowners accounts for about 10 percent of its annual sales volume of $1.4 billion and operates in the black. Hewlett-Packard has held down its calculator service costs by centralizing repair facilities, and now makes money (despite a policy of low markup on repair work). General Electric, also, treats service as a profit center, and claims its service business profits are growing at a rate of 20 percent a year.

Western Union did an in-depth analysis of the service on teleprinters in its Telex and TWX networks, and found that other companies were making lots of money maintaining these machines, while its own technicians and repair facilities were under-utilized. Several years ago, the company spun-off a separate service business, which is now quite profitable.

SUMMARY OF SELF-AUDIT RATINGS AND FUNCTIONAL IMPROVEMENT GOALS

If you wish, you may summarize the ratings for each function at the end of each section, on this "Summary Rating" form. (A "function" is the equivalent of a chapter.) The rating is simply an arithmetic average of the ratings on Checklists A through I—that is, the total divided by 9. This form also provides space for listing the Improvement Goals for each function.

Under each function, enter the rating percentage for each Checklist section, A through I. "Function Number 1," for example, is the first (1st) chapter in the section, regardless of its number in the book—5, 11, or so on. The Summary Rating is the total of each column divided by 9, to give you an average rating for the total function. The lower portion of the form can be used to list your improvement goals for each function.

	FUNCTION NUMBER					
CHECKLIST	**1** %	**2** %	**3** %	**4** %	**5** %	**6** %
A	_____	_____	_____	_____	_____	_____
B	_____	_____	_____	_____	_____	_____
C	_____	_____	_____	_____	_____	_____
D	_____	_____	_____	_____	_____	_____
E	_____	_____	_____	_____	_____	_____
F	_____	_____	_____	_____	_____	_____
G	_____	_____	_____	_____	_____	_____
H	_____	_____	_____	_____	_____	_____
I	_____	_____	_____	_____	_____	_____
SUMMARY RATING (%)	_____	_____	_____	_____	_____	_____

IMPROVEMENT GOALS

_____

_____

_____

_____

_____

_____

_____

_____

(Use separate sheet as required)

Epilogue

MAKE THE SELF-AUDIT AN ANNUAL EVENT

The self-audit is not a "one-shot" effort; it is intended to be a continuous process. A dynamic, growing business is constantly changing as it responds to the markets it serves and the environment in which it operates. As a result, your job as a professional *marketeur* is constantly changing and growing as well. So, too, are the jobs of every manager who reports to you.

Because of this, you need to reappraise every marketing activity regularly—at least once a year. The proper time for this will depend on the nature and seasonality of your business, of course, but normally the best time is just prior to the time that marketing plans and annual budgets are firmed up—during the fourth quarter, probably. The self-audit gives you good factual input to the planning and budgeting process.

Be sure to provide sufficient time for yourself and your staff to conduct these self-appraisals. Evaluating your own operation is not an easy task, to be done whenever there is a free hour to spare from the daily routine. A good self-audit requires concentration and takes time—as much as several days in some cases. It is important, as well, to get away from the distractions and interruptions of the daily workplace while making the self-audit.

A couple of cautions are in order. First and most important, don't be tempted to use the deficiencies and weaknesses that might be exposed by your subordinate's appraisals against them. If you do, they'll find ways to hide them from you, and the value of the process will be lost. Also, don't solve their problems for them; the whole point of the process is to develop your subordinates into responsible, mature decision-makers.

Finally, make it clear to your managers that they cannot correct every deficiency, solve every problem, cure every organizational ailment. The purpose of the self-audit process is to identify the most critical areas needing improvement, so managers can concentrate their skills and energies on these. This is the famous "80/20 rule" at work—the rule that says 80 percent of your results usually comes from 20 percent of the tasks you do. By helping you to isolate the most important aspects of the job and putting your talents to work on these, you'll generally accomplish better and more lasting results. The 80/20 rule also says that about 80 percent of your profit comes from 15 or 20 percent of the products in the line; that 80 percent of your business comes from about 20 percent of your customers, or dealers; and that the great majority of your problems arise from a small percentage of the people you deal with. By concentrating your energies and resources on the really critical tasks, you will make a more important and lasting contribution to the enterprise.